PENGUIN BOOKS

1705

A HISTORY OF
POLAR EXPLORATION

L. P. KIRWAN

A HISTORY OF
POLAR EXPLORATION

L. P. KIRWAN

PENGUIN BOOKS

Penguin Books Ltd, Harmondsworth, Middlesex
AUSTRALIA: Penguin Books Pty Ltd, 762 Whitehorse Road,
Mitcham, Victoria

—

First published as *The White Road* by
Hollis and Carter 1959
Published in Penguin Books 1962

—

Copyright © L. P. Kirwan, 1959

—

Made and printed in Great Britain
by Hazell Watson & Viney Ltd
Aylesbury and Slough
Set in Linotype Granjon

CONTENTS

Preface   11

PART I
THE AGE OF DISCOVERY

1 Greeks, Norsemen, and Monks   15
2 A Northern Passage to Cathay   26
3 Dutch and English Rivalry in the Arctic   40

PART II
THE AGE OF EXPLORATION

4 Arctic and Antarctic:
  The Age of Strategy and Exploration   55
5 Cook and the First Crossing of the Antarctic Circle   73
6 After the Napoleonic Wars   88
7 The Royal Navy Takes the Lead   96
  The first attack on the North-West Passage   99
  Parry's attempt on the Pole   106
  The discovery of the North Magnetic Pole   109
  Land explorations of the Canadian Arctic coast   111
8 The First Sightings of the Antarctic Continent   115
9 Russia Enters the Antarctic   125
10 A British Sealer Circumnavigates the Continent   137
11 The United States Exploring Expedition   143
12 Europe Revives Antarctic Exploration   157

13 The Arctic Cruise of *Erebus* and *Terror*:
The Mystery of Sir John Franklin   176

PART III

THE AGE OF ADVENTURE
AND RESEARCH

14 New Men and New Motives –
America Approaches the Pole   197

15 The Scandinavian Ascendancy:
Nordenskiöld and Nansen   210

16 The Scandinavian Ascendancy:
Sverdrup and Amundsen   226

17 The Turn of the Century:
The Revival of Antarctic Exploration   234

18 Scott and the *Discovery* Expedition   253

PART IV

THE HEROIC AGE

19 The Conquest of the North Pole   273

20 Shackleton Returns   288

21 The Race to the South Pole   305

22 Coast and Continent   318

PART V

POSTSCRIPT TO POLAR HISTORY

23 Between the Two World Wars   339

24 The Second World War and After:
The Significance of the Polar Regions   360

Bibliography (with notes)   380

Index   390

LIST OF PLATES

1 The Dutch prepare for the first Arctic wintering, 1596

2 From Peter Apian's *Cosmographia*, 1551. Showing the supposed relationship between America and Antarctica

3 Cook's Antarctic 'Ice Islands', January 1773
   From Cook's *Voyage towards the South Pole . . .*, pp. 36–7, London, 1777

4 Bellinghausen's Russian Antarctic Expedition, 1819–21
   From the Atlas of the Voyage of Capt. Bellingshausen, St Petersburg, 1831

5 Weddell's brig *Jane* and 65-ton cutter *Beaufoy*, typical early nineteenth-century Antarctic sealers
   From Weddell's *Voyage towards the South Pole*, 1825

6 Parry's 'Attempt to reach the North Pole in Boats Fitted for the Purpose', 1827
   From Parry's *Narrative of an Attempt . . .*, p. 90

7 'View of the Antarctic Continent.' As seen by Wilkes's United States Exploring Expedition, January 1840
   From Wilkes's *Narrative . . .*, II, p. 325
   Philadelphia, 1845

8a Top-hatted officers of Franklin's Second Expedition explore the Arctic coast of America. Drawn by Capt. Back, 1826
   From Franklin's *Narrative of a Second Expedition . . .*, p. 10

8b 'Critical Position of H.M.S. *Investigator* ...' The
Franklin Search, August 1851

> From a drawing by Lieut. S. Gurney Creswell in
> the possession of the Royal Geographical Society

9a James Clark Ross discovers Mount Erebus,
January 1841

> From Ross, *Voyage . . . in the Antarctic Regions*,
> I, p. 216.

9b 'A gale in the pack.' H.M.S. *Erebus* and *Terror* in
the Antarctic, January 1842

> From Ross, *Voyage . . . in the Antarctic Regions*,
> I, page 216

10   'Crossing the Ice Belt at Coffee Gorge.' Kane's
Yankees in the Arctic, 1854

> From Elisha Kent Kane, *Arctic Explorations*, I,
> p. 92

11   The Peary Arctic Club's S.S. *Roosevelt*, 1906

> From R. E. Peary, *Nearest the Pole*, p. 358

12   The Navy advances across the 'Great Ice Barrier'.
Scott's Antarctic expedition, 1901–4
By courtesy of the Royal Geographical Society

13   On the Polar Plateau. Scott's last expedition,
1910–13

> Copyright, Paul Popper Ltd

14a Amundsen's dog-teams reach the South Pole,
December 1911

> From R. Amundsen, *The South Pole*, John
> Murray, London, 1912

14b Scott and his men find the Norwegian flag flying at
the Pole, January 1912. From a film found at Scott's
last camp

> Copyright, Paul Popper Ltd

15 Scott's hut at Cape Evans, built in 1911 and last
    used by Shackleton's Trans-Antarctic Expedition in
    1916. Photographed through a broken window-pane
    during the U.S. 'Operation Deepfreeze' in 1956

    Photograph by John E. Fletcher © National
    Geographic Society

16 The United States Navy lands at the South Pole,
    31 October 1956

    Copyright, Planet News Ltd, London

MAPS AND DIAGRAMS

Ice Drift in the Central Polar Basin   219
    After V. F. Burkhanov, *New Soviet Investigations in the
    Arctic*, Moscow, 1955

The Ross Dependency   293

The Partition of the Antarctic   357

The South Polar Regions   376–7

The North Polar Regions   378–9

The North-West Passage   inside back cover

PREFACE

It may seem an impertinence that one who has no personal experience of the polar regions, whose own field-work in fact has been in hot and not cold deserts, should write a book about polar exploration. However, I can claim at least some close acquaintance with polar affairs over the past twelve years. In this book moreover – and I believe the treatment to be relatively new – I have been more concerned with the evolution of polar exploration in its historical and social context than with an analysis of geographical achievement or with the development of polar techniques. And I have been concerned especially with the motives and impulses – economic, strategic, personal, and political – which have given rise to polar exploration. This has of course involved working outwards from the centre, from the hub, of polar activity in each case. It has similarly involved an attempt to weave Arctic and Antarctic into one continuous story instead of treating each region separately as has generally been done. The events of the last forty years are an exception and, largely because of the difficulty of achieving historical perspective at such close range, these have been more summarily described, reference being made only to the main happenings and to some of the principal influences and trends.

The bibliography at the back of the book gives some idea of the extent of my debt to those on whose published work I have so much depended. It also contains references to certain unpublished material in the possession of the Royal Geographical Society or of the Scott Polar Research Institute at Cambridge, England. To the authorities of both these oganizations I am likewise much indebted for permission to use this.

The opinions expressed in this book are my own. But I must – like so many other writers on polar exploration – record my gratitude to Dr Brian Roberts of the Scott Polar Research Institute for many valuable factual comments at proof stage, made out of his encyclopaedic knowledge of polar exploration. I am also grateful to Mr G. R. Crone, Librarian and Map Curator at the Royal Geographical Society, for helpful comments on the introductory Part I; to Mr G. S. Holland and his colleagues at the Royal Geographical Society for their expert preparation of the maps; and to Miss Frederica Estill for much assistance in the preparation of the manuscript.

Finally, I must acknowledge my debt to my wife, not only for her encouragement and her patience during the writing of a book done at the cost of a good many leisure hours, but also for her skill in helping to clarify the final proofs.

L. P. K.

Chelsea and Longmore, 1959

Preface to the Penguin Edition

I should like to acknowledge my gratitude to those who have so kindly suggested corrections and amendments to the original edition; in particular to Sir James Marshall-Cornwall, Captain J. K. Davis, Professor Hans Ahlmann, Dr T. Armstrong, and Dr Charles Swithinbank.

I must mention that, as from 3 March 1962, by an Order of Council the Falkland Islands Dependencies (excluding South Georgia and South Sandwich Islands) have been re-named British Antarctic Territory. Similarly, the Falkland Islands Dependencies Survey is now known as the British Antarctic Survey.

L. P. K.

London, 1961

PART ONE

THE AGE OF DISCOVERY

GREEKS, NORSEMEN, AND MONKS

It is not surprising that the Age of Aristotle, alight with the restlessly inquisitive spirit of the Greeks, should have seen the birth of the first polar explorer: Pytheas, from the Greek colony of Massilia, the modern Marseilles. Pytheas was more than a bold adventurer determined to chance a voyage through the allegedly haunted seas which lay beyond the limits of the 'Habitable World' of his time. He was an intellectual, a scientific explorer, a meticulous observer, a skilled navigator learned in astronomy, and the ingenious inventor of an instrument, a 'gnomon', which enabled him to calculate the latitude of his native city with extraordinary accuracy for those days.

In origin, the motives of this first polar expedition were, like those of most expeditions to the polar regions until the eighteenth century, primarily economic. When Pytheas sailed about 320 B.C., he sailed in search of the tin which had mysteriously appeared from time to time in the markets of Massilia, coming, so rumour said, south through Gaul from some remote and unknown northern land. He sailed, also, in the interests of his sponsors, the merchants of the colony, on an attempt to break the blockade of the Atlantic trade routes which for years had been monopolized by Phoenician ships.

Navigating by sun and stars, Pytheas steered his square-sailed Greek galley out of the sunlit Mediterranean, past the warning pillars traditionally set up by Hercules (at the Straits of Gibraltar), and on through grey and boisterous seas to Brittany and to Cornwall, the source of tin.

Pytheas is famous in history for his discovery and circumnavigation of the land of the 'painted' Britons. It was during his exploration of Britain that he first heard of a land, far to the north, called Thule. To explore towards the Arctic was no part of his original mission, but he determined nevertheless to search for Thule, and after sailing for six days he sighted land; a land, its inhabitants told him, which lay at times on the very edge of a 'frozen' or 'curdled' sea. It was evidently an Arctic land, probably Iceland, for Pytheas gives a very recognizable description of the Midnight Sun, and he witnessed there a phenomenon to which he gives the curious and much disputed name of 'sea-lung', a substance neither land nor air nor water which was impassable to men and boats; a word-picture, perhaps, of the gentle and rhythmical undulation of the ice rising and falling with the movement of the sea, linked possibly with some suggestion of the exhalations of the sea-mist which so often hangs, cold and dank, above the ice edge in the Arctic.

It has been the sad fate of many polar explorers that their claims to discovery should have been contemptuously rejected by later generations. In Roman times, the geographer Strabo, who could not tolerate even the inclusion of Ireland within the limits of his definition of the Habitable World, refused to believe that man could survive so far to the north on the very edge of a world of ice and he rejected Pytheas's story as an extravagant traveller's tale. This first polar discovery thus passed into oblivion. Only in comparatively recent times has Pytheas been recognized as the first civilized man to travel north as far as the Arctic Circle.

This first contact with the new world of ice and snow was followed, though not until the early centuries of the Christian era, by the discoveries of Irish monks and Norsemen pirates, seldom the result of deliberate exploration. The Irish monks, descendants of those who had followed St Patrick, were intent not on adding to geographical knowledge but on the discovery of remote islands to the north and east of Ireland to which they might escape from a too gregarious community life to one of solitude and contemplation. Sailing in hide-covered coracles or curraghs, flung about on the tumbling seas, they found refuge among the western isles of Scotland and from there, driven out by the Norsemen, spread to the Orkneys, Shetlands, and Faroes. Some, hardier and more adventurous seamen, had a more ambitious plan. Living in monasteries round the mouth of the Shannon, they had seen how each year at the first sign of spring flock after flock of wild geese migrated northwards to summer breeding grounds, and it was probably by following the flight of these spectacular and noisy birds that the Irish monks reached Iceland. When the Norsemen, the Vikings, reached Iceland about A.D. 870, they found, the Sagas record, monks and priests, 'papar' with their 'bells, books, and croziers', already there.

The Norsemen discovered Iceland when the longship of the Viking chieftain Garda was blown westwards off its course on a journey from Norway to the Faroes. Discovery led to settlement, and settlement to colonization, as year after year the Vikings, making landfall by releasing ravens and other shore-sighting birds, spread their stone farmsteads and churches over the island. On these now regular voyages from Norway, the Norsemen experienced all those hazards which were to bewilder and exhaust and often to destroy the Arctic navigator through the ages; the impenetrable fog, the roving menace of ice, the blustering, freezing squalls, the violent storms. On one Norse voyage twelve ships, conveying colonists, their wives and children, their cattle, all their meagre and threadbare possessions, sank out of a fleet of twenty-five. During one of these storms, in the tenth century A.D., a Norseman, Gunbjorn, was swept past Iceland to within sight of the Greenland coast.

Gunbjorn's discovery led to the first landing on Greenland by a Viking chieftain, Eric the Red. He had been outlawed from Iceland as the result of a blood-feud and appears to have landed somewhere near the modern Angmagssalik, on the south-east coast, about A.D. 985. But this coast was (and remained for many centuries) too barren and icebound for settlement, so the Norsemen moved round to the west and along the deep fjords there, so like the fjords of their native Norway. Farms of stone and peat multiplied as new colonists arrived from Norway and Iceland, and in a climate much milder than today, they appear to have flourished. In summer there was deep green grass for the cattle; hares and reindeer and foxes were hunted; and it was not long before the Norsemen began to trade with the 'Skraelings' or Eskimoes, exchanging corn and iron from Norway for walrus ivory and the skins of bear and seal.

It is not easy to elicit from the stark and enigmatic language of the Sagas the precise extent of Norse explorations in the

Arctic. In their search for new hunting grounds, the Norsemen voyaged, no doubt, far up the west coast of Greenland. Greenland, moreover, was the base for the great Norse discovery of the New World, for the epic voyages to Wineland and Markland, the voyages of Bjarni Jerjulfsson, of Lief Ericsson (son of Eric the Red who brought Christianity to Greenland) and Thorfinn Karlsefni which carried the high-prowed and grotesquely figured ships of the Vikings to Baffin Island, to Nova Scotia and Labrador, and even as far south as the coast of Maryland.

In A.D. 1261 the Norse settlements in Greenland became a crown colony of Norway. But already this Arctic prelude was drawing to a close. The milder climate which had enabled farming to flourish in Iceland and Greenland in the Viking Age began gradually, and unaccountably, to change. The cold returned. Ice closed slowly in over land and sea. At the same time, Norwegian sea-power began to decline in the face of the thrustful competition of the growing northern seaports of the Hanseatic League. Oppressed by the new harshness of the climate, deprived of the resources of the mother-country, the Norse farmers in Greenland in A.D. 1345 were excused payment of tithes by the Pope. Ten years later, alarming (but unwarranted) rumours reached Norway that in their desolation they had forsaken Christianity for the pagan beliefs of the Eskimoes, and missionaries were sent to their rescue. But the sight of the sails of a ship off Greenland was now a rare event. In 1492, a letter of Pope Alexander VI declared that the Norse settlers in Greenland were eking out a miserable existence on dried fish and a little milk and that no ship had reached them from either Norway or Iceland for eighty years. And, indeed, excavations of the Norse cemetery of Herjolfness in South Greenland show vividly to what straits the abandoned Norsemen had been reduced. Their bodies, mummified by the ice, were found to be emaciated, diseased, and deformed by years of intermarriage. Many had obviously been the victims of Eskimo attacks. Beneath the ice encasing their rough wooden coffins were traces of happier days in the form of tree roots and plants, relics of the warmer climate which their ancestors, the early colonists, had once enjoyed. A few survivors may have lived on until the early sixteenth century, for about A.D. 1550 there is a record of a ship bound for Iceland, but blown off her course, whose captain landed on one of the small islets or skerries off the Greenland coast which the Viking Gunbjorn had first seen six centuries before. Clambering over the ruins of an old stone farmhouse, he came suddenly upon the body of a Norseman wearing a hood and cloak of coarse wool and sealskin. This man was the last of the Norse settlers of Greenland to be seen by a European.

Iceland and Greenland and the eastern fringes of the Canadian Arctic were not the only Arctic lands to be discovered by the Norsemen. About A.D. 880, soon after the first Norse settlement in Iceland, a Viking named Ochtere, then living in northern Norway, sailed from Hålgoland on a voyage of exploration and trade in walrus tusks, round North Cape and eastwards round the Kola Peninsula into the White Sea. The exploits of the Norsemen of Iceland and Greenland were for generations recited annually at Scandinavian 'Things' or festivals and were not committed to writing until long after the event. The story of Ochtere's voyage, however, with its details of the tribes he encountered along the north Russian coast, has survived as a contemporary record because on his return he told it personally to King Alfred of England, who inserted it in his translation into Anglo-Saxon of a history of the world which had been written by a Spanish priest, Orosius, in the fifth century A.D. There, it replaces the wholly fabulous description of the Far North which Orosius had compiled. It is the first surviving contemporary record of an Arctic expedition.

What memory, what knowledge of these early Arctic wanderings persisted in later medieval times? To judge by the works of the schoolmen, of the geographers, the cosmographers, and the historians, writing in Latin, immersed in the intricacies of dusty argument, the Norse voyages might never have happened. But these men moved in a world of royal courts and palaces, of castles and manor-houses, a world of books and of learning derived from Greece and Rome. They were remote from the salt smell of the sea and from the talk of seamen, and it was among the seamen, on the cobbled quays or in the smoky taverns of a port like Bristol, that the legends of the great Viking voyages in the Arctic survived.

But knowledge of these earliest Arctic discoveries was not only a matter of verbal tradition. From the days of Henry III until the fifteenth century, English and Scottish merchants and shipowners were constantly in Norway and kept agents there and contrived to share in the profits of the fisheries off Iceland and Greenland, especially in whaling: an increasingly profitable luxury trade since it was the source of blubber-oil for lighting and provided perfume (ambergris) and whalebone for the ladies of the court. There is negative evidence, moreover, that the English themselves fished and hunted in Greenland waters until the second quarter of the fifteenth century. In A.D. 1432, for example, in the reign of Henry VI, when the Scandinavian kingdom established by treaty its rights to the Greenland trade, it was stipulated that all English ships should be excluded from these waters. Visits of the Bristol fishing fleet in search of cod and herring off Iceland were also an annual event.

What geographical discoveries these fishermen made is unrecorded. There are, however, two Arctic voyages of the fourteenth century of which some contemporary record has survived. One was by a young Franciscan minor friar, Nicholas of Lynn (mentioned in Chaucer's Essay on the Astrolabe), fragments of whose works were preserved by sixteenth-century writers. From these it appears that about A.D. 1360 Nicholas, sailing from Norway, reached a sea, far to the north, which froze in winter; and a land whose inhabitants were no more than four feet high and where along the coast timbers of ancient ships and the ruins of ancient homesteads could be seen. This strongly suggests that Nicholas of Lynn reached southern Greenland, met the Eskimoes, and saw vestiges of the old Viking settlements there. On his return, he drew up a scheme for the broad geography of the Arctic. The Pole he pictured as glistening black magnetic rock standing in the midst of a whirlpool, the whole surrounded by a circle of mountainous lands divided by numerous channels through which the sea, sucked towards the central whirlpool, rushed so swiftly that no ship could survive. It is by no means a wholly imaginary scheme of the general arrangement of Arctic land and ocean, and it is considerably nearer the truth than some of the fantastic theories about the geography of the Arctic basin evolved during the eighteenth and nineteenth centuries.

Another Arctic voyage, reputed to have been made in the fourteenth century by two Venetian brothers, Niccolo and Antonio Zeno, was published with a map by their descendants in 1558. This dubious voyage has a unique place in Arctic history, not for its alleged discoveries but for the way in which the Zeno map, a maze of fact and fancy, was to mislead future generations of Arctic explorers. On it, in deference perhaps to a cherished medieval theory that since civilization sprang from one centre or cradle, all lands must be linked together, Greenland is shown swinging round to the east and south, to meet the northernmost coast of Norway. Enclosed within this great bend of land lies Iceland and other islands, while far to the west numerous islands are strung about, carrying a variety of fanciful names. It was disastrous that so much of this ingenious piece of cartography should have been incorporated in the maps and globes of the great Flemish cartographers Mercator and Ortelius in the sixteenth century because these for centuries were accepted as the cartographical basis of Arctic exploration. The course of Arctic exploration from that time might indeed have been very different had it not been for the fabrications in 1558 of the descendants of the brothers Zeno.

In the fifteenth century, a fresh impulse to Arctic exploration appears, involving a new and quite specific objective: the search for a northern route to the Indies, to China, to Japan; those kingdoms, as they were called, of Cathay, news of whose unimagined wealth, brought back by Marco Polo's desert caravans, had dazzled the civilized European world of the thirteenth century. Here, in the vision of these lush and opulent lands, the adventurer saw fortune, and governments the answer to all their economic ills. For many years, however, Cathay was thought by men of learning (though not by seamen) to be unapproachable by sea, for did not the Scriptures teach that the earth was not a globe as the Greeks believed, but a flat disk, four-square, centred on Jerusalem, an earth surrounded by a continuous and impassable ocean which divided mankind from Paradise? Seen thus,

Cathay could only be reached by land, and the way by land, over the mountains and the torrid deserts which Marco Polo had crossed, was barred, and had long since been barred, by the warriors of Islam. By the fifteenth century, all this was changed. The idea of the sphericity of the earth was, by educated people at all events, generally accepted, and in 1409, a development which transformed geographical thought and cosmographical ideas occurred, the translation into Latin of Ptolemy's *Geography*. With its lists of longitude and latitude, this provided cartographers with a basis for the fixing of positions on the terrestrial globe. Rudimentary as navigation was bound to be until the solution of the problem of longitude in the eighteenth century, the Age of Discovery by long sea voyages could now begin. With globes in use and charts and maps beginning to take modern shape, voyages of circumnavigation round the world (foreseen by some as early as the fourteenth century) became generally accepted as being possible and seamen sailing under the rival flags of Portugal and Spain embarked on a host of great voyages to east, west, and south to seek a way to the Orient. To the south and east, the explorations promoted by Prince Henry the Navigator and those of Bartholomew Diaz on the west coast of Africa led in 1497 to the rounding of the Cape of Good Hope by Vasco da Gama; a feat already accomplished by Arab seamen, as some geographers of the time appear to have known. Here was one seaway to Cathay. In the west, too, there was hope. There the discovery by Columbus of islands of the so-called West Indies – territories in a region where, it was thought, wealth must necessarily be created by the life-giving rays of a perpetual sun – suggested that these were outliers of Cathay and that in this westward direction a way through to Cathay would be found. This hope, however, was short-lived. The Genoese John Cabot, from Bristol, sailed west and north as far as Newfoundland and Labrador but found no way through. Indeed, from Cabot's voyage and from those of others searching for a western passage to Cathay it soon appeared that not islands but an entire continent barred the way.

With this westward route thus closed, what were the alternatives confronting the three principal nations engaged at the end

of the fifteenth century in planning voyages to Cathay? There
was the way south down the Atlantic, and thence eastwards
round Africa or westwards (if a way could be found) round the
southern extremity of America. Or, as could be seen from the
globe, there was a possibility of a northern ice-infested route, a
route across the summit of the world, but a poor alternative to
the temperate and torrid waters of the South Atlantic. These
waters lay however within the domain of Spain and Portugal
whose relative roles in their exploration were defined by the
Treaty of Tordesillas in 1494; in time, but only just in time, to
prevent a rivalry which seemed likely to lead to a catastrophic
split in Christendom. A line of demarcation running south
roughly along the meridian through the centre of the north
Atlantic Ocean was agreed, the right to exploration and discovery on the west being granted to Spain, and on the east to
Portugal. For these great seafaring countries, this division was
not unsatisfactory. But for the merchants and seamen of other
countries, excluded by this joint monopoly, only the northern
routes to Cathay, through the ice and fogs and blizzards of the
Arctic, remained. 'Out of Spain', an Englishman, Robert
Thorne, complained in 1541, 'they sail all the Indies and seas
occidentals, and from Portugal they sail all the Indies and the
seas orientals, so that between the way of the Orient and the way
of the Occident they have encompassed the world ... also by
way of the meridian there is a great part discovered by the
Spaniards. So resteth this way of the north only for to discover. ...' For Englishmen like Robert Thorne this was a
dismal prospect. For was it not generally acknowledged that the
frozen lands of the north, far from the rays of the equinoctial
sun which nourished the precious metals of the torrid zone,
could not in themselves offer hopes of wealth? But a way
through them must be found, a North-East or a North-West
Passage to Cathay. It was thus that the search for a northern
passage became the dominant motive behind the English, Dutch,
and French explorations of the Arctic for two centuries or more.

The search for a route to Cathay from the South Atlantic by
Portugal and Spain led also to another kind of polar exploration,
towards the search for an Antarctic Continent, conceived not as

the glaciated, virtually lifeless land which it has since been found to be, but as a rich and fertile continent stretching northwards into the temperate zone. The idea of a great southern continent, lying at the opposite extreme of a spherical earth, was of ancient origin. Aristotle had argued that just as a habitable zone existed below the Arctic Pole, so the symmetry and balance implicit in the concept of the earth as a perfect sphere required equally a habitable zone in the south. In this global scheme northern and southern habitable zones were pictured as divided by an impenetrable belt of fire, the belt of the torrid equatorial regions. It was a scheme which found much favour in Roman times, and Cicero and Pomponius Mela both allude to a southern habitable zone. But to the fathers of the Church, for whom the earth was a flat disk, it was generally anathema, and St Augustine in particular objected to the notion that men could thus 'plant their footsteps opposite to our feet'. Nevertheless, throughout the Middle Ages, there were men who, whatever the Church might say, adhered to the Greek view of the sphericity of the earth, and one of them in the fourteenth century, Sir John Mandeville, author of the *Travels*, echoed the classical argument for an Antarctic Continent. 'For ye wit well,' he declared, 'that they that be toward the Antarctic, they be straight, feet against feet, of them that dwell under the Transmontane (the immovable north star). For all parts of the sea and lands have their opposites, habitable and trespassable. . . .'

That men could reach this southern or Antarctic habitable zone seemed at first inconceivable because of the intermediate torrid regions. But the crossing of the Equator by Lopo Gonçalves in the third quarter of the fifteenth century brought the Antarctic within the realms of human exploration. Seamen and merchants, geographers and governments began then to watch keenly for the first sight of a rich and fertile southern continent, and until 1488 when the temperate coasts of south-west Africa were navigated by Bartholomew Diaz, more than once the idea arose that these might prove to be the northward projection of that great southern continent which the logic of geography demanded.

Belief in the existence of a continent adjoining Africa vanished finally when Vasco da Gama rounded the Cape in 1497. But the southern coasts of America had yet to be explored. When Ferdinand Magellan, on his first voyage of circumnavigation, saw in 1520 beyond the strait which bears his name the land he called 'Land of Fires', Tierra del Fuego, he concluded, from the sound and movement of the sea, that this new land was an archipelago. But the geographers, as so often in the history of exploration, knew better. As the years went by, the legend of a temperate Antarctic continent grew and on maps such as that of Orontius of 1531 Tierra del Fuego appears as the northern tip of a continent, *'Terra australis recenter inventa sed nondum plene cognita'*, separated only by the narrow Strait of Magellan from the mainland of South America.

Until the eighteenth century, the main motive of voyages in the Arctic was penetration rather than discovery; the search for a northern passage through the Arctic to the Pacific and the oriental kingdoms of Cathay. In the Antarctic, discovery was the aim; the discovery of a continent which, geographers imagined, would prove no less rich, no less seductive than those kingdoms of the East which English and Dutch aimed to reach in the sixteenth and seventeenth centuries by way of the Arctic seas.

A NORTHERN PASSAGE TO CATHAY

RICHARD CHANCELLOR, a great Arctic voyager of the Elizabethan Age, once explained (to the young schoolmaster commissioned to write the story of his adventures) the reasons which
first impelled his countrymen to search for a sea route to Cathay.

'At that time', he said, 'our merchants perceived the commodities and wares of England to be in small request with the
countries and people about us, and near unto us, and that those
merchandises which strangers in the time and memory of our
ancestors did earnestly seek and desire were now neglected, and
the price thereof abated, although by us carried to their own
ports, and all foreign merchandises in great account and their
prices wonderfully raised, certain grave citizens of London and
men of great wisdom and careful for the good of their country
began to think with themselves how this mischief might be
remedied. Neither was a remedy (as it then appeared) wanting
to their desires. For seeing that the wealth of the Spaniards and
Portuguese by the discovery and search of new trades and countries was marvellously increased, supposing the same to be a
course and mean for them also to obtain the like, they thereupon
resolved upon a new and strange navigation.'

In such circumstances, the result of a decline in England's
traditional trade with France and with the Netherlands, the first
English voyages into the Arctic of the sixteenth century, no less
than those to the New World, can be seen as part of the general
expansion of overseas enterprise which wrought such changes,
social, economic, and intellectual, in the pattern of life in
Elizabethan England.

Like the voyages to discover and colonize the New World, the
Arctic voyages were no haphazard, impetuous adventures. On
the contrary, they were most carefully planned. The men behind them included not only the Court, the city companies, the

rich merchants who were the principal investors of funds, but
a highly efficient group of technical advisers, specialists in
economics, in navigation, and in the geography of distant lands,
many of whom were also shrewd men of business. Outstanding
amongst these planners was Richard Hakluyt, author of the
great collection, *The Principall Navigations, Voiages, and Discoveries of the English Nation*, whose publication the year after
the Armada filled the minds of Englishmen, young and old,
with thoughts of adventure, and of profit, overseas. A percep-
tive geographer, Hakluyt was admirably qualified to sift from
a great mass of picturesque but often fictitious travellers' tales
the geographical and economic facts essential to his plans for
exploration. His cousin, Richard Hakluyt, another planner, was
a lawyer and an expert in dyes and oils and in the woollen
goods which were England's principal export. No less important, in planning the new Arctic voyages, was the training
of seamen in the theory and practice of navigation, in which
England lagged so far behind her rivals, Portugal and Spain.
New text-books had to be written, new instruments devised.
And professional pilots had to be instructed in the latest navigational developments. In this field, the leading adviser was a
brilliant young Welshman, John Dee, a mathematician from
Cambridge who had studied at Louvain with the great European
cosmographers and cartographers, German Frisius and Gerhard
Mercator. John Dee became the principal instructor in astronomy and navigation to almost all the Arctic captains and pilots
of his day.

The first question confronting the planners, as they studied
their globes (now in general use), was in which direction the
first expeditions should be sent. Should they search for a North-
East or a North-West Passage to Cathay? Until the year 1558
when the famous map of the Venetian brothers Niccolo and
Antonio Zeno was published, the north-east appeared more
hopeful. As far as the North Cape of Norway, the seas were
familiar to English ships and had been found to be ice-free; beyond North Cape, Russian fishermen were known frequently
to sail at least as far as the River Ob. The north-east route,
moreover, offered some compensation if an expedition failed to

reach Pacific waters. Along it, along the shores of the Old World, 'civill people', prospective customers, were known to live, while beyond the Ob – if the cartographers who showed Tartary and Scythia joined to north-east Asia were correct – there were possibilities of an even more lucrative trade with the outlying kingdoms of the East.

To the west, by contrast, the outlook was less hopeful. John Cabot from Bristol, probing northwards in 1497 as far as Labrador, found no trace of any passage or strait to Cathay. Nor could the two Portuguese brothers Miguel and Gaspar Cortereal in A.D. 1500 find any limit to the northward-stretching coast of the American continent. If the discovery by the Breton seaman Jacques Cartier of the mouth of the St Lawrence had been known when he returned from his voyage in 1536, those who argued in favour of a western route might have been more encouraged, for thirty years later when Cartier's Canadian discoveries first appeared upon the maps, it looked as if here at last was the opening of a North-West Passage. However, as so often, publication lagged far behind geographical discovery. The north-east, therefore, was the direction chosen.

The next problem for the planners was finance. They had a host of powerful friends at Court and in the City, and with their help 'The Mysterie and Companie of the Marchants Adventurers for the Discoverie of Regions, Dominions, Islands, and Places unknowen' was established on 12 December 1551, its first Governor being Sebastian Cabot, son of the John Cabot who had explored the coast of Labrador at the end of the previous century. This Company of Merchant Adventurers became the focus and hub of all the earliest activities directed towards the search for a North-East Passage and one of the Company's first acts was to appoint the leader of their Arctic expedition, and to recruit as his second-in-command a professional Chief Pilot. As Captain-General they chose, according to custom, a distinguished soldier, a courtier, Sir Hugh Willoughby, who knew nothing of navigation. His second-in-command was a professional seaman, Richard Chancellor, who was known throughout England as 'the odde (i.e. outstanding) man of his time for matters touching the sea'.

Willoughby, who was to sail in the 'Admiral of the Fleet', the *Bona Esperanza* of 120 tons, had William Gefferson as master of his ship, while Chancellor in the *Edward Bonaventure* carried as master a man destined to become famous as an Arctic pilot, Stephen Borough. The third ship of the Arctic squadron, the *Bona Confidentia*, had a Dutch master, Cornelius Durforth. These men, with the merchants who hoped to trade along the route and in Cathay, and those generally known as 'the ignorant and unruly mariners', comprised the expedition.

All Willoughby's ships, armed merchant ships, shallow enough in draught to be able to navigate the great rivers which some maps showed flowing into the Arctic from central Asia, were specially strengthened, a sheathing of lead being devised to protect their bottoms against the attacks of a particularly virulent and piercing worm which was said to infest the torrid waters off Cathay. It was a precaution characteristic of the robust optimism with which these Elizabethan seamen, in sailing ships of a hundred tons or less, set out on a voyage through the Arctic to the Far East, along a route heavily encumbered with ice, obscured continually by fog and mist; a seaway which was not completely navigated until late in the nineteenth century.

Among the documents of permanent importance to the polar historian are the instructions given to the leaders of polar expeditions. The instructions drawn up by the Governor of the Company for the use of Sir Hugh Willoughby (and preserved by Richard Hakluyt) are worth recording briefly because they give not only a vivid picture of what was expected of a sixteenth-century expedition voyaging through Arctic and other unknown regions, but throw light on some of the problems, internal as well as external, confronting the leader of an Arctic expedition at this time. One of the great problems, evidently, was the preservation of discipline among the crew, and there are strict injunctions that 'no blaspheming of God, or detestable swearing, be used in any ship, nor communication of ribaldry, filthy tales, or ungodly talk to be suffered in the company of any ship, neither dicing, carding, tabling, nor other devilish game to be frequented, whereby ensueth not only poverty to the players, but also strife, variance, brawling, fighting, and oftentimes murder. ...' It is no wonder that not only in the oaths, *juramenta*, taken by each man to the Captain-General, but throughout the Instructions (which were to be read aloud each week) 'unity, love, conformity, and obedience' are constantly enjoined.

More important, because so revealing of the shrewd and practical attitude of those who drafted them, are the clauses laying down rules of behaviour for the expedition on its arrival in a new land. The use of force was forbidden except in the last resort; women above all were to be respected; courtesy combined with caution were to be the watchwords of the landing parties; and tolerance, especially in religious matters. 'If the people', Willoughby is told, 'shall appear gathering of stones, gold, metal, or other like on the sand, your pinnaces may draw nigh, marking what things they gather, using and playing upon the drum or such other instruments as may allure them to harkening, to fantasy, or desire to see and hear your instruments and voices. But keep you out of danger, and show to them no sign of rigour or hostility.' Only so could these Arctic navigators of the sixteenth century expect to obtain what the Company wanted, a full account of the new peoples and countries, detailed information about natural resources, and opportunities to develop trade.

In May 1553, through the warm air of an English summer day, the three ships of Willoughby's Arctic expedition moved slowly down-river from Deptford. The Court was in residence at Greenwich at the time, and as the ships came in sight, there was great excitement. 'The courtiers', an onlooker relates, 'came running out, and the common people flocked together, standing very thick upon the shore. The Privy Council, they looked out at the windows of the Court, and the rest ran up to the tops of the towers.' The ships, in response to this ovation, fired a salvo in salute 'in so much that the tops of the hills sounded therewith, and the waters gave an echo', and the sailors 'shouted in such sort that the sky rang again with the noise thereof. One stands on the poop of the ship, and by gesture bids farewell to his friends ... another walks upon the hatches, another climbs the shrouds, another stands upon the mainyard, and another in the top of the ship.' After 'divers gentlemen and gentlewomen' had come aboard to drink the health of ships and crews (to whom they gave 'right liberal awards'), Sir Hugh Willoughby's Arctic fleet made for the open sea.

For Willoughby the expedition ended in tragedy, a personal tragedy of the kind which was to darken many another expedition to the polar regions. Off the west coast of Norway, a great storm swept the ships apart, and Willoughby's ship, the *Bona Esperanza*, after days of wandering, crippled, in the Barents Sea, made landfall on the north coast of the Kola Peninsula, somewhere in the neighbourhood of Murmansk. There, because of the weather and the battered state of his ship, Willoughby and his men were forced to winter, and there, one by one, they died; probably of scurvy, the enfeebling and eventually killing disease which was to be the scourge of generations of polar explorers. In 1554, a year after they had sailed from Greenwich, their bodies were found in this desolate spot by Russian fishermen, and with them a note in Willoughby's own hand, describing their adventures, the seals, the deer, the bears, and foxes they had seen, the unceasing storms of snow and hail which they had endured on their voyage, so violent that they would have been expected only in the depths of winter. Day after day, Willoughby wrote, they had searched the bleak and snowbound coast, to the east, to the west, to the south. But they found no human being.

Richard Chancellor, meanwhile, in the *Edward Bonaventure*, had managed to put in at Wardhouse (Vardö) in Finnmark, and there met some Scottish merchants. When he told them of the object of his voyage, to search for a North-East Passage to Cathay, they did their utmost to dissuade him from so insane an enterprise. But Chancellor was adamant. 'Nothing at all discouraged with the speeches and words of the Scots', he sailed and held on his course until 'he came at last to a place where he found no night at all, but a continual light and brightness of the sun shining clearly upon a huge and mighty sea. ...' At length, the *Edward Bonaventure* put into a great bay, a hundred miles wide; the bay in the White Sea at the estuary of the Dvina River, where Archangel now stands.

The rest of the story of the Willoughby-Chancellor expedition is one of Russian rather than of Arctic discovery, for not far from where he landed Chancellor was met by emissaries from the Tzar Ivan the Fourth, the Terrible, who invited him to return with them by sledge on the fifteen-hundred-mile journey to Moscow. For the merchants and for the government of England, it was a momentous journey. It led in 1555 to the foundation of the Muscovy Company for the development of the highly lucrative Muscovy and Persian trade by way of the northern Dvina route. And it led three years later to the foundation of the famous port of Archangel. In the realm of Arctic exploration, however, Chancellor's voyage added little to geographical knowledge. Indeed, it carried the search for a North-East Passage no further than the Viking Ochtere had done in the days of Alfred the Great.

The search for a North-East Passage was now taken over by the newly-established Muscovy Company, and Stephen Borough, former master of the *Edward Bonaventure* (Chancellor having been drowned at sea), was invited to follow up the explorations which Willoughby and Chancellor had begun. Like Chancellor, under whom he had served, Borough was a professional seaman, an expert at his trade, trained in the latest practice of navigation by John Dee. In 1556, after a banquet with music and dancing given at the Sign of the Christopher at Gravesend by the aged Sebastian Cabot, Borough sailed in the *Searchthrift*, a tiny ship, smaller even than Chancellor's *Edward Bonaventure*. He had better fortune than Chancellor, and reached as far east as the Kara Sea. But at its entrance, south of Novaya Zemlya, his way was blocked by a mass of ice churned up by the winds, an impenetrable barrier which was to be the despair of many an expedition during the sixteenth and seventeenth centuries.

For twenty years the new and immensely profitable trade with Russia wholly preoccupied the merchants of the City of London. Nevertheless there were many, among the nobility, among the landed gentry, and in the learned world, who were not so concerned with immediate gain, men for whom the study of geography, of cartography, and of navigation had become a fashionable intellectual pursuit, and who were prepared to support a further search. In Elizabeth's reign, however, the direction of the search was changed. The quest was now for a North-West Passage. There were reasons for this change of policy. On the one hand, the publication in 1558 of the Zeno map showed Greenland swinging eastwards, thus barring the eastern route; on the other, was the incorporation in the Flemish geographer Ortelius's map of 1564 of Jacques Cartier's discovery of the mouth of the St Lawrence River. Then 1569 saw a great event in the history of man's mapping of the world: the publication of Gerhard Mercator's world map on the new Mercator projection. This finally decided the direction of the new explorations, for it showed in its outline of Arctic geography (which was all the new projection could permit) not only the start of a passage to the west but a formidable land barrier to the east, thus lending the great weight of Mercator's authority to the fabrications of the Zeno map.

For twenty years thereafter Arctic exploration was directed westwards. And in the spring of 1576, Martin Frobisher, a bold and practised seaman who was to win fame during the Armada, a man who was the quintessence of the Elizabethan adventuring spirit, sailed with two pinnaces, each of only twenty tons, on another Arctic enterprise. Frobisher's first landfall was the southern tip of Greenland, but Greenland being on his maps far away to the east, he called his new land West Friezeland, identifying it with one of the many islands dotting the Western Arctic on the Zeno map. From Greenland, Frobisher sailed westwards until he reached a 'Strait' now known as Frobisher Bay, at the south-east end of Baffin Island. These are the 'straits' or 'streights' to which Richard Hakluyt refers in his account of Frobisher's voyage: 'And that land upon his right hand as he sailed Westward he judged to be the continent of Asia, and there to be divided from the firme of America, which lieth upon the left hand over against the same. This place he named after his name, Frobishers streights.'

As Frobisher and his men approached the coast of this new Arctic land, they saw an astonishing sight. For, darting out from the ice-bound shore, came a fleet of skin-covered canoes, the 'kayaks' of the Eskimoes, the first they had ever seen. The appearance of these small men especially excited them. With their pronounced Asiatic, Mongoloid features, surely these, they thought, must be men from Marco Polo's Cathay. As proof that here was Cathay at last, or at least an outlier of it, an Eskimo and his kayak were hauled aboard and were brought back in triumph to London.

Martin Frobisher's arrival in London with his 'Pyknean' or 'Strange Man of Cathay' caused a considerable sensation. 'And so', said a contemporary, 'they came to London with their ship Gabriel the sixth day of October; and they were joyfully received with the great Admiration of the people, bringing with them their strange man and his Bote, which was such a wonder unto the whole city, and to the rest of the Realm that heard of it, as seemed never to have happened the like great matter to any men's knowledge. ...' The Eskimo (who died of a cold soon after he landed) was not the only, nor indeed the most sensational, prize brought back by Frobisher's men from the Arctic. Some brought back Arctic flowers, and some green grass. One brought back a piece of black stone. It looked like coal, but when thrown into the fire, according to Humphrey Gilbert, the author of *Discourse of a Discovery for a New Passage to Cathaia*, 'It glistered with a bright marquesset of golde'.

Martin Frobisher was convinced that, in his westward-heading 'Strait', he had found the entrance to a North-West Passage, and his charts and the Mongoloid appearance of the Eskimo convinced even his instructor in navigation, the learned and discriminating John Dee. But when rumours spread that the black stones of Baffin Island had been identified as gold, all thought of the North-West Passage was forgotten. A Cathay Company was formed. The Queen bought shares. Miners from the tin mines in Cornwall – the mines which Pytheas had sought in Aristotle's time – were hastily recruited, and Frobisher and his officers, after kissing the Queen's hand at Lord Warwick's house in Essex, sailed in 1577 on a second expedition to the Arctic.

This time, on his outward voyage, Frobisher landed in Greenland, the West Friezeland of the Zeno map, to which he gave the homely name of West England, and there he established friendly relations with the Eskimo inhabitants, trading 'bells, looking-glasses, and divers of our country toys' for their dogs. He noted, too, among objects brought by the Eskimoes that some were of iron; evidence of contact with 'civill people', relics of trade or plunder perhaps, dating from the days of the old Norse colonies, or proof of more recent contact with whalers or fishermen whose voyages had never been recorded. Frobisher took possession of this new land of West England 'to the use of our sovereign lady the Queen's Majesty'. He was optimistic about the prospects for further exploration; it was a country, he said, which promised 'good hope of great commodity and riches, if it may be well discovered'. He then sailed for Baffin Island and returned with two hundred tons of the black ore.

Frobisher's third and last voyage to Baffin Island was in 1578, the year in which Drake, in his ship the *Golden Hind*, was the first to round Cape Horn. This time it was a colonizing and not an exploring expedition, the first of its kind in the Canadian Arctic; and the fifteen ships which sailed from the Port of London carried miners, settlers, massive planks and timbers, and a large prefabricated wooden house to establish a mining settlement in Frobisher Bay. But no sooner had they entered the so-called 'Strait' than disaster overwhelmed the fleet. A storm arose, sweeping down upon the ships a mass of churning, grinding ice-floes which sank most of the supply ships and ended the whole enterprise. When the remnants of the fleet, scattered by Atlantic gales, arrived at a number of different English ports, they were confronted by another and quite unexpected catastrophe. The famous ore, identified by an unscrupulous Italian assayer as gold, proved to be worthless iron pyrites. The Cathay Company was bankrupt, Martin Frobisher was disgraced, and his discoveries, his claims to have found a North-West Passage and to have reached the very frontiers of Cathay, were utterly discredited. 'The passage to Cathay', commented sourly a contemporary, 'is left unto us as uncertain as at the beginning, though thereupon hath followed great charges to the Company.' Only from Russia was there any comfort for the disgraced explorer. In January 1579, the Russians protested violently to the

English Government. Frobisher's Eskimo, the 'Strange Man of Cathay', they declared, was none other than a Russian Asiatic subject, kidnapped by a pack of English adventurers.

The bankruptcy of the Cathay Company, in which the Court and the City of London were heavily involved, put an end for some years to expeditions to the western Arctic. The planners now turned eastwards again, and in 1580 two sturdy and experienced English mariners, Arthur Pet and Charles Jackman, sailed in the pinnaces *George* and *William* to try for a North-East Passage. But just as Stephen Borough had been held up a quarter of a century earlier, so their way was barred by the same impenetrable wall of pack ice which loomed up out of the fog at the entrance of the Kara Sea. It was the last English attempt to seek a North-East Passage during the sixteenth century.

The Frobisher fiasco, however, had not robbed the north-west of all its protagonists, and there were still among geographers and courtiers men who felt, like Frobisher, that only in the north-west lay the solution to the problem of Cathay. In 1584 they obtained from the Queen a charter for a new North-West Company and selected as the leader and chief pilot of the new enterprise a remarkable man, John Davis. Davis, a splendid seaman, was a quiet and modest man with no gallant flourish to his name like Frobisher. But he was by far the most accomplished navigator of his day, with an intimate knowledge of the new and ingenious navigational instruments, of the new techniques of navigation at sea which the Age of Discovery had compelled the English to invent. Moreover, in providing the first detailed descriptions of Eskimo life in Greenland, he shows a power of acute and meticulous observation, a capacity for vivid description, which in polar literature are hard to match.

Frobisher, it will be recalled, had been optimistic about the prospects for exploration in Greenland (West Friezeland, or 'West England', as he called it), and Davis, on his first voyage in the *Moonshine* and the *Sunshine* in 1585, determined on a systematic exploration of the coasts. He landed first in south-west Greenland, near the modern Godthaab in Gilbert Sound, then sailed across Davis Strait to Cumberland Sound in Baffin Island, north of Frobisher's 'Strait', or bay. The following year,

1586, Davis divided up his four ships for simultaneous voyages along the eastern and western coasts, but the south-east coast, against which the pack ice is swept and massed by southward-flowing cold currents from the Arctic Sea, presented a formidable and frightening sight. 'The loathsome view of the shore and the irksome view of the ice', Davis wrote, 'was such as to breed strange conceits among us, so that we supposed the place to be wast and voyd of any sensible or vegitable creatures whereupon I called the same Desolation. . . .' The east coast of Greenland, indeed, as many later expeditions were to find, proved both desolate and unapproachable and the two ships working there were forced by eastward-branching currents over towards the coasts of Iceland. Davis, meanwhile, after failing to land on the southernmost promontory of Greenland (called, in happy commemoration of escape from shipwreck, Cape Farewell, now Kap Farvel), made for his old anchorage on the south-west coast, in Gilbert Sound. The Eskimoes, remembering the music and dancing with which Davis's sailors had delighted them the previous year, welcomed the Englishmen enthusiastically. They were, Davis found, a gay and simple but also a mischievous and 'thievish' people, who cut the ships' cables and stole the *Moonshine*'s boat and pilfered, like jackdaws, anything in sight. Davis made some curious discoveries in Greenland. Like Frobisher, he saw many relics of trade with Europe, iron objects which the Eskimoes greatly prized, and was shown 'a grave with divers buried in it, only covered with sealskins having a cross laid over them', the grave of a Viking colonist, or of some Eskimo family converted by the Norsemen to Christianity.

Davis took careful note of all he saw in south-western Greenland, of the trees, fir, spruce, and juniper, birch, and willow, of the great swarms of seals wallowing in the sea or basking sleepily in the sunshine on the islands off the coast. He explored the deeply-cut fjords along which the Viking colonists had built their farms, fjords so numerous, penetrating so far to the east, that he thought the land must be 'a great number of islands standing together'. Inland, along this western coast in summer, he found 'a plain champaign country, with earth and grass, such as our moory and waste grounds of England are . . . but found nothing, nor saw anything, save onely gripes, ravens, and small birds, as larkes and linnets. . . .'

John Davis, on his return, was optimistic about prospects for the discovery of a North-West Passage. On 3 October 1585, he wrote to Mr Secretary Walsingham: 'Right honorable most dutyfully craving pardon for this my rashe boldness, I am hereby, according to my duty, to signyfy unto yor honor that the north-west passage is a matter nothing doubtfull, but at any tyme almost to be passed, the sea navigable, voyd of yse, the ayre tollerable, and the waters very depe.' It was therefore with high hopes that in 1586 and 1587 he made two further voyages westwards from Greenland, venturing northwards on one occasion into the unexplored waters of Baffin Bay to which a great English explorer of the early seventeenth century was to give his name. Twice he crossed over towards Baffin Island but was swept southward by drifting ice beyond Frobisher Bay. On the second of these voyages, drifting south, he found his small ships caught up and spinning in 'a mighty overfall', probably the turbulent waters at the entrance to Hudson Strait.

In 1587 John Davis returned to England, having contributed to geographical knowledge of the Arctic more than any of his predecessors. But for the English, Arctic exploration was now at an end. In July of the following year, the high castles of the Armada of Philip of Spain were sighted from the English coast and Elizabeth's seamen, Martin Frobisher, John Davis, indeed all those tested and trained in great voyages of discovery, were needed for more vital and immediate tasks than Arctic exploration or a search for an Arctic passage to Cathay.

John Davis, in *The Seaman's Secrets*, admirably summed up sixteenth-century views about the polar regions, bringing all his own personal experiences to bear in his remarks about the Arctic. 'The frozen zones', he wrote, 'are contained within the polar circle, the Antarctick frozen zone within the Antarctick polar circle which are also reported not to be habitable by reason of the great extremity of colde supposed to be in those parts because of the Sunnes far distance from those zones, but in these our dayes we find by experience that the auncient Geographers had not the due consideration of the nature of these zones, for

three times I have been within the Artick frozen zone, where
I found the ayre very temperate, yea and many times in calme
wether marveilous hot; I have felt the Sunne beames of as
forcible action in the frozen zone in calme neere unto the shore,
as I have at any time found within the burning zone; this zone
is also inhabited with people of good stature, shape, and tract-
able conditions, with whom I have converced and not found
them rudly barbarous, as I have found the Caniballs which are
in the straights of Magilane and Southerne parts of America.'
Davis's observations, the observations of an active and not a
sedentary geographer, serve as an encouraging if optimistic preface to the Arctic explorations of the seventeenth century.

DUTCH AND ENGLISH RIVALRY
IN THE ARCTIC

TOWARDS the end of the sixteenth century, the Dutch, bold and adventurous seamen, resourceful merchants so opulent that the wealth of their great trading cities, Antwerp and Amsterdam, had made the Netherlands the treasury of their Spanish overlords, emerged as rivals to the English in the search for an Arctic route to Cathay. Since 1555 when the English Muscovy Company was established, the merchants of the Netherlands had looked with growing envy at the riches flowing into the coffers of the City of London from Russia and lands further east. But to the Dutch as to the English the kingdoms of Cathay were closed, barred by the Spanish–Portuguese monopoly of the South Atlantic routes. So they too began to look to the north, for a north-east sea or land passage to Asia, which might also enable them to share in the intermediate Russian trade.

In 1565, on the eve of the great revolt which was to liberate the Netherlands from Spain and lead, under William of Nassau, Prince of Orange, to the rise of the Dutch Republic, a Dutch White Sea Trading Company was formed under an enterprising manager, Oliver Brunel. Brunel had already established a Dutch trading post on the Kola Peninsula (Kol'skiy Poluostrov), and with Russian fishermen, whose contributions to Arctic exploration were probably far more extensive than has ever been recorded, had not only reached the islands of Novaya Zemlya which enfold the Kara Sea but after a remarkable eastward journey overland had travelled as far east as the River Ob. In an attempt on the North-East Passage, however, Brunel in 1584 did no better than the Englishmen, Pet and Jackman. He was forced back, like them, by the ice barrier at the entrance to the Kara Sea. Nevertheless, he had high hopes and raised support for another attempt, sponsored this time by the rich merchants of

Amsterdam, in commerce and sea-power the leading city of a Holland now supreme among the seven small republics federated by the Union of Utrecht of 1579.

The outstanding figure in this first Dutch Arctic enterprise was, however, not Brunel but Willem Barents, the chief pilot on three successive voyages; voyages (according to Gerrit de Veer's account, published in England in 1609) 'so strange and wonderful that the like hath never been heard of before; done and performed in three years, one after another by ships of Holland and Zeeland ... towards the kingdoms of Cathaia and China. ...'

Barents sailed with four ships in 1594, carrying with him (through the good offices of Richard Hakluyt, the English geographer) a Dutch translation of Pet and Jackman's log with its terrifying description of the great ice barrier stretching across the entrance to the Kara Sea. Because of this, no doubt, he made first for Novaya Zemlya, hoping to find an alternative way into the Kara Sea by rounding its northern point. All the way up the western coast he located the most prominent features of the land with remarkable accuracy. But on reaching the northern limit, he was held up by the pack which lay for miles ahead 'as if it had been a plain field of ice'. Barents then returned by the same route, noting on his way the channel, Matochkin Shar, which divides Novaya Zemlya in two, to find to his astonishment that his other ships had not only penetrated the dreaded Kara Strait but had actually entered and found completely free from ice the Kara Sea. This was a great stride forward in the navigation of a North-East Passage – it was not bettered until the nineteenth century – and indeed the Dutch if they had pressed forward might well, in the favourable ice conditions then existing, have reached the Bering Strait. Instead, they stopped. Greatly elated by their breaching of the notorious Kara Strait and further encouraged by a meeting with Russian fishermen who claimed that they made easy and frequent voyages along the coast as far as the mouth of the Yenisey River, they decided to return at once to Amsterdam with the great news that a way through to the East had been found.

The Dutch Government itself launched the next expedition which sailed in 1595 with a fleet of seven ships. But it was a bad ice year, and rather than risk their ships in a fresh attempt on the Kara Strait, the Dutch fleet returned to Amsterdam. The States of the United Provinces were too discouraged to venture again, but they let it be known that if any town corporations or merchants were prepared to put up funds for another expedition, the Government would offer a handsome reward to the finders of a passage. It was a sufficient inducement to the merchants of Amsterdam, and in 1596 a third Dutch expedition sailed, this time with only two ships. The leader was Jacob van Heemskerck, a landsman, a man, like Willoughby, of noble birth. With him went Barents, in Richard Chancellor's role, as chief pilot of the fleet.

There was no reason this time why the Dutch should not have anticipated by nearly three hundred years the navigation of the North-East Passage. But the pilots of the fleet disagreed. Some, like Barents, emboldened by earlier success, urged a fresh attempt across the Kara Sea. But others were still fearful of ice risks in the Kara Strait and in the end instead of making for the Barents Sea they veered away to the north, aiming to reach Novaya Zemlya by a more northerly route than the previous expeditions. There was, however, some reward for this unduly cautious decision. These were seas never before explored and if they contributed nothing to the problem of a North-East Passage they yielded important discoveries. Early in June 1596 the Dutch saw the first ice-floes in these new waters floating, in the words of Gerrit de Veer, like white swans on the surface of the sea, a sea so green that they thought they must be nearing Greenland. On 9 June Bear Island was discovered, a small snow-covered island so called from the Dutchmen's battle with a great white bear which they slaughtered with muskets, halberds, and hatchets. Ten days later, still sailing northwards through the ice, they came upon the first of a group of islands pinnacled with ice which they called Spitsbergen, and coasting along the western ice-bound shores to beyond 80° of north latitude, they reached the most northerly point yet reached by man. These were desolate lands. But, in the seas around them, seals, walrus, and whales abounded, maritime wealth which soon was to provoke fierce rivalry, amounting even to open warfare, between

English and Dutch whalers and sealers; each nation, and others too, Arctic pirates like the Basques, determined to monopolize these Arctic riches.

Off the Spitsbergen coast, Heemskerck and Barents (who had always favoured an attack on the Kara Strait) decided to make for the Strait by way of the north and west of Novaya Zemlya and to leave Jan Cornelison in the other ship to his own devices. It proved, however, an unfortunate decision. Days of twisting, turning, winding through narrow leads in the ice were followed by days of gales which churned up the pack, threatening to crush them. Near Novaya Zemlya, the wind died down, but the ice continued to mount against the ship, its iron grip tightening inch by inch, pressing the hull upwards, until suddenly 'the ship burst out of the ice with such a noise and so great a crack, that they verily thought they were all cast away, knowing not how to save themselves'. It was of safety and not of the Kara Strait that they were thinking now. The coast being within reach, the Dutchmen abandoned ship and just managed to reach an indifferent refuge, Ice Haven, before the onset of the Arctic winter.

The first wintering by Europeans in the Arctic is described in vivid detail by Gerrit de Veer, the chronicler of these Dutch expeditions. Their house, built out of driftwood and timbers from the forecastle of the ship, was surmounted by a high and tapering chimney. It was elaborately furnished. There were wooden sleeping bunks for the men, and, on the advice of the surgeon-barber, a Turkish bath made out of a wine barrel. From the ceiling hung a large lamp, lit with the fat of the 'cruell beares' which prowled around the house during the winter, and by its light the Dutchmen could sit around the central fire, reading such books as *The Chronicle of Holland, Zeeland, and Friezeland*, by Albert Hendricus, or *The History or Description of the Great Empire of China*, to search for which by way of the Arctic they had left their comfortable, gabled houses along the canals of Amsterdam. When the bear-fat ran out and they could no longer read, when the smoke from the fire became too suffocating, they lay in their bunks with hot stones at their feet listening to the thudding of the foxes across the snow-covered roof and to the cracking of ice-floes out at sea.

As the winter wore on, the cold became intense; the Dutch clock stopped, the wine froze, the sheets became stiff as boards. As they sat close around the fire, Gerrit de Veer wrote: 'We froze behind our backs, and were all white as the countrymen used to be as they come into the gates of the town in Holland with their sledges, after travelling all night.'

By the New Year, scurvy had set in and one man had already died. But there was still no pale gleam from the Arctic sun to presage the coming of spring, no lessening of the ice which was piled high round the ship 'as if there had been whole towns made of ice, with towers and bulwarks round them'. Barents all along had been convinced that their only hope lay in a boat journey to the nearest mainland, the Kola Peninsula, sixteen hundred miles away, and in mid June they determined to take this risk. Loading the ship's boats with all the cargo they could hold, including the cloth, the linen, and rich velvets destined for Cathay, the Dutchmen then set out, rowing, sailing through heavy seas, dragging the overladen boats from one water channel to another over hummocky and precipitous ice until they had completed a remarkable journey to the Kola Peninsula. But they arrived without Willem Barents who was not only the pilot but the dominant personality in these great Dutch voyages of the sixteenth century. He had died of cold and exposure while still within sight of Ice Haven, the scene of this first Arctic wintering.

Nearly three hundred years later, there was a curious sequel to the Barents expedition. In the eighteen-seventies, some Norwegian sealers, rounding Novaya Zemlya, put into Ice Haven and there, still standing, they found the balks and timbers of Willem Barents' winter house. Its contents had been scattered far and wide by generations of marauding bears, but digging amidst the rocks and melting snow they found copper pans, swords, gun-barrels, flutes and drumsticks, and the remains of the Dutch chiming clock. Among the charts and books still recognizable was a copy of the Dutch translation of Pet and Jackman's log which Barents had obtained from Richard Hakluyt, and among the other discoveries which bring to life this sixteenth-century Arctic expedition was an old sea-chest. In this, frozen together in the ice, were prints and copper engravings depicting in elaborate Renaissance style classical scenes such as Pallas, Juno, and Venus in the presence of Paris, and biblical events such as the meeting of Esau with Jacob, all intended for the edification of the people of Cathay.

These Dutch expeditions, which had achieved not only access to the Kara Sea but the discovery of Bear Island and Spitsbergen and a reconnaissance of the unknown western coast of Novaya Zemlya, came to an end with the return of the Barents expedition. The reason lies in the course of Dutch history. The year 1597 when Barents and his men escaped from their winter quarters in Novaya Zemlya marked a great event, the liberation of Holland from the Spanish Army by the son of William of Orange, Maurice of Nassau. The Dutch in their war of freedom from Spanish rule had already defied Spain in the East. A Dutch fleet had visited China and Siam. Dutch factories had been established in the Spice islands of Cathay. Now, in open defiance of the Spanish monopoly, the liberated Dutch established their own East India Company. They were, in consequence, no longer much concerned with an Arctic route to Cathay, and it was left to the English to resume the search for a northern passage in the persons of two great Arctic navigators and discoverers, Henry Hudson and William Baffin.

The discoveries of Hudson and Baffin in the western Arctic exceeded all those of previous expeditions and laid the first foundations of Canada's Arctic territories. Hudson, a professional seaman, had already gained a high reputation with the Dutch as a navigator and pilot in Arctic waters and had, as an employee of the English Muscovy Company, made an historic voyage in 1607, the first directed towards the North Pole. On this, in the waters west of Spitsbergen, he reached a latitude of 80° 23′ N. This was not exceeded by any ship until the voyage of Captain Constantine Phipps in 1773. Hudson, homeward bound from this voyage, rediscovered Spitsbergen, calling it Newland (though he carried copies of Barents's charts), and south-west of Barents's Bear Island, added another territory to the Arctic map, a small island which he called 'Hudson's Tutches'. This was soon to be rediscovered by a Dutchman, Jan

May, and named Jan Mayen island. On this first voyage Hudson carried with him not only Barents's charts but – as Barents himself had done – a translation of the sailing directions for a voyage from Norway to Greenland compiled by a Norse colonist living in Greenland towards the end of the fourteenth century. Nevertheless, though Hudson sighted the east coast of Greenland more than once during his exploration of the waters west of Spitsbergen, each sighting he identified with one of those numerous islands which had decorated the western Arctic on the Zeno map.

On 15 September 1607 Henry Hudson returned to 'Tilberie Hope in the Thames'. His employers, 'certaine worshipfull merchants of London', were not too disappointed, for he had advanced northwards further than any man before him and had, moreover, confirmed Barents's reports of the rich fisheries waiting to be exploited in the waters around Spitsbergen and Bear Island. They had reason enough, therefore, to support another voyage, a voyage this time further to the east, in the waters explored by the Dutch north and east of Novaya Zemlya. Its main object was to achieve what the Dutch had failed to achieve: the navigation of a North-East Passage.

For this voyage, in the *Hopewell*, Henry Hudson had choice of three possible routes into the Kara Sea: by way of the north of Novaya Zemlya, past Barents's old winter quarters at Ice Haven; by the channel called Matochkin Shar which, as Barents discovered, separates the two islands of Novaya Zemlya; or finally, by way of the Vaigach Strait, which, like the adjacent Kara Strait, leads directly into the Kara Sea from the west. But by none of these did he succeed. Between Spitsbergen and Novaya Zemlya, even in June, Hudson found (as Barents had found) that the sea was a mass of ice stretching to the horizon. The narrow channel dividing Novaya Zemlya he missed entirely. As to the Vaigach Strait, Hudson was in favour, but the crew, led by Hudson's new mate, a sly elderly man by the name of Robert Juet, resolutely refused. The incident is important only in that it provides the first evidence of a fatal weakness in Hudson's character, a weakness in leadership which was to end in his death. Mutiny, not the ice of the Kara or Vaigach strait, forced Hudson to bring the *Hopewell* back to England.

Hudson's failure discouraged the Muscovy Company from supporting another venture, and he sought employment elsewhere, first in France, then with his old employers the Dutch and the newly established East India Company of the Chamber of Amsterdam. With them, on the 8 January 1609, he signed a contract undertaking 'to search for a passage by the North, around by the North side of Novaya Zemlya'. At the last minute, however, the directors of the East India Company changed their plans, from an eastward to a westward voyage, to explore not the North-East Passage but, in rivalry with the English, the North American coast. There were good reasons for this change. In 1609, the year in which Hudson signed his contract with the East India Company, Holland forced Spain to grant her full rights to trade in Eastern waters. The Company thereupon abandoned the now needless Arctic adventure for a very much more lucrative project, colonization in the New World. This third voyage of Hudson's therefore belongs to the history of the discovery of North America rather than of the polar regions. It is the story of trading and fighting with Indians, of landfalls off Maine, off Cape Cod and in Chesapeake Bay, and of Hudson's penetration of the great Hudson River as far as Albany, a discovery which led to the foundation of the colony of New Amsterdam, later named New York. This voyage, however, made one negative contribution to the great unsolved problem of Arctic exploration. Hudson was convinced as he sailed up the Hudson River that such shallow and narrow waters as these could not possibly lead to a northern passage.

The merchants of the City of London, determined that so brilliant an English explorer should not again be employed 'to the detriment of his own country', now themselves commissioned Hudson 'to try if, through any of those inlets which Davis saw, but durst not enter, any passage might be found to the other ocean called the South Sea'. This last voyage of Hudson's, which led to the discovery of Hudson Bay and to the explorations and Arctic trading of the Hudson's Bay Company whose stations dot the map of the Canadian Arctic today, led also to his death.

From the day Henry Hudson entered Hudson Strait (John Davis's 'mighty overfall') and sailed on into the waters of the

'great and whirling sea' which was Hudson Bay, he was convinced that he had discovered the western route to Cathay. He
contrived, despite the fog and drifting ice in the strait, to explore Ungava Bay and the north coast of the Ungava peninsula,
and during early autumn he struck out into Hudson Bay to the
west and north, aimlessly it seemed to his already murmuring
crew. He then turned south to James Bay and the mouth of the
Rupert River. It was now November, too late to turn back, for
'the nights were long and cold, and the earth covered with
snow', and his ship was soon frozen in, beset for the winter.
Already Hudson's men had witnessed omens of approaching
disaster: a savage sacrifice of 'fowles hanged by the neck' on
Digges Island, a thunderstorm which broke over the jagged
cliffs as they landed, scattering the slowly encircling sea-birds.
During the winter, the carpenter died; scurvy broke out; supplies, it became tragically clear, could not last the homeward
voyage, and by June when at last *Discovery* weighed anchor,
suspicion, mistrust, accusations of hoarding food, led inexor-
ably to the final tragedy, the marooning of Hudson, his son,
and five loyal men, without food, without weapons, at dawn off
Charlton Island.

The mutineers had been led by Robert Juet, mate of the *Hopewell*, and Abakuk Prickett, servant of Sir Dudley Digges, author
of *The Circumference of the Earth or a Treatise of the North-
West Passage*, a patron of Hudson's expedition. On their return
they were brought before the Masters of Trinity House and the
High Court of the Admiralty to answer for their crime. They
were saved from the gallows only because of their foresight in
bringing back Hudson's charts which recorded the great discoveries of the man whom they had so callously condemned to death.
Somewhere along the north-western shores of Hudson Bay, they
maintained, 'by a great flood or billow' which swept in from
that direction, lay the entrance to the North-West Passage. Their
arguments were so convincing, their optimism so infectious, that
the mutiny on the *Discovery* was forgotten, and in 1612 a new
expedition under Sir Thomas Button, consisting of the *Discovery* and another ship, the *Resolution*, was launched by the
Governor and Company of the Merchants of London, Dis-

coverers of the North-West Passage. Its object was 'to search and find out a passage by the north-west of America to the Sea Sur, commonly called the South Sea'. Bylot, mate of the *Discovery* under Hudson, was the chief pilot of the new venture, and in the course of two voyages, in 1612 and in 1615, Button explored the western shores of Hudson Bay as far north as Southampton Island.

Sir Thomas Button was followed four years later by Jens Munck, a Dane, who wintered near where Churchill town now stands, at the mouth of Churchill River. In 1631, Captain James, following in Hudson's wake, gave his name to James Bay, and another Englishman the same year, Luke Foxe – 'Northwest Foxe', he called himself – explored the waters round and north of Southampton Island and is commemorated in Foxe Peninsula and Foxe Basin. Further gaps in the great work of exploration of Arctic Canada were filled in by British voyages to Hudson Bay in the middle of the eighteenth century. Needless to say, no exit from the bay to the west was ever found, but in the perspective of history, that is relatively unimportant. For the discoveries by Hudson and his immediate successors in the first half of the seventeenth century led to the founding in 1670 of the Hudson's Bay Company. Just as in the central Arctic the discoveries of Barents and Hudson had given rise to the whaling and sealing industry, so in the west a great fur trade was developed by men – hunters, trappers, traders, voyageurs, pioneers – who in the succeeding centuries were to be primarily responsible for expanding the land frontiers of the Canadian North.

In 1616, while the coasts of Hudson Bay were being explored, a very remarkable English navigator and explorer, William Baffin, in his voyages north and west of Baffin Island, came nearer to solving the problem of the North-West Passage than any until the nineteenth century. It is one of the misfortunes of polar history that owing to the negligence and parsimony of a popular anthologist, Samuel Purchas, only the bare outline of Baffin's explorations are known. Baffin was a highly accomplished navigator with experience of both Hudson Bay and Spitsbergen waters. He was also the first to take a lunar observation at sea. His detailed map and journals, if Purchas

had ever cared to preserve them, would certainly have
shortened by many years the search for a North-West
Passage.

Baffin knew from his own experiences of Hudson Bay that
there was little prospect there of any outlet to the west; tides,
currents, the movement of ice were all more in keeping with the
conditions of an enclosed sea. He decided therefore to try
further north and to follow Davis's tracks up the west coast of
Greenland and into Davis Strait where Davis had thought there
were a number of possible directions where the entrance to a
North-West Passage might be found. Baffin's ship was the same
Discovery which Hudson had navigated into Hudson Bay and
his mate was Bylot, one of the mutineers, a man who, whatever
his part in the murder of Hudson may have been, appears to have
played an important part in a number of these Arctic expeditions. Keeping to the Greenland side of Davis Strait, Baffin
anchored the *Discovery* near the present Danish station of Upernavik, and then forced his ship, of only fifty tons, northwards
through the pack to Melville Bay and beyond to where the
United States air base of Thule now stands. In this region and
westwards, Sir Thomas Smith's Sound – through which many
American and British expeditions were to approach the Pole in
the nineteenth century – 'Sir Francis Jones his Sound', and Sir
James Lancaster's Sound were all discovered by Baffin on this
one voyage; the last two leading, if he had but known it, westwards through the Canadian Arctic archipelago to the open
waters of the Beaufort Sea. Near Smith Sound, Baffin noted the
greatest variation in the compass known at that time, and must
then have been in the vicinity of the ever-shifting North Magnetic Pole.

Baffin returned to England in August 1616, with news of
discoveries which were greater in extent and importance than
any in this part of the Arctic until the nineteenth century.
But unsupported by maps or journals, it was not long before
they were discredited or forgotten. Neither Smith Sound, nor
Lancaster Sound, nor Jones Sound, nor even Baffin Bay, appears
on the maps of the Arctic which were published in England
after the Napoleonic Wars; maps which were to serve as the

basis for the great revival of British naval exploration in the Arctic in the first quarter of the nineteenth century.

No further progress in the navigation of the North-East Passage was made during the seventeenth century, nor any attempts beyond a futile and farcical expedition led by two drunken Englishmen, Wood and Flawes, in 1676. This served only to discourage further effort. In the eighteenth century, however, Arctic explorations were renewed, though less by English or Dutch ships than by the new Imperial Navy of Peter the Great, Tzar of the expanding empire of Russia.

PART II

THE AGE OF EXPLORATION

ARCTIC AND ANTARCTIC:
THE AGE OF STRATEGY AND
EXPLORATION

BY the end of the seventeenth century, the broad pattern of Arctic geography had begun to take shape. Eastwards, along the desolate north Russian coast, English ships had reached, the Dutch had entered, the Kara Sea. In the Barents Sea, the western coasts of the twin islands of Novaya Zemlya had been reconnoitred while, further west, Spitsbergen, Bear Island, Jan Mayen island had all been discovered and on their coasts and in the waters around them a great rivalry between Dutch and English in the slaughter of whales, seals, and walrus had broken out. West of these snow-peaked islands, though knowledge continued to be greatly confused by the distortions of the Zeno map, the southern parts of the land-mass which the Norsemen called Greenland (the English, misled by the cartographers, West Friezeland or West England) had emerged from a forgotten past. Along the southern coasts of Greenland, John Davis, the discoverer of Davis Strait, was the first to attempt some systematic explorations.

The most spectacular advance during this period, however, was in the Canadian Arctic. There, not only had the eastern frontiers of modern Canada (Labrador and Baffin Island) been roughly defined, but Hudson Strait, first detected by Davis, had been found by Hudson to lead into the broad waters of an open sea. This discovery, in reality Hudson Bay, gave new hope to those searching for an entrance to a North-West Passage. More relevant, however, to the future of polar exploration was William Baffin's discovery, north of the Arctic Circle, of Baffin Bay and of the three large sounds leading from it. These, when they were rediscovered in the nineteenth century, were to provide routes of access both to the North-West Passage and the Pole.

These maritime expeditions, launched by merchant guilds and city companies seeking a trade route through the Arctic to the rich oriental kingdoms bordering the Pacific Ocean, were not the only Arctic ventures during the seventeenth century. Other discoveries, though unrecorded, must have been made by the whalers which followed in the wake of these Arctic expeditions. Meanwhile, on land, the men of the Hudson's Bay Company, trappers and hunters, guides and voyageurs, who lived off the country and were learning from the Eskimo and the Indian how best to travel and survive, had already started, as they laid the foundations of a great fur industry, to push the Canadian frontiers towards the north.

The Antarctic, of which little has so far been said, remained throughout the seventeenth century in the realm of academic argument and speculation about the existence of a fertile southern continent. Each new discovery, every rumour of new lands in the southern oceans, was hailed as confirmation of all that the geographers had predicted. When the Solomon Islands – endowed, their discoverers insisted, with all the wealth of Solomon – were discovered by the Spaniard Alvaro de Mendana and his Portuguese pilot Pedro Fernandez de Quiros in 1568, they were at once identified as outliers of some continental El Dorado, projecting northwards into the Pacific from a central position round the Antarctic Pole. Not only the Solomon Islands, but the Carolines and Marianas, the New Hebrides, the Marquesas Islands, discovered by Mendana and Quiros in 1595 and 1605, all these were thought to presage a neighbouring southern continent which might at any moment emerge.

Indirectly, the Solomon Islands made at least a negative contribution to the problem, though it went quite unheeded at the time. When the news of Mendana's discovery reached the civilized world, Sir Richard Grenville and a group of enterprising West-Country gentlemen in England, with the discreet approval and support of their Queen, were laying the first plans to break into Spanish preserves in the Pacific and along the prohibited Atlantic trade routes to Cathay. Their ambition was to sail through the Strait of Magellan and up the west coast of America in search of a Strait of Anian or a North-West Passage. They now added to this programme another project, 'the discovery, traffic, and enjoying for The Queen's Majesty and her subjects, of all and any lands, islands, and countries southwards beyond the equinoctial, to where the Pole Antarctic hath any elevation above the horizon'. These plans, made probably in 1573, are thought, like so many of the plans for Elizabethan discovery, to have been the work of the cousins Hakluyt. As far as Grenville was concerned, they proved abortive, the Queen withholding her permission because of temporarily improved relations with Spain. Four years later, however, when relations worsened once again, these same plans were revived and led to Drake's great voyage of circumnavigation of 1577–80.

Emerging from Magellan's Strait – where his ship the *Pelican* was renamed the *Golden Hind* – Drake was borne away by high winds to the south of Cape Horn and into the passage, Drake Passage, which bears his name. Of Magellan's archipelago to the north of him, Drake wrote: 'The uttermost cape or hedland of all these ilands stans neere in 56° without which there is no maine or iland to be seene to the southwards, but that the Atlanticke Ocean and the South Sea meete in a most large and free scope.' With this one statement, Drake disposed of one fashionable theory, namely that a southern continent adjoined South America. Nevertheless, as was the case with Magellan when he rejected the notion that Tierra del Fuego was the tip of a southern continent, the geographers, not the seamen, were believed, and two hundred years later geographers were still speculating about the existence of a fertile southern continent stretching northwards into the temperate zone. Such speculation persisted despite the claims of seamen, notably the English buccaneers Bartholomew Sharpe, Ambrose Cowley, Edward Davis, and William Dampier, who roamed freely in these southern waters during the seventeenth century, that often on their voyages they had sailed their ships where continental land was plainly marked on the map.

While geographers were debating these extravagant notions, some truly Antarctic discoveries were probably being made. Dirck Gerritz of the Dutch East India Company, who it is claimed saw in 1599 the snow-clad mountains of a continent in 64° S., may, though it is very doubtful, have been the first to set eyes on peaks of the South Shetland Islands, which lie south of Drake Passage and Cape Horn. In 1675, probably, a merchant captain, Antonio de la Roché, first saw the coasts of South Georgia, an island often wrongly supposed to have been sighted nearly two centuries earlier by the Portuguese Amerigo Vespucci. However, such an isolated chance discovery as this was bound to be shifting and uncertain in the days before the solution of the vital problem of longitude enabled the position of ships and the position of landfalls to be accurately fixed. This was not accomplished until late in the eighteenth century.

Such, broadly speaking, was the state of discovery in the Arctic and Antarctic regions at the end of the seventeenth century. With the opening of the new century, under the influence of new political and strategic conditions and in response to new intellectual, new social, and new technological developments, not only the motives but the methods of polar exploration changed. Spain as the dominant imperial power, Holland as England's principal commercial rival, had faded from the European scene, to be replaced by France, the France of Louis XIV, determined not only to succeed to the former position of Spain, but to establish an even more extensive and more magnificent maritime, colonial, and commercial empire. During the long series of Anglo-French wars – the War of the Austrian Succession, the Seven Years' War, the American War of Independence – which were waged continuously throughout the eighteenth century, the Arctic and sub-Arctic lands of Canada, the trade routes across the southern ocean, even the prospect of colonial gains in the as yet undiscovered southern continent, played some part in the maritime and colonial strategy of the two great powers.

In this period of strategic exploration, Arctic territory was also involved in another direction, when Peter the Great, Tzar of Russia (1682–1725), launched into Asia the first of a series of grandiose national projects for colonial expansion and development. These led in time to a spread of Russian settlements south of Bering Strait and along the Asian coast. To a Tzar so

eager to emulate, indeed to eclipse, the exploratory achievements
of the West, who was, moreover, the founder of the Russian
Navy, the discovery and navigation of a North-East Passage
was in itself a sufficient challenge and inducement to display,
for the admiration of the West, Russian prowess in exploration
and Russian technical skill. But as her remote Pacific settlements
grew and spread, the North-East Passage gained for Russia a
new and special and more urgent significance as a possible
route by which such colonies and trading posts might be sustained more economically than by the long and wearisome
caravan journeys through the forests and across the endless
Siberian plains.

This new concern of governments with exploration led in turn
to some basic changes in organization. In Holland, in England,
in Russia too in her first advances towards the fur and sealing
frontiers of Siberia, expeditions of discovery had been organized by private groups and corporations, merchant adventurers
hiring vessels and seamen for purposes of private gain. But
when exploration became, in the eighteenth century, largely
an instrument of policy, it became the task of the ships and men
of the national navies, British, French, and Russian alike. In
Britain this use of the Navy in polar exploration became a
traditional and established practice. From the time of Cook to
the first expeditions of Robert Falcon Scott early in the twentieth
century, officers of the Royal Navy played a dominant – some
have thought, a too exclusive – role in the organization and
conduct of polar exploration.

The most striking innovation, however, during the eighteenth
century, when science began to approach its modern form, was
the injection into polar exploration of a scientific motive. The
eighteenth century saw the beginning of scientific exploration,
and James Cook, who in the course of his three great Pacific and
Antarctic voyages was to build for Britain a new maritime and
commercial empire greater than the world had ever seen, was
the first to show how effectively science and strategy could be
blended. In the development of scientific exploration, the new
national academies of science which sprang up in England,
France, and Russia late in the seventeenth and early in the eight-

eenth century played an exceedingly important part as advisers of governments in all scientific matters. The foundation by royal charter of the Royal Society in England in 1660 was followed in 1666 by the foundation of the Académie des Sciences. But Russia, for centuries isolated in medieval darkness, remained untouched by this new national concern with scientific studies until, in 1697 and 1717, Peter the Great, the first Russian emperor to travel outside Russia, came to consult (so that he might rival) the scientists and technologists of the West. It was not, however, until 1725, the year of his death, that the Imperial Academy of Sciences was founded, not only to promote studies in the physical and natural sciences but to promote the active exploration of the vast resources of Russia's new and expanding territories.

In the remarkable advance of science which the eighteenth century witnessed, an advance which was now for the first time to influence polar exploration, no branch (except chemistry) developed more rapidly than the study of magnetism. Magnetic studies had been given a new and quite revolutionary aspect a century before when William Gilbert published in 1600 his great discovery that the earth itself was a globular magnet. This in turn led to the demand for the formulation of general laws or principles which could, it was apparent, only be deduced from an analysis of widespread, coordinated, and simultaneous observations of magnetic variation and magnetic dip. These magnetic discoveries greatly stimulated scientific exploration, and in 1699 a British naval expedition, the first scientific expedition to leave English shores, sailed in His Majesty's ship, the pink *Paramour*. This was led – disastrously – by a landsman, Edmund Halley, the Astronomer Royal, who was rashly placed in command of the ship by the Admiralty. It produced, nevertheless, from observations in the South Atlantic, the first map of magnetic variation. Following this precedent the recording of magnetic observations during the eighteenth and nineteenth centuries became a primary duty of naval expeditions.

The long exploring voyages so characteristic of the eighteenth century could never have been achieved without considerable advances in hygiene, in navigation (of which magnetic studies were a vital part), and in the choice of ships. In hygiene, the most notable development since the introduction in 1601 of fruit juice as an anti-scorbutic was the publication in 1753 of James Lind's *Treatise of the Scurvy*. In navigation, the invention of John Hadley's reflecting quadrant (later, the sextant) in 1731; the publication by Nevil Maskeleyne in 1767 of the first nautical almanac; and notably the testing in 1762 of John Harrison's chronometer, remarkably accurate for its day; these were the principal advances, each in turn contributing to the greatest of all the mariner's needs, the solution of the problem of longitude. In the choice of ships, the most notable development was in the use by Cook of ships specially selected and adapted for exploration. There are, indeed, few clues to the motives of exploring expeditions more revealing than the choice of ships. In the sixteenth and seventeenth centuries, cargo ships large enough to carry bulky merchandise were needed for the Arctic voyages to Cathay. In the eighteenth century, a century of war, when exploration was closely linked with strategic operations, warships were in general use. When, however, in the second half of the century the first voyages of scientific exploration began under Cook, he chose his ships accordingly. Small but robust, roomy but of shallow draught, they were capable not only of withstanding the strain of long ocean voyages but of working along unknown coasts close inshore. It was in these, north-country colliers of three hundred tons or so, that Cook was able to undertake the first hydrographic surveys in Antarctica.

One other facet of exploration during the eighteenth century, in the polar as in other regions, and one too often disregarded, was the steady growth of public concern with exploration which tended to mould its course and direction. Following the publication of the pirate William Dampier's *New Voyage around the World* in 1697 – a best-seller in its day – works about travel and exploration came second only to those on theology in public popularity, and this trend continued and became especially marked towards the end of the eighteenth century when with the voyages of Cook there opened the greatest era of geographical exploration since the Age of Discovery. In England it was fostered in a number of ways: through the foundation of private societies to promote travel and exploration, such as the Linnean

Society and the African Association in 1788 for the support of botanical journeys and African travel; through the spread to the provinces of newspapers and lending libraries; and through the publication not only of those ornate but costly volumes with which the wealthy furnished the libraries of their country houses, but of inexpensive reprints or, as in the case of G. W. Anderson's edition of Cook's *Voyages* of 1784, of works in cheap periodical parts.

Included in this growing popular literature of exploration were a number of collections of voyages and travels, not the speculations or moralizings of geographers and philosophers, but personal stories of discovery and adventure like Dampier's *New Voyage*. Two works of this kind, published in England and in France, did much, as indeed their authors intended, to focus the attention of peoples and of governments on the problem of the existence of a fertile southern continent and thus to direct attention to Antarctic exploration. In England, Dr John Campbell's *Complete Collection of Voyages and Travels* appeared in a second edition in 1745. It was addressed to the merchants of Britain for whom, the editor declared, a great new southern world, rich in prospects for trade, for colonies, and for the enhancement of British naval prestige, lay open. In France, at the instigation of the naturalist Buffon, a foremost protagonist of the idea of a southern continent, M. Charles De Brosses, president of the Parliament of Dijon, published in 1756 his *Histoires des navigations aux terres australes*. In both countries – and in France the territorial losses and the humiliations suffered under the Treaty of Paris of 1763 made the discovery of a southern continent all the more imperative – these works aroused great public enthusiasm and excitement, and concern that national expeditions should at once be sent out to probe the undiscovered Antarctic regions.

Against this background of trends and influences, we must turn first of all to the Arctic. The eighteenth century was principally a century of Russian achievement in the Arctic, Britain being preoccupied with the great Pacific and Antarctic voyages of James Cook. But British ships were also active in the Arctic, especially in the waters of Hudson Bay, and there a number of voyages in search of the entrance to a North-West Passage took place, several towards the middle years of the century when Britain was engaged in a series of powerful maritime operations to oust the French and secure dominion over Canada.

Since Hudson's last and tragic voyage there had been a number of attempts to discover a North-West Passage leading out of Hudson Bay, voyages made the more attractive to promoters in the City of London because of the prospect of a direct sea-route to the fur-bearing lands of the Canadian North which were to be harvested by the Hudson's Bay Company. The English voyages between 1615 and 1617, the Danish expedition to Churchill River in 1619–20, and the expeditions ten years later of Captain Thomas James and Captain Luke Foxe, sponsored respectively by the merchants of Bristol and of London, have already been mentioned. Geographically perhaps they made no great advances, but they were important because they built up among English seamen a traditional skill in Arctic navigation. In the second half of the seventeenth century, to the motives behind these voyages – trade, strategy, discovery – there was added the new and growing concern with science, stimulated in Britain by the new Royal Society whose Fellows had from the start shown an increasing concern with Arctic phenomena and observations and with the problems of Arctic navigation. During these and subsequent years, however, trade probably remained the most powerful motive. It was, it is true, often viewed by the colonists and the Company on one side and by the Government on the other in a very different light, the colonists and the Company being concerned with profit, the Government rather with trade as a weapon of strategic and commercial expansion. Nevertheless, to both sides it was of the highest importance, for the fur trade was to the northern colonists what the tobacco trade was to the colonists in the southern parts of the United States, it provided the means, the 'cash-crop', with which the manufactured goods of the mother-country could be purchased.

The routes by which this trade should be conducted had an important bearing on the prospect of British voyages to seek a North-West Passage. Towards the end of the seventeenth century the Government and merchants of England were persuaded that trade in furs could best be carried not through the normal, and geographically more logical, route up the St Lawrence River but by direct sea voyages from England by way of Hudson Strait to Hudson Bay. To the colonists and trading stations to the south of the Bay this, because it would be less profitable, was unpopular. But in London these new proposals, first put forward, oddly enough, by two disgruntled French-Canadian backwoodsmen, gained much support. Voyages by this route would strike a blow at French trade and at the French trading areas in the south, while to the City of London such direct access would be more profitable. It offered possibilities, moreover, of associating with trading voyages, expeditions for the purpose of Arctic discovery and scientific research, and in particular expeditions to seek a North-West Passage. This continued to be a constant enthusiasm, indeed an absorbing passion, of governments, merchants, scientists, and the general public alike.

To counter this projected English offensive the French themselves planned some voyages in search of a passage, aiming to exclude the British from the northern trade. But the Treaty of Utrecht of 1713 put an end to such ambitions, for by it the French lost all their ports along the shores of the Bay. However, even with the field thus open, new obstacles arose to the promotion of voyages into the north of Hudson Bay, for the Company showed themselves strongly averse to the new policy of expansion and penetration. They had, they declared, neither the resources nor the men to thrust forward and hold trading posts in the unknown and hostile interior and preferred to consolidate rather than expand, leaving it to the Indians to bring their furs to the posts along the shores of the Bay. In the second decade of the eighteenth century this opposition on the part of the Company to voyages of exploration and expansion was temporarily overcome under the influence of a former governor of the Company, Captain James Knight, and in 1719 he led an expedition of three ships to the north of 64°, seeking not only to expand trade and discover a North-West Passage but also to discover the gold and copper mines said to exist in these far-northern regions. Knight's expedition ended in disaster, and in the last stages of exhaustion, he and his men, as a subsequent search expedition discovered, were massacred by Eskimoes. This was a turning-point in the Company's interest in a North-West Passage and it decided that it would do nothing further to encourage such ambitious adventures.

In London, however, in the second half of the eighteenth century a very different opinion developed. There were fears that the renewed and widespread expansion by French hunters and scouts northwards and round the Bay might soon pin the English to their posts along its shores with the French holding the hinterland. These fears led to a clamour for a more active, a more offensive, policy involving not the passive tenure of trading posts but voyages of discovery and penetration inland such as the search for a North-West Passage would require. The leader of this growing body of opinion was Arthur Dobbs, an Ulsterman and a Member of the Irish Parliament, one of those remarkable men who from time to time have emerged as insistent and persevering champions of polar discovery.

Dobbs, an enthusiast for northern exploration of all kinds, was keenly interested in the problem of a passage and he picked upon one of the Company's servants, a Captain James Middleton, a man sufficiently well versed in the current studies of magnetic variation to become in 1736 a Fellow of the Royal Society, as the ideal man to lead an expedition. No doubt because of the strategic significance of the voyage, Dobbs proposed that this time the expedition should be sponsored by the Admiralty. In June 1741, accordingly, Captain Middleton sailed from the Thames for the Arctic in His Majesty's bomb-carrier *Furnace*, accompanied by the sloop *Discovery*. But once again the voyage was a failure. The crew was mutinous. Scurvy broke out. And the officers of the ships proved for the most part to be as useless at sea as they were unqualified for such an arduous and complicated task of navigation. Following Foxe's route, Middleton's ships reached and penetrated Wager River, so called after the First Lord of the Admiralty. Indeed, they thrust even further north, as far as Repulse Bay on the Arctic Circle. But Middleton returned convinced that no passage of any kind lay along that shore of Hudson Bay.

Arthur Dobbs, convinced that Middleton had been bribed to come to a conclusion so agreeable to the Company, refused to give up the struggle. In 1745, the year when the British capture of Vauban's great fortress of Louisburg demolished the French defences of their main artery, the St Lawrence, he persuaded Parliament to vote the sum of £20,000 to reward the discovery of a North-West Passage by way of Hudson Bay; and two years later an expedition under Captain Moore set forth, at public expense, to search for the mysterious passage. They probed deeply into Wager's inlet but they discovered that it only dwindled into two minor waterways instead of expanding into the great seaway they had hoped for, leading to the distant East. Middleton's findings being thus confirmed – as indeed they were again to be by the British explorer, Parry, early in the nineteenth century – English interest in the Passage died away. The next expeditions to seek it came not from London but from Philadelphia, in 1753 and 1754. Four years later, the fortress of Louisburg, which had been returned to France under the peace of 1748, was retaken, and this was followed by the capture of Quebec and Montreal, the keys to French Canada. With the French threat thus removed, there were no longer any strategic reasons for promoting further attempts on the North-West Passage. In England, nevertheless, there was a slight revival of interest in the second half of the eighteenth century, and in 1761 and 1762 Middleton, with Captain Norton, followed up a suggestion made by Captain Moore that they should explore Chesterfield Inlet. But these were the last important voyages of exploration in the eighteenth century into the northern waters of Hudson Bay. In 1763 the Peace of Paris brought the Seven Years' War to a close, and the pressure in London for voyages of discovery to counter French expansion consequently and finally ceased.

Before turning to the great Russian explorations in the Arctic, one other British Arctic expedition deserves to be mentioned because it shows, in its concern with science and in its general equipment, the influence of the more specialized attitude towards exploration for which Cook, as we shall see, was so largely responsible.

The moving spirit in this enterprise was the Honourable Daines Barrington, a lawyer and a keen naturalist and student of Arctic history, who persuaded the Royal Society to submit through the First Lord of the Admiralty, the Earl of Sandwich, a memorial to King George III urging the dispatch of a scientific expedition to the North Pole by way of Spitsbergen. 'The great French enterpriser', the Chevalier de Bougainville, was known to be launching a similar expedition that same year and in adding to the armament of the two British ships, the Admiralty had the attractive prospect of an encounter with him in mind. The British expedition was commanded by Captain the Honourable Constantine Phipps in the *Racehorse*, while in the *Carcass*, under Commander Skeffington Lutwidge, there was among the young gentlemen of the quarter-deck Midshipman Horatio Nelson. The *Racehorse* carried a civilian astronomer, Israel Lyon, and two ice-pilots, masters from the Greenland whaling fleet. The expedition, of which there is a lively account in the private journal of Midshipman Thomas Floyd, established new standards in British Arctic exploration. The ships chosen, two 'bombs', so-called from their bomb-carrying mortars, had bows and bottoms strengthened against the ice. Great ice-saws and hatchets, ice-cables and anchors were carried, and a large quantity of bricks, sand, and lime in case of shipwreck on the Arctic coasts. Special clothing was issued by the Admiralty; jackets, waistcoats, and breeches of flannel, and mittens and stockings of lamb's wool. The surgeon on the expedition, Dr Irving, 'justly noted for his knowledge in Natural Philosophy', invented – the melting of ice for water not then being the practice – an ingenious machine for distilling fresh from salt water. He insisted, moreover, that butter and rice instead of cheese and oatmeal should be taken, the better to fortify the daily beef or pork diet of the crews.

Constantine Phipps sailed in 1773, and although he contributed little to the accurate mapping of Spitsbergen, he reached remarkably far north up the west coast and indeed exceeded Hudson's farthest north by several miles. His expedition had its share of adventures. Both ships had a narrow escape from being beset, and Horatio Nelson, playing truant from his

ship one night under cover of a fog, decided rashly to challenge
a bear. Although his musket had flashed in the pan, and his
ammunition had run out, he resolutely refused to return to his
ship until, Commander Lutwidge having ordered the ship's
guns to be fired, the bear was scared away.

These British voyages to Hudson Bay and the waters of
Spitsbergen were, however, small affairs by comparison with the
great panorama of Arctic exploration which the eighteenth century witnessed in the East: the culmination of Russian colonial
and trade expansion through the forests and across the great
waterways and prairies of Siberia to the Bering Strait and the
north Pacific Ocean. In grandeur of scale and range, these
Russian expeditions were characteristic of the physical and intellectual energy and ambition of their principal architect, Peter
the Great, a ruler who was determined to match and outstrip
the West by 'the finding of a passage to China and India through
the Arctic Sea', a North-East Passage leading into the Pacific
Ocean.

The first problem confronting the Russian explorers, whether
Asia and America were joined by land or separated by sea, had
– though this was not known until the second quarter of the
eighteenth century – already been solved three-quarters of a
century earlier by a Siberian Cossack, Simon Dezhnev, one of a
band of Cossacks fleeing to the east to escape serfdom. In 1644,
he reached the Kolyma river which flows into the East Siberian
Sea. Four years later, in six flat-bottomed boats, Dezhnev set
out again, following the coast towards the east until he reached
East Cape (Mys Dezhneva) overlooking the Bering Strait. This
was the land of the warring Chukchi tribes. Only Dezhnev and
his boat's crew escaped, and, rounding the Chukchi Peninsula
(Chukotskiy Poluostrov), they reached the mouth of the Anadyr
river. Some reports, vague and unconfirmed, of this first discovery of the Bering Strait may have reached the Imperial Court
across the vast wilderness which separated the Russian outposts
in east Siberia from the new capital, St Petersburg; and, indeed,
a map presented to Peter the Great by a Swedish prisoner of
war in Siberia is said to have recorded a Russian penetration of
the Bering Strait and even Russian penetration as far south as

the Kamchatka peninsula. It is possible that such rumours may have stimulated the grandiose project which Peter the Great was about to launch.

This first great Russian Arctic expedition was as different from earlier pioneering efforts as were the British expeditions of the eighteenth century from those of the Merchant Adventurers. In planning and execution it was a national enterprise, combining with national strategic motives, as in the West, objectives of geographical and scientific discovery. It was natural, therefore, that the ships used and the leader appointed, Vitus Bering, a Dane, should belong to the new and progressive Imperial Russian Navy.

Six months before his death in 1725, Peter the Great put the finishing touches to his great Arctic plans. To Vitus Bering and his men they must have presented a formidable prospect, for they entailed not only an initial overland journey of 5,000 miles across Europe and Asia to Okhotsk on the Pacific coast, which meant the transport of men and supplies by raft over the swirling waters of four of the mightiest rivers in Russia, but at the end of it a sea voyage northwards round the Kamchatka peninsula, and a landing on the American coast. By the summer of 1725, Bering and the twenty-five men of his expedition had reached the settlement of Yakutsk on a curving branch of the Lena river. Already it had been an immense and wearisome journey. But worse was to come. So far they had travelled mainly over steppe land, but between Yakutsk and Okhotsk lay seven hundred miles of country broken by rivers, mountains, and swamps and swept by the blizzards of an early winter. Of the two hundred horses in Bering's caravan many died of the cold, and cumbrous loads of equipment and provisions had to be hauled on sleds to the coastal township of Okhotsk.

There Bering soon found himself tangled in the web of petty officialdom whose procrastination and corruption and secret manoeuvres were to prove throughout his explorations such a barrier to progress. However, one of the ships for the northern voyage, the *Fortune*, had been built and in the summer of 1727, two years after leaving St Petersburg, the sea route to Kamchatka was explored. In the following summer, the second ship, the *St Gabriel*, was finished after intolerable delays and in the summer of 1729 Bering was able to circumnavigate the Kamchatka peninsula as far as the Gulf of Anadyr.

The Chukchi tribes, from whom Simon Dezhnev had so narrowly escaped, this time proved friendly, and their stories of journeys northwards across the peninsula to the Kolyma River, which, they said, flowed out into an ice-covered sea, encouraged Bering to persevere. Sailing out of the Gulf of Anadyr (Anadyr'-skiy Zaliv), the *St Gabriel* passed St Lawrence Island, named by Bering after his patron saint, and entered the Bering Strait. To the west, Dezhnev's East Cape (Mys Dezhneva), the furthermost point of Asia, loomed above the sea. But to the east over the Alaskan coast fog hung heavily over the water and no sign of land could be seen. In part, Bering's mission had been accomplished, for a sea passage linking the Pacific with the Arctic Ocean had been found. But the passage had still to be navigated and the coast followed to the west for the discovery to be beyond all doubt. To go on, to turn back: it was no easy decision for Bering to take. Bering Strait was free of ice, but it was dangerously late in the season and winter and the ice might at any moment close in. In any event they faced a long and hazardous voyage to Okhotsk. Disaster, Bering well knew, would mean disgrace and worse. He therefore turned back.

A fruitless voyage eastwards the following summer completed Bering's five years of exploration and he returned in triumph to St Petersburg to report to the Tzarina Ann. But applause quickly turned to scorn as Bering told his story. The charting of the Kamchatka peninsula, the discovery of new islands, the revelation of a strait separating Asia and America about which the geographers had speculated, all these achievements were submerged in the flood of public accusation at Bering's apparent timidity. It was fortunate that there were men at court who still believed in him sufficiently to support his plea to be allowed to redeem his reputation by leading another expedition.

Bering's next expedition was on an even more majestic scale, and it exceeded in scope and complexity anything that had yet been attempted in Arctic exploration. The whole Arctic coast from the Gulf of Ob (Obskaya Guba) to the Anadyr River was to be systematically mapped. Bering was to search for land to the east of Kamchatka across the Bering Sea. South of Kamchatka Martin Spanberg, his Danish second-in-command, was to chart the Kurile islands and the islands of Japan. This was the plan. But even the Admiralty College, when it took over direction of the vast enterprise in 1733, thought this more than one man could possibly control, and Bering was left with the principal exploring expedition, from Kamchatka across the Bering Sea.

When Bering arrived in Okhotsk late in 1734, it was no longer the frontier settlement of his first visit. It was now a township, thronged with the colonists, the technicians, the innumerable officials sent out by the Imperial Government. Here he was immobilized for six years, bewildered and frustrated by the procrastination and the intrigues, by the multiplication of dossiers, by the stream of inquiries, of orders, and of counter-orders dispatched across the vast expanses of Siberia by a central government determined to exercise remote control over every detail of his operations. Not until 1740, seven years after he had left St Petersburg, were Bering's new ships, the *St Peter* and *St Paul*, ready to sail eastwards on the new explorations. The *St Peter* carried as surgeon the German naturalist, Georg Wilhelm Steller. Louis Delisle de la Croyère, related to Guillaume Delisle, geographer to Louis XV, sailed with Chirikov, the Russian captain of the *St Paul*.

Bering's last voyage ended in both triumph and disaster. The broad beaches and dark forests of north-west America were reached and in the one day spent on shore, Steller the naturalist found time to make copious notes on fauna and flora and to gather specimens of Alaskan native arts and crafts for the Imperial collections. But the plan to winter had to be abandoned, for Bering, among others, was weakening rapidly from scurvy. Both ships therefore, despite the threatening weather, put out to sea and made for home. But Bering's ship, the *St Peter*, sailing through fog and storms of torrential rain, was wrecked on the beach of Bering Island. And there the greatest Arctic explorer of the eighteenth century died.

Bering's discovery of the strait which bears his name, and of the islands south of it, his charting of the Kamchatka and Anadyr peninsulas and his two landings on the American coast are among the great achievements of Arctic exploration. And to them must be added the immense and systematic work of charting the whole length of the northern Russian coast eastwards from the Ob which was carried out simultaneously and was continued after Bering's death by the Imperial Admiralty College. All these complicated and extensive operations, successfully completed despite the hindrances of a highly centralized and often incompetent administration, disposed once and for all of the fantastic ideas about the Arctic geography of north-east Asia and north-west America current in the first half of the eighteenth century. They were also more indirectly to affect the course of Arctic exploration. In the east as in the west (in Hudson Bay), exploration was followed by trade, and by the formation of trading companies. In the footsteps of the Russian explorers, a new brand of Russian imperialism at the instigation of Catherine the Great began to spread during the second half of the eighteenth century across the Bering Strait and down the North American coast. By the first quarter of the nineteenth century, Russia – in the form of the government-sponsored Russian-American Company – was firmly established in Alaska. She thus became a strategic factor in the problem of a North-West Passage round the northern extremity of British Canada. The search for this was to preoccupy the British Navy for more than half the century which followed the Napoleonic Wars.

COOK AND THE FIRST CROSSING
OF THE ANTARCTIC CIRCLE

AN Antarctic voyage early in the eighteenth century, made by
a young Frenchman, Bouvet de Lozier, came for the first time
close to discovering the true nature of Antarctic geography.
Bouvet had persuaded the French East India Company to equip
two ships to discover and annex the Southland and, reaching
latitude 48° 50′ S. in the Atlantic section of the Southern Ocean,
he was able to describe for the first time the great flat-topped
tabular icebergs, the seals, and the penguins, familiar elements
in the Antarctic scene. On New Year's Day 1739, a snowy land
loomed out of the fog through which his two ships, the *Aigle*
and the *Marie*, had been steering a tortuous course. This was
Bouvet Island. Then as now it was so difficult to approach that
Bouvet was forced to bear away to the south until he reached
the edge of the pack. This great belt of ice, he surmised, girdled
a distant and inaccessible continent, a continent of ice and
snow, in harsh and disagreeable contrast to the rich lands
promised by the geographers in Britain and France.

Not until after the Seven Years' War was exploration in the
southern hemisphere renewed. It was then that the British
Navy entered the field, with results which were before the end
of the eighteenth century to transform the whole problem of a
southern continent and, in so doing, to provide a true and
rational basis for future Antarctic exploration.

Charles Byron in 1764, Samuel Wallis and Philip Cartaret in
1766, each sailed with secret orders from the Admiralty to go
'in search of the Land or Islands supposed to lie in that part of
the Southern Hemisphere'. Each carried precise instructions as
to the making of surveys, the proper treatment of natives, and
the annexation of newly discovered territories to the British
Crown. Byron, great as was his voyage, contributed little to the

problem of a southern continent. But Wallis's discovery of Tahiti, with its sands and placid lagoons, its verdant slopes and graceful casuarinas, once again filled the minds of men like De Brosses and John Campbell with hopes no less extravagant than those aroused by the discovery of the Solomon Islands and other island groups in the eastern Pacific during the sixteenth and early seventeenth centuries.

France now also joined in the search, eager to rival British naval achievements and, in compensation for the losses of the recent peace, to have some share in this new and rich colonial world. The leader chosen for the French expedition was the Chevalier de Bougainville, of noble birth and an intellectual turn of mind, and a fervent disciple of Charles De Brosses. Accompanied, as was now the fashion, by scientists, Commerson the botanist and Verron the astronomer, De Bougainville reached Tahiti in 1767 and explored numerous new islands in the flamboyant archipelago of which Tahiti was the central jewel. Follower of De Brosses though De Bougainville was, his views about the probable discovery of a great southern continent in these seas were not encouraging to the optimists at home. 'I agree', he declared, in an objective analysis reminiscent of Cook, 'that it is difficult to conceive so great a number of low islands and, as it were, drowned pieces of land, without supposing a continent in their neighbourhood. But geography is a science of fact; no man in his study ventures on system-making except at the risk of the largest mistakes, which are subsequently corrected only at the expense of the practical sailor.' Tahiti might be La Nouvelle Cythère but that was no proof that a continent lay nearby. To seek that proof was to be the task of one who, among other and greater qualities, amounting in aggregate to genius, was just such a practical sailor as De Bougainville had in mind.

In England at this time one of the most ardent champions of the southern continent was Alexander Dalrymple, an obdurate, cantankerous Scot, of some ability, much self-conceit, and no sense of proportion. He had served for some years in the East India Company and on his return had devoted himself in a general way to a variety of studies, such as astronomy, cartography, the history of the Spanish voyages, and the formation of coral reefs, and had gained sufficient distinction in these diverse fields to win a Fellowship of the Royal Society. His principal passion, however, was the history of exploration of the Southern Hemisphere. A friend and correspondent of De Brosses, he soon became convinced, like De Brosses, of 'the necessity of a Southern Continent to maintain a conformity in the two hemispheres' – a concept peculiarly attractive to the formal eighteenth-century mind – and took as his mission the task of persuading the people and government of Britain to launch expeditions to discover, as he called it, the Southland.

In 1766 an opportunity arose for Dalrymple to direct the search himself. The Royal Society had sought the support of the Treasury and the Admiralty for an expedition to observe the transit of Venus across the sun, a rare astronomical phenomenon known to occur in 1769. For such observations, Tahiti was regarded as the perfect base, and Dalrymple seized the opportunity to plead that with these astronomical tasks there should be combined a thorough search for the Southland. He drew up plans and, indeed, instructions for the voyage. In 1767 he published a memoir on the Spanish voyages in the Pacific to draw attention to the problem. And when the appointment of a leader of the expedition came to be considered, he applied for the post himself.

Dalrymple was no inconsiderable astronomer. He was well known to the Royal Society, moreover, as a diligent student of southern exploration and he seemed, therefore, the obvious man for the post. The Admiralty, dubious at first, refused him outright when Dalrymple insisted that he had 'no thoughts of making this voyage as a passenger or in any other capacity than having the total management of the ship to be sent'. True, only seventy years earlier the astronomer Halley had been given command of a naval ship; but in the Admiralty Halley's incompetence in naval matters had not been forgotten, and the First Lord, hearing of Dalrymple's demand, roundly declared that he would lose his right hand rather than see one of His Majesty's ships commanded by one not a naval officer. Dalrymple was outraged. But it was a wise, indeed historic, decision.

For instead, an officer then on leave from a marine surveying mission off Newfoundland was selected: a Master in the Royal Navy, James Cook.

It must to many have seemed surprising that Cook, then only a warrant officer and nearing forty, should have been selected for so important a mission. But he was already well known, not only in the Navy but to the Royal Society as well. His charts of the St Lawrence which had played such a vital part in making possible the assault on Quebec, his marine surveys of Nova Scotia and Newfoundland, had already caused senior officers to speak of 'Mr Cook's genius and capacity'. And in 1766, the very year in which the Royal Society had approached the Admiralty with plans for the new astronomical expedition, Cook's achievement in accurately observing an eclipse of the sun and in calculating the longitude of Newfoundland had, when communicated to the Royal Society, established his reputation as 'a good mathematician and very expert in his business'. So the tall, angular, enigmatic Yorkshireman became Lieutenant James Cook and in May 1768 assumed command. When on 25 August of that year he sailed out of Plymouth, he carried plans and instructions in scope infinitely greater than the Royal Society had ever conceived. It was, as Dr Beaglehole, Cook's distinguished biographer, has said, 'the beginning not of one voyage but of three voyages that were going to change the face of geography and a number of other departments of human learning, as well as to affect the politics and strategies of empires'.

In equipment, in attention to scientific needs and to the requirements of health and hygiene, the preparations and the planning for Cook's first voyage became the pattern for future voyages of polar exploration until the middle of the nineteenth century. There was first the choice of a ship. It must be one, Cook maintained, 'in which the officers may, with the least hazard, venture upon a strange coast'. She must be 'of a construction that will bear to take the ground; and of a size, which ... may be safely ... laid on shore'. These were qualities, Cook reflected after his second voyage, 'not to be found in any ships of war of forty guns, not in frigates, nor in East India Company's ships, nor indeed in any other but North-country-built ships, or such as are built for the coal-trade'. These were the ships, 'cat-built' colliers from Whitby used as transports and storeships by the Navy, in which Cook had served as a merchant seaman in the North Sea. It was in one of them, the *Endeavour*, a 'cat-built' barque of some 370 tons with a wide bluff bow, that Cook sailed on his first great voyage.

Since the expedition was in inspiration a scientific enterprise, a number of scientists, including Cook himself (for navigation, charting, astronomy) were numbered in the *Endeavour*'s complement of eighty-five. There was Mr Green, the astronomer, 'the ingenious Mr Green', whose observations of the transit of Venus were to be the main work of the expedition at King George III Island or Tahiti. There was the portly and garrulous Dr Solander, a pupil of Linnaeus and the ablest botanist in England; with another Swede, Herman Sporing, as assistant naturalist. And there was the young and elegant Mr Joseph Banks, one of those rich dilettantes who adorned the Royal Society of that time, 'a gentleman of large private fortune, well versed in Natural History' who, preferring exploration to the routine diversions of the Grand Tour, had eased the problem of his acceptance by a contribution of £10,000 to the expedition's funds. The inclusion of so fashionable a young man had its drawbacks, for Banks insisted on bringing with him a small retinue of servants, including two Negroes, Richmond and Dorlton, for all of whom space had to be found in the cramped and dingy quarters of the East Coast collier. He also brought two members of the expedition essential before the days of photography. These were the draughtsmen; for botany the young and virtuous Sydney Parkinson, for 'landskip' Alexander Buchan whose delicate drawings have charmed successive generations of readers of Cook's travels.

Natural History, a term in the eighteenth century almost synonymous with Science, was a principal preoccupation of the expedition and a contemporary remarked: 'No people ever went to sea better fitted out for the purpose of Natural History. They have got a fine Library of Natural History; they have all sorts of machines for catching and preserving insects; all kinds of nets, trawls, drags, and hooks for coral fishing, they even have a curious contrivance of a telescope, by which, put into the water, you can see the bottom at a great depth, when it is clear . . .'

But these scientific studies, in astronomy, in natural history, though of primary concern to the Royal Society, were secondary in the minds of the Admiralty. More important were Cook's own work in charting and survey, and the exact geographical descriptions which he was instructed to make, of mineral resources, of 'the Genius, Temper, Disposition, and Number of the Natives, if there be any . . .' In the long run, trade and colonization were the objects of this as of most exploratory voyages in the eighteenth century. Discovery and exploration, the preamble to Cook's Instructions reads, 'will redound greatly to the honour of this nation as a maritime power, as well as to the dignity of the Crown of Great Britain, and may tend directly to the advancement of the trade and navigation thereof'. As for colonization, 'You are also with the consent of the natives to take possession of convenient situations in the Country in the name of the King of Great Britain.'

There is no need here to retell the story of Cook's first great voyage of circumnavigation from Cape Horn to Tahiti, or to describe the charting and circumnavigation of New Zealand, the journey up the east coast of Australia, or the return journey by way of New Guinea and Java. From the point of view of polar exploration, what is important are Cook's views about the legendary southern continent (for which from Tahiti he had secret instructions to search) after this first voyage of 1768–71. That such a continent, if it existed at all, could only be found in a high latitude, Cook was now certain. With an eye on Dalrymple and De Brosses and their followers, this voyage, Cook declared, 'must be allowed to have set aside the most, if not all, the arguments and proofs that have been advanced by different authors to prove that there must be a Southern Continent – I mean to the northward of 40 degrees South, for what may lie to the southward of that latitude I know not. Certain it is that we saw no visible sign of land, according to my opinion, neither in our route to the northward, southward, or westward, until a few days before we made the coast of New Zealand . . .'.

The problem had now at last been reduced to manageable

proportions. But Cook was not content to leave it there. 'Thus,' he wrote in his journal for March 1770, 'I have given my opinion freely and without prejudice not with any view to discourage any future attempts being made towards discovering the Southern Continent; on the contrary, as this voyage will evidently make it appear that there is left but a little space to the northward of 40° where the Grand Object can lay, I think it would be a great pity that this thing which at times has been the object of many ages and nations should not now be wholy clear'd up, which might very easily be done in one voyage without either much trouble or danger. . . .' The direction in which such a voyage must be made Cook explained in his report to the First Lord of the Admiralty in 1772: 'Therefore, to make new discoveries the Navigator must traverse or circumnavigate the globe in a higher parallel than has hitherto been done. . . .' The search, in other words, had now to be directed towards the heart of the Antarctic regions.

None of these sober and logical reflections, however, reached the general public or Dr Dalrymple. On the contrary, sensational rumours flew around the town that the greatest of the discoveries from which Cook had just returned was nothing less than the continent itself, inhabited, so it was said, by peoples 'hospitable, ingenious, and civil' who were eagerly awaiting his return. Dr Dalrymple was greatly encouraged. In 1772, the year after the *Endeavour*'s return, he took up the cudgels again with his customary violence, using language which shows the full measure of his fantasy. Why, he asked angrily in his *Collections of Voyages to the South Seas,* why should the Government bother with the North American colonies when all the wealth of the Southern Continent lay to hand; a land more spacious 'than the whole civilized part of Asia, from Turkey to the eastern extremity of China'. 'The scraps from this table', he declared, 'would be sufficient to maintain the power, dominion, and sovereignty of Britain.'

In France the followers of De Brosses were no less vocal nor were their claims less absurd. When, that same year, the Breton nobleman Yves Joseph de Kerguelen-Trémarec returned from his discovery of the sub-Antarctic Kerguelen Island (on the fringes

of the Indian Ocean), he claimed, on the basis of one brief and
hazardous landing, no less than the discovery of La France
Australe. 'The lands which I have had the happiness to discover',
Kerguelen declared, 'appear to form the central mass of the
Antarctic Continent ... and the land which I have called South
France is so situated as to command the route to India, the
Moluccas, China, and the South Seas ... South France can
henceforth give new life to the Île de France and Bourbon,
tripling their sea-trade, provisioning and enrichening them ...
the latitude in which it lies promises all the crops of the Mother
Country ... no doubt, wood, minerals, diamonds will be found
... if men of a different species are not discovered, at least there
will be people in a state of nature living in their primitive manner, ignorant alike of offence and remorse, knowing nothing of
the artifices of civilized society. In short, France Australe will
furnish marvellous physical and moral spectacles.' At first glance,
this Rousseauesque vision was exhilarating and full of promise.
The following year, however, Kerguelen returned for a more
extensive exploration. He found his island cold and barren, with
fog lying heavily upon its mountains, and named it the 'Land
of Desolation'.

In England, too, illusions were shattered (though not those of
Dr Dalrymple) for, in 1773, the full story of Cook's voyage was
published in two volumes. Here was the problem of the Southern
Continent clearly set out, and the way to its solution pointed.
It was inevitable that Cook should be asked to lead a second
expedition so that the matter could, as he put it, 'now be wholly
clear'd up'.

Dalrymple in his abortive plans had argued that 'a thousand
motives recommend a single ship for discovery', but Cook this
time knew better. In his single ship, the *Endeavour*, he had been
perilously near disaster on the Great Barrier Reef. For this second
voyage, therefore, two ships were taken, the *Resolution* of 462
tons and the *Adventure* of 336 tons; both, like the *Endeavour*, of
the sturdy, East Coast, collier type. The sole motive this time
was exploration, the solution of the specific geographical problem which Cook himself, in his sparse, laconic way, had so
clearly defined. To take advantage of new discoveries scientists

were again invited, but they were different from those who had voyaged in the *Endeavour*. Mr Green, the astronomer, who had persisted with his astronomical observations even when on the verge of shipwreck on the Great Barrier Reef, had died. 'He had been ill for some time,' the *General Evening Post* reported, 'and was directed to keep himself warm, but in a fit of the phrensy he got up in the night and put his legs out of the portholes, which was the occasion of his death.' This time the astronomers were Mr William Wales, in the *Resolution*, and Mr William Bayley, in the *Adventure*.

Joseph Banks had used all his considerable influence to join the new expedition and had, with Dr Solander, planned to take an even larger party, twelve in all, including Zoffany the painter and Dr James Lind, Fellow of the Royal Society, a distinguished geologist and astronomer with an extensive 'knowledge of Natural Philosophy and Mechanics'. It was a large party to fit into a small Whitby collier like the *Resolution*, and the alterations which had to be made caused her to be so unseaworthy – 'so crank', in Cook's words, – that she had to be restored to her original condition. Banks was indignant. He now found the ship to be 'neither roomy enough nor convenient enough for the purpose, nor no ways proper for the voyage', and he wrote a tempestuous letter to the Earl of Sandwich, First Lord of the Admiralty. 'Shall I then, my Lord,' he complained, 'who have engaged to leave all that can make Life agreeable in my own Country and thrown on one side all the Pleasures to be reaped from three Years of the best of my life . . . be sent off at last in a doubtful ship with Accommodations rather worse than those which I at first absolutely refused and after spending £5,000 of my own Fortune in the Equipment upon the Credit of those Accommodations which I saw actually built for me? . . . 'Tis our Great Cabbin which is too small and that is in reality our Shop where we are all to work . . . To explore is my Wish but the Place to which I may be sent almost indifferent to me whether the Sources of the Nile or the South Pole are to be visited I am equally ready to embark in the Undertaking whenever the Public will furnish me with the means of doing it properly. . . .'

The comments of the Navy Board were explosive, and Banks's

criticisms and his proposal that Cook should find another ship provoked the bluntest of replies. This acrimonious correspondence left Cook unmoved. But he did not entirely get the best of the matter for instead of Banks he had foisted upon him a gloomy and complaining pair of German naturalists, Mr Johann Reinhold Forster and his son. A draughtsman completed the scientific team, the celebrated William Hodges, and the scientific equipment carried included not only a theodolite, level, and chain but an ingenious oceanographical apparatus for obtaining the temperature of the sea at different depths. For navigation and survey, too, the new expedition was excellently equipped, better perhaps than any that had sailed on a voyage of exploration. All the new and handy instruments were carried, the reflecting sextant, the chronometer, the station pointer. Of these the chronometer, a copy made by Larkum Kendall of John Harrison's No. 4 chronometer, was of supreme importance for the solution of the vital problem of longitude.

Early in December 1772, less than a month after the two colliers had set a southerly course from Cape Town, the first of Cook's famous Ice Islands were seen, great flat-topped bergs, moving silently through the water, some with high colonnaded sides, perfect in their glistening symmetry, others of elaborate design with pinnacles and arches, caverns and grottoes, carved and hollowed by the ceaseless motion of the sea. Keeping as far south as the drifting ice allowed, the two ships held their course, their officers on the watch day and night for the new land which might at any moment be sighted. Only the Forsters were unstirred by the tension in the air. 'We were', they recorded gloomily in their journals, 'almost perpetually wrapped in thick fogs, beaten with showers of rain, sleet, hail, and snow, surrounded by innumerable islands of ice against which we daily ran the risk of being shipwrecked, and forced to live upon salt provisions which concurred with the cold and wet to infect the mass of our blood.' Banks with all his retinue must to Cook have seemed preferable to this dismal pair.

On 17 January 1773 the Antarctic Circle was crossed by man for the first time. In his *Voyage towards the South Pole and around the World*, published in 1777, Cook describes this landmark in the history of polar exploration. 'I continued to stand to the south,' he wrote, 'and on the seventeenth, between eleven and twelve o'clock, we crossed the Antarctic Circle in the latitude of 66 degrees 36 minutes 30 seconds south. The weather now was becoming tolerably clear, so that we could see several leagues around us: and yet we had seen only one island of ice since the morning. But about 4 p.m., as we were steering to the south, we observed the whole sea in a manner covered with ice . . . in this space, thirty-eight ice islands, great and small, were seen, besides loose ice in abundance so that we were obliged to luff for one piece and bear up for another; and as we continued to advance to the south, it increased in such manner that . . . we could proceed no farther, the ice being entirely closed to the south in the whole extent from east to west-southwest, without the least appearance of any opening.' In these passages is the first complete picture of Antarctica; the whales wallowing and blowing in the water-holes; the darting petrels, brown and white and blue; the iron-grey albatrosses swooping over the mastheads, while beyond the two ships, which lay dark and motionless at the edge of the pack, ice stretched as far as the eye could see.

No trace having been discovered of a continent on this voyage, in December 1773, after a spell in New Zealand, the search was renewed and on the twentieth of the month the *Resolution* and the *Adventure* crossed the Antarctic Circle for the second time. Steering past ice islands more than two hundred feet in height, they reached a latitude of 67° 31′ S., but still there was no sign of land. In January, the following year, the search was widened. This time, after a third crossing of the Circle, the *Resolution* (the *Adventure* having returned to England) reached the farthest south to be attained in the eighteenth century, 71° 10′ S. in 106° 54′ W. But with no better success. On this third attempt, the pack ice, of which the first signs had been seen in clouds to the south of an unusual snow-white brightness, proved to have been rafted by thrust and pressure from afar to monumental heights. On the crew, meanwhile, the incessant foul weather, the monotony of the salt food, and the strain of a hazardous voyage were beginning to tell. For once Johann Reinhold Forster was probably justified when he wrote, 'A gloomy, melancholy air loured on the brows of our shipmates, and a dreadful silence reigned amongst us ... the hour of dinner was hateful ...' Confronted by such physical and psychological obstacles, Cook decided to turn back.

The terms of his decision, as Cook's biographer has pointed out, are among the most revealing of the character of this great seaman. 'I will not say', he confessed, 'that it was impossible anywhere to get in among this Ice, but I will assert that the bare attempting of it would be a very dangerous enterprise and what I believe no man in my situation would have thought of. I whose ambition leads me not only farther than any other man has been before me, but as far as I think it possible for man to go, was not sorry at meeting this interruption. ... Since therefore we could not proceed one inch further south, no other reason need be assigned for our tacking and stretching back to the north. ...'

Cook did not turn back without clarifying in his own mind the problem which future explorers would have to face. 'It was, indeed, my opinion as well as the opinion of most on board', he wrote in a passage of remarkable perception, 'that this ice extended quite to the Pole, or perhaps joined to some land to which it had been fixed from earliest time; and that it is here – that is, to the south of this parallel – where all the ice we find scattered up and down to the north is formed, and afterward broken off by gales of wind, or other causes, and brought to the north by the currents, which we always found to set in that direction in high latitudes.' Cook's final conclusion dealt one last and fatal blow at the sanguine speculations of Dalrymple and De Brosses, for he declared himself 'now well-satisfied no continent was to be found in this ocean but must lie so far south as to be wholly inaccessible on account of ice'.

However inaccessible the continent – if such it was – might be, Cook was sure that 'there remained ... room for very large islands in places wholly unexamined; and many of those which were formerly discovered are but imperfectly explored, and their situations are imperfectly known'. The elusive snow-capped lands doubtfully sighted by wandering ships in the sixteenth, seventeenth, and eighteenth centuries were now to be systematically tracked down.

In November 1774 Cook sailed once again from New Zealand and discovered (or probably rediscovered) to the south-east of Tierra del Fuego, early in 1775, the first typical Antarctic land. This was the Isle of Georgia, the island of South Georgia as it is now known; an island first sighted by a Spanish ship, the *León*, in 1756, and today a famous whaling base and port of call for Antarctic expeditions. Three landings were made, the flag was hoisted and Cook 'took possession of the Isle of Georgia in His Majesty's name, under a discharge of small arms'. It was the first British claim to territory in the newly discovered region of Antarctica.

A rapid charting by Cook of its coastline soon proved that the Isle of Georgia was no part of any continent; nor did the appearance of this 'savage and horrible' land give any promise of the riches expected by Dalrymple. From the ice-cliffs of the coast, masses of ice tumbled with a thunderous roar. Lichen clung in patches to the inhospitable rocks and inland the only vegetation seen was a coarse long-bladed grass. 'The wild rocks', Cook wrote, 'raised their lofty summits until they were lost in the clouds, and the valleys lay covered with everlasting snow. Not a tree was to be seen, nor a shrub even big enough to make a tooth-pick.' No doubt Cook expressed the feelings of every man and boy on board the *Resolution* when he declared 'the disappointment I now met with did not affect me much; for to judge of the bulk by the sample it (i.e. the continent) would not be worth the discovery.'

The *Resolution* sailed from the Isle of Georgia without regrets, and Cook set course south-eastwards and then north-eastwards to escape much floating ice which lay about 60° S. and 30° W. Soon afterwards another desolate island emerged, one of the South Sandwich islands which was charted and named Sandwich Land after the then First Lord of the Admiralty. After a fruitless search for Bouvet Island whose longitude Bouvet had evidently sadly miscalculated, the *Resolution* sailed for Cape Town, and thence for Spithead. There at the end of two great voyages during which Cook had for the first time circumnavigated the 'continent' in high latitudes, the *Resolution* dropped anchor on a summer's day, in July 1775.

Cook's conclusions were as convincing as they were discouraging and put an end, as has been said, to one of the great chapters of human speculation. Ocean after ocean had been systematically searched, but of Dalrymple's continent there was no sign. If it existed, then it lay impregnable far to the south in the midst of encircling battlements of ice. If it were found, would it be worth the lives of men, the loss of ships which would be the price of its discovery? On this point Cook had no doubts. 'Should anyone', he bluntly declared, 'possess the resolution and fortitude to elucidate this point by pushing yet further south than I have done, I shall not envy him the fame of his discovery; but I make bold to declare that the world will derive no benefit from it.' As for the Antarctic lands discovered, what were these but 'countries condemned to everlasting rigidity by Nature, never to yield to the warmth of the sun', countries for whose wild and desolate aspect Cook could find no words. The Antarctic seas certainly were rich in life and in promise of wealth. But the lands, to judge by these discoveries, were dead.

Cook's pioneer voyages across the Antarctic circle were not his last to the polar regions. In 1776, a year after his return, Parliament, as it had done in 1745, offered a reward for polar discovery, this time for the discovery of a North-West Passage by way, not of Hudson Strait, but north of the 52nd parallel of north latitude. A further reward was offered for a sea voyage as far as 89° north. Cook meanwhile had accepted a vacant captain's berth at Greenwich Hospital. Nevertheless, tired as he was by so many years continuously and hazardously at sea, he accepted the Admiralty's invitation to lead a new expedition.

Sailing northwards across the Pacific, Cook came in 1778 within sight of the Bering Strait. His intention had been to sail through the Strait, then north-eastwards past Point Barrow into the Beaufort Sea, but towards Alaska the ice was thick and he therefore crossed over from the American side northwards and westwards towards Asia and Dezhnev's East Cape. Here again ice blocked the way. Bering, confronting an ice-free sea, had chosen to turn back. For Cook there was no choice. The whole strait was frozen over. But Cook saw what Bering had never seen because of the fog which obscured the peaks and promontories of Alaska. In *A Voyage to the Pacific Ocean*, published in 1784, he wrote, 'At this time, the weather which had been hazy, clearing up a little we saw land extending from South to South East by East, about three or four miles distant. The Eastern extreme forms a point which was much encumbered with ice; for which reason it obtained the name Icy Cape. Its latitude is 70°29', and its longitude 198°20'. The other extreme of the land was lost in the horizon; so that there can be no doubt of its being a continuation of the American continent.' Meanwhile the main body of ice to windward was drawing down upon his ships and threatening to force them on to the shore so, with this sight of the two continents achieved, Cook withdrew again towards the central Pacific and there met his death on a Hawaiian beach.

On this last voyage the tracks of Russian and British, Arctic and Antarctic, ships had crossed as if in preparation for one of the greatest ages of polar exploration. This, in both Arctic and Antarctic, opened in the second decade of the nineteenth century, after the Napoleonic Wars.

6

AFTER THE NAPOLEONIC WARS

NEVER had conditions been so favourable for exploration as during the years of the *Pax Britannica* which followed Waterloo. Because of the abandonment of mercantilism in favour of free trade – a revolution in British policy – the seas were for the first time free. In science, and in technology too, the period was one of extraordinary progress though it was not until well into the second half of the nineteenth century that the greatest advance in maritime technology, the transition from wood and sails to iron and steam, was to benefit polar exploration.

In Britain, which took the lead in exploration after the Napoleonic Wars, the advance of science was an overwhelming influence in the general shaping of ideas and as education spread among the new literate classes which had emerged from the aftermath of the Industrial Revolution, the need for centres arose in which this popular enthusiasm for science could be focused and where new knowledge could be accumulated and diffused. Just as the intellectual interests and desire for improvement of the new technical working class found a focus in the Mechanics Institutes which spread rapidly in the second quarter of the century, so the preoccupation with scientific knowledge of the broadening middle class became concentrated in a number of private societies which combined scientific aims with a popular, rather than a professional, membership.

These new popular enthusiasms, concerned especially with science in relation to exploration, arose fundamentally from the broadening, in new social conditions, of a trend which had originated, as we have seen, in the late eighteenth century when Cook's startling revelation of a new and unknown world powerfully stimulated a general desire to promote geographical discovery. The foundation of the Linnean Society and of the African Association in 1788 was followed in 1804 by that of the

Palestine Association for the exploration of Syria and the Holy
Land. In 1828 the Zoological Society was founded, and in 1830
and 1831 respectively the Geographical Society of London and
the British Association for the Advancement of Science. These
societies, supported by the private subscriptions of members
who came for the most part from the professional and commercial classes, fulfilled two important requirements. As science
moved early in the nineteenth century towards the modern
pattern of specialized research, broad studies grouped in the
eighteenth century under such general names as 'Geography'
and 'Natural History' came to be discarded by the national
academies of science in favour of more precise and specialized
investigations. In this respect the new societies filled a gap.
More important, however, was the psychological need arising
out of the circumstances of the Revolutionary and Napoleonic
Wars. In so far as the new societies were concerned with the
promotion of travel and exploration and with the accumulation
of knowledge about foreign or unknown lands, they provided a
most welcome avenue of actual or vicarious escape after thirty
years of national isolation.

Of these various societies, the geographical societies not only
in Britain but in Europe are in many ways most characteristic
of these new developments in contemporary taste. As centres of
influential and informed public opinion they became during the
nineteenth century powerful if somewhat reactionary protagonists of polar exploration; with a role initially comple-
mentary to, but as they grew in popularity gradually diverging
from, that of the more specialized national academies of science.
The first of the geographical societies was the Société de
Géographie of Paris, founded in 1821. This was followed in
1828 by the foundation of the Gesellschaft für Erdkunde in
Berlin and two years later by that of the Geographical Society
of London. A memorandum of 24 May 1830 proposing that a
society should be founded in London for 'the promotion and
diffusion of that most important and entertaining branch of
knowledge – geography' illustrates in sympathetic language the
point of view (making allowance for national prejudice) of the
founders of a nineteenth-century geographical society. It was

needed, its promoters declared, on the grounds 'that the interest excited by this department of science is universally felt, that its advantages are of the first importance to mankind in general, and paramount to the welfare of a maritime nation like Great Britain, with its numerous and extensive foreign possessions; that its decided utility in conferring just and distinct notions of the physical and political relations of our globe must be obvious to everyone, and is the more enhanced by this species of knowledge being obtained without much difficulty, while at the same time it affords a copious source of rational amusement. ...' This blend of intellectual interest, national bias, and enlightened entertainment is fairly typical of the atmosphere in which the principal geographical societies were founded.

Polar exploration during the first half of the nineteenth century was, in the tradition established by Cook, predominantly a naval affair and naval officers with experience of polar voyages were among the most active members of the new geographical societies. Through them a wealth of practical knowledge was accumulated, and just as the national academies of science continued to advise governments in matters of polar science, so the geographical societies became centres of advice on the organization and technique of polar exploration. The geographical societies also included a large proportion of the new and expanding commercial and industrial class, among them the owners of whaling and sealing ships. The remarkable contribution which these men and their carefully selected captains made to geographical knowledge is one of the most striking features of polar exploration during the first half of the nineteenth century.

One of them, William Scoresby, whose father William Scoresby of Whitby achieved a farthest north of 81° 31′ to the east of Spitsbergen in 1806, may be said without exaggeration to have laid the foundations of modern Arctic geography by the publication in 1820 of his *Account of the Arctic Regions with a History and Description of the Northern Whale Fisheries*, and by his *Journal of a Voyage to the Northern Whale Fisheries*, which appeared in 1823. No less remarkable in their disinterested services to exploration were the Enderby brothers, one of whom, Charles Enderby, was a founder of the Geographical Society of London. Sacrificing the secrecy inevitable in a highly competitive industry, in which knowledge of new fishing bases and fishing grounds, of tides and currents and ice conditions, was jealously guarded from rivals, these men not only made available the knowledge they or their captains had acquired, but also diverted their ships for the purpose of geographical discovery, often at considerable financial loss. The discoveries made by sealers of the Enderby brothers, some of the most impressive discoveries of the nineteenth century, prepared the way for a great campaign of Antarctic exploration in which the navies of Russia, Britain, the United States, and France in turn participated.

The broad scientific interests, the zest for travel, for exploration, and for geographical discovery which inspired men of different kinds and nationalities in this age of peace and of freedom of the seas, were not, however, untarnished by thoughts of national prestige or strategic advantage. The advent of free trade and freedom of the seas brought with it no corresponding decline in nationalism, on the contrary, and in a period when polar exploration was predominantly sponsored by governments and carried out by navies, it was inevitable that politics and strategy should creep in.

The British Navy took the lead in the revival of polar exploration after the Napoleonic Wars and its ambition was the discovery of a North-West Passage. It was a challenge inherited from past generations of British seamen and for this reason it had a traditional and a romantic appeal. But this was no longer the North-West Passage of the sixteenth and seventeenth centuries, the North-West Passage to Cathay. It was now envisaged in terms of the circumnavigation and exploration of the Arctic coast of British Canada and of the discovery of any new lands which might be found to the north of the American continent, including (because Baffin's discoveries were no longer acknowledged) the ice-covered mass of West Greenland.

Such a project, so closely bound up with the exploration and extension of British territory, was one in which Britain, supreme in naval as in economic and financial power but keenly alive to potential rivals, could not allow herself to be forestalled by any foreign nation. In fact, some apprehension of foreign activity along the borders of Canada in the first quarter of the nineteenth century was not unwarranted. The strategic position was far from reassuring. British colonists were relatively few and widely scattered. Relations between British and the remaining French settlers were easily inflammable. To the south lay a youthful and ebullient United States which had already threatened the Canadian frontier during the war of 1812. To the west was apparently a greater danger: Russia, fervently nationalist and with imperial ambitions which had been greatly encouraged by the events of 1812–15. She was in total occupation of Alaska (overlooking one extremity of the North-West Passage) and had by 1820 spread her trading posts and settlements so far south along the American coast (as far indeed as San Francisco) that it almost seemed as if three nations not two might soon divide the North American Continent.

British suspicion of Russian intentions and of the true nature of her recent exploratory operations in Arctic and Pacific waters was reported by the Austrian Archduke Ludwig after his visit to England in 1816.

'A Power', he wrote, 'which is not in friendly esteem is Russia. The Englishman, calculating and jealous of his trade, knows that that Empire, which is so vast, provided with all resources, and touching all seas, might one day come forward as a Sea Power. England has been made attentive of late by repeated Russian sea voyages, which had for their purpose more than discovery; by the establishment of settlements on islands between Asia and America, and even on the North-west Coast of this continent [i.e. America], by the connexion with Kamchatka, the Continent of Russia; by the mission to China, and by the conquests over Persia.'

Similar suspicions were hinted a year later by John Barrow, Secretary to the Admiralty, a principal founder of the Geographical Society and the father, as he came to be called, of British Arctic exploration in the nineteenth century. In an anonymous article in the *Quarterly Review* for October 1817 Barrow (who had access to the latest intelligence about Russian movements)

wrote, 'The Russians have for some time been strongly impressed with the idea of an open passage round America. ...
It would be somewhat mortifying if a naval power but of yesterday should complete a discovery in the nineteenth century, which was so happily commenced by Englishmen in the sixteenth.'

In 1818 an Act of Parliament similar to that of 1776 offered substantial rewards for the discovery of a North-West Passage, or for a farthest north towards the Pole if no westward route to the Bering Strait could be found. Great as was the British anxiety to forward exploration and discovery it is difficult to avoid the suspicion that the desire to forestall and counteract Russian operations in the Arctic, if not a major factor, was at least in the minds of the Board of Admiralty when they agreed to make men and ships available for Arctic exploration.

International rivalry was also much in evidence in Antarctic waters early in the nineteenth century. There the first discoveries after the Napoleonic Wars were made by the sealers, American and British, working in fierce competition in their search for ports and bases and the most profitable fishing grounds. In political terms, this rivalry among the sealers (who were surreptitiously supported by their Governments) was a reflection, an extension, of the Anglo-American economic and commercial war which had begun with the first expansion of British trade in South America in the eighteenth century. After the Napoleonic Wars, when Europe was impoverished and Canada still too scantily populated to provide profitable openings for British goods, this sharpened to a bitter conflict as Britain strove by every means to capture the South American trade. The Monroe Doctrine of 1823 was directed at Britain rather than at France or Russia, and Canning for one was convinced that it was the American intention to supplant Britain in navigation throughout the world, but especially in all seas adjacent to America. When rumours reached London in the thirties that the United States Navy was preparing to explore Antarctica, this news had accordingly a powerful effect in persuading the British Admiralty to launch the first naval expedition to the Antarctic since the voyages of James Cook.

At one stage in this Anglo-American struggle, Antarctic territory nearest to South America assumed for British merchants engaged in the South American trade an importance which had nothing to do with sealing. On the mainland their future was precarious for, quite apart from the hostility of American interests whose agents were active in all ports and cities, there were many doubts about the fate of the old Spanish colonies. They began therefore to look about for adjacent islands from which they could, if need be, carry on the struggle. The Falkland Islands, the nearest, had been abandoned for reasons of economy in 1774 and were not reoccupied until 1833. When the South Shetlands were discovered by Britain in 1819, more than one of these merchants saw in them a possible base to which they might retire and carry on British trade.

To conclude this preface to the story of the first polar explorations of the nineteenth century, a word must be said – because the British Navy took the lead – about the special position and functions of the Navy in exploration at this time, and about the characteristic pattern of life on these first British naval expeditions.

The doctrine of the freedom of the seas which Britain had proclaimed and of which her Navy, supreme on all seas, was the principal guardian, carried with it a special obligation. This was not only to ensure the protection of the seas but to provide for their safety by exploring and charting unknown coasts and waters for the benefit of the shipping of the world. Hydrographic survey had made great strides since the days of Cook. In 1811 a separate Hydrographic Branch was established. After the wars, charting and survey, with magnetic observations which assumed an importance greater even than during the eighteenth century, became the principal task of British naval expeditions and, indeed, so great was British technical advance in this field that London became the world's chief centre for the purchase of charts and hydrographic instruments, as it remains to this day.

The first British naval expeditions to the polar regions provided in their organization and their conduct the pattern for British polar exploration for many years to come. Officers and men, ambitiously or adventurously minded, volunteered for polar service not as 'explorers' in the twentieth-century idiom but as part of an ordinary naval career and they sailed for an unknown world of ice and snow full of the robust confidence of the Victorian Age. Their uniforms, of standard naval pattern, were more appropriate to Portsmouth than to the Poles, and samples of the heavy Victorian plate with which their wardroom tables were laden have survived among the more curious and moving relics of the Arctic tragedies of the nineteenth century.

On board, rollicking performances by the ship's company of the latest London farce, magic lantern shows, and a heavily humorous weekly magazine, like Parry's *North Georgia Gazette and Winter Chronicle*, kept up morale during the months of winter darkness. But discipline was stern, and the moral tone set by officers drawn from the new middle class was strictly Evangelical and Sabbatarian. Religious education featured largely in the ship's routine on these expeditions and large additional stocks of bibles were hopefully carried for distribution to the Eskimoes.

But despite this stubborn adherence to traditional naval ways in most unsuitable conditions, despite their inadequate equipment, their ignorance of how best to live and how best to travel in the polar regions, the achievements of these expeditions, now to be described, are among the most remarkable in polar history. At sea their supreme skill in the handling of cumbrous sailing ships, turning and twisting through the pack at the mercy of the winds and the ice, was a miracle of navigation. On land, their heroic journeys hauling, officers and Jack Tars alike, heavy sledge boats across the tumbled and shifting Arctic floes were for generations the inspiration of British polar explorers.

7

THE ROYAL NAVY TAKES THE LEAD

THROUGHOUT polar history there have been men – John Barrow, Jeremiah Reynolds, Henry Grinnell, Clements Markham – who gave, like the Hakluyts in Elizabethan days, a new turn and thrust to polar exploration. The moving spirit in British Arctic exploration of the first half of the nineteenth century was John Barrow. Industrious, highly capable, widely travelled in his younger days, Barrow served as a decisive and influential Secretary to the Admiralty for forty years from 1804, and became moreover in later years President of the Geographical Society of London. He was born of humble Westmorland stock. As a boy while working in a foundry at Liverpool he contrived to be the first in England to make an ascent with the famous Italian aeronaut Lunardi in his balloon. He followed this adventure by a summer cruise to the Arctic in a whaler and from that day he became an ardent enthusiast for polar exploration and a great student of its literature, especially of the Elizabethan Age.

When Barrow, after many years in China and South Africa, joined the Admiralty in 1804, he found himself in an exceptionally strong position to influence polar affairs. The year 1817, as he describes in his autobiography, appeared ordained by circumstance to be the one in which the great traditions of British Arctic exploration might be revived. There was little demand on the Royal Navy at the time. The Arctic geography of North America, the discovery of a North-West Passage (on which the Russians had their eyes), even the insularity of Greenland, were all problems yet unsolved. Indeed, how little was then known of Arctic geography despite the explorations of the last two hundred years can be seen from the map accompanying Barrow's own *Chronological History of Voyages in the Arctic Regions*, published in 1818. At the mouth of the Mackenzie River, at points northwards of Great Bear Lake, the sea had been reached late in the eighteenth century by Alexander Mackenzie and Samuel Hearne, men of the Hudson's Bay Company. But farther north, except for a vague and shadowy outline of Greenland's west coast, the Arctic map, despite William Baffin's discoveries, was blank.

But there was another and more immediate reason for the renewal of Arctic exploration. Ice conditions, because of some temporary climatic fluctuations, were in 1817 quite exceptionally favourable and as Barrow recorded in his article in the *Quarterly Review* (already quoted), William Scoresby the younger, the whaling captain, had that very summer reported the extraordinary disappearance of an immense quantity of ice. 'I observed', Scoresby had written to Sir Joseph Banks, 'on my last voyage (1817) about two thousand square leagues (18,000 square miles) of the surface of the Greenland seas, included between the parallels 74° and 80°, perfectly void of ice, all of which had disappeared within the last two years.' This was an opportunity not to be lost. Barrow at once proposed to Lord Melville, First Lord of the Admiralty, a plan for two voyages 'for the advancement of geography, navigation, and commerce' and this, with strong support from the Royal Society on scientific grounds, was rapidly approved.

Barrow's plans were on a grand and multiple scale. One naval squadron was to sail northwards between Spitsbergen and Greenland and then as close to the Pole as possible and on to the Bering Strait. This was in the direction of Captain Constantine Phipps's expedition of 1773. The second and principal squadron was to search for an entrance to a North-West Passage along the traditional avenue of Davis Strait while other ships waited off Bering Strait to welcome or rescue any survivors who might get through. This was the plan for the first maritime operations. In addition, there was to be a land exploration of the almost unknown Arctic coast of North America.

In May 1818 the naval squadrons sailed. Captain David Buchan, with orders for the northern journey, commanded two bomb-built sailing ships, the *Dorothea* and the *Trent*. His second-in-command was an officer whose name was soon to become a household word, Lieutenant John Franklin. This voyage, however, was a total failure. Off the west coast of Spitsbergen a violent gale fell upon the ships, forcing them to make for land. Venturing out again to the north, they were beset for days in heavy pack along the edge of the Arctic Sea, then escaped, and returned, battered by the ice, to Spitsbergen. A coastal map of north-west Spitsbergen, but nothing else, came out of this first attempt.

The voyage of the second squadron, under the stocky, red-headed Commander John Ross, who had a very remarkable young naval officer, Lieutenant Edward Parry, as his second-in-command, ended inexplicably. Ross's ships, the *Alexander* and the *Isabella*, sailing up Davis Strait, restored to the map the discoveries of the great Elizabethan seaman, Baffin: Baffin Bay, and Smith, Jones, and Lancaster Sounds, which Baffin had named after his supporters in the City of London. But after arriving on 30 August 1818 off Baffin's Lancaster Sound, the most likely of the three to lead to a North-West Passage, Ross sailed westwards for a day, then stopped. Ahead of him, he insisted, he 'distinctly saw land round the bottom of the bay forming a chain of mountains connected with those which extended along the north and south side'. Indeed, so convinced of their existence was he that he named them after a Secretary of the Admiralty, the 'Croker Mountains'. To Parry and his fellow officers, however, the 'Croker Mountains' seemed no more than a fantastic optical illusion. They could see nothing. The sea ahead was clear. They felt certain that they were on the very verge of a great discovery. When Ross, therefore, insisted on turning back, it seemed an incomprehensible, a lamentable, decision.

Amusing and malicious stories about Ross and his mythical 'Croker Mountains' were soon going the round of the drawing-rooms of London. Some found it impossible to doubt the word of so capable and trustworthy an officer. But there were many who hinted slyly that the Croker Mountains were a happy excuse to retreat to safer waters. So damaging was this gossip not only to Ross but to the Navy that the Admiralty decided to settle the matter by the dispatch of another expedition. The commander chosen was Ross's second-in-command, Lieutenant Edward

Parry. The elegant and ambitious young commander of the North-West Passage expedition was only 29 years of age. But his talents and achievements were already considerable. His knowledge of hydrography, nautical astronomy, and magnetic research had won him a Fellowship of the Royal Society and he had at the same time already won a name in the Navy for seamanship and navigation and for leadership of men.

THE FIRST ATTACK ON THE NORTH-WEST PASSAGE

To follow in any detail the fortunes of Parry's first great Arctic expedition, or for that matter the manoeuvres of any of the many expeditions seeking a North-West Passage during the nineteenth century, some knowledge is necessary of the intricate pattern of islands and icy channels which spreads across the map between the north-western extremity of Greenland and the Arctic coast of the American continent. Below the ice and around the rock masses, geologically related to those of the Yukon and Alaska, Atlantic waters mingle with those of the Beaufort Sea. Beyond lies the Bering Strait through which warm currents stream from the Pacific into the Arctic Ocean. On the map, the ways to the west looks easy. But to Parry, as he sailed, the region westwards of Baffin Bay was utterly unknown, a world of lands perhaps, or of sea, where navigation must be a matter of tedious and repeated probing, where a day's sailing might end in besetment in the ice, or imprisonment in some land-locked bay. Parry's ships were the Hull-built bomb *Hecla* of 375 tons and a gun-brig of 180 tons, the *Griper*; both ships, to save men, being barque-rigged, with bows, bottoms, and keels strengthened against the ice, and with provisions for two years. Parry had with him in the *Hecla* young Captain Sabine of the Royal Artillery who was to gain a reputation as 'the most persistent and the most successful magnetic observer of his day'. Lieutenant Liddon commanded the *Griper*. It was a very young expedition, for apart from Parry and Sabine, no officer was more than 23 years of age.

The two ships sailed from the Thames on 11 May 1819 with

one question uppermost in the minds of those on board. Did Ross's Croker Mountains exist or not? By the beginning of August, they were nearing the answer. To the north lay the cliffs of South Devon Island, overhung with clouds; to the south the snow-covered mountains of northernmost Baffin Island. Ahead, free of ice and dark as the ocean, were the waters of Lancaster Sound. The *Hecla* was the faster ship. As she waited for the *Griper* under easy sail, she pitched so heavily in the westerly swell that the sea was thrown up against her stern windows. To Parry this immediately was a hopeful sign, the sign of an open sea and not of the land-locked bay which Ross thought he had seen.

As they sailed towards the new waters there was much scientific work to be done: there were soundings to be made with the new deep-sea clam invented by Captain Ross, there were sea and air temperatures to be noted, the movement of tides and currents, the angle of dip of the horizon, the effects of the Aurora Borealis on the electrometer and magnetic needle, and many other phenomena to be observed. Magnetic observations were an important part of the scientific programme recommended by the Royal Society and Captain Sabine of the Royal Artillery, 'a gentleman well skilled in Astronomy, Natural History, and various branches of knowledge', was fully occupied. Charting and survey and drawing were assigned to Lieutenant Beechey and Lieutenant Hoppner, the Admiralty having decreed that no professional civilian draughtsman should be carried on this purely naval expedition.

As the *Hecla* and the *Griper* sailed westwards into Lancaster Sound, two questions filled the minds of Parry and his men. Was this the North-West Passage? Or were they at any moment to be confronted by the barrier of Ross's Croker Mountains? In his *Journal of a Voyage for the Discovery of a North-West Passage from the Atlantic to the Pacific*, Parry describes the scene:

'It is more easy to imagine than to describe the almost breathless anxiety which was now visible in every countenance while, as the breeze increased to a fresh gale, we ran quickly up the sound. The mastheads were crowded by the officers and men

Were these two Englishmen, then, Edward Bransfield and William Smith, the discoverers of the Antarctic Continent? That in retrospect they were, that in this first sighting of the mainland coast of the Graham Land peninsula they were the first men to approach within landing distance the perimeter of a continent larger than Europe, twice as large as the continent of Australia, may seem in relation to the great sea voyages of Cook, of Bellingshausen, of James Clark Ross, or to the land explorations of Scott, Shackleton, and Mawson a fact of only moderate importance. Of recent years, however, Antarctica has been brought more closely into the realm of international politics. American historians and Russian historians have in turn put forward rival claimants to this first continental discovery. Out of the archives of the Library of Congress of the United States an American sealer Nathaniel Palmer, of Stonington, Connecticut, has emerged as the alleged first discoverer of the mainland and in commemoration of this legendary achievement (which Nathaniel Palmer himself never claimed) the whole of the Graham Land peninsula is named Palmer Peninsula on American maps. Soviet historians and geographers, furthermore, supported by the Soviet Government, have since the last war claimed similar priority for Captain Baron Fabian Gottlieb von Bellingshausen of the Imperial Russian Navy. The claims with which Bellingshausen has been credited will be discussed in a later chapter. Here we are only concerned with the voyage of Nathaniel Palmer.

In 1820, the year of Bransfield and Smith's discovery, Palmer, then mate of the sloop *Hero*, sailed from the New England port of Stonington. His log preserved in the Library of Congress is, from the available facsimiles, a laconic and restrained document compared with the *Literary Gazette*'s graphic account of the British voyage. From the slopes of a mountain on Deception Island, one of the South Shetlands group, Palmer – it records – caught glimpses of Trinity Island and possibly also of the mainland beyond. Having thereupon decided to follow up his discovery, he approached close to the Trinity Peninsula but because of ice thought it prudent not to attempt to land. 'Laid on and off until morning', his log records, 'at 4 a.m. made sail in shore and discovered – a strait – trending SSW. and NNE. – it was literally filled with ice and the shore inaccessible – we thought it not prudent to venture in ice ... the latitude of the strait was 63° 45′ S.' These events took place on 16 November 1820, ten months after Bransfield's discovery.

A more picturesque account of Palmer's voyage is contained in the veteran American sealing captain Edmund Fanning's *Voyages Around the World*, published in New York in 1833. From this it appears that while the sloop *Hero*, one of a fleet of five sealing vessels under the command of Captain Benjamin Pendleton, lay at anchor in 'Yankee Harbour', Deception Island, in 1820–21, Palmer saw from the top of a mountain on a very clear day a range of mountains far to the south, one of which was an active volcano. In the *Hero*, a ship of less than 40 tons, Nathaniel Palmer was then sent out to explore. He found, according to Fanning, 'an extensive mountain country, more sterile and more dismal if possible, and more heavily laden with ice and snow than the South Shetlands. There were sea-leopards on its shore but no fur seals. The main part of its coast was ice-bound, although it was midsummer in this hemisphere, and a landing consequently difficult.'

The rest of Fanning's story is worth repeating not only because it reveals that Palmer, though an enterprising sealer, knew nothing of Bransfield's discovery but because it introduces one of the most remarkable of Antarctic explorers, the Russian Captain Bellingshausen. The sloop *Hero*, the story continues, while on her way back to the South Shetlands, became enveloped in thick fog and when it cleared Palmer was astonished to see, towering on either side of his small sealer, a frigate and a sloop of war hoisting the Russian colours. These two ships, commanded by Captain von Bellingshausen, had been sent, Palmer discovered, by the Emperor Alexander I of Russia on a voyage of circumnavigation. Palmer was immediately invited on board and was able to tell the Russians that the islands they could see ahead of them were the newly discovered islands of New South Britain or New South Shetland.

According to Fanning, Bellingshausen was astounded by this news. 'Previous to our being enveloped in fog', Fanning reports the Russian commodore as saying, 'we had sight of those islands and concluded that we had made a discovery, but behold, when the fog lifts, to my great surprise, here is an American vessel apparently in as fine an order as if it were but yesterday she had left the United States; not only this but her master is ready to pilot my vessels into port. We must surrender the palm to you Americans.' This anecdote is more picturesque than accurate for Bellingshausen's journals have been fully published and it is abundantly clear that he already knew of the existence of New South Shetland.

Fanning then goes on to describe how Palmer told the Russians 'of the existence of an immense extent of land to the south, whose mountains might be seen from the masthead when the fog should clear away entirely ... and the commodore was so forcibly struck by the circumstances of the case that he named the coast then to the south, Palmer Land. By this name', Fanning declares, 'it is recorded on recent Russian and English charts and maps which have been published since the return of these ships.' Here again Fanning's narrative is misleading. Neither in Bellingshausen's journal nor on his maps is Palmer Land once mentioned. And it certainly never appeared on any English maps or charts. In the United States, however, the Palmer-Fanning legend became firmly entrenched. Eighty-six years after the meeting between Bellingshausen and Palmer, Palmer's neice, a certain Mrs Loper, published an even more highly coloured account of these events, allegedly based on Palmer's journals. In this also Palmer features as the discoverer of the Antarctic Continent. Nevertheless, suspect as Fanning's account evidently is, there is no reason to doubt the bare facts of Palmer's voyage as recorded in his log. In the following year, 1821, in company with a British sealer, Captain George Powell, in the sloop *Dove*, Palmer shared in a new and important discovery, that of the South Orkney Islands which lie east of the island group discovered by William Smith.

The discovery of the South Shetlands, of the Antarctic mainland, and of the South Orkneys gave a strong impetus to American sealing activities during the second quarter of the nineteenth century and American sealers may have added further lands or islands to those discovered by Smith, Bransfield, Palmer, and

Powell. Little is known about their discoveries. One claim made by an enterprizing and imaginative young sealer, Benjamin Morrell, whom Charles Enderby regarded as notoriously unreliable, was certainly invented. This was a claim to have discovered islands in the Weddell Sea; a fiction to which the German explorer Filchner put an end early in the twentieth century. On the other hand, there is good reason to believe that the American Captain Davis landed from the *Cecilia* in the Hughes Bay area in February 1821, the first recorded landing on the mainland of Antarctica.

RUSSIA ENTERS THE ANTARCTIC

'EMPEROR ALEXANDER PAVLOVICH of glorious memory, desiring to help in extending the fields of knowledge, ordered the dispatch of two expeditions, each consisting of two vessels, for the exploration of the higher latitudes of the Arctic and Antarctic Oceans.' With these words the President of the Scientific Committee of the Imperial Naval Staff introduced the first Russian edition of the 'Voyage of Captain Bellingshausen to the Antarctic Seas 1818–21'; the same Captain Bellingshausen whose ships were last seen towards the end of this voyage appearing out of the fog off the South Shetlands on either side of Nathaniel Palmer's sealer.

The Russian Arctic expedition consisting of a corvette and a transport under Commander Vasilev was ordered to search for the North-West Passage by way of the Alaskan coast. It was a project which (as the British had suspected) the Russians had for some time had in mind and to the Tzar it might well have seemed the more urgent of the two for reports of Ross's abortive voyage had already reached St Petersburg and rumours were now coming in of Parry's imminent departure, and of British sea and land operations in the Western Arctic on an unprecedented scale. Little is known, however, about this Russian North-West Passage expedition except that it failed. It returned to Russia in 1822, a year later than the Antarctic expedition under Captain Baron von Bellingshausen.

In the words of the Tzar, 'the great object' of the Antarctic expedition 'was exploration in the closest vicinity to the South Pole'; or as Bellingshausen explained more precisely, 'to explore those parts of the Antarctic Sea into which as yet navigators had not penetrated, and to survey, in regions which were already known, such islands as had not previously been visited'. In his concern for the advancement of science, as in his efforts to promote higher education, the Tzar Alexander I was perhaps the most liberal-minded of all the rulers of pre-Soviet Russia. The rewards expected however from this Antarctic project, the first of its kind undertaken by Russia, were by no means wholly intellectual.

For some years the problem of nourishing the remote Pacific settlements, not only those on the Kamchatka peninsula and on the shores of the Sea of Okhotsk but since the foundation of the Russian-American Company in 1798 those in North-West America and in the Aleutian Islands as well, had been the source of much anxiety in St Petersburg. Inadequate and costly communications lay at the root of the problem; communications which until early in the nineteenth century were virtually restricted to the land route across Siberia. It was not only that the distance to be travelled was immense. The cost of maintenance and of the transport needed, more than four thousand horses every year, was prohibitive. Furs exported westwards from Siberia, merchandise and equipment of every kind sent from Europe to the Pacific coast, even cables and anchors for the shipyard at Okhotsk, had to be carried, piece by piece, by waggon and packhorse, through the forests, across mighty rivers, over plains and over prairies by this trans-Siberian route, at a cost so exorbitant as to threaten the whole economic future of these Russian colonial settlements.

But what were the alternatives? The northern sea route, infested with ice, was dangerous and unpredictable. The long sea route down the Atlantic and across the Indian Ocean was exceedingly costly because goods had to be carried in foreign ships. Only if Russian seamen in Russian ships could explore this route, only if they themselves could learn the secrets of trade and navigation in these waters, could this economic problem be solved. It was for this reason that a young Russian nobleman, A. J. Kruzenstern, who in his four years with the British Navy during the War of the Revolution had made several voyages in British ships to the Far East, persuaded Alexander I in 1802 to give him command of a three-year expedition, the first from Russia to circumnavigate the World.

After the Napoleonic Wars these Russian reconnaissances

were continued by the famous Otto von Kotzebue and others. On such long ocean voyages, however, the Russians, unlike the British and French, suffered one serious disadvantage: the lack of Russian-owned harbours, ports, and bases, along the route. In the Indian Ocean, in the South and Central Pacific, France and Britain were already in possession. But further south, along the perimeter of the Antarctic seas, there might still be territories undiscovered or unclaimed and in Bellingshausen's instructions from the Imperial Admiralty Department great stress is laid accordingly on the importance of harbours and on 'the possibilities of establishing future sea-communications or places for the repair of ships'.

This first Russian Antarctic expedition sailed from Kronshtadt (an island off Leningrad) on 26 July 1819. There had been little enough time for preparation, for only in April had the Tzar's orders (issued on 25 March 1819) reached the Marquis de Traversay, his Minister for Naval Affairs. During these three months a volume of instructions, repetitive, verbose, and sometimes misleading, poured in on Captain Bellingshausen. There were the instructions from the Marquis de Traversay on behalf of His Imperial Majesty. There were instructions from the Imperial Admiralty Council, others from the Imperial Admiralty Department. A special memorandum of advice was provided for the draughtsmen of the expedition by the President of the Imperial Academy of Fine Arts. The Imperial Academy of Science produced nothing, 'owing to lack of time'. But this scientific gap was filled by a second series of instructions from the Minister of Naval Affairs. The array of scientific studies to which attention was drawn, geodesy, astronomy, gravity observations, observations on winds, tides, and weather, auroral observations, oceanography, ice studies, geology, mineralogy, anthropology, must have seemed to Bellingshausen an encyclopedic undertaking.

In the political sphere the accent was on peace and a great and curious variety of gifts – hussar jackets and tambourines, huntsmen's horns, knitting needles, kaleidoscopes, and silver and bronze medals with the Emperor's effigy for important personages – was to be carried to placate the people of foreign or

newly discovered lands. There was also a military side to the
instructions. Detailed intelligence was to be collected about other
travellers, and about the war strength, the harbours, forts, and
armament of foreign countries visited.

The ships of Bellingshausen's Antarctic expedition were an
oddly assorted pair. The *Vostok* (East) in which Bellingshausen
sailed was an armed sloop of unseasoned pinewood, sheathed in
copper underwater against the ice, very similar to the sloop
Kamchatka in which Captain Golovnin had sailed round the
world. The second ship, the *Ladoga,* renamed the *Mirnyi* (Peaceful), was commanded by Mikhail Lazarev. She was a transport of 230 tons, a sluggish ship very much slower than the
Vostok, and Bellingshausen was constantly delayed throughout
his voyage waiting for the *Mirnyi* to catch up.

The *Vostok*'s company of one hundred and seventeen included
an astronomer, Professor Ivan Simanov of Kazan University,
and Paul Mikhailov, Academician of the Imperial Academy of
Fine Arts. The *Mirnyi* carried a ship's company of seventy-two.
Each ship was to carry a naturalist and the Tzar on the advice
of the Academy of Sciences had nominated two German naturalists, Dr Mertens of Halle and Dr Kuntze of Leipzig. At the
last moment, however, both refused to join. Bellingshausen's
comment on the excuses they gave was characteristically blunt.
'They had refused', he wrote, 'on the ground that too little time
had been given them to complete preparation for the voyage.
Perhaps they were right; but I, as a naval officer, cannot help
thinking that all that a scientist need bring with him is his
scientific knowledge; books were to be found at Copenhagen of
every kind in quantities, and even if some had been found un-
obtainable all the bookshops in London would have been at their
service. . . .' Bellingshausen proposed instead that two Russian
scientists should be invited. But his request was flatly rejected.
This incident is an interesting commentary on the state of
Russian science at the time. Founded by the Germanized Russian
Peter the Great, the Academy of Science had been for many
years exclusively German in membership and though a few Russians were later reluctantly admitted, German influence was still
predominant in Bellingshausen's day. Faced by the Academy

of Science's refusal to appoint any but 'unknown foreigners' as Bellingshausen called them, the expedition sailed without a naturalist to the great disadvantage of its scientific work and to Bellingshausen's lasting regret.

It is not easy to draw out from the laconic and official prose of Bellingshausen's journals any very clear picture of Bellingshausen or of his second-in-command, Mikhail Lazarev. Born in 1779 in Estonia, of a family as aristocratic as that of Cook was humble, Bellingshausen first appears in the context of exploration in the pages of Kruzenstern's narrative of his voyages. 'The choice of Baron Bellingshausen, my fifth lieutenant,' wrote Kruzenstern, 'I made without being personally acquainted with him. His reputation as a skilful and well-informed officer in the different branches of navigation, which I found to be perfectly just, induced me to propose to him to sail with me.' Bellingshausen was then twenty-four. In April 1819 when he was summoned by Alexander I to St Petersburg, he was engaged in a survey of the Black Sea as commander of a frigate under Vice-Admiral Sir Alexis Samuilovich Greig whose father, Sir Samuel Grieg, born in Fifeshire, had been one of the many Scots who distinguished themselves in the service of the Imperial Russian Navy. Little about Bellingshausen's character and personality can be gauged from the carefully impersonal prose, from the clipped phrases customary with serving officers, which mark his journal. His admiration for Cook – 'the great explorer, Captain Cook' – his admiration for learning and for its patrons like Sir Joseph Banks, his professional pride, high competence, and passion for accuracy are evident. It is evident too, from his reference to the works of Alexander von Humboldt for example, that he had some acquaintance with the scientific literature of his day. His portrait, done about the time of the expedition, may be a little more revealing. Here he is seen, sharp-eyed, a little arrogant perhaps, evidently a somewhat forbidding man and something of a martinet; a contrast to his genial, bluff, and sociable second-in-command Mikhail Lazarev who had like Kruzenstern served four years in the British Navy.

Copenhagen and Portsmouth were the expedition's first ports of call and it was in Copenhagen that Bellingshausen heard the

news that the German naturalists refused to join him. The visit
to England was more profitable, though Bellingshausen was no
more successful there than in Copenhagen in finding replace-
ments for the missing naturalists. First, there was the welcome
sight of Golovnin's ship, the *Kamchatka*, lying in Spithead
Road, homeward bound from North America. Then in Portsmouth harbour the Russians were able to salute the gilded yacht
of the Prince Regent 'accompanied by warships and a great
number of spectators in gaily decorated boats of all sorts'. 'Only
in England', Bellingshausen wrote in his journal that night, 'is
it possible to see such a picture of animation.'

In England, however, the Russians had to wait nearly a
month for the instruments and charts which the Imperial
Admiralty Department had instructed them to buy; sextants
from Mr Troughton, chronometers from Arnold and Barraud,
telescopes from Mr Dolland, and charts from Mr Arrowsmith,
one of the founders of the Royal Geographical Society. But the
days passed quickly. They called on the aged Sir Joseph Banks
at the Royal Society in the vain hope that he could find them a
naturalist. They toured the City, saw the Tower, visited West-
minster Abbey, Vauxhall Gardens, and the theatres. And early
in September they sailed for the South Atlantic on a day so hot
that fresh meat sufficient only for three weeks could be brought
on board.

From Teneriffe and Rio de Janeiro, the two ships had a
straight run down the South Atlantic and towards the end of
December 1819 Cook's Isle of Georgia came in sight, the peaks
of its mountains obscured by dark and heavy clouds, their slopes
white with snow. As the ships approached, whales spouted, blue
and white and small black petrels flew about or rested upon the
water, and numerous crested penguins, with cries of alarm,
jumped off the floating ice into the sea. In Port Mary (Undine
Harbour or Queen Maud Bay), two British whalers, the *Indes-
pensable* (sic) and the *Mary-Ann*, commanded by Captains
Brown and Short, lay at anchor. They had been there for four
months extracting blubber from seals and Bellingshausen cross-
examined them closely on their technique, helped in interpretation by one of their sailors who proved to be a deserter from

a Russian ship. Bellingshausen then turned to his principal task, a survey of the island. In two days he completed a survey of the south coast, linking up with Cook's survey of the northern coast done forty-four years before. It was an admirable piece of work later included in British Admiralty charts and unrivalled until recent years.

The *Vostok* and the *Mirnyi* then set course south-east by east for the northern extremity of Cook's Sandwich Land, now known as the South Sandwich Islands. Cook had thought Sandwich Land to be 'either a group of islands or else the point of a continent'. But Bellingshausen settled the matter. He discovered Sandwich Land to consist of two groups of islands and named the northern group the 'Marquis de Traversay Islands' after the Minister of Naval Affairs. The islands were carefully surveyed; sketches, precise and elegant, were made of coastal profiles by Paul Mikhailov, the Academician, and these have continued to decorate the British Admiralty's 'Antarctic Pilot' down to the present day.

There were lesser tasks still to be completed, no less methodically, before Bellingshausen embarked on the first stage of his great voyage of circumnavigation. The position of the Candlemas group of islands was firmly fixed. Saunders Island, Cook's Cape Montague, was proved to be an island. These and other islands, including Cook's Cape Bristol, were mapped and their insularity proved.

On 27 January 1820 the *Vostok* and the *Mirnyi*, the first ships to do so since Cook, crossed the Antarctic Circle; an achievement not even mentioned in Bellingshausen's journal. Then followed a sequence of discoveries, exaggerated of recent years far beyond the limits of Bellingshausen's modest claims, which brought the Russians, though they never realized it at the time, within sight of the Antarctic Continent. On 28 January (16 January by the Russian Calendar), the two ships in a heavy swell were in latitude 69° 21′ S. and longitude 2° 14′ W., when Bellingshausen saw through the falling snow 'a solid stretch of ice running from east through south to west'; a veritable 'icefield strewn with hummocks'. But the weather was rapidly worsening and Bellingshausen turned north-west by west in search of the open sea, leaving behind him – for discovery more than a century later – the ice cliffs of Kr. Prinsesse Märtha Kyst, part of the Norwegian Antarctic territory of Dronning Maud Land. Only two days later, away to the west, Edward Bransfield and William Smith in the brig *Williams* became the first to recognize this same Antarctic mainland in the form of the Trinity Peninsula.

Sailing east and south, by 21 January (2 February, new style) Bellingshausen was again within sight of the ice cliffs of the Continent and wrote, 'As we surveyed the extent of the icefield around us to the east, south, and west, we were unable to see its limits; it was precisely an extension of that which we had seen in thick weather on the 16th (i.e. 28 January, new style), but had been unable to examine properly on account of the mist and snow.' They were now in clear weather. Nevertheless, Bellingshausen from his narrative seems to have been quite unaware of the true nature of his discovery. In his journal for 5 and 6 February (17th and 18th, new style), when the two ships still in clear weather were in latitude 69° S., longitude 16° E., Bellingshausen once again gives a very recognizable description of the ice cliffs of the mainland and of the ice slopes beyond, gently rising towards the polar plateau; the cliff edge, he says, 'was perpendicular and formed into little coves, whilst the surface sloped upwards towards the south to a distance so far that its end was out of sight even from the masthead'. These coves, he thought, marked places from which the ice-bergs floating round the ships had broken away. On the following day, Bellingshausen, then off the coast of Prinsesse Ragnhild Kyst which was discovered by the Norwegian Riiser-Larsen in 1931, saw in the farther distance 'ice-covered mountains'. But he makes no claim even then to any discovery of the Antarctic Continent.

Bellingshausen's Antarctic expedition because of its bearing on Russia's historic right to a say in the future of Antarctica has recently been the object of much research in the Soviet Union and new documents have been unearthed and published. These include a lecture delivered by Professor Simanov, the astronomer, in 1822 at Kazan University; a letter from Mikhail Lazarev, captain of the *Mirnyi*; the diary of Yegor Kiselev, a seaman on the *Vostok*; and a book, not published until 1853, which was probably the work of P. M. Novosil'skiy, a midshipman on the *Mirnyi*. One might expect such private documents to be less guarded and cautious in expression than Bellingshausen in his official narrative. But none contains any claims to continental discovery. Nor are there any assertions of Russian sovereignty over these parts of Antarctica; a remarkable omission on the part of Bellingshausen and his men in a century when national claims were made with such alacrity.

Continuing eastwards and clockwise round the Continent, Bellingshausen penetrated further south than any previous explorer in these waters and after crossing and recrossing the Antarctic circle reached almost to Enderby Land, today part of Australian Antarctic Territory. The two ships then made for Australia and visited New Zealand, Tahiti, and the Central Pacific before returning to the Antarctic regions.

Early in November 1820, with men rested and ships refitted, Bellingshausen embarked on his second phase of discovery in the Antarctic, approaching by way of the sub-Antarctic Macquarie Island, south of the Tasman Sea, where he found British sealers from Sydney were very active. He then sailed westwards through the Southern Ocean and approached the Continent through the waters of the Bellingshausen Sea. On 21 January 1821 the first signs of land were seen, heralded by a dazzling white light, the ice-blink familiar to Antarctic explorers, lighting the sky to the south.

The following day, a dark shape seen through the haze to the north-east was transformed as the sun broke through the clouds into a land of black rock and snow, the first recognizable land they had seen within the Antarctic circle. This small island, as it proved to be, protected by an encircling belt of ice, Bellingshausen called Ostrov Peter I after, 'the great name of the founder of the fleet of the Russian Empire'. In 1929 Norwegians, within whose territory the island now falls, made the first landings there. But it retains its Russian name, Peter I Øy, today.

Towards the end of the month, heading for the east, the *Vostok* and *Mirnyi* sailed close to a great and mountainous headland. 'I called this discovery "land"', wrote Bellingshausen, 'because its southern extent disappeared beyond the range of our vision'; he named it Bereg Aleksandra I (Alexander I Coast); it is now known as Alexander Land. This, the most extensive Antarctic discovery made by the Russians, is not part of the mainland, as Bellingshausen thought, but an island separated from the mainland by a narrow, ice-covered sound.

Bellingshausen had now almost completed his circumnavigation of the Antarctic Continent and he turned to his last mission, the survey of New Shetland, the South Shetland Islands, 'to ascertain whether this recently discovered land belongs to the supposed Southern Continent'. Bellingshausen, unlikely as it may have seemed to Captain Edmund Fanning, already knew all about William Smith's discovery through a message he had received while in Australia from the Russian Minister in Rio de Janeiro. He had also heard the news from the captain of an East India merchantman he met in Sydney Harbour. As usual no time was wasted. In six days he surveyed with his customary accuracy all the islands of the group and thus disposed of the continental theory. Bellingshausen had now proved beyond doubt that neither the South Sandwich Islands nor the South Shetland Islands belonged to a Southern Continent.

It was in the course of this survey, early in February 1821, that Bellingshausen met Captain Nathaniel Palmer and it is worth while comparing his version of this encounter with the picturesque version perpetuated by Captain Edmund Fanning. Bellingshausen, as he approached Deception Island, met one of the several American sealers lying off the coast. 'I lay to,' he writes, 'despatched a boat, and waited for the Captain of the American boat. . . . Soon after Mr Palmer arrived in our boat and informed us that he had been here for four months' sealing in partnership with three American ships. They were engaged in killing and skinning seals, whose numbers were perceptibly diminishing. There were as many as eighteen vessels about at various points, and not infrequently differences arose amongst the sealers, but so far it had not yet come to a fight. Mr Palmer told me that the above-mentioned Captain Smith, the discoverer of New Shetland, was on the brig *Williams* and that he had succeeded in killing as many as 60,000 seals, whilst the whole fleet of sealers had killed 80,000. As other sealers were also competing in the destruction of the seals there could be no doubt that round the South Shetland Islands just as at South Georgia and Macquarie Islands the number of these sea animals will rapidly decrease.' After some further talk about sealing and about the dangers to ships in these waters 'Mr Palmer soon returned to his ship'. There is no word, in this Russian version of the episode, of Palmer Land, or of Palmer's discovery of a continent.

This survey of the South Shetland Islands completed, Bellingshausen turned for home. It was the end of a great voyage of circumnavigation and of Antarctic discovery. In the east, he had been the first, though he had not realized it, to set eyes on the continental coast in the Norwegian sector of Antarctica. In the west, he had discovered Peter I Øy and the great and mountainous expanse of Alexander Land, an island barely separated from the mainland. In the west, too, in his surveys of South Georgia, of the South Shetlands, and of the South Sandwich Islands, Bellingshausen completed, extended, and perfected the work begun by Cook. It it indeed with Cook whose example he so closely followed, whose achievements he so much admired, that Bellingshausen can most fittingly be compared in his leadership and conduct of this first Russian Antarctic expedition.

It is remarkable that Bellingshausen's great contributions to Antarctic discovery should, on his return to Russia in 1821, have been so tardily recognized. In 1824 when he presented to the Imperial Admiralty his report and the maps of his two-year voyage, the Emperor refused to sanction the cost of its publication. Three years later the work was somewhat reluctantly taken in hand out of fear that 'the scientific discoveries of Captain Bellingshausen, if not now made known, may be claimed by others as their own, and that the honour of them will go to foreign and not to Russian navigators'. In 1831, the report and maps were published. But it was not until 1836 that Bellingshausen's charts were available outside Russia to guide the course of future exploration.

Waning maritime ambitions, a diversion of strategic and economic interest from the Far to the Near East, these no doubt were factors in Russia's failure to profit in the nineteenth century from the brilliant lead in Antarctic discovery which Bellingshausen gave. Indeed, whaling apart, Russian Antarctic exploration was not renewed until after the Second World War when the Soviet Union in 1957–8 contributed on a great scale to the Antarctic investigations of the International Geophysical Year. Bellingshausen, meanwhile, largely because of the great significance of his voyages in connexion with Russia's claims to the status of an Antarctic power, has at last been restored to his rightful place in the history of polar exploration. The names of his ships, *Vostok* and *Mirnyi*, have been given to Soviet Antarctic stations set up for the Geophysical Year. And Soviet plans are already (1959) in hand for a scientific journey across the Antarctic Continent towards the waters which Bellingshausen was the first to explore, the waters of the Bellingshausen Sea.

Along the line of this trans-continental journey, in Dronning Maud Land and on the shores of this sea, two Russian scientific bases are to be established and named, in the words of the Soviet Press, 'in honour of the famous Russian sailors who discovered Antarctica – Thaddeus Bellingshausen and Mikhail Lazarev'.

A BRITISH SEALER CIRCUMNAVIGATES
THE CONTINENT

AFTER this magnificent Russian interlude we can return to the explorations of the British sealers who continued to promote science and discovery under the diligent guidance of such owners as the Enderby brothers. Their long voyages in the twenties and thirties of the century, in brigs and cutters manned often enough by no more than a dozen men, were in distance covered no less extensive, in discovery often as fruitful as those of many of the heavily manned naval ships which took part in the subsequent revival of national Antarctic exploration towards the end of this period. The names of Powell, Weddell, John Biscoe, John Kemp, and John Balleny are those which stand forth among the British sealers at work in the Antarctic between 1822 and 1839.

In 1822, the year after Bellingshausen's return, James Weddell in the 160-ton brig *Jane* and the 65-ton cutter *Beaufoy* penetrated deeply into the Weddell Sea, normally one of the most dangerous of Antarctic seas because of the tremendous pressure of the circulating ice within it, and reached the latitude of 74° 15′ S., two hundred and fourteen nautical miles nearer the Pole than Cook. Weddell, a retired Master from the Royal Navy, was in his devotion to science typical of these sealing captains of the first three decades of the nineteenth century. Despite the lack of proper instruments and the disgruntlement of his sailors at so apparently profitless an occupation, he did what he could, testing the strength and direction of currents, taking temperatures of the sea until his thermometers were smashed in a gale, puzzling over differences in magnetic variation, scrupulously observing even in moments of immediate danger the nature, form, and movement of the ice. To persevere with such tasks in vessels cruelly exposed to the violence of Antarctic weather required a singular devotion. The experiences, however, of Weddell's ships on this lengthy pioneering voyage were not unusual. A whale boat over-board; a rudder frozen into immobility; bulwarks, decks, and rigging so heavily encrusted with ice that the ship could scarcely rise to the sea – such experiences were common in the brigs and cutters of the Antarctic sealers in the early years of the nine-teenth century.

Eight years later, John Biscoe, who is the best known of the Enderby sealers, circumnavigated the Antarctic Continent and the log of his voyage of 1830–2 was presented by Charles Enderby to the newly founded Geographical Society of London. Biscoe's mission was to search for land in the Southern Ocean east of the meridian of Greenwich where it was thought the great icebergs originated which had recently been seen, to the alarm of shipping in the South Atlantic Ocean, as far north as 35° 50′ S. By 22 January 1831 Biscoe's brig the *Tula*, with the cutter *Lively*, had crossed the Antarctic Circle. The edge of the pack must have receded considerably since Bellingshausen's voyage through these same waters ten years earlier, for Biscoe was able to sail well south of Bellingshausen's track of which, of course, he had no knowledge. East of the Greenwich Meridian, Biscoe's ships were pounded fiercely against the pack. Only, as he calmly recorded, 'by careful management of the sails' were they able to escape disaster. On 25 February 1831, the first doubtful land was seen, 'an appearance of land ... nearly similar to the North Foreland'. 'I should think', Biscoe wrote, 'that the cliffs of it, which bore the marks of icebergs having been broken off from it, and which was exactly similar to their sides in every respect, were as high, or nearly so, as the North Fore-land; it then ran away to the southward with a gradual ascent, and with a perfectly smooth surface, and I could trace it in extent to at least from thirty to forty miles with a good telescope; it was then lost in the general glow of the atmosphere.'

Biscoe is clearly describing, just as Bellingshausen had de-scribed, the ice cliffs of the continent and the ascending slope of the ice beyond, rising towards the polar plateau. But on this first view he was very doubtful of his discovery. He had unortho-dox views on the origins of Antarctic ice and imagined that it was all engendered from the sea. Antarctica he prophesied would prove to be not an ice-girt, ice-covered land-mass, but a solid mass of sea ice, though islands might be found embedded in it. In accordance with this hypothesis to which he obstinately adhered, Biscoe concluded that the great ice wall he had seen, which reminded him so much of the white cliffs of the North Foreland, was 'nothing more than a solid body of ice'.

But on 3 March 1831, undeniable land appeared which Biscoe identified from the foretop as the dim black shapes of mountain summits. As the *Tula* and *Lively* edged dangerously through the pack, this new discovery was heralded by an Aurora Australis so brilliant that it emblazoned the whole night sky, and of such a marvellous variety of pattern and colour that Biscoe and his sailors, seeing these Southern Lights for the first time, had no eyes for the ice hazards in the sea below. 'Nearly the whole night', John Biscoe wrote in his log, 'the Aurora Australis showed the most brilliant appearance, at times rolling itself over our heads in beautiful columns, then as suddenly forming itself as the unrolled fringe of a curtain, and again suddenly shooting to the form of a serpent, and at times appearing not many yards above us.' Under this canopy of colour the brig and the cutter moved cautiously towards a prominent and sombre headland which Biscoe named Cape Ann. Suddenly the sublimity of the scene was shattered. A south-easterly gale arose, boats were swept away, bulwarks were stove in, and before a wind which had turned ice-cold, the brig trapped in the whirling pack was swept a hundred miles out to sea. Of the cutter no vestige could be seen.

When the storm subsided, Biscoe returned to this coast which he named after his owners, Enderby Land. It lies in the north-west of Australian Antarctic Territory. But it was then mid March, the new ice forming on the sea marked the approach of winter, and scurvy had broken out among the exhausted crew of the brig. Biscoe in his log for this stage of the voyage gives a picture of the hardships endured by the men who manned these small sealers; 'the land inaccessible, heavy gales frequent every day, some of the people getting sick, the carpenter for some time past having lost the use of his legs, and two others at this time in the same condition, and two or three more under medicine for the same complaint ... the vessel is very uncomfortable in bad weather and ships a great deal of water, and is now on her outside, both hull and ropes, where the spray can reach, one mass of ice.' By April so weakened were they by scurvy and the incessant rolling and pitching of the brig in the south-easterly gales that only three men on board could work, but nevertheless Biscoe managed to bring her into port, at Hobart, on 10 May 1831. By some miracle, the cutter *Lively* too survived and her effective crew, reduced to the captain, one seaman, and a cabin boy whose hand had been crushed by a falling boat, brought her into Port Philip, near the modern Melbourne.

Leaving Tasmania in October 1831, Biscoe on the second stage of his voyage of circumnavigation entered the region of Bellingshausen's discoveries. Knowing nothing of these, Biscoe sailed westwards and, approaching the continent from north of the Bellingshausen Sea, wrongly claimed that his first new discovery Adelaide Island, an island 'of a most imposing and beautiful appearance, with one very high peak running up into the clouds' was 'the farthest known land to the southwards'. To the north, beyond this island named after William the Fourth's Queen, he could see other islands fringing a mountainous mainland coast, and on 21 February 1832 he made his first landing on Antarctic territory. It it difficult to be certain precisely where Biscoe landed but it was probably on Anvers Island off the central stretch of the coast of the Graham Land peninsula south of Bransfield's 'Trinity Land' and 'Palmer's Land'; the latter, a name to which Biscoe himself refers though he seems to have been vague about its position. On his return to England, this central stretch of coast was given the name of Graham Land after Sir James R. G. Graham, then First Lord of the Admiralty; and, with slight justification considering the prior discoveries of Bransfield and Smith and Palmer himself, the name was later applied to the whole of this northward projecting Antarctic peninsula.

The brig *Tula* anchored in the Thames on 30 January 1833. Biscoe, despite the great extent of his voyage, had been singularly unsuccessful as a sealer. But as an explorer he had won

fame and he received, in company with no less a traveller than
Richard Lander, the explorer of the Niger, one of the two gold
medals of the Geographical Society. His owner Charles Enderby
meanwhile, despite heavy financial loss, was so encouraged by
Biscoe's achievements that he forthwith planned further voyages
of Antarctic exploration. One by Biscoe himself is unrecorded.
But another, a no less costly and hazardous venture by a British
sealer, John Kemp, resulted in the discovery of Kemp Land,
adjoining Enderby Land (and also part of Australian Antarctic
Territory). Yet another Enderby expedition sailed in 1838. In
this, seven other London merchants joined with Enderby in
sharing the cost. Enderby's captain this time was John Balleny.
He sailed due south from New Zealand to discover in 1839 the
Balleny Islands – five large and two small islands to which the
names of Enderby's partners were given – and subsequently,
though less certainly, discovered the stretch of coast called, after
Balleny's cutter, Sabrina Land. It is shown on modern maps in
the western part of Australian Antarctic Territory.

A historian of Antarctica, the late Hugh Robert Mill, has
aptly summed up the remarkable contributions of these British
sealers in the second quarter of the nineteenth century. 'Balleny's
cruise', he wrote, 'proved for the first time the existence of land
within the Antarctic Circle south of New Zealand, and by means
of it the firm of Enderby forged still more links in the strong
chain of evidence that either the edge of an extensive continent or
a long series of islands lay to the south of the Indian Ocean just
within or on the Antarctic Circle, portions of which appeared
in the Balleny Islands on the east, Enderby Land on the west,
and at Kemp Land and possibly Sabrina Land between the two.'

A more eloquent and no less justifiable tribute to the disinterested devotion to exploration of the Enderby brothers was paid
after Charles Enderby had retold Balleny's story to the Fellows
of the Royal Geographical Society. 'It would be impossible',
declared the speaker, 'to close the simple but apparently faithful
narrative of this voyage without adverting to the progress made
in discovery in the Southern Seas through the spirited exertions
of Mr Charles Enderby, and other British merchants, so honourable to the commercial enterprise of our country. Graham Land,

Enderby Land, Kemp Land, and now the Balleny Isles, are all discoveries made by the ships belonging to the disinterested and praiseworthy owner. The results of this voyage', he continued, 'must tend to keep alive the supposition of the existence of either a great southern land or a vast mass of islands, whose northern limits would seem to range between the 67th and 69th parallels, a part of which we trust, ere long, to see laid down in our charts, and not improbably rendered subservient to the interests of science, if not to the prosperity of our fisheries.'

THE UNITED STATES EXPLORING
EXPEDITION

IN origin, American concern with Antarctic exploration was a reaction to these great advances made by the British sealers in the Antarctic for the far-ranging voyages of the latter, revealing as they did how widespread were Antarctic lands and how extensive were the possibilities for future exploration, had for some time aroused an interest sharpening to suspicion among the merchants and financiers of the United States. They feared indeed that America was being outpaced and outmanoeuvred in the race for bases, for fishing grounds, and trade routes and that American commercial prospects were being endangered in a traditional zone of American interest, in the Southern Ocean south of Cape Horn.

During the first twenty years of the nineteenth century American interests in these sub-Antarctic and Antarctic waters had been upheld by shipowners and sealers alone, the Government remaining in the background. But in 1821 the United States Government displayed open concern and on 21 May of that year the House of Representatives 'Resolved, That it is expedient that one of our small public vessels be sent to the Pacific Ocean and the South Seas, to examine the coasts, islands, harbours, shoals, and reefs in those seas, and to ascertain their true situation and description'. When President John Quincy Adams (the principal architect of the Monroe doctrine) entered office in 1824, he went ahead with preparations and in his message to Congress of 6 December 1825, tried to gain support for a project of southern exploration by discoursing in general terms on the duty of nations to advance scientific knowedge by sending out naval expeditions.

Meanwhile others were striving to bring public pressure to bear on the Government to promote American exploration both in the Pacific and in Antarctica. The most remarkable, and certainly the most indomitable, was Jeremiah N. Reynolds of Ohio, the first active promoter of American polar exploration, less judicious, less successful, but no less worthy of the name than his British contemporary, John Barrow. From the start he had been the great protagonist of President Adams's project and his one ambition was to see an American expedition to the Antarctic sail, with himself as historiographer. He was, however, less concerned with forwarding American commercial interests or competing with the British than with the advancement of American discovery and research. When the Senate under President Jackson's new Democratic administration refused in 1828 to ratify such an exploratory project, Reynolds sailed with a Government sponsored expedition (the first to the Antarctic) under the sealing captains, Palmer and Pendleton, and on his return in 1831 after a cruise round the South Shetlands he was more than ever convinced of the urgency not only of promoting American exploration but of making known to the world American achievements through a national expedition not bound by the commercial secrecy which surrounded sealing operations.

For the next six years Reynolds, convinced of the rightness of his cause, embarked with immense energy on a stormy public campaign to whip up support for a large scientific expedition to explore the Antarctic. The Stonington sealing community were among his most enthusiastic backers and in 1833 the veteran sealing captain Edmund Fanning succeeded in presenting a memorial to Congress 'praying that a national discovery and exploring expedition be sent to the South Seas'. Reynolds himself addressed Congress in support of the motion. He solicited supporting testimony from scientific organizations and commercial bodies. And he engaged in a spate of newspaper publicity. But his campaign made slow progress. Outside a few intellectual centres like Philadelphia imbued with the spirit of Benjamin Franklin, his impassioned speeches in the cause of science made little impression. Nor beyond the sealing towns did the Antarctic arouse much enthusiasm. To the public and to the politicians, the Pacific with its known promise of new whaling grounds and trade routes to the lucrative markets of China, was a far more attractive proposition.

In 1836 Reynolds was again permitted to address Congress. This time he heavily emphasized the Antarctic theme. In an eloquent passage he urged attention to 'the extensive group of islands lying north of the coasts of Palmer's Land, the extent of which neither we nor any subsequent navigators have as yet ascertained'. 'A British vessel', he added in an acid reference to John Biscoe's landing on Anvers Island off Graham Land, 'touched at a single spot in 1832, taking from it the American and giving it a British name.'

At last, Reynolds's unflagging campaign aroused a sufficient pressure of public opinion and this, reinforced by rumours reaching Washington that the British Navy was shortly to launch a national Antarctic expedition, stirred Congress into action. On 14 May 1836, an Act of Congress authorizing a United States Exploring Expedition was passed. For Reynolds, however, it was the beginning as well as the end of a battle. For on that day there was born an expedition which, however important its achievements, was the most ill-prepared, the most controversial, and probably the unhappiest expedition which ever sailed the Antarctic seas.

At the start, all went well. Captain Thomas ap Catesby Jones was appointed by the Navy Department to command. Scientific societies and organizations throughout the country were called upon to advise on equipment, to draw up programmes of research, and to recommend scientists for the expedition. A squadron of ships was earmarked. And a member of the expedition, a Lieutenant Charles Wilkes, of the Department of Charts and Instruments, was sent to London to purchase (as Bellingshausen had purchased) charts and scientific equipment. Then followed two years of charges and counter charges, of personal feuds and political intrigues. The ships selected were unsuitable and the budget inadequate; when the Senate was approached for additional funds, they refused on the grounds that they had been insufficiently consulted by the Navy. Accusations of corruption and fraud, some of which later proved quite justifiable, were flung from side to side. The principal battle, however, was between Reynolds and the Department of the Navy. In his eyes the expedition was to be a scientific expedition and societies like the Philosophical Society of Philadelphia had on his invitation composed lengthy memoranda of advice on scientific research. But the Navy Department in so far as they were interested at all in such matters considered that science was a matter for the Navy and viewed with the greatest of mistrust Reynolds's proposal to include a contingent of civilian scientists in a purely naval expedition. In Reynolds's mind, moreover, the object of the expedition had been discovery as far south as possible. Now even this was changed, the emphasis being placed on Pacific and not on Antarctic exploration. Embittered by these successive defeats, Reynolds vented his grievances in a stream of pamphlets and newspaper articles and ended by accusing Mahlon Dickerson, Secretary of the Navy, of a deliberate intention to wreck the expedition.

This indeed very nearly happened and *Niles' National Register* for 28 October 1837 declared with some truth that 'Success alone can efface the recollection of the bickerings and the heartburnings, and delays and blunders, which have marked the progress of this expedition from its inception to the present time'. Officer after officer resigned, including the commander, Captain Jones. The men recruited, being idle all this time, became increasingly disgruntled. The public, exasperated by the quarrels and the vacillations of all concerned, proclaimed the expedition a failure before it started.

In March 1838, command of the expedition was offered to Charles Wilkes, a comparatively junior lieutenant who had already resigned from the expedition because he had been offered a scientific and not an executive role. Wilkes's appointment produced another storm. He was accused of intriguing to obtain the post. His seniors in the service complained that they had been passed over. Many of the officers previously selected now refused to serve. Nevertheless, it was a justifiable appointment. Wilkes, a descendant of John Wilkes, the champion of the people, the firebrand English politician who had battled on behalf of the American colonists in the reign of George III, was – as his subsequent career made all too plain – impetuous and dominating. But his scientific attainments were far above those of the average naval officer of his day, and he was a resolute and determined man, of great driving power.

Wilkes's orders were to reorganize the whole expedition, and in particular to reduce the number of vessels and the number of scientists, twenty-five, selected. The choice of ships was unfortunate. Three were warships, the *Vincennes* and the *Peacock*, sloops of 700 tons, and the *Porpoise*, a gun-brig of some 200 tons. None were fortified against the ice and in heavy weather their large square gun-ports lay wide open to the surge of the sea. Of the *Peacock*, her captain was later to say, she 'has been fitted (as far as the Navy-yard are concerned) with less regard to safety and convenience than any vessel I have ever had to do with'. The remaining vessels were the *Sea Gull*, an old New York pilot boat serving as a tender, a curious vessel to take on an Antarctic cruise; the tender *Flying Fish* of 100 tons; and a store-ship, the *Relief*, so slow that she was sent home early on in the voyage. It is not surprising that only two of Wilkes's ships survived the expedition. Their capacity was no less inadequate than their design or equipment. Provisions for twelve months, and fuel for seven was all that they could carry, by contrast with the two or even three years' supplies of the British and Russian expeditions.

The reduction in the number of scientists was easier than Wilkes anticipated for, sickened by the endless feuds, several had already thrown up their posts. Of those remaining, the first to be dismissed was Jeremiah Reynolds; 'for the sake of harmony', the Navy Department not unjustifiably said. An applicant for his post was the American novelist, Nathaniel Hawthorne. One of the dismissed scientists was a Mr Johnson who had resigned his professorship at the Franklin Institute in order to join the expedition. His reported comments on the new arrangements were probably typical of the attitude of his scientific colleagues to the Navy's reorganization. 'The dignity and efficiency of the scientific corps, in particular', Johnson declared, 'was so much curtailed that it was with disappointed hopes and lowered expectations that those who were retained, embarked on the voyage; and it was with satisfaction rather than regret, that Mr Johnson finally received notice from the Secretary of the Navy that his services would not be required.'

Although, in the words of the Secretary of the Navy, 'the important interests of our commerce embarked in the whale fisheries' were to be the chief objectives of the expedition, science was not entirely excluded. 'All occasions will be taken', Wilkes's instructions read, 'not incompatible with the great purpose of the undertaking, to extend the bounds of science, and to promote the acquisition of knowledge. For the more successful attainment of these, several scientific gentlemen will accompany the expedition, for the departments of philology, zoology, conchology, geology, mineralogy, and botany, with suitable artists, and a horticulturalist.' Professor Johnson had originally been placed in charge of magnetism, electricity, and astronomy. Now, however, 'astronomy, hydrography, geography, terrestrial magnetism, meteorology, and physics' were entrusted to the Navy. Furthermore, the reduced scientific staff which was finally permitted to sail with the expedition was itself bound by an impossible regulation. For the Navy Department had ordered Wilkes to forbid 'all communications except to this Department, from any person attached to the Expedition, referring to discoveries, or any circumstances connected with the progress of your enterprise'. It is not surprising, therefore, that the civilian scientists, suspect from the start, were allowed no part in the Antarctic cruises of the expedition on which alone new geographical discoveries were likely to be made.

In the Antarctic programme of the United States Exploring Expedition, the effect of the discoveries of the British sealers, Weddell, Biscoe, and Balleny is very evident. Broadly, it envisaged two summer voyages. The first, from Tierra del Fuego to the south of Powell's Group (the South Orkney Islands) and between the latter and Cook's Sandwich Land, was directed towards the greatest possible penetration of the Weddell Sea, 'following the track of Weddell as closely as practicable'. The second voyage was to be southwards from Australia or Tasmania to the Balleny Islands and thence westwards as far as John Biscoe's Enderby Land. The United States Exploring Expedition was, however, no longer primarily concerned, as Reynolds had hoped, with Antarctic exploration. The Antarctic voyages, therefore, were no more than interludes in a series of Pacific voyages ranging from Valparaiso to Fiji and Sydney; from the Sandwich Islands to the north-west of America; and thence to Japan, Singapore, and back to the Cape of Good Hope.

On 18 August 1838 Wilkes's squadron sailed from Hampton Roads. For Wilkes it was a gloomy moment. 'It required', he confided to the pages of his private journal, 'all the hope I could muster to outweigh the intense feeling of responsibility that hung over me. I may compare it to that of one doomed to destruction.' Six months later the ships were assembled at Orange Harbour, Nassau Bay, in the extreme south of Tierra del Fuego, the starting point for the first Antarctic voyage. Almost at once Wilkes in the *Porpoise* and Lieutenant Johnson in the old New York pilot boat set off for James Weddell's sea. They sighted the northern islands of the South Shetland group early in March 1839 and three days later fixed the 'eastern extremity of Palmer's Land or Mount Hope' – at the tip of the Graham Land peninsula – in 63° 25' S. and 57° 55' W. They did not know that only a year before a French national expedition, the first of the nineteenth century, had under Captain Dumont d'Urville explored these waters and named Mount d'Urville at that very spot.

The ships then swung round towards the Weddell Sea. But any hopes they had of beating Weddell's furthest south were rapidly dissipated. The extent of the ice cover in the Weddell Sea has fluctuated strangely from year to year. In Weddell's time, only a decade or so earlier, the sea must have been extraordinarily free of ice to have enabled him to achieve such a high latitude. Wilkes found conditions very different. Along the north-east coast of Graham Land, the weather was so thick, the ice pressed against the coast by the westerly drift so massive, that he soon despaired of penetrating further, or of landing. The men were in great discomfort. The brig, her gun-ports wide open to the heavy south-westerly gales, every rope, every inch of deck thickly encrusted with ice, was too small to accommodate so large a crew even in moderate conditions. The clothing issued to the men, moreover, was absurdly inadequate for a polar journey. 'Although purchased', Wilkes wrote later, 'by the Government at great expense, it was found to be entirely unworthy of service, and inferior in every way to the samples exhibited. This was the case with all the articles of this description that were provided for the expedition.' An outbreak of scurvy among the crew of the *Porpoise* was decisive. After a hasty visit to Deception Island both ships, in some distress, headed for Orange Harbour.

An attempt, meanwhile, by the *Peacock* and the *Flying Fish* to exceed Cook's *Ne Plus Ultra*, in longitude 105° W., was astonishingly almost successful. The *Peacock*, the sloop of war of which her commander Lieutenant Hudson had so bitterly complained, managed somehow to struggle through the ice made the more dangerous by dense fog, as far as 68° S., 95° 44' W. when there emerged the outlines of the 96-ton tender, the *Flying Fish*, with the triumphant news that by riding above the ice and slipping through narrow leads she had only just failed to reach 71° 10' S., Cook's most southerly point. To have voyaged so far west and south, almost to within sight of the inaccessible coast of Marie Byrd Land (as it is now called) was a remarkable achievement in such ill-found vessels. But the Antarctic season was now over. When the squadron was assembled again off the South Shetlands, they returned to Valparaiso, and in May 1839, to Wilkes's relief, sailed for the warm waters of the Pacific.

In December 1839 the United States Exploring Expedition lay in harbour at Sydney, after seven months of Pacific exploration, preparing for their principal Antarctic voyage southwards towards the Balleny Islands and thence westwards round the continent towards Enderby Land. This was a voyage from which the civilian scientists were excluded. Wilkes did what he could to prepare his ships for the test. Tarred canvas and sheet lead was used to patch rotten bulwarks and keep cabins and quarters dry. Patching and restoring went on night and day. Wilkes, meanwhile, in his anxiety gained no comfort from the comments of the inhabitants of Sydney. They had already heard rumours of the new, elaborate, and ingenious equipment soon to be used by Sir James Clark Ross in a great British Antarctic venture and they expressed open astonishment at Wilkes's make-shift

fleet. 'They inquired', Wilkes ruefully admitted, 'whether we
had compartments in our ships to prevent us sinking? How we
intended to keep ourselves warm? What kind of anti-scorbutic
we were to use? And where were our great ice-saws? To all of
these questions I was obliged to answer, to their great apparent
surprise, that we had none, to agree with them that we were
unwise to attempt such a service in ordinary cruising vessels;
but we had been ordered to go, and that was enough . . . go we
should. . . . This want of preparation certainly did not add to the
character for wisdom of our government, with this community
. . . and, altogether, as a gentleman told me, most of our visitors
considered us doomed to be frozen to death. . . .'

Depressed but resolute, Wilkes's squadron left Sydney on
26 December 1839 and the first Antarctic land was seen on
15 January 1840; a small island of the group discovered by John
Balleny, of which Wilkes seems to have had no knowledge. The
next few days sailing on a westerly course they met the full
impact of the Antarctic weather, with heavy gales and huge seas
succeeded, ominously, by smooth water strewn with scarcely
moving pack-ice. The air was still and a dense fog hung over the
sea, and Wilkes, beset in the *Vincennes* (the sloop of war serving
as the flag ship) spent many hours listening anxiously 'to the low
and distant rustling of the ice'.

However, the pack shifted and they made sail and on 19
January land was seen stretching far to the south-south-east and
south-west, visible above the ice islands which lay ahead of the
ships. It had, Wilkes noted, 'the appearance of being 300 feet in
height, forming a sort of amphitheatre, looking grey and dark,
and divided into two distinct ridges or elevations throughout
its entire extent, the whole being covered in snow'. This new
coast, possibly the coast of Oates Land adjoining the Ross Dependency, was their first sight of the Antarctic continent. The
Peacock and the *Vincennes* then steered westwards along the
edge of a belt of close pack-ice, weaving a way between great
tabular icebergs and Wilkes wrote in his journal of these with
a true touch of neo-Gothic fantasy, 'Some of the bergs were of
magnificent dimensions, one third of a mile in length, and from
150 to 200 feet in height, with sides perfectly smooth as if they

had been chiselled. Others, again, exhibited lofty arches of many coloured tints, leading into deep caverns, open to the swell of the sea, which, rushing in, produced loud and distant thunderings. The flights of birds passing in and out of these caverns recalled the recollections of ruined abbeys, castles, and caves, while here and there a bold, projecting bluff, crowned with pinnacles and turrets, resembled some Gothic keep. A little farther onwards could be seen a vast fissure, as if some powerful force had rent in twain these mighty masses. Every noise on board, even our own voices, reverberated from the massive and pure white walls ... if an immense city of ruined alabaster palaces can be imagined, of every variety of shape and tint, and composed of huge piles of buildings grouped together, with long lanes or streets winding irregularly through them, some idea may be formed of the grandeur and beauty of the spectacle.'

Wilkes was still in the midst of this reverie when the *Peacock*, attempting to free herself from the ice closing in on her bows, drove backwards into the pack. But her rudder was smashed in this manoeuvre and she became so unmanageable that all sails were furled and ice-anchors were used to make her fast to a floe. Then a sudden squall tore her away. Her port quarter was smashed. A boom and davit were carried off. Her stern boat was crushed. And she lay, rotten and helpless, the pack surging round her at the whim of the sea. Wilkes, however, had no hesitation in leaving her to her fate. The one thought in his mind was to advance westwards as far as Enderby Land and in the flag-ship, the *Vincennes*, with the gun-brig, the *Porpoise*, he carried on, charting the ice-islands as he went, thinking that they would change their position so little that he would be able to return the same way.

Wilkes was convinced that if he could penetrate the ice belt which lay unbroken to the south of the ships, he would – as he had already done farther east – reach land. On 30 January 1840, in bright sunlight, still advancing westwards through a 'sea so smooth that a yawl could have passed over in safety', he saw his chance. Under full sail, the ships threaded their way through a glistening forest of bergs and ice-islands towards a bay, enclosed by rocks and ice, with land rising towards the south and stretching from east to west for sixty miles. 'I make this bay', wrote Wilkes in his log, 'in longitude 140° 30′ E., latitude 66° 45′ S.; and, now that all were convinced of its existence, I gave the land the name of the Antarctic Continent.' The bay, named Piner's Bay after Wilkes's signal-quartermaster, must have been in the vicinity of Terre Adélie.

This first confident announcement of the existence of an Antarctic continent was followed by a crisis in the fortunes of the United States Exploring Expedition. The hardships of the voyage, the unbearable condition on board, the remorseless discipline of Wilkes himself, a martinet of the old sea-going school, had reduced the crew of the *Vincennes* to a state so wretched that two of the three surgeons in the ship (the third Wilkes had personally suspended from duty) were forced to certify in writing that illness would soon so reduce their numbers 'as to hazard the safety of the ship and lives of those on board'. The men pleaded that they should return. Only fear of their formidable commander prevented mutiny. But Wilkes was merciless and adamant. 'It was my duty', he wrote in his journal, 'to proceed, and not to give up the cruise until the ship was totally disabled, or it should be evident to all that it was impossible to persist any longer.'

Throughout February 1840 the *Vincennes*, now alone, with the *Porpoise* far behind, advanced slowly westwards within sight of the coast, glimpsing from time to time high land stretching southwards beyond the ice cliffs. One landing was made, on an island, to make magnetic observations and collect geological specimens, but no landing could be made on the coast. Wilkes had passed west of Balleny's Sabrina Land to longitude 106° 40′ E. in the vicinity of Knox Coast. But even Wilkes had now to give up hope of reaching Enderby Land and of linking up there with Biscoe's eastward voyage. Winter was approaching, and he could not risk his ships with work still to do in the Pacific, work far more important from the Navy Department's point of view. So he decided to turn north. 'I have seldom seen', he wrote, 'so many happy faces or such rejoicing as the announcement of my intention to return produced.' By 11 March Wilkes was back in Sydney Harbour, at the end of a turbulent but remarkable voyage in the course of which he had explored and charted, intermittently at all events, fifteen hundred miles of Antarctic coast.

The remaining ships of Wilkes's squadron added little to these discoveries. The *Peacock* struggled back to safety. But the *Porpoise* was involved in an incident which is worth recalling because it introduces for the second time in this narrative France's first Antarctic expedition under Captain Dumont d'Urville. Towards the end of January 1840 the gun-brig *Porpoise* was cruising off the present King George V Land when her captain, Lieutenant Ringgold, saw two ships ahead, standing to northward. Seeing that they were strangers, he hoisted his colours and attempted to cut them off. He thought that they might be the ships of the rumoured British expedition under Captain James Clark Ross and was, as he said, 'preparing to cheer the discoverer of the North Magnetic Pole' when to his surprise they ran up French colours and made sail 'without exchanging the usual and customary compliments incidental to naval life'. Wilkes, when he heard of the incident, of which Dumont d'Urville gives a different version, expressed himself with unwonted restraint. 'It cannot but excite surprise', he wrote, 'that such a cold repulse should have come from a French commander, when the officers of that nation are usually so distinguished for their politeness and attention.'

Although subsequent expeditions were able to show that some of Wilkes's claims to have seen land were unfounded, the voyage of the United States Exploring Expedition was, considering the quality of its ships and equipment, an extraordinary achievement and greatly supplemented and extended the discoveries of John Balleny along the coast of what is now Australian Antarctic Territory. Wilkes, however, received no hero's welcome on his return. On the contrary, he was immediately court-martialled on a variety of charges bred of the quarrels and discontentments of the voyage. He was accused of having exceeded his authority, of undue harshness to his crew, of falsehood, of wearing a captain's uniform when only a lieutenant. On all these he was acquitted except on that of 'illegal punishment of subordinates'. But this was only the first of the misfortunes which beset the leader of the United States Exploring Expedition. During the Civil War, while commanding the U.S. sloop *San Jacinto* in African waters, he intercepted the two Confederate Commissioners, Mason and Slidell, on their way to Britain, then sympathetic with the Confederate cause. At first he was a national hero. But the British Government intervened to such effect that his act was disallowed. This was typical of a number of his precipitate actions on the high seas which brought Britain and the United States almost to the verge of war. In the end, though not before he had once again been court-martialled for insubordination and for personal abuse of no less a person than Gideon Welles, Secretary of the Navy, he was retired to work on the publication of the results of his explorations. To this considerable task he dedicated the rest of a no less stormy life.

Ill-judged though his conduct no doubt often was, one cannot help admiring Wilkes's devotion and persistence in this culminating phase of the United States Exploring Expedition. In August 1842 a law was passed providing funds for a limited publication of the expedition's scientific work on condition that American scholars only contributed, without European help. But a limited publication was not at all what Wilkes had in mind. He had all along been obsessed by the idea that the Whig administration which had been in office since his return was determined to minimize his achievements and he was all the more inclined to consider this a derisory and humiliating proposal. For thirty years, indeed until after the Civil War, he clamoured for funds to publish new and more sumptuous volumes until the Senate, which had sufficiently unhappy memories of the Expedition's early days, became exasperated under this incessant bombardment. 'Throw it into the Potomac; that is the best thing', said Senator Toombs of Georgia in the course of one debate. But perhaps Senator Simon Cameron's comment during the appropriation debate of 1861 best summed up official feeling about the United States Exploring Expedition. 'I am tired', he declared, 'of all this thing called Science here.'

Nevertheless Wilkes, by a tenacity no less than he had displayed on his Antarctic voyage, got his way. 'I am, my dear Sir,' he wrote to a correspondent soon afterwards, 'beginning to feel very proud of our work ... we shall now produce a work that every American will be proud of, and which will show those across the Atlantic that we can compete with them in many more ways than they have as yet given us credit for, and that too under every disadvantage.'

Bitter memories of the feuds surrounding the United States Exploring Expedition dissuaded the United States Government from involvement in polar exploration for more than a quarter of a century. To generations of the people of the United States, however, Charles Wilkes was a national hero, another Columbus, the discoverer of a strange, new world. His books were read and re-read, especially by the young. And Mark Twain relates in his autobiography that when he was a boy on the Mississippi, Wilkes was then as famous as Theodore Roosevelt in later years.

EUROPE REVIVES ANTARCTIC
EXPLORATION

WHILE Jeremiah Reynolds of Ohio was demanding that the people and Government of the United States should launch an exploring expedition, a powerful movement developed in Britain which urged the resumption of Antarctic exploration on a national scale comparable with the great Arctic enterprises of the British Navy promoted by John Barrow. The object was to be not only geographical discovery but also, and as many thought even more important, the advancement of magnetic research.

From a navigational as well as from a theoretical point of view, the study of magnetism was one of the most pressing scientific problems of the first half of the nineteenth century because this was the beginning of a new maritime era, an era of iron and steam, of speed and naval expansion. In these new conditions accurate compass navigation involving a better understanding of magnetic phenomena was all the more essential. In England, by the eighteen-thirties, considerable advances had been made in this branch of science, chiefly during voyages of exploration in the Arctic. In 1823 Captain Sabine of the Royal Artillery, the magnetic specialist on Parry's Arctic expeditions, had been the first to demonstrate the correlation of magnetic variations on a chart. In the Arctic, too, Ross had discovered the location on Boothia Peninsula of the Magnetic Pole. In the Antarctic, however, little had been done. Here a new and exceedingly valuable scientific motive for further exploration was provided by the German mathematical physicist Johann Karl Friedrich Gauss who discovered a formula whereby he claimed to be able to deduce at any given time the magnetic elements for any part of the earth's surface. On this basis Gauss predicted (with remarkable accuracy) that a South Magnetic Pole would be discovered in the Antarctic in the neighbourhood of latitude

66° S. and longitude 146° E. The discovery of the South Magnetic Pole accordingly became the principal object of the British Antarctic expedition which was about to be proposed, the first since the days of Cook.

The first public appeal to the British Government to sponsor a national Antarctic expedition for the discovery of a South Magnetic Pole came at a meeting at Dublin in 1835 of the newly fledged British Association. At this meeting Captain Sabine was a dominating figure. The following year reinforcement, eloquent and powerful, came from another and at first a mysterious source in the form of an anonymous pamphlet composed, it became known, by Captain Washington, R.N., the Secretary of the Royal Geographical Society, and addressed to his President and Council, though from its contents it was evidently also intended for a much wider and even more influential audience.

This pamphlet, which appealed to the British Government to revive Antarctic exploration, was prompted, the author said, by the news that at that very moment the United States of America was preparing to launch a great national Antarctic exploring expedition, namely the expedition led by Charles Wilkes. Was England, Washington demanded, to stand passively by and allow a 'foreign and in some points a rival nation ... to step in and bear away the palm of glory' which Cook, Weddell, and Biscoe had by their achievements so magnificently won? Washington marshalled a formidable array of arguments in support of his case: the traditions of the Navy; the great example of the Russian Bellingshausen; the urgent need for magnetic investigation; and finally, and in the last resort, the commercial benefits to be derived, the profits to be made, from a renewal of Antarctic exploration. As to magnetic research, the author of the pamphlet maintained, 'the safety of our ships, the value of our commerce, the lives of our fellow creatures are all risked by the unknown agency of this mysterious power which seems to baffle investigation'. And as for commerce and industry, 'the expense of the outfit of an expedition to search for a new spot for British enterprise and capital to exert itself' would be covered five times over by the discovery of new sealing grounds and new and lucrative sources of sea-elephant oil.

On his own Society, Washington's letter had no effect whatsoever. Its President was now Sir John Barrow, the Secretary to the Admiralty, who was as deeply as ever immersed in the history of the Elizabethan adventurers and was in the throes of planning yet another naval voyage to discover the North-West Passage. Barrow had no intention of allowing the Society to be diverted to Antarctic exploration. But strong support came from the British Association. At meetings in 1837 and in 1838, first Sabine and then Washington (in a paper to the newly established Geographical Section) urged the dispatch of an Antarctic expedition and in veiled terms proposed, as Washington in his pamphlet had quite obviously hinted, that the leader should be James Clark Ross, discoverer of the North Magnetic Pole. Progress was now rapid. In May 1838 the Royal Society, which had been granted large funds by the Government to purchase magnetic instruments, set up a committee to consider the whole matter of magnetic stations and of a South Polar voyage. In this they were greatly influenced by a letter (said to have been prompted by Captain Sabine) which the great German geographer Baron Alexander von Humboldt had addressed to their President, the Duke of Sussex. This proposed the establishment of a chain of such stations 'with the hope of enabling the philosophers to approximate to some of the general laws by which this extraordinary phenomenon is regulated'.

Washington's pamphlet had a more immediate effect in France than in England. There, one of the founders of the Paris Geographical Society, the naval officer, Jules Sebastien César Dumont d'Urville, an explorer, linguist, and ethnologist who in the course of a varied career had rescued for posterity the Venus de Milo, was preparing an ethnological expedition to his favourite Pacific islands. His plans had been approved by the French Admiralty but when they were submitted to Louis Philippe he proposed that Dumont d'Urville should undertake a preliminary expedition in the Antarctic, aimed at surpassing (as Wilkes had tried to do) James Weddell's farthest south in the Weddell Sea.

King Louis Philippe was a shrewd assessor of public opinion. Possibly he calculated that such an adventurous exploit would have a tonic effect on a jaded and dispirited people. Possibly the ubiquitous Baron von Humboldt, a geographer of international fame and a frequent visitor to the French court, may have had a hand in it as he had had in the Antarctic discussions in Britain. In any event, Dumont d'Urville was at first very dubious about this royal proposal, though he admitted 'it must at least give occasion for interesting observations'. Meanwhile, Captain Washington's pamphlet had been sent to the Paris Geographical Society. On reading this, Dumont d'Urville was convinced, as indeed the whole Society was convinced, that France too must play her part in Antarctic exploration and in the advancement of magnetic research.

For Dumont d'Urville, as for James Clark Ross, magnetic studies were the main objective. 'An important discovery remained to be made,' he wrote of the voyage of his two ships, the *Astrolabe* and the *Zélée*, 'the position of the magnetic pole, the knowledge of which is so important for the great problem respecting the laws of terrestrial magnetism. From the outset I had always wished to shape my course with this end in view.' His enthusiasm for such scientific discovery however can have found no response in the French Government for when the French ships sailed from Toulon early in January 1838 they carried only orders, the orders of Louis Philippe, to penetrate as far south as possible in the Weddell Sea, to the greater glory of France.

In this attempt Dumont d'Urville (whose two warships were as unsuitable for Antarctic service as those of Wilkes) was largely unsuccessful. Islands and channels previously discovered by sealers were rediscovered, accurately mapped, and renamed: Louis Philippe Land, Orléans Channel, the Sieur de Joinville's Island. A mountain was named in tribute to the discoveries of Lieutenant Edward Bransfield. But the Weddell Sea proved, as Wilkes had found, impenetrable with the pack extending far to the north. For two months or more the two ships hovered about the ice edge. Observations on the formation and movement of the ice were made in accordance with the instructions of the Academy of Sciences in Paris. Young M. Goupil, the artist, who was destined to die on a voyage to which 'his passion for art and travel' had committed him, made delicate drawings of the shapes of passing bergs. Then the *Astrolabe* and the *Zélée* retreated.

After more than a year of ethnology in the Pacific, Dumont d'Urville returned to the Antarctic early in 1840 to attempt, entirely on his own initiative, the discovery of the South Magnetic Pole. His plan was to sail as far south as possible between 120° and 160° E., in accordance with the predictions of Johann Gauss. On 19 January land was sighted. It was a scene very similar to that described by Bellingshausen, Biscoe, and Wilkes, a panorama of ice and snow fronted by towering ice-cliffs which formed a columned façade stretching far to east and west, broken here and there by deep recesses where the icebergs which littered the sea had fallen away. To this desolate landscape, scoured by winds of unimaginable power, Dumont d'Urville gave the name 'Terre Adélie' after 'the devoted companion who has three times consented to a painful separation in order to allow me to accomplish my plans for distant exploration'.

The land, so called, was unapproachable because of the tumbled masses of ice which littered the coast. But there were numerous rocky snow-covered islets accessible, and on one of these Dumont d'Urville landed with a boat's crew from the *Astrolabe*. The landing was made with Gallic verve and gaiety. With loud cries, the sailors, armed with pick-axes and hammers, leapt ashore, hurling resentful penguins from their path. Then the Tricolor was unfurled. 'Following the ancient custom, faithfully kept up by the English', Dumont d'Urville relates, 'we took possession of it [the island] in the name of France, as well as of the adjacent coast. ... Our enthusiasm and joy were such that it seemed to us that we had just added a province to French territory, by this wholly pacific conquest. ... We regarded ourselves, therefore, at once as being on French soil. ...'

The *Astrolabe* and the *Zélée* then moved east towards, as their compasses showed, the South Magnetic Pole. They were in about 65° S. and 135° E. when suddenly out of the fog in which they lay they saw running towards them before the wind, a strange ship, by her lines and pennant an American man-of-war. This was the *Porpoise* of Wilkes's squadron. She was moving fast through the water and fearing that she might pass them the French ships too made sail. We can now compare Dumont d'Urville's version of this international Antarctic incident with that of Charles Wilkes. According to Dumont d'Urville, the American ship immediately bore off to the south and disappeared. 'We had no object', Dumont d'Urville afterwards declared, 'in keeping secret the results of our operations, and the discoveries for which we had nearly paid so heavily. Besides, these are no longer the days when navigators, impelled by the interests of commerce, think themselves obliged to hide carefully their route and their discoveries in order to avoid the concurrence of rival nations.'

Dumont d'Urville, abandoning his eastward course, turned south-westwards. It was an unvarying and monotonous scene, and there seemed no end to the wall of ice cliffs which stood here, as in Terre Adélie, a hundred feet or more above the level of the sea. To this stretch of coast he gave the name of Côte Clarie after the wife of Captain Jacquinot, captain of the *Zélée*. That its existence has since been confirmed is a tribute to the high accuracy of this great French explorer's charting and observations.

The exact nature of this ice-bound coast was the subject of much excited discussion on board the two French ships. Some like John Biscoe held that it 'was a mass of compact ice independent of all land'. Others, including Dumont d'Urville himself, argued more justifiably 'that this formidable belt was at least an envelope, a crust covering a solid base, either of rock, or even of scattered shoals round a vast land'.

In England, meanwhile, the discussions about the renewal of Antarctic exploration came to a head at a meeting of the British Association at Newcastle in the summer of 1838. A formal resolution calling upon the British Government to dispatch a naval expedition to the Antarctic, for magnetic investigations between the meridians of New Holland (Australia) and Cape Horn, was enthusiastically approved. The Prime Minister, Lord Melbourne, was sympathetic. The Royal Society, a strong supporter from the start, was wholly favourable. Parliament voted the funds. And the joint exertions of Captain Sabine and of Captain Washington, the Secretary of the Geographical Society, ensured (as, throughout, they had intended) that the leader appointed was James Clark Ross, the discoverer of the North Magnetic Pole.

In its exclusive concentration on Antarctica, in the long polar experience of its leader, in the excellence of its ships and equipment, the British expedition enjoyed all the advantages which the French and American expeditions had so unhappily lacked. Ross, a determined and an ambitious Scot, was better suited than any officer in the Navy to supervise all the different aspects, naval and scientific, of the expedition's work. The ships, H.M.S. *Erebus* and H.M.S. *Terror*, were three-masted barque-rigged bombs, without engines, 'of strong build and with a capacious hold', of a type whose value for ice navigation had already been well tested in the Arctic. Each had a double deck and a double coppered hull. Each was fitted with watertight bulkheads and strengthened internally with massive timber beams. The *Erebus* of 370 tons was commanded by Ross himself. Captain Francis Moira Crozier, a shipmate of Ross on his Arctic voyages and earlier of Parry on his North Pole expedition, commanded the 340-ton *Terror*.

This was to be a purely naval expedition and ostensibly no civilian scientists were taken. The surgeons, however – McCormick, Robertson, Lyall, and Joseph Hooker, son of the eminent botanist, Sir W. J. Hooker – were in reality civilians in naval guise who had volunteered for the expedition, for work in zoology, geology, and natural history, because of the great opportunities for scientific discovery and research.

The instructions issued to Ross by the Admiralty in September 1839 were framed in the broadest terms. To ensure the maximum coordination of simultaneous magnetic observations, stations and observatories were first of all to be set up at points as far apart as St Helena, the Cape of Good Hope, Hobart, and Sydney. And provided that all this could be completed by February, Ross was then to proceed as far as the ice permitted to the south 'to examine those places where indications of land have been noticed, and to make the requisite observations of any outlying islands. ....' The principal Antarctic explorations were to start the following summer. Their object would be the discovery and attainment of the South Magnetic Pole. This, said the Admiralty, would be 'one of the remarkable and creditable results of this expedition'.

That was the plan for the Antarctic summer of 1841. The programme for the Antarctic summer of 1842 allowed even wider scope to the experienced commander and was on an even more considerable scale. 'On the breaking up of the succeeding winter', Ross was told, 'you will resume the examination of the Antarctic seas in the highest latitude you can reach, and proceeding to the eastward from the point at which you had left off the preceding year, you will seek for fresh places on which to plant your observatory in all directions from the Pole.' Throughout, the prominent features of new coast were to be charted. The positions of Graham Land and (the officials of the Admiralty apparently having little regard to distance) of Enderby Land were to be checked, and a variety of scientific tasks were to be carried out, in meteorology, geodesy, oceanography, astronomy, geology, and botany in accordance with the great weight of advice which Ross received from the busy committees of the Royal Society.

In September 1839, eighteen months after Dumont d'Urville had left Toulon for the Antarctic, the *Erebus* and *Terror* sailed from Margate Roads on the greatest Antarctic expedition of the nineteenth century. Hobart, Tasmania, was reached in August 1840, after numerous magnetic stations had been established on the way and deep-sea soundings had been made with new equipment in the South Atlantic. The Governor of Van Diemen's Land (Tasmania) was the Arctic veteran, Sir John Franklin and Ross's ships were greeted with the greatest enthusiasm. Balls and dinners, special meetings of the Tasmanian Natural History Society, picnics from which the fragile Dr Hooker snatched such moments as he could to pursue his studies in natural history, were organized with indefatigable energy by the Governor's lady, who was herself to achieve independent but tragic fame in the course of polar history. Despite this multitude of social diversions, science, the principal theme of the expedition, was not allowed to flag. The magnetic observatory was completed in record time by allegedly enthusiastic convict gangs and within it, the Governor, Sir John Franklin, a keen follower of the recent advances in terrestrial magnetism, found 'infinite relaxation'.

For Ross, however, the smooth passage of life in Tasmania was marred by some disturbing news; news that both the Frenchman Dumont d'Urville and the American Wilkes had been exploring where according to Gauss the South Magnetic Pole was most likely to be found. Ross had heard criticisms of the secrecy surrounding the activities of the United States Exploring Expedition. Wilkes, however, was remarkably generous with his information, more generous than Ross was later to give him credit for, and went so far as to enclose, with much other valuable material, a tracing of his chart. This served to confirm Ross's forebodings.

Ross's reaction to these developments was unhesitating and full of the pride of the Navy which since the War had been supreme on the seas. 'That the commanders of each of these great national undertakings should have selected the very place for penetrating to the southward, for the exploration of which they were very well aware at the time that the expedition under my command was expressly preparing did certainly greatly surprise me. ... They had, however, the unquestionable right to select any point they thought proper, at which to direct their efforts, without considering the embarrassing situation in which their conduct might have placed me. Fortunately, in my instructions, much had been left to my judgement under unforeseen circumstances; and, impressed with the feeling that England had ever *led* the way of discovery in the southern as well as in the northern regions, I considered it would have been inconsistent with the pre-eminence she has ever maintained if we were to follow in the footsteps of the expedition of any other nation. I therefore resolved at once to avoid all interference with their discoveries and selected a much more easterly meridian (170° E.) on which to endeavour to penetrate to the southward, and if possible reach the magnetic pole.' It was a momentous and far-reaching decision for it was to lead to discoveries, more

remarkable and more extensive than any that had yet been
made in Antarctica, and in consequence to the first land explorations of the Continent by Scott, Shackleton, and Amundsen early
in the twentieth century.

The *Erebus* and *Terror* sailed from Hobart on 12 November
1840, and on 30 December, then in 64° S. and 10° E., they
crossed Bellingshausen's track. So far they had met only loose
ice, easily brushed away by the blunt bows of the ships. But the
great test of Ross's specially strengthened ships was yet to come
in the form of the main pack, the encircling ice belt which had
kept so many ships at bay. This now stretched out before them,
white, motionless, and menacing, for over a hundred miles.
Ross had an anxious time, waiting for the most favourable conditions of wind and weather. He had, however, full confidence
in the heavy sheathing and giant timbers with which *Erebus* and
Terror had been reinforced and he determined to try his luck.
At first, as if in solemn warning, he was held off by a heavy
swell, by fog, and by thick snow-showers which fell like a
curtain across the ships. Then on the morning of 5 January,
side by side, under full sail, *Erebus* and *Terror* went into the
attack. Looking astern, they watched the open water north of
them gradually disappear. On all sides there was only ice.

To their great surprise, the pack proved nothing like as impenetrable as had been prophesied. An occasional collision with
massive floes sent a violent shudder through the ships. But for
the most part they made a slow and stately progress through the
narrow leads in the ice which opened up under pressure from
the bows. In a few days they saw that the sky ahead of them was
darkening, a sure sign of open water. Momentarily the pack
grew denser and their progress unbearably slow. But in another
four days they were through.

This conquest of the notorious ice belt – a feat which he
was sure neither Wilkes nor Dumont d'Urville could ever have
achieved – was a triumph for Ross and the British shipyards.
Meanwhile the increasing dip of the magnetic needles showed
that they were all the time nearing the main objective of the
expedition, the South Magnetic Pole. Then astonishing news
came from the officer of the watch. A strong land-blink, he re-

ported, could be seen on the horizon, much paler than Ross or any of his shipmates of the North-West Passage expeditions had ever seen in the Arctic, and on 10 January 1841 wholly unexpected land was distinctly seen, rising in lofty, snow-covered peaks, possibly a hundred miles away.

This discovery of new land was not only unexpected but disconcerting. Ross when he so flatly refused to follow foreign tracks and chose instead a course further to the east, along the 170th parallel of latitude, must have known that such a course would carry him well to the east of the region where Gauss had predicted the South Magnetic Pole would be found. Had he decided in a moment of exasperation, to sacrifice science to the interests of national prestige? Or had he hoped ultimately to turn west again, through seas which Balleny had found free of ice and of land, towards his original objective? Whatever he may have hoped, the situation now looked like forcing his hand. He was not only east but also south of Gauss's region. There was land appearing on his port bow. Only if these new lands proved to be islands, around which he might later make his way towards the west, could he expect to return towards the predicted region of the Magnetic Pole.

If these were islands which *Erebus* and *Terror* were approaching, then they were hewn on a scale far nobler and more majestic than any yet seen in the Antarctic. Their great mountains, deep valleys, and sweeping rivers of ice were of an austere and inviolate beauty. To the men on board the two ships the slow revelation of this silent landscape, never before seen by man, seemed like crossing the threshold of a new and undiscovered world.

'It was a beautiful clear evening', wrote Ross, 'and we had a most enchanting view of the magnificent ranges of mountains, whose lofty peaks, perfectly covered with eternal snow, rose to elevations varying from seven to ten thousand feet above the level of the ocean. The glaciers that filled their intervening valleys, and which descended from near the mountains' summits, projected in many places several miles into the sea, and terminated in lofty perpendicular cliffs. In a few places the rocks broke through their icy covering, by which alone we could be assured that land formed the nucleus of this, to appearance, enormous ice-berg.' Ross named the most prominent features as they came into view; a high mountain after Lieutenant-Colonel Sabine; the northernmost cape, high and dark, after Viscount Adare, M.P. for Glamorganshire; another more southerly, at Commander Crozier's special request, 'after his kind and lamented friend, the late estimable Marquis [of Downshire]'; yet another was named after Sir John Barrow, Bart., 'the father of modern Arctic discovery, by whose energy, zeal, and talent our geographical knowledge of those regions has been so greatly increased; we may hope he may live to see the great object of his heart, the discovery of a North-West Passage through the Barrow Strait into the Pacific Ocean, accomplished'.

Off Cape Adare, Ross had to make a decision of the greatest importance for the future of Antarctic discovery. The South Magnetic Pole, he calculated, lay about 500 miles to the southwest, in latitude 76° S. 145° 20′ E. Should he now follow the new coast to the south in the hope that a channel might be found leading westwards towards the Magnetic Pole? Or should he turn westwards at once towards the ice cliffs discovered by Wilkes and Dumont d'Urville, namely along the northern coast of Victoria Land and beyond? A channel might then be discovered cutting through them to the south which would enable him to reach the Magnetic Pole from this direction. Ross's picture of the choice confronting him shows how little he was thinking in terms of the continuous land-mass of a continent. All his previous polar experience had been in the Arctic, among the mountainous islands and ubiquitous channels of the North-West Passage. Here too he was thinking in terms of islands, of channels, of a passage; a passage which sooner or later would probably be found, leading southwards or westwards to Gauss's Magnetic Pole.

Of the two, the prospects towards the west, towards the region of the American and French discoveries, was the less hopeful. The ice cliffs in that direction sighted by Wilkes, Dumont d'Urville, and Balleny might extend for a great distance; they were moreover exceedingly difficult to approach through the outer girdle of ice. Ross therefore decided to follow the new coast towards the south. This was, he said, 'preferred as being more likely to extend our researches into higher latitudes, and as affording a better chance of afterwards attaining one of the principal objects of our voyage'. 'Although', he added, 'we could not but feel disappointed in our expectation of shortly reaching the magnetic pole, yet these mountains being in our way restored to England the honour of the discovery of the southernmost known land, which had been nobly won by the intrepid Bellingshausen, and for more than twenty years retained by Russia.'

Slowly, with men crowding decks and rigging, H.M.S. *Erebus* and H.M.S. *Terror* moved south. As they moved, new mountains, new and glistening glacier streams curving majestically and terminating in giant tongues projecting far into the sea, successively appeared. No sound came from this cold and lifeless land; only the persistent surge and beat of a heavy surf could be heard as it broke on the fallen ice blocks which barricaded the beach. There was life, however, in the sea and the sight of whales – the 'right' or Greenland whale, he thought – reminded Ross of the wealth awaiting the enterprising merchants of Britain. From the deepest waters, moreover, the biologists brought up many minute marine creatures in their new dredge, several very similar to those they had found in the deep waters of the Arctic.

Ross continued to name the new features of the landscape, the peaks and promontories and glaciers, after those closely associated with the expedition. Two ranges were named after the members of the committees of the Royal Society and of the British Association. Mount Melbourne was named after the Prime Minister upon whom 'the representations of the great philosophers of the day had their due influence'. A headland to the south of Cape Melbourne Ross called after Captain Washington, R.N., 'the able Secretary of the Royal Geographical Society'.

In order that these new lands might be properly claimed for the British Crown, a landing had to be made. The coast of the mainland was quite inaccessible for no ship's boat could have penetrated its heavy ice defences. A landing was made, therefore, on a rocky islet named Possession Island, against a strong tide which swept a mass of loose ice through the channel separating it from the shore. There, on this isolated outpost of a new world, on 12 January 1841, 'the ceremony of taking possession of these newly discovered lands, in the name of our Most Gracious Sovereign, Queen Victoria, was immediately proceeded with'. Victoria Land, and with it the British Ross Sea Dependency over which New Zealand was later to claim sovereignty, thus came into being. Ross in his journal describes the celebrations which followed, the hearty cheers of officers and men, the toasts to the Queen and to Prince Albert. For the young Queen, declared Dr Hooker, this great but wholly unexpected discovery was 'surely the whitest if not the brightest jewel in her crown'.

By 22 January 1841 the two ships were in latitude 74° 20' S., further south than James Weddell had reached on the other side of the continent, and another landing was made on an islet which Ross called after Sir John Franklin. Soon afterwards, on a day of clear cold air and sparkling brightness, Mount Erebus and Mount Terror were seen far away to the south. Dr Hooker, in a letter to his father, describes his first sight of these Antarctic mountains, such familiar and impressive landmarks for many exploring expeditions travelling in this region from the time of Borchgrevink and Scott to that of the recent Commonwealth Trans-Antarctic Expedition. Mount Erebus was then an active volcano emitting dense smoke and spurts of flame. 'The water and the sky', Hooker wrote, 'were both as blue, or rather more intensely blue, than I have ever seen them in the tropics, and all the coast one mass of dazzlingly beautiful peaks of snow which, when the sun approached the horizon, reflected the most brilliant tints of golden yellow and scarlet; and then to see the dark cloud of smoke, tinged with flame, rising from the volcano in a perfectly unbroken column, one side jet-black, the other giving back the colours of the sun, sometimes turning off at a right-angle by some current of wind, and stretching many miles to leeward. This was a sight so surpassing everything that can be imagined, and so heightened by the consciousness that we had penetrated into regions far beyond what was ever deemed practicable, that it really caused a feeling of awe to steal over us at the consideration of our own comparative insignificance and helplessness, and at the same time, an indescribable feeling of the greatness of the Creator in the works of His hand.' It was indeed a most impressive sight. On occasions the column of smoke from Mount Erebus seemed to reach fifteen hundred, possibly two thousand feet above the rim of the crater. Then it would fall back and condense into mist or snow and gradually disperse, leaving the crater rim clearly visible, a sharp black irregular line against the scarlet flames.

But even as Ross watched he was planning his next move towards, if possible, the South Magnetic Pole which lay on the map more than two hundred and fifty miles away. His hope was to sail south of the island on which the mountains stood – High Island, now called Ross Island – then westwards and north, through what no doubt he imagined to be an archipelago on the Arctic pattern, towards the vicinity of the Magnetic Pole itself.

But once again he was frustrated. As his ships moved south under all studding sails, Ross saw stretching eastwards from High Island, as far as the eye could see, a long, low, white line. 'It presented', he says, 'an extraordinary appearance, gradually increasing in height as we got nearer to it, and proving at length to be a perpendicular cliff of ice, between one hundred and fifty and two hundred feet above the level of the sea, perfectly flat and level at the top, and without any fissures or promontories on its even seaward face.' What lay immediately to the south of this gigantic barrier of floating ice, which 'crushes the undulations of the waves and disregards their violence', Ross could not say, for its top lay far above the mastheads of the ships. But in the remote distance they could see – or, as Scott later discovered, imagined they could see – the dim shapes of mountain peaks, and that was all, that and the unending line of the Barrier; the Victoria Barrier as Ross named it, the Ross Ice Shelf as it is called today. As to finding a way through, in pursuit of his plan, 'we might', said Ross, 'with equal chance of success try to sail through the cliffs of Dover, as to penetrate such a mass'. There was no hope of wintering for there was no harbour safe for sailing ships. Nor was there any hope of landing and travelling, as Ross thought they might easily have travelled, overland to 'the brilliant burning mountain' and on perhaps to the Magnetic Pole. Instead, all he could do was to bow 'to the will of Him who had so defined the boundary of our researches'. He decided to follow the Barrier eastwards in the hope that some hidden channel or passage might ultimately appear.

For day after day H.M.S. *Erebus* and H.M.S. *Terror* sailed eastwards close to the groined and hollowed cliffs of ice. By 5 February they reached their furthest point, in longitude 167° W., and a few days later, fearful now because of the denser ice and the lateness of the season, they turned back to the coast of Victoria Land, making for McMurdo Sound. Ross at first had some hope that there or between there and Cape Adare, he might find a winter harbour so that he could renew his explorations as early as possible the following spring. But none was found. And by 6 April 1841, he and his men were back in the Derwent River, Tasmania, his ships unscathed, every man aboard them as fit, after one hundred and forty-five days in the Antarctic, as on the day on which they had sailed.

The soft green of the hills, the colours, the scents of garden flowers, the comforts and hospitality of colonial Tasmania, were intensely pleasurable after so many months of ice and snow, of gaunt mountains and bitter winds. To the people of Hobart, Ross and his men were the heroes of the hour. There were dinners and receptions. There was a grand ball on the *Erebus*. But the highlight of these celebrations was a new nautical drama given at the Royal Victoria Theatre. Act II presented 'a splendid view of the Volcanic Mountain'; Act III 'A grand allegorical tableau, of Science crowning the distinguished navigators Captain Ross and Crozier at the command of Britannia, and Fame proclaiming their success to the World'.

The second Antarctic cruise of H.M.S. *Erebus* and H.M.S. *Terror* began in November 1841 after six months of refitting. This gave the surgeon-scientists excellent opportunities for magnetic observations and botanical surveys in Australia and New Zealand. The aim of this second voyage was the solution of 'The Great Barrier Mystery' and Ross accordingly struck this time towards the east, along the meridian of 146° W., hoping that he would hit the eastern extremity of the Barrier (the Ross

Ice Shelf) and thereby continue, as his instructions ordered, his explorations of the previous season. But conditions were very different from those of 1840 with thick fog blanketing the Ross Sea, rendering the ships invisible to each other. In mid December, sailing together within hailing distance, *Erebus* and *Terror* entered the pack and steered south-west where the ice appeared more open. It was tedious going, forty-four days moving from water-hole to water-hole, enlivened only by the sudden surfacing of whales to breathe. For safety, the ships were moored on either side of a large floe. This made an admirable sports ground and it was the scene on New Year's Day 1842 of 'a grand fancy ball, of a novel and original character', the centre piece of which was 'The Antarctic Hotel' flanked by an array of allegorical figures representing Bacchus and Britannia, 'The Pilgrims of the Ocean' and 'The Pioneers of Science'. No display could have better symbolized the spirit of mid Victorian polar exploration.

Towards the middle of January, the monotony of the voyage was suddenly and most disagreeably broken when a strong westerly swell snapped hawser after hawser and the two ships were driven by high winds deep into the heavy pack; high winds which rose soon afterwards to the full violence of an Antarctic storm. 'Soon after midnight', wrote Ross, 'our ships were involved in an ocean of rolling fragments of ice, hard as floating rocks of granite, which were dashed against them with so much violence that their masts quivered as if they would fall at each successive blow; and the destruction of the ships seemed inevitable from the tremendous shocks they received.' The rudder of the *Erebus* was put out of action, that of the *Terror* was wrenched away from the stern-post by the battering of ice blocks flung about by the tremendous seas. As he listened through the wind to the straining and working of decks and timbers, to the crashing of the ships against the floes, Ross – calmness itself – found time to admire 'the coolness, steady obedience, and untiring exertions' of his seamen. But he thought 'there seemed to be but little probability of our ships holding together ... so frequent and violent were the shocks they sustained'.

The storm as suddenly subsided and on 19 February, after a voyage of eight hundred miles through the ice, the Barrier was seen. The cold was intense, the decks and rigging of the *Erebus* and *Terror* were heavy with frozen spray, and already young ice, the first portent of winter, could be seen forming gelatinously between the older floes. The Barrier as they approached seemed to trend north-eastwards and to merge at its eastern end with a range of snow-covered mountains. These were the mountains of Scott's King Edward VII Land. But Ross had no time, with winter so near, for extended exploration. After a brief survey, he ordered his squadron to sail for the Falkland Islands. There they arrived in April 1842.

In November 1842 Ross received permission from the Admiralty to spend a third and final year of exploration. His ambition this time was to combine a survey of the east coast of Graham Land with an attempt to achieve what both Wilkes and Dumont d'Urville had failed to achieve, a new record for a farthest south in James Weddell's Sea. Not a man on board the *Erebus* or *Terror* had the slightest doubt that they would succeed. Had they not already made discoveries of Antarctic land greater than the world had ever seen? Had they not in the Ross Sea reached a latitude of 78° 9′ 30″ S., in longitude 161° 27′ W., the highest southern latitude attained by man? By comparison with such feats, to which they could add the approximate location though not the attainment of the South Magnetic Pole, the Weddell Sea presented no great challenge; 'a *bonne bouche*', Dr Hooker called it.

But they had not reckoned with the unaccountable vagaries of Antarctic ice and weather. The pack extended almost as far north as Wilkes or Dumont d'Urville had found it and of all their three seasons in the Antarctic, the weather that season was the worst. It was a year, old Dr Hooker used to recall, 'of constant gales, fogs, and snow-storms. Officers and men slept with their ears open, listening for the look-out man's cry of "Berg ahead." followed by "All hands on deck". The officers of the *Terror* told me that their commander (Commander Crozier) never slept a night in his cot throughout that season in the ice, and that he passed it either on deck or in a chair in his cabin. They were nights of grog and hot coffee, for the orders to splice the mainbrace were many and imperative if the crew were to be kept up to the strain on their nerves and muscles. Of discovery there was nothing, but the fact that Weddell's route was effectively closed. ...' James Weddell in his unprotected sealer had reached 75° S. in 1823. A little beyond 70° S. was all that could be achieved by Ross's sturdy, copper-sheathed bombs which had thrust a way so easily through the Ross Sea pack. Turning back with better grace than Dumont d'Urville in the face of such hopeless odds, Ross (after making several important discoveries in North Graham Land) reached England in September 1843.

To his contemporaries in England, indeed throughout the world, the Antarctic discoveries of James Clark Ross were the greatest geographical discoveries of modern times; discoveries, in the words of the President of the Royal Geographical Society, which had 'secured to the name of Ross a distinguished place amongst the most successful votaries of Science, and the brightest ornaments of the British Navy'. Seen in the perspective of history, they had an even greater significance. From the moment Ross returned to England, the Arctic became the focus of the polar world. But when Antarctic exploration was resumed, after a lapse of fifty years, in a great renaissance in which Britain took the lead, it was to the Ross Sea sector, scene of former triumphs of the British Navy, that the British effort was directed. There the first inland explorations of the continent were launched. There also, because in this region lay the most accessible and the shortest route to the heart of the continent, the tragic race for the South Geographical Pole began.

THE ARCTIC CRUISE OF *EREBUS* AND *TERROR*: THE MYSTERY OF SIR JOHN FRANKLIN

No sooner had he returned than Ross, now Sir James Clark Ross, was offered the command of another great naval expedition, destined this time for the Arctic. It is surprising that the Admiralty, which had so recently diverted ships to the Antarctic, should have been prepared to equip yet another costly project of polar exploration. From the Admiralty's point of view, however, the moment was in one respect opportune, for the Navy was about to embark on an exciting and critical experiment, the introduction of the screw propeller. For years the greatest obstacle to the use of steam had been the huge paddle boxes which, installed amidships, deprived the British of their favourite weapon, their beloved broadside. The new screw propeller now allowed both mobility and fire-power and what better testing ground could there be for it than the Arctic with all its intricate problems of navigation amidst the ice? The Arctic veteran, Sir Edward Parry, who had become Comptroller of Steam Machinery, was full of optimism and he and another Arctic enthusiast, Captain Beechey, were convinced that the new invention would revolutionize polar exploration.

What form was the new expedition to take? Captain Beechey, who had just returned in H.M.S. *Blossom* from a voyage along the American coast eastward of Bering Strait, urged an attempt on the North Pole, an attempt to reach along the line of a northern passage a record high latitude comparable with Ross's Antarctic achievement. But Sir John Barrow had other and quite definite ideas, formed thirty or more years ago. His sole concern was with the North-West Passage.

During the past thirty years the search had little by little been narrowed into two main directions, westwards and southwards from Barrow Strait. Westwards, the outlook was least inviting, Parry, the Admiralty's principal technical adviser in polar matters, having never forgotten the massive barrier of ice against which his sailing ships had battled so resolutely but so vainly south-west of the rugged promontory of Cape Dundas, on Melville Island. But south and west of Barrow Strait and Lancaster Sound the prospects were more hopeful. Here, across seventy-thousand square miles still unexplored, there lay the shortest stretch of land or sea between the extremities of the lands which had been discovered. This was the direction, Barrow and Parry decided, in which the new expedition must go.

In December 1844 Barrow laid his plans before Lord Haddington, First Lord of the Admiralty. As of old, his reasons were cogent, his arguments skilfully adapted to the mood and susceptibilities of a Board with whose members he had been on terms of personal friendship for many years. He appealed in moving terms to the illustrious precedents of history, to the brilliant lead given by the great Elizabethan seaman William Baffin, the discoverer of the gateway to the North-West Passage, Lancaster Sound. He pleaded the cause of science, pointing to the high importance of magnetic observations in these latitudes and to the great geographical and hydrographical discoveries which might be made, discoveries he urged 'well deserving the attention of a power like England'. Finally there were the political arguments less potent now, but no less attractive to the Admiralty in terms of national prestige. To be the first nation to link the Atlantic with the Pacific by way of this Arctic route would be a feat which 'if left to be performed by some other power, England by her neglect of it, having opened the East and West doors, would be laughed at by all the world for having hesitated to cross the threshold'. The American fleet was young, progressive, adventurous. Russia, which since the death in 1825 of Bellingshausen's sponsor, the liberal Alexander I, had been subject to a succession of barbaric and ruthless despots, had an active and ambitious fleet. 'It should not be overlooked', Barrow therefore reminded Their Lordships, 'that there are in the Pacific at the moment two fleets of the only two naval powers likely to undertake the enterprise in question, and it is extremely probable that some of their ships will make trial of this nearest passage home when they leave the Pacific station.' But most appealing to a Board who viewed with gloom the passing of the old days of sail were the advantages of Arctic training to the Navy. 'It is admitted', Barrow declared, 'that the Arctic expeditions have produced a finer set of Officers and Seamen perhaps than in any other branch of the Service ... we have much need of increasing such men, now that Steamers are supplanting our best Seamen.'

Barrow's plans, on the insistence of the Prime Minister, Sir Robert Peel, were most carefully scrutinized, twice by the Royal Society, and by a host of Arctic experts including Parry, Ross, and Sir John Franklin who had recently relinquished his post as Governor of Tasmania. The only amendment was proposed by Ross who suggested that if the expedition failed in the southwest, they should try and discover a northern route by way of Parry's unprobed Wellington Channel. The next problem, the choice of a leader, was far more contentious. Ross, though he had received tempting offers of a baronetcy and an especially generous service pension, had already refused, having promised his wife that once home from the Antarctic his active polar days would be over. There remained of the available Polar men of national distinction only Sir John Franklin.

Throughout the country, Franklin's Arctic exploits were still legendary. His polar experience, moreover, had been acquired in the very region to which the new expedition was bound. Nevertheless, there were strong arguments against him. His age, almost fifty-nine, was not exceptional perhaps for a naval officer before the days of the Retired List, but for the leader of an Arctic expedition he was, many thought, dangerously old and Barrow for one openly preferred a much younger man even though without Arctic experience. Nor was Franklin's reputation entirely without blemish. The circumstances of his recent recall from the Governorship of Tasmania – engineered in fact by a malicious and intriguing subordinate whom Franklin had suspended – had been left, to those who did not know, strangely unexplained by the Colonial Secretary. Had he been weak or incompetent? Had he been indecisive perhaps, or lacking in energy? No one knew for certain. And no official statement came to clear his name.

It was indeed for this very reason, to clear his name and re-establish his reputation of earlier Arctic days, that Sir John Franklin strove so desperately to obtain command of the new expedition. With such a surplus of unemployed officers encumbering the Navy's Active List, it was indeed likely to be his last chance to obtain a sea-going appointment of any kind. 'I dread exceedingly', wrote his second wife Jane Franklin to James Clark Ross, 'the effect on his mind of being without honourable and immediate employment.' In the end after, for Franklin, days of agonizing waiting, Sir Edward Parry's voice was decisive. 'He is a fitter man to go', he declared to the First Lord of the Admiralty, 'than any I know, and if you don't let him go, the man will die of disappointment.'

'We are commanded', wrote young Lieutenant Irving to his sister, 'by a fine old fellow, of whom you have read, I daresay, eating his boots.' It was no doubt a fair description of his new and elderly commander, robust, honest, God-fearing, who was with truth to write 'the highest object of my desire is faithfully to perform my duty'. A fuller, indeed a very life-like picture of Franklin emerges from the letters of his two remarkable wives. His first wife was Eleanor Porden, a young poetess in the romantic mode who had dedicated to John Franklin in their courting days 'An Esquimaux Girl's Lament'. She was the moving spirit in an earnest literary coterie 'The Clouds' and an assiduous attender at Mr Baker's lectures at the Royal Society on the fashionable topic of terrestrial magnetism. Devoted as she was to him, Franklin appears in her letters as reserved, stiff, conventional, provincial, a man whose narrow evangelicalism proved on occasions an embarrassing obstacle to one of Miss Porden's sophisticated and convivial taste. His second wife, Jane Franklin, whom we have seen as the arbiter of social life in Tasmania, must have seemed a less puzzling companion. With the same resolute energy which Ross and Hooker had observed in Hobart, she plunged into the battles of social and official life in London and she was tireless in her efforts to get Franklin appointed to command the Arctic Expedition.

The ships selected were once again H.M.S. *Erebus* and H.M.S. *Terror*, and their refitting and strengthening after their Antarctic voyages was the pride of the naval dockyards. Sheet iron covered their bows. A new and ingenious hot water system warmed the cabins. Adapted railway engines of twenty horse power were installed. And the Master Shipwright of Woolwich Dockyard invented a special device for raising the screw propellers to avoid entanglement with the ice.

Despite the optimism of Sir John Barrow who was quite confident that twelve months would ensure the conquest of the North-West Passage, the expedition was equipped for three years on an unprecedented scale. Enormous quantities of provisions and fuel were carried; china, cut glass, and heavy Victorian silver encumbered the wardrooms; each ship had a library of twelve hundred volumes ranging from treatises on steam engines to the works of Dickens and Lever and volumes of *Punch*. Franklin was particularly concerned for the educational and spiritual welfare of his men while isolated in the Arctic wastes. Slates and arithmetic books, pens, ink, and paper were provided for classes during the winter; testaments and prayer-books were available for all; and a hand-organ, playing fifty tunes, ten of which were psalms or hymns, was purchased for each ship. Of special Polar equipment, except for scientific research, there was none apart from large supplies of warm underclothing and a few wolf-skin blankets. The Arctic clothing of the Franklin expedition was the stout blue cloth of Her Majesty's Navy.

Late in the spring of 1845, H.M.S. *Erebus* and H.M.S. *Terror* moved from Woolwich towards the sea. 'We tried our screws,' wrote Lieutenant Irving of H.M.S. *Terror*, 'and went *four* miles an hour. Our engine once ran somewhat faster on the Birmingham line ... it has a funnel the same size and height as it had on the railway, and makes the same dreadful puffings and screamings, and will astonish the Esquimaux not a little.' This first experiment in an Arctic ship was an unhappy augury for the protagonists of steam and screws. 'We can carry twelve days coal for it', added Irving, 'but it will never be used when we can make any progress at all by other means.' Ten years before, the men of Ross's paddle-steamer the *Victory* had expressed a similar distrust of the new machinery.

For a few days in the middle of May the two ships lay at Greenhithe, near Greenwich, their freshly painted black hulls, yellow upper works, and white masts glinting in the early summer sun. The expedition had yet to start but no one, neither the Government nor the public, least of all its officers and men, had the slightest doubt of the outcome. Was this not the best, the most lavishly equipped expedition ever to set forth for the Arctic? Out of the 134 men of the ships' companies, had not many already been fully tried and tested by the rigours of Arctic service? As for any predictions of disaster, had any polar expedition manned by the Royal Navy ever met with a major disaster? Talk, the mere suggestion, that plans at least should be made for a relief expedition was quickly brushed aside and the general optimism was voiced by Sir Roderick Murchison, President of the Royal Geographical Society, who proclaimed that Franklin and his men would do everything 'for the promotion of science and for the honour of the British name and Navy that human efforts can accomplish'. Only one discordant but distant voice was raised, that of Dr Richard King who had been with Back down the Great Fish River. 'I have contended', he warned Franklin, 'against the present attempt by sea from an honest conviction of its impracticability in the present state of our knowledge of Arctic lands.' King had already submitted an alternative plan for overland exploration to the Royal Geographical Society. But his prophecy of disaster and his alternative plans were alike contemptuously ignored.

Yet disaster lay awaiting the Franklin Expedition as the two ships towards the end of June crossed the Arctic circle west of Greenland, weaving their way through the ice in continuous daylight amazing to those new to the Arctic regions. There were certainly no premonitions among those on board. Spirits were high. The weather through Baffin Bay had been remarkably fine. And Dr Goodsir, the assistant surgeon on board the *Erebus,* had already achieved a notable scientific success with his deep sea equipment in dredging up live animals from three hundred fathoms. Far from premonitions, there was talk only of completing the expedition in a summer, of celebrations when they passed in triumph through the Bering Strait. Towards the end of July the two ships were seen by Captain Martin of the whaler *Enterprise*, moored to an iceberg in Lancaster Sound, and Martin spoke to Sir John Franklin and several of his men. But he was the last man to do so. For from that date the Franklin Expedition, bound for the North-West Passage, disappeared.

Few exercises in historical detection have been more fascinating, and none more ingenious, than the reconstruction by Dr Cyriax of the fate of Sir John Franklin. Only a brief summary need be given here for the story is largely the story of the multitude of search expeditions which were in the next twenty years or so to preoccupy the whole attention and the whole resources of the polar world. From Lancaster Sound, Franklin passed into Barrow Strait and from there, following perhaps prematurely Parry's suggestion of an alternative northern route, he appears to have sailed northwards up Wellington Channel and thence back to Barrow Strait by way of Crozier Strait which separates Cornwallis Island from Bathurst Land. The winter of 1845-6 was spent at Beechey Island, then they sailed again, through Peel Sound, Franklin Strait and on into Victoria Strait. There, on 12 September 1846, the *Erebus* and the *Terror* were beset in heavy ice borne down from Melville Sound through McClintock Channel. This was for the winter of 1846-7.

The part of the Canadian Arctic Archipelago, known today as 'The District of Franklin' is – as we have seen from the voyages of Parry and Ross – a complex network of channels, straits, and sounds. It can be seen from the map (inside back cover) that by linking Barrow Strait with the upper part of Victoria Strait, part at least of a North-West Passage had by this time been discovered by the Franklin expedition. All that now remained was to link Victoria Strait with Simpson Strait and the coastal waters of Arctic Canada. In May 1847, this too was achieved when a small party led by Lieutenant Gore set off for King William Island to bridge this final gap. The North-West Passage had not been completely navigated. But by land and sea it had been discovered and explored.

On 11 June 1847 tragedy began to darken this first discovery of a North-West Passage for on that day Sir John Franklin died and Captain Francis Rawdon Moira Crozier, who had served with Ross on his great Antarctic voyages, took command. Yet another winter, the winter of 1847-8, was spent in the grip of the ice, as the ships drifted southwards down Victoria Strait. Scurvy had already begun insidiously to sap the strength of the men, and provisions, provided for three years on what to Sir John Barrow had seemed such an excessive scale, were by August 1848 nearing exhaustion.

By the end of this third winter in the Arctic, Crozier was forced to abandon ship and on 25 April 1848 he and his second-in-command Captain James Fitzjames added to a record previously left by Lieutenant Gore which they found in the north of King William Island. 'H.M. Ships *Terror* and *Erebus*', they said, 'were deserted on the 22 April, 5 leagues NNW. of this, having been beset since 12 Sept. 1846. . . .' One hundred and five officers and men out of the original complement of one hundred and twenty-nine were then alive.

Crozier's plan apparently had been to travel along the west and south coasts of King William Island in the hope of reaching the nearest post of the Hudson's Bay Company, Fort Resolution, by way of the Great Fish River. A few men, unable to face such a journey, may have turned back to the shelter of the drifting ships but the majority, weak with hunger, with scurvy steadily draining away the last vestige of vitality, followed Crozier on this tragic march. Graves, skeletons, relics of the dead men were later found marking the route from King William Island and across to the Great Fish River (the Back River). This was the route of the last journey of the men of the Franklin Expedition, a journey from which not a man survived.

The fate of the drifting ships is less certain. It seems probable that they foundered somewhere to the south-west of King William Island in or later than 1849 for even then there may still have been a few survivors on board. Or they may have drifted, like Backs' ship the *Terror* had drifted in 1836-7, out into Baffin Bay and through Davis Strait to the Atlantic. In April 1851, the story goes, the mate of an English brig the *Renovation* saw two three-masted ships very similar to the *Erebus* and *Terror* stranded on a large ice-floe off the east coast of Newfoundland. It is just possible that these were the ships of the lost expedition of Sir John Franklin.

In London there was no knowledge of these disastrous events. Indeed, in 1847, while H.M.S. *Erebus* and H.M.S. *Terror* were drifting helplessly with the ice down Victoria Strait, Lord Francis Egerton wrote (anonymously) in the *Quarterly Review*:

'With interest which accumulates by the hour do we watch for the return of these two vessels which are perhaps even now working their way through Bering Strait into the Pacific. Should the happiness be yet allowed us of witnessing that return, we are of opinion that the *Erebus* and *Terror* should be moored henceforth on either side the *Victory*, floating monuments of what the Nelsons of discovery can dare and do, at the call of their country in the service of the world.'

In some minds, however, there were the stirrings of anxiety. Sir John Ross, whose suggestion that a relief expedition should at least be planned Franklin had rejected 'as an absurdity', urged the dispatch of an expedition in January 1847. In April Captain Beechey proposed that a relief expedition be sent down the Great Fish River in the direction of Prince Regent Inlet. A few months later a similar proposal by Dr Richard King, whose warnings of impending disaster the Geographical Society had so briefly discarded, was conveyed to Earl Grey, the Colonial Secretary. Earl Grey referred the matter to the Admiralty, the Admiralty sought the advice of the two most famous of living Arctic explorers, Sir Edward Parry and Sir James Clark Ross. But neither thought anything of Dr King's plan. They could conceive, they said, of no conditions in which the missing men would make for the Great Fish River. And even if they had done so, how, they demanded, could Dr Richard King, with a party to be carried in one canoe, possibly be of the slightest assistance? Reassured, the Board of Admiralty turned its mind to more urgent matters, confident that they could rely in the last resort on the whalers and posts of the Hudson's Bay Company.

Nevertheless as the months passed by, there was evidence of a growing public alarm and in the end Their Lordships were forced into action. A plan of search was prepared based on a thorough exploration of the route Franklin had been ordered to take and with this was combined the stationing of relief parties on the continental coast and of relief ships at the Bering Strait. It was the beginning of a search by land and sea on a tremendous scale, a scale, as far as fleet operations were concerned, that had not been witnessed since Barrow's Arctic campaign after the Napoleonic Wars. But this was only the beginning. In the next ten years forty expeditions set out to find the missing ships, six of them travelling by land along the coast of the Canadian Arctic, and on one occasion a fleet of no less than fifteen ships was simultaneously deployed. In the course of these operations, not only was the fate of Sir John Franklin and his men revealed in all its tragic circumstances, but the North-West Passage which had challenged British seamen for so many centuries was twice to be traversed, though on neither occasion entirely by sea. Nor was this the most important geographical discovery. For by 1878, the date of the last Franklin search expeditions, the intricate geography of the south and west parts of the Canadian Arctic archipelago, with its multitudinous islands, its maze of ice-strewn channels and straits, had almost wholly been elucidated. Such extensive discoveries of new land were not made again in this region until the explorations of the Norwegian Otto Sverdrup in 1898–1902.

The complicated manoeuvres of these various search expeditions, though they added greatly to the detail of Arctic geography and to the development of polar techniques, did not constitute any notable advances in the broad evolution of polar exploration. They will, therefore, only briefly be recalled. Of the three simultaneous expeditions launched by the Admiralty in 1847, the Bering Strait expedition, consisting of the *Herald* and the *Plover* in command of Captain Kellett, occupied their time in exploring the coastal waters north and west of the Strait, discovering on these voyages Herald Island (near Wrangel Island) to the north of the Chukchi Sea. The mainland group, led by Sir John Richardson with the Hudson's Bay Company official Dr John Rae, was in 1848 largely immobilized by ice and storms and Richardson returned in 1849 leaving Rae to continue work.

The third group, approaching from the east by sea, was led by Sir James Clark Ross of Arctic and Antarctic fame.

Ross's two ships, of between four and five hundred tons, were the *Enterprise* and the *Investigator* and on board the latter was a young Lieutenant Leopold McClintock. The name of McClintock stands high in the development of Arctic exploration for not only did he play ultimately a distinguished part in solving the Franklin mystery but he evolved, through his unusual readiness to learn from the Eskimoes, a new sledging and travel technique far in advance of his conservative contemporaries, staunch supporters of the old naval polar school. Ross sailed in 1848, the last year probably in which any of the Franklin survivors might have been found alive. After a winter, the winter of 1848–9, spent at the north-east end of Somerset Island, a bare seventy miles from Beechey Island where Franklin had wintered in 1845–6, they travelled, manhauling sledges, down the east coast as far as Fury Beach, along the north coast, and then west as far almost as Bellot Strait, the unlucky John Ross's 'Brentford Bay'. These spring journeys added almost two hundred miles of new coast of Somerset Island, and Ross only just stopped short of the waters now known as Franklin Strait. The Franklin mystery however remained unsolved.

Sir John Franklin had now been missing for more than four years and his fate and the failure of these expeditions to discover it had become matters not only of national but of world-wide concern. Throughout Europe and North America, public interest became wholly absorbed in the Arctic regions; in England, books of Arctic travel and adventure were in great demand; in London, in Brighton, crowds, admiring but alarmed, gazed at the panoramas of polar landscapes displayed in the shop-windows, picturing in their minds the hardships and horrors of life in the Arctic wastes. The central attraction in London's pleasure gardens at Vauxhall in the sultry summer of 1852 was an immense and dramatic diorama of Arctic scenery. Meanwhile, throughout these hours and days and months of tension, Jane Franklin clung to hope and wrote letter after letter to her husband only to receive them back months later from one or other of the search expeditions. 'My dearest love – May it be the will of God if you are not restored to us earlier that you should open this letter and that it may give you comfort in all your trials ... dearest, if you ever open this, it will be I trust because I have been spared the greatest of all ...' At her suggestion, public prayers were offered in 1849 throughout the country for the safety of those serving in the Arctic regions.

Meanwhile the Admiralty, perplexed as to what should now be done, were bombarded by suggestions, by rumours, and by false messages purporting to be from the lost expedition. Some were found in bottles cast up on the seashore. One was attached to a small balloon which floated gently to the ground near Gloucester. Among the rumours, however, there were gleams of hope. Eskimoes, reported the *Morning Herald*, travelling along the Franklin route had heard ships' guns reverberating over the frozen seas. Two abandoned three-masted ships, the *Limerick Chronicle* declared, had been seen adrift off the coast of Newfoundland. But nothing was proved, nothing was certain, about the fate of the missing men.

At length, the gathering force of public anxiety compelled the Admiralty to take further action, this time on a most impressive scale, and the second half of the century opened with plans for a host of relief expeditions, most of them officially but some privately sponsored. To stimulate their efforts, the British Government offered a reward of twenty thousand pounds to any person of any nationality who rescued the missing men; a reward of ten thousand pounds to the rescuer of any one of them, or to any who provided information leading to such a rescue; and a reward of ten thousand pounds to the first man to solve the mystery of the expedition's fate.

Sir James Clark Ross having had no success in his attempt from the east, the Admiralty now decided to try from the west and to combine with this search from the direction of the Bering Strait another but much more formidable attack from Baffin Bay and Lancaster Sound. In the autumn of 1850, therefore, a great concourse of ships put to sea. The squadron moving eastwards from the Bering Strait consisted of Ross's ships, the *Enterprise* and the *Investigator*, commanded respectively by Captain Collinson and McClure, with Captain Kellett in the *Plover* to stand by at Bering Strait. Moving westwards from Lancaster Sound were the barques *Resolute* and *Assistance*, under Captain Austin, with Captain Erasmus Ommanney as his second-in-command. With them were two screw-steamers, the *Pioneer* and the *Intrepid*, the first full-powered steamers to be employed in ice navigation. Other ships in this eastern squadron were the brigs *Lady Franklin* and *Sophia* both commanded by a whaling captain William Penny, and the schooner *Felix* and a supply ship fitted out by the Hudson's Bay Company and commanded by the veteran Sir John Ross. This fleet was later joined by two small American brigs, manned by the United States Navy and commanded by Lieutenant E. J. D. Haven, which had been bought and largely equipped by a retired New York shipping magnate, Henry Grinnell, who had been greatly moved by Lady Franklin's world-wide appeals for help. This American addition to the eastern squadron, which left New York City in May 1850, has its own place in polar history for it was the first American polar expedition since the tumultuous days of Wilkes; in launching it, and subsequent Arctic expeditions, Grinnell, who became the first president of the American Geographical Society of New York, stimulated the revival of American exploration as John Barrow had done in England earlier in the century. There was one more addition to the eastern squadron, the sailing ship *Prince Albert*, equipped privately by Lady Franklin and a group of friends.

The strategic plan behind these fleet manoeuvres was that the two main squadrons should converge from east and west thereby narrowing the search to the general area of Melville Island and Banks Island. An initial search of Wellington Channel was to be carried out, as a subsidiary operation, by the eastern squadron. Meanwhile, Dr John Rae of the Hudson's Bay Company agreed to explore parts of Wollaston Land and Victoria Island to supplement the search by sea. With so much simultaneous effort involved, it seemed impossible to those who read of these elaborate, costly, and far-ranging enterprises, that the Franklin mystery should not be solved.

Yet, from 1850 to 1854, though important geographical discoveries were made, little enough was found out about Franklin.

Sailing from the west, McClure in the *Investigator*, by linking Prince of Wales Strait with Parry's Melville Sound, proved the existence of a North-West Passage and was the first man alive to have done so. Collinson in the *Enterprise*, following closely in his wake, repeated his junior officer's discovery, and after a winter in Cambridge Bay went on in 1853 to explore part of the coast of Victoria Island and the west side of Victoria Strait. In the great expanse of Arctic sea covered for the first time by such large ships, and in sheer navigational skill, these are among the most remarkable voyages in the history of Arctic exploration. But from the point of view of the Franklin search it was, on McClure's side, an ill-conducted expedition. McClure, an ambitious officer more concerned it seems with being the first to discover the Passage than with the fate of Franklin and his men, arrived first at Bering Strait from the Pacific (by a short cut through the Aleutian Islands), refused to wait for his senior officer and set off on his own for Point Barrow. One expedition therefore became two and when Collinson came to search the vital area of Victoria Strait, only one side could be searched for only one ship was available. The Eskimoes tried to put Collinson on the track but he failed to understand them for the only interpreter was miles away on board the *Investigator* with McClure. At one point, Collinson was only thirty miles away from the principal clue to the Franklin mystery. But a metal bolt with The Queen's Mark and a fragment of door-frame from a cabin were the only relics found of the Franklin Expedition.

Collinson must be reckoned one of the most magnanimous of commanders. Reviewing these voyages, he said of McClure, 'To him belongs the honour of first navigating the Arctic Sea along the American coast, and the discovery of Prince of Wales Strait ... neither of us have succeeded in the grand object which animated our endeavours; but he, being first in the field, has added greatly to our geographical knowledge'. McClure was accordingly awarded £5,000 by the House of Commons Committee, with another £5,000 for his officers and crew, for the first discovery, as it was then thought, of a North-West Passage.

More success, as regards the discovery of Franklin relics, attended the other participants in the Admiralty's campaign, notably De Haven, the leader of Henry Grinnell's expedition. Landing on Beechey Island, near the entrance to Barrow Strait, he discovered clear evidence of the first wintering of the Franklin Expedition; a forge, a storehouse, a shooting gallery; hundreds of tins of meat, well-preserved, arranged meticulously in rows and discarded for some unknown reason; all the litter, the bottles, rope, scraps of newspaper, of an Arctic camp-site occupied for months. Nearby, three tombstones roughly carved commemorated Leading Stoker John Torrington of the *Terror*, and a seaman and a marine from the *Erebus*. Running away from the coast De Haven saw the deep marks of heavily laden sledges which had evidently been hauled with the greatest labour over the frozen ground.

On the mainland Dr Rae, confident all along that the mystery would be solved in the neighbourhood of Victoria Strait, searched its west coast (as Collinson did two years later) and found relics from the *Erebus* and *Terror* which had drifted down from the north. The remaining expeditions made only geographical discoveries: Austin and Ommanney along the coast of Prince of Wales Island; a Frenchman Bellot and Kennedy (who had replaced Commander Forsythe as captain of Lady Franklin's ship, the *Prince Albert*) by sledging to Bellot Strait, John Ross's 'Brentford Bay'. Yet another expedition set out in 1852 commanded by the elderly Sir Edward Belcher whom Dr Richard King in his caustic way described as a man who 'had spent a whole life in proving himself to be the very last man fitted for so honourable a service'. On this expedition, McClintock, commanding the steam tender *Intrepid*, made some fine sledging journeys in the lands north of Barrow Strait. The expedition is also memorable for the rescue in April 1853 of McClure and his men who had been forced to abandon ship. But in the following year the expedition was recalled. The Admiralty was tiring of the Franklin search.

On 20 January 1854 notice was given that unless news was received before the end of March, the officers and men of the Franklin Expedition would be considered to have died on Her Majesty's Service. Lady Franklin's reaction was characteristic. She refused her widow's pension. 'She changed', it was said, 'the deep mourning she had been wearing for years for bright colours of green and pink as soon as the Admiralty notice was gazetted.' And suspecting that the Admiralty had lost interest in the search after McClure's discovery of the North-West Passage, she wrote, 'My Lords, I cannot but feel that there will be a stain on the page of the Naval Annals of England when these two events, the discovery of the North-West Passage, and the abandonment of Franklin and his companions, are recorded in indissoluble association.' The people of London at least showed sympathy with her sorrow and admiration for her indomitable courage.

> My Franklin dear long has been gone
> To explore the northern seas,
> I wonder if my faithful John,
> Is still battling with the breeze;
> Or if e'er he will return again,
> To these fond arms once more
> To heal the wounds of dearest Jane,
> Whose heart is grieved full sore.

So ran the ballad, 'Lady Franklin's Lament', on sale in the streets of London.

In October 1854 startling, indeed horrifying, news came from Dr Rae of Hudson's Bay Company. He had heard that the Eskimoes had seen a party of white men hauling boats towards the Great Fish River and there, near its mouth, he had found the remains of thirty of the men of Crozier's party who had left the drifting ships. Guns, silver spoons and forks, were marked with the crests and initials of missing men. The fate of some at least of Sir John Franklin's expedition was known; a fate, in the words of Dr Rae, 'as terrible as imagination can conceive ... from the mutilated state of many of the corpses, and the contents of the kettles, it is evident that our miserable countrymen had been driven to the last resource'. It was an outrageous suggestion and it caused an uproar in the British Press. Lady Franklin alone was, outwardly, unmoved. If Franklin's men had reached the Great Fish River from Beechey Island, she declared at once, John Franklin and not McClure must have been the discoverer of the North-West Passage.

The public conscience was deeply stirred and an expedition to settle so grave a matter was clearly an urgent national duty. But Britain was now involved in the Crimean War and in 1855 Chief Factor James Anderson of the Hudson's Bay Company, at the request of the Government, undertook investigations. More relics were found, a snow-shoe marked 'Mr Stanley', a letter-clip, part of a backgammon board presented to *Erebus* by Lady Franklin; but there, as far as the Admiralty was concerned, the search ended and £10,000 was paid to Rae for discovering the fate of Franklin's men.

But this was not the end for Lady Franklin. A public appeal was launched, the steam yacht *Fox* of 177 tons, built for a member of the Royal Yacht Squadron in 1855, was purchased and in her, a vessel more appropriate to the clear and open waters of the Solent than to Arctic seas, Captain Leopold McClintock, available largely through the intervention of the Prince Consort, left Aberdeen on 1 July 1857. After two winters beset, first in Baffin Bay, then in Bellot Strait, McClintock with his second-in-command, Lieutenant Hobson, marched southwards across Boothia Peninsula and on across the ice to King William Island. There, on the west coast at Point Victory, a cairn was found with the record, stained by the rust of its tin case, which had been deposited by Captain Crozier eleven years before. It told the story of the end of the Franklin expedition, of the first winters, of the besetments, of the death of Franklin, of the abandonment of the ships on 22 April 1848, of the death of twenty-four officers and men, as already described. On that day, Captain Crozier was about to start on the tragic march to the Great Fish River.

The discoveries of McClintock and Hobson on both sides of King William Island and south as far as the Great Fish River revealed in all their tragic detail the fate of the Franklin Expedition. Irrespective of the earlier award to Dr Rae, McClintock and the men of the *Fox* were voted £5,000 by Parliament. And the claims of the members of the Franklin Expedition (several had evidently managed to reach Simpson Strait) to have preceded McClure in the discovery of the North-West Passage were formally recognized by the Royal Geographical

Society in the award to Lady Franklin of its Founder's Medal. For her, the years of tension were over. The battle which she had fought so bravely against inert, or as it so often seemed, insensitive officialdom had been won. Franklin had been vindicated at last.

Over the next twenty years the full measure of the tragedy was revealed by the discoveries of Captain Charles Francis Hall of Cincinnati and Lieutenant Schwatka of the United States Army. Their expeditions, inspired by the Franklin search, will be described in greater detail when we consider American explorations in the Arctic in the second half of the nineteenth century. All the way from Point Victory, skeletons, graves, relics of the dead marked the direction of Crozier's last march. Fifty miles to the south (sixty-five from the abandoned ships) a ship's boat lying on a sledge contained two skeletons side by side. Stowed away were guns, chronometers, knives, much heavy table silver belonging to Franklin, Crozier, Dr Goodsir, and others, but no papers and no food beyond a little chocolate and some tea. Farther south, at Cape Herschel, lay the skeleton of Harry Peglar, Captain of the Foretop of H.M.S. *Terror*, fallen forward as if in sleep. Papers, including the parody of a sea-shanty written at the end of the second winter, proved identity and the remnants of uniform enabled a reconstruction to be made. Trousers and jacket were of fine blue cloth, the jacket being double-breasted and edged with silk braid, with sleeves slashed and bearing five covered buttons each. Over this uniform the dead man had worn a blue greatcoat, with a black silk neckerchief. This was the Arctic clothing of a Petty Officer of the Franklin expedition.

During their travels around King William Island, Captain Hall and Lieutenant Schwatka heard many Eskimo stories about the last days of Franklin's men. At 'Starvation Cove', as Schwatka named it, Eskimoes had found the remains of thirty-five men who had been dragging a boat with an awning. At Terror Bay were thirty more lying huddled together inside a tent. There were stories, too, about the ships. One was found, the Eskimoes told them, near the entrance to Simpson Strait, with awnings screening her decks and a gangplank still resting on the ice. In great fear, they crept on board. But there was no sound and they saw only the body of a white man lying on deck. They prised open the closed hatches and ransacked the cabins. But when they returned later to collect their plunder, the ship had foundered. Only the tops of her masts were visible above the ice.

Among the Eskimoes interrogated by Captain Hall were many who told him how thin the white men had been, how their mouths had been 'dry and black and hard', how they had complained of loose teeth and spongy gums. These were sure signs of scurvy and there is no doubt, as McClintock had surmised, that scurvy, its enfeebling effects accelerated by starvation and by exhaustion from the tremendous effort of hauling heavy boats and sledges on the long march towards the mouth of the Great Fish River, lay at the root of the Franklin tragedy.

PART III

THE AGE OF ADVENTURE
AND RESEARCH

NEW MEN AND NEW MOTIVES– AMERICA APPROACHES THE POLE

WITH the solution, macabre as it was, of the Franklin mystery Arctic exploration in the second half of the nineteenth century entered a new phase. Now that the North-West Passage had been traversed by sea and on foot not only by Franklin's men but by both McClure and Collinson, eyes were turned towards the larger Arctic islands; to Greenland whose vast interior was quite unknown; to the adjacent Ellesmere Island; and to Spitsbergen and the waters to the east washing the undiscovered archipelago of Franz Josef Land. In all these islands – one, Greenland, of continental size – there were still large areas unexplored and unmapped. In all there were high prospects for scientific investigations, in geology, in geophysics, in meteorology, and natural history. To those moreover to whom polar exploration appealed less as a labour of geographical or scientific discovery than as a race to be won, a tremendous contest in human courage and human endurance, these islands were essential stepping-stones to what was now to become the most coveted of trophies, the North Geographical Pole. Nevertheless, although the exhaustive experiences of half a century left little hope that the North-West Passage would ever be of practical value as a seaway, it had still to be completely navigated and, in this respect, it remained a sporting challenge until early in the twentieth century. In 1875–76 Allen Young, a British merchant officer who had served with McClintock in the *Fox*, tried and failed, and it was left to the Norwegian Roald Amundsen to be the first in 1903–5 to link the Atlantic with the Pacific by this route. Of more practical importance, as it transpired, was Baron A. E. Nordenskiöld's earlier voyage through the North-East Passage which had been forsaken by all except Russian fishermen and native craft since the brave but abortive efforts of the seventeenth-century seamen. This led some years later to the opening up of a northern sea route for Russia and provided at long last a relatively short (though uncertain) passage between Russia and the Far East.

The mid nineteenth century which saw the start of the explorations thus briefly surveyed was a period in Europe when the gathering forces of liberal opinion, when stifled impulses to personal freedom, broke through old barriers standing since the Napoleonic Wars. In the midst of this general fermentation of ideas, it witnessed new and widespread advances in scientific thought which had disturbing social and intellectual repercussions. It witnessed also, paradoxically with the greater emphasis on individualism, an intensification of nationalism which the new and amazing instruments of closer human intercourse – the steamships, the spreading railways, the electric telegraph – did little to allay. To offset this, however, there was in science the beginning of international cooperation and the first International Polar Year of 1882 (the forerunner of the International Geophysical Year) was a striking advance in a field of intellectual endeavour in which the development of cooperative and international effort was becoming all the more essential because of increasing specialization.

Some reflection of these broad movements can be perceived in the evolution of polar exploration; in the decline, for example, of the national naval expedition in favour of private and independent enterprise; in the rise, first evident in North America, of the individual adventurous explorer who was little concerned with scientific motives; and in sharp contrast to this, in the development of the purely scientific expedition concerned not with exploration but with research.

The advent of the independent private explorer, engaged in adventure or research or a combination of both, with plans and projects which were his own and not those of governments, is a distinguishing characteristic of the second half of the nineteenth century. The leaders and promoters of such private expeditions in America and in Europe were not supported, as the earlier expeditions had been, wholly by government funds, though governments were often called upon to contribute. They relied to a new and large extent on public subscriptions, on handsome donations from the newly arisen capitalist class, and on subventions from the proprietors of the new popular newspapers in return for exclusive rights of publication. A North American newspaper, the *New York Herald*, whose proprietor James Gordon Bennett in 1872 commissioned Stanley 'to find' Livingstone, was the first to appear as a substantial sponsor of exploration of this kind when it sponsored Lieutenant Frederick Schwatka's expedition of 1878 in search of Franklin relics.

It was fitting that the United States, where in the fifties and sixties the pioneer was striking out across America's own last frontier (the frontier of the Far West), should have been foremost in encouraging the independent Arctic explorer. The first American Arctic expeditions were sponsored by Henry Grinnell, the wealthy New York shipping magnate who had made a fortune through buying the business of a man curiously named Preserved Fish. He had already (as related) sent out Lieutenant De Haven to take part in the Franklin Search. Two years later Dr Elisha Kent Kane, the surgeon on De Haven's expedition, who had in his youth explored the Philippines, submitted to the newly founded American Geographical Society of New York and to Grinnell, its first president, his plans for a new expedition. Its purpose was to combine a further search for Franklin with an attempt – and this was Kane's real object – to reach the North Pole across the great barrier of ice which, he argued, would be found to surround an open polar sea. The search for Franklin had, as Kane well knew, a powerful humanitarian appeal and Grinnell's response was no less generous than it had earlier been to the heart-rending letters of Lady Franklin.

In 1853, therefore, the second Grinnell expedition set forth, with Elisha Kent Kane in command, following the route up the west coast of Greenland taken in 1852 by Commander Inglefield in the *Isabel*. On this, the expedition which brought back Sir Edward Belcher and rescued McClure and his men, Inglefield named what is now known as Ellesmere Island; he was able to show, moreover, that Smith Sound, discovered by William Baffin, was a channel leading northwards to the Pole. Kane reached nine miles beyond Inglefield's farthest north and spent two winters in these high latitudes.

In May 1854 the doctor on the Kane expedition, Isaac Israel Hayes, led a party westwards across Smith Sound and named Grinnell Land while Kane with another party explored northwards up the Greenland coast and named Kane Basin, north of Inglefield Land. In the course of these last explorations Kane and his party became the first white men to set eyes on the great Humboldt Glacier, sixty miles long, so called after the German geographer and traveller already mentioned in connexion with Antarctic discovery. It rose, Kane wrote, 'in a solid glassy wall three hundred feet above sea level ... a long ever shining line. ... Here was a plastic, moving, semi-solid mass, obliterating life, swallowing rocks and islands, and ploughing its way with irresistible march through the crust of an investing sea'.

Kane, moving westwards, reached a channel (Kennedy Channel) leading out of Kane Basin towards the north but when he returned he found his base in sore distress. The *Advance* was beset. Food was nearing exhaustion. The upper works of the ship had had to be burnt for fuel. And scurvy had broken out among the crew. Eventually, in 1855, being unable to hold out any longer, they made an adventurous journey in three small boats to a Danish settlement in south-west Greenland and there were rescued by a relief expedition dispatched, with the help of Congress, by the American Geographical Society and the New York Chamber of Commerce.

Kane has been described as 'the outstanding American polar idol of the mid century'. His *Arctic Explorations*, acclaimed by Washington Irving, could be seen on every parlour table in his native city of Philadelphia and lovers of Byron, it appears, were enthralled by his picture of these newly discovered 'Icy halls of cold sublimity'. Kane's notoriety, however, was not solely on account of his Arctic adventures. At an early age he had fallen in love with thirteen-year-old Margaret Fox, one of a trio of spiritualist sisters from Rochester to whose 'obscure and ambiguous profession' he was accustomed to refer. This secret liaison was the target of a scandalous and exceedingly popular book, *The Love-Life of Dr Kane*.

Two years after Kane's return, Isaac Israel Hayes put forward a plan of his own for an attempt on the Pole; an enterprise, he declared, which would be greatly to the credit of 'our national character'. The Pole, however, had none of the appeal of the Franklin Search and despite the exertions of the American Geographical Society, not only were funds hard to raise but there was some sharp criticism of Hayes's proposed adventure. Eminent authorities, one New York newspaper remarked, considered that 'all pretence, either of mercantile value or scientific discovery, had been exhausted with reference to the Polar seas'; if a sea-passage across the Pole linking the Atlantic and Pacific Oceans was Hayes's object, why then 'the Pacific railroad would be built before Dr Hayes could return'. Only a powerful and portentous intervention by Dr Gould of Harvard saved the situation. 'It is the duty of mankind', he declared, 'to explore these strange and yet uncomprehended portions of our globe; and more than this, it is a duty which seems to devolve properly upon our nation. Europe has contributed more than her just proportion of geographical expeditions. . . . We Americans now owe it to the world and to ourselves to prosecute these researches.'

Once again Henry Grinnell came to the rescue and with further help from a group of prominent New York business men, Hayes sailed from Boston in July 1860, nine months before the bombardment of Fort Sumter by Southern guns began the Civil War. On the day of departure, Henry Grinnell presented Hayes with the flag of Wilkes's United States Exploring Expedition with the injunction, 'Now I, Sir, entrust it to you. Unfurl it to the breezes of the North Pole, and having done so you will take special care of it and return it to me.' A slight extension of Kane's explorations up the east coast of Ellesmere Island, however, was the nearest to the North Pole that the Hayes expedition could reach.

Meanwhile, in March 1860, on the eve of Abraham Lincoln's nomination by the Republican Convention, another American Arctic explorer appeared, Charles Francis Hall, already mentioned in relation to the Franklin Search. An impoverished printer from West Cincinatti, he had no exploring experience, no scientific knowledge, no commercial or political influence or standing. Nor did he have any of the geographical ambitions of Kane or Hayes; he was moved solely by a deep distress at what he considered to be the shameful relaxation of effort in the search for Franklin. He was far from being discouraged by the findings of the British expeditions. Was there not, he asked, even now a glimmer of hope that a few men might still be found alive? And even if he failed in this, was there not a chance that he might find journals, log-books, diaries which might reveal for the future guidance of the world all the secrets of this dreadful tragedy. Improbable as such arguments would have seemed to McClintock who had by then returned from the last British expedition of the Franklin Search, Hall convinced the warmhearted citizens of Ohio and Connecticut that he might yet be in time and with further aid from Henry Grinnell, 'the honored father of American Arctic discovery', he sailed in the *Rescue* in May 1860, passing on his way out of Boston Harbour the schooner *United States* with Hayes on board.

The cost of Hall's first Arctic expedition was less than a thousand dollars of which Grinnell contributed a third. He had no ship. He travelled in a New London whaler, sailing on a routine trip. His expedition was indeed a striking contrast to the massive and costly expeditions dispatched by the British Navy. Living for two years among the Eskimoes of Baffin Island, wearing Eskimo dress, eating raw seal-meat, living in their snow-houses, and travelling with dogs and sledge, Hall became convinced that the Arctic explorer of the future must learn, especially in the eating of raw food, 'to Esquimeaux-ise himself'. He found no relics of Sir John Franklin. He made, however, one astonishing discovery, bringing back to America many relics of Frobisher's unfortunate sixteenth-century expedition, all of which have since and quite unaccountably disappeared.

With a family of Eskimoes sitting cheerful but silent by his side, Hall lectured all over America to raise funds for a more ambitious expedition 'to solve the mysteries enshrouding the fate of Franklin's men'. Grinnell contributed generously to the support of the Eskimoes. But, like many another potential patron, he had been hard hit by the Civil War. However, with the help of the whaling companies and of the newspapers Hall obtained enough for a modest expedition and in another whaler he set off in high spirits in July 1864 to spend five years without a break in the Arctic; for a white man, living and travelling alone with the Eskimoes, an extraordinary feat of endurance. During this long sojourn, Hall added considerably to the geography of the Melville Peninsula (to the north of Hudson Bay), and sledging across the Rae Isthmus to King William Island, he discovered, as related, a great many relics of the Franklin expedition.

Hall had now become, like Elisha Kent Kane, an Arctic hero to the people of the United States and his expedition in 1871, in which he sailed with his Eskimo companions and the German naturalist Dr Bessels in a naval tug the *Polaris*, was considered worthy of support by the United States Government. There was no question this time of any Franklin search. Following Kane and Hayes, Hall's aim was no less than 'the discovery of the northern axis of the great globe if possible, or the absolute proof of its inaccessibility'. As in the case of Hayes's North Pole adventure, Grinnell saw to it that Hall carried with him the flag of the Wilkes Expedition.

Hall's achievements on this, his last expedition, brought nearer than it had ever been the possibility of an assault on the Pole. In a number of great sledging journeys, he reached the northernmost limits of the Greenland ice sheet and discovered at the foot of its glaciated escarpments Hall Land, green, pleasant, plentiful in game, a delight to the eye after the desert of ice over which he and his men had sledged so wearily. North of Hall Land lay the frozen Lincoln Sea. Crossing Kennedy Channel (discovered by Kane) Hall travelled up the east coast of Ellesmere Island and reached two hundred miles beyond Kane's farthest north, to latitude 82° 11'. But these were the last of the Arctic journeys made by the printer from Cincinatti who died before reaching the ship, exhausted from the strain of such tremendous sledging efforts. The *Polaris*, homeward bound out of Smith Sound, was struck by an enormous floe. And just as stores, records, clothing, equipment, were being flung from the reeling ship, she was swept away through the Arctic twilight, with most, but not all, of her crew on board. Those left behind drifted for thirteen hundred miles on an ice-floe until they were rescued, starving and dazed, off the coast of Labrador.

The survivors of Hall's last expedition reached New York in 1874, the year of the birth of Ernest Henry Shackleton who as a boy was enthralled by Hall's books. So narrow an escape from total disaster however did not discourage Henry Grinnell from looking forward to the day when the greatest of all Arctic triumphs would crown the efforts of American explorers. Receiving back the flag of the Wilkes Expedition he declared himself willing 'to send it again if there is any American expedition fitted out for the discovery of the Pole'.

In Britain and in Europe meanwhile, polar exploration was developing along very different lines; in Britain traditional, in Europe experimental under the influence of new and unorthodox ideas. The British Arctic Expedition of 1875-6 was probably no very exceptional example of the conservative, indeed complacent spirit of the late Victorian Navy. It consisted of two ships, the *Alert* and the *Discovery*, and was commanded by Captain George S. Nares who, in curious contrast to his new post, had been recalled by the Admiralty from command of H.M.S. *Challenger* in the Antarctic, a ship then being used as a floating laboratory by a group of civilian scientists engaged in the most important oceanographical investigations to be conducted in polar waters during the nineteenth century. The expedition which Nares joined was the very antithesis of such a progressive, scientific enterprise. Far indeed from looking forward, it was in conception, in its organization, and methods, a reversion to the ideas of fifty years ago. Only in the carriage of some Eskimo dogs, in the attachment of one of Hall's Eskimoes, Hans Hendrick, and in the use of fresh musk-ox meat to supplement the heavy tins of preserved food provided from Admiralty Stores, were any concessions made to the new techniques of travel and survival perfected mainly by North American explorers.

The intention of the British expedition was to plant the Union Jack beyond America's farthest north and at the same time, by showing the flag, to counter the drive of the American

XLV.
DOMVS A NOBIS EXTRV-
CTA ET ERECTA, QVA PER HYEMEM
commodè lateremus. 10.

Ebus omnibus desperatis cum animaduerteremus, ante æstatem futuram nos Oceano glaciati haudquaquam ereptum iri: collectis votis decreuimus, loco quodam commodè dispecto, domicilium quoddam, mansioni hybernæ aptum, extruere. Cui instituto mira quoque gratia Deus nobis fauere visus est. Etsi enim tota illa insula, nec ligna, nec stramen, nec folia, aut gramen ferret: ripam tamen quandam ad littus illud indagauimus, tot arboribus, ramis & radicibus, alluuione fortuita, eò illatis obsitam, vt & ad ædes parandas, & hyemis iniurias foco mitigandas ligna abundè sufficerent. Quæ fortuna nisi singulariter nobis alluxisset, propter intensissimum frigus operis cœptis peruacare nullo modo potuissemus. Et quod mirum erat, acerbissimum gela ita iam inualuerat, vt forte clauo occasione aliqua ori indito cutis tam pertinaciter adhæreret, vt extraclum eã expeditè cum certa hæmorrhagia sequeretur.

The Dutch prepare for the first Arctic wintering, 1596

From Peter Apian's *Cosmographia*, 1551

Cook's Antarctic 'Ice Islands', January 1773

Bellingshausen's Russian Antarctic Expedition, 1819–21

4

Weddell's brig *Jane* and 65-ton cutter *Beaufoy*

Parry's 'Attempt to reach the North Pole in Boats Fitted for the Purpose', 1827

'View of the Antarctic Continent'. As seen by Wilkes's United States Exploring Expedition, January 1840

a Top-hatted officers of Franklin's Second Expedition explore the Arctic coast of America

b. 'Critical Position of H.M.S. *Investigator* . . .'

a. James Clark Ross discovers Mount Erebus, January 1841

b. 'A gale in the pack'. H.M.S. *Erebus* and *Terror* in the Antarctic,
January 1842

9

'Crossing the Ice Belt at Coffee Gorge'. Kane's Yankees in the Arctic, 1854

The Peary Arctic Club's S.S. *Roosevelt*, 1906

The Navy advances across the 'Great Ice Barrier'. Scott's Antarctic expedition, 1901-4

On the Polar Plateau. Scott's last expedition, 1910-13

13

a. Amundsen's dog-teams reach the South Pole,
December 1911

b. Scott and his men find the Norwegian flag flying at the Pole,
January 1912

Scott's hut at Cape Evans

The United States Navy lands at the South Pole

whalers who had followed in the wake of Kane and Hall to the
rich whaling grounds north of Smith Sound. The tactics designed to achieve these objectives will be familiar to those who
remember Parry's explorations. The ships were first to ram
their way through the ice to the highest possible latitude. Then
officers and seamen would take to the ice, man-hauling ponder-
ous boats and sledges until they could haul no more. Nevertheless, the outcome of these heroic efforts was remarkable, no less
so than in Parry's day. Having imposed upon themselves
these intolerable but customary conditions, the officers and men
of the Navy proceeded by sheer courage, endurance, and
patriotic fervour to beat all Arctic records.

Nares, first of all, following Hall's route up the west coast
of Greenland and through the ice-strewn narrows of Smith
Sound, brought his ships with superb skill to the very edge of
the Arctic Ocean. Then the man-hauling parties set out along
the Ellesmere Island and Greenland coasts. One party, the first
summer, rounded Cape Columbia, the northernmost point of
Ellesmere Island and explored westwards for two hundred and
twenty miles. Exhausted by the strain and weakened by scurvy
– from which the American expeditions, thriving on their
Eskimo diet of raw fish and seal meat, had been so remarkably
free – only two men had strength enough to haul the sledges
on return. A second party that same summer, led by Lieutenant
Albert Markham, advanced across the sea ice towards the Pole.
Making no more than two miles a day, they struggled on and
by 11 May reached latitude 82° 48', beating (by a mile or two)
the high latitudes achieved by Parry and by Hall. The return
journey had all the possibilities of final tragedy. One boat had
to be abandoned, for five men had to be carried on sledges, leaving only six men and two officers to haul, and once again the
toll of scurvy was devastating. Out of the hundred and twenty-
one men of the Nares Expedition, there were fifty-six cases of
scurvy.

The following summer another party, again led by Lieutenant
Albert Markham, carried the record still farther north, forty-
eight geographical miles beyond the point reached the previous
year, and there it stood until an American expedition of 1882.

Remarkable as these achievements were, the Nares Expedition was the last expedition of its kind. Never again in the nineteenth century were such heavily manned naval vessels working under purely service conditions to explore the polar seas.

Meanwhile a German scientist, the industrious and prolific geographer Petermann, evolved a theory which gave some hope of a less arduous approach to the North Geographical Pole. Because of a branching of the warm waters of the Gulf Stream north of the Bering Strait, Petermann argued that there was some probability in this part of the eastern Arctic of a relatively ice-free route towards the north. Two young Austrian scientists, Lieutenant Karl Weyprecht of the Austrian Navy and Lieutenant Julius Payer of the Austrian Army, were greatly attracted by this notion and with the support of a rich patron, Count Wilczek, set off on a reconnaissance along the coasts of Novaya Zemlya in the summer of 1871. They met little ice and were so encouraged that they sailed again the following year in the steamer *Tegethoff* on a voyage which, though it gave little enough support to Petermann's theories, resulted in the discovery of Franz Josef Land.

In October 1872 the *Tegethoff* was beset and all winter drifted helplessly with the ice to the north-west. All the following spring and summer, Weyprecht and Payer tried desperately to escape by boring and sawing a way through ice nearly thirty feet in thickness and had indeed given up all hope when on 30 August 1873 they saw on the horizon what seemed in their relief to be nothing less than 'a radiant Alpine land', the snow slopes of the archipelago of Franz Josef Land.

It was October before they made landfall on one of a cluster of islands, a dismal, anything but radiant, place of rock and snow and broken ice; without game, without indeed any sign of life except the sparse lichens which were the only trace of vegetation. During the winter they explored and mapped and when April came they decided to abandon their ship and make by boat for their base on Novaya Zemlya. There, off the coast, they were rescued by a Russian vessel fishing, on 24 August 1874. The discovery of the islands of Franz Josef Land – one of which Weyprecht and Payer called Wilczek Island after their patron

– filled the unexplored gap between the very much earlier discoveries of Spitsbergen and Novaya Zemlya. Most important, however, for the future evolution of Arctic exploration was the hypothesis Weyprecht and Payer put forward on their return: that these islands were perhaps outliers, on the Antarctic model, of some greater land-mass, possibly even a continental land, in the midst of which was the Pole. This proposition, strange but perhaps no stranger than Kane's obsession with an open polar sea, reveals the total ignorance which existed even as late as this in the nineteenth century about the true nature of the Polar Basin.

This same belief in a southward stretching central polar land mass led Lieutenant George Washington De Long of the United States Navy to select Wrangel Island in the East Siberian Sea as a likely stepping-stone to the Pole; an island which was also near enough to the Bering Strait to be affected by Petermann's warm Japanese current. De Long was no scientist like Weyprecht or Payer. His expedition was an ambitious adventure, spectacular enough to attract the backing of James Gordon Bennett, the proprietor of the *New York Herald*, who had sponsored Lieutenant Schwatka's expedition the previous year. Bennett had at first thought of using balloons to reach the Pole. Finally however he bought a yacht, the *Pandora*, in which Allen Young had unsuccessfully attempted the North-West Passage in 1875–6, and in this, manned and equipped by the United States Navy, De Long sailed from San Francisco in 1879. He renamed his ship the *Jeannette*.

The expedition was in itself a total failure. The *Jeannette* was caught in the ice near Captain Kellett's discovery, Herald Island, was swept westwards past Wrangel Island (which proved to be relatively small) and then drifted in a north-westerly direction for seventeen months, only to be crushed in the ice north of the New Siberian Islands on 12 June 1881. Her crew managed to reach the estuary of the Lena river, but hunger and cold killed all but two, including De Long himself. For the future of Arctic exploration, nevertheless, this expedition was of the greatest significance. In 1884, three years after the sinking of the *Jeannette*, a pair of oilskin breeches and other wreckage from the same ship were found on the extreme south-west coast of Greenland. This curious and chance discovery was to lead to the most ingenious of all the attempts on the Pole, Fridtjof Nansen's drift across the polar basin.

Of all these various attempts to approach the Pole the last to be described, the one led by the American, Major Adolphus W. Greeley, is most oddly out of context for it originated in a project, an international project, which was the very antithesis of exploration of the record-breaking kind. Lieutenant Karl Weyprecht, when he returned from the Franz Josef Land expedition, proposed to a meeting of the German Scientific and Medical Association at Graz in 1875 that a new direction should be given to polar exploration. He considered that far too much effort had been devoted to hazardous feats of exploration and that these had been inspired too often not by any desire to advance scientific knowledge but by considerations of national and personal prestige. What was required, Weyprecht argued, now that so much especially in the Arctic had been explored, was not only more intensive scientific exploration but some coordination of national and individual effort within the framework of a general and carefully integrated scientific plan. He proposed therefore that coordinated and simultaneous scientific observations, using comparable means and comparable methods, should be made in both the Arctic and Antarctic regions; observations which, on analysis, might lead to the discovery of fundamental laws and principles. These would be to the benefit not of particular nations but of the whole of mankind.

There was much opposition at first to Weyprecht's ideas. But the young Austrian scientist was a determined man. Four years later, in 1879, his proposals were approved by the first International Polar Conference at Hamburg and they led to the first International Polar Year of 1882–3. Fifteen scientific stations were planned; four of them in the Antarctic though little came of these. Of the Arctic stations, on Ellesmere Island, Greenland, Baffin Island, Spitsbergen, the Kara Sea, and at the mouths of the Yenisey and Lena, that on Ellesmere Island was the task of the United States and was in charge of Major Adolphus W. Greeley of the United States Army. In composition (apart from two Eskimo hunters) a military expedition, its principal function was the making of meteorological and magnetic observations in Hayes's Grinnell Land in accordance with the international plan. In the mind of its leader, however, there was also another objective, and one quite out of tune with the spirit of Weyprecht's Polar Year. This was no less than an American assault on the Pole, or at least an attempt to beat the record gained for Britain by Lieutenant Albert Markham of the Nares Expedition. In this Greeley was strikingly successful. In April 1882 sledging journeys with dog-teams carried Lieutenant Lockwood, Sergeant Brainard, and the Eskimo Frederick north-eastwards from Ellesmere Island along the unexplored coast of north Greenland and north as far as latitude 83° 24', four miles beyond the point reached by Markham in 1876. The rest of the story of this expedition, which planted the United States flag nearest the Pole, forms both a tragic and, in its home administration, a discreditable chapter in the history of American polar exploration. At home, indecision, incompetence, and corruption worse even than that of the Wilkes Antarctic Expedition; in the field, great courage, starvation, madness, death. When eventually, after innumerable and disgraceful delays, relief arrived in June 1884, only seven men including Greeley himself survived, barely alive. 'Did what I came to do,' Greeley found strength to tell his rescuers, 'beat the best record!' It was the spirit which drove on another American, Robert E. Peary, to the conquest of the Pole in the first decade of the twentieth century.

THE SCANDINAVIAN ASCENDANCY:
NORDENSKIÖLD AND NANSEN

THE explorers and scientists Nordenskiöld and Nansen, who
were the founders of a new Scandinavian school of Arctic exploration in the last thirty years of the nineteenth century, came
from countries where the urge to explore, to cross the frontiers
of the unknown world, had since Viking days been part of the
national heritage. It was indeed a national impulse as characteristic in its way as that which had created the American frontiers-
man and pioneer. Baron A. E. Nordenskiöld, though born in
Finland, came of an old Swedish family. He had been compelled
as a young man to leave Finland (at that time part of Russia)
for political reasons, and it was in Stockholm that he first embarked upon his Arctic studies. He was by training a scientist, a
chemist and a mineralogist, and gained his first Arctic experience
on a scientific expedition to Spitsbergen in 1858, led by the
Swedish geologist Professor Torell. The geographical and geological problems of Spitsbergen, whose coasts had been visited
by Russian expeditions sent by Catherine the Great in the seven-
teen-sixties, had been explored over three centuries by a succession of Dutch and British whalers (including William Scoresby)
and had attracted Swedish scientists ever since the visit in 1827
of the Norwegian geologist, Professor Keilhau.

In 1861 and again in 1864 (with the help of his wealthy patron
Baron Oscar Dickson) Nordenskiöld returned to Spitsbergen:
to measure an arc of the meridian and to map parts of the
archipelago 'with an accuracy', the American explorer Greeley
affirmed, 'hitherto unattained in any Arctic land'. Two years
later he moved westwards to explore a region which was by
comparison almost unknown: the vast and lofty ice sheet, fifteen
hundred miles long and six hundred miles wide, which almost
covers Greenland, and spills over in the form of cliffs and

glaciers, into the sea. One or two desultory Danish expeditions in the eighteenth century had made no impression on this great desert of ice and in the nineteenth century it seemed no more than a gigantic waste land until a Danish inspector for southern Greenland, Dr Henry Rink, began to ponder on its geographical significance and on the possibility that it might be the source of Atlantic icebergs, and a relic perhaps of the last Ice Age. There-after scientists and explorers of many nations were drawn to Greenland to explore the ice sheet, and to investigate its history, formation, and movement, and the influence of this vast and persistent expanse of ice on weather.

With a Swedish botanist and two Lapps, Nordenskiöld in 1870 tried unsuccessfully to cross the ice sheet at its narrow, southern end. This first scientific reconnaissance was followed by numer-ous Danish expeditions and on one of these, Jensen's expedition of 1879, the first ice-free rock outcrops, known as 'nunataks', of which rumours had been current in the eighteenth century, were discovered. The discovery of these, the ice-free peaks of sub-glacial mountains, faintly coated with earth, gave rise to a curious and exciting idea. Might there not be deep in the interior of Greenland not ice but stretches of cultivable land, rich agri-cultural land where corn and grass might grow in the midst of this desiccated field of ice?

After another visit to Spitsbergen in 1872 on which after failing to approach the Pole with reindeer teams and sledges, he crossed the ice-cap of North East Land, Nordenskiöld turned to a very different problem, the navigation of the old North-East Passage. For the Western world, the North-East Passage had long lost its attraction as a possible seaway to the East. In North America, trans-continental railways were spreading fast. Indeed, as Nor-denskiöld in the steamship *Vega* moved towards the Bering Strait in 1878, the Colombian Government granted de Lesseps his concession to build the Panama Canal. Nevertheless, for Russia, Nordenskiöld was convinced, the navigation of the North-East Passage could be of vital importance; it might open up a com-mercial highway along the Siberian coast over which the mineral resources, scarcely probed, of the immense territories of eastern Russia might be brought cheaply to industrial Europe and in particular to Scandinavia; it might even link the north Russian ports with the ports of the Pacific Ocean. There were in addition strong scientific arguments in favour of the voyage since it would enable him not only 'to carry on researches in geography, hydrology, geology, and natural history' along the coast but 'to survey an almost unknown sea of enormous extent'. In July 1877, these arguments gained Nordenskiöld the support of the King of Norway and Sweden, of his patron Baron Oscar Dickson and, notably, that of a rich Russian merchant A. Sibiriakov. He like Nordenskiöld saw considerable commercial prospects for Russia in the opening up of the North-East Passage.

A year later, after two reconnoitring voyages into the Kara Sea, Nordenskiöld in the three-hundred-ton steam and sailing ship the *Vega*, with the *Lena* in consort as far as the Lena River and two of Sibiriakov's cargo boats bound for the Yenisey, sailed from the Norwegian port of Tromsö. In response perhaps to Weyprecht's plea for greater international cooperation in polar exploration Nordenskiöld's expedition had a distinctly international flavour and lieutenants of the Swedish, Danish, and Italian navies, a lieutenant of the Russian Army, Swedish sailors, and Norwegian sealers were all included among the scientists and crew.

Nordenskiöld, remembering the disaster of the *Tegethoff* off Novaya Zemlya, decided from the start to keep close to the North Siberian coast being confident that 'the open navigable water, which two years in succession had carried me across the Kara Sea ... extended in all probability to the Bering Strait'. Thereafter his voyage, carefully, meticulously, planned, was singularly devoid of the tragedies, the dramatic escapes, the tales of hardship and endurance by which polar exploration is so often only remembered. It was indeed remarkably uneventful. By 6 August the convoy was at the mouth of the Yenisey, at a secure and ample island anchorage close to the mainland which Nordenskiöld had marked down on his reconnaissance voyages. Just as he named an adjacent island after his Russian patron Sibiriakov, so this, an anchorage which he prophesied would one day be of 'great importance for the foreign commerce of Siberia', was named after Baron Dickson; an anchorage now known as

O. Diksona (Dickson Island), a most important harbour on the Soviet Northern Sea Route.

Beyond the Yenisey, the ships launched into waters unknown except to the small native craft of the north Siberian tribes. But fog rather than ice was their worst enemy. Through August, Nordenskiöld wrote, 'we continued to sail and steam along the coast, mostly in very close fog, which only at intervals dispersed so much that the lie of the coast could be made out. In order that they might not be separated, both vessels had often to signal to each other with the steam whistle. The sea was as bright as a mirror. Drift ice was seen now and then, but only in small quantity and very rotten; but in the course of the day we steamed past an extensive unbroken ice-field, fast to the land, which occupied a bay on the west side of the Chelyuskin peninsula . . . the northernmost promontory of Asia. . . .' Nordenskiöld then resolved to sail north-eastwards to discover if land lay between the peninsula and the New Siberian Islands. But the mist thickened into fog and finding the *Vega* facing a labyrinth of ice he returned on his tracks to where he first entered the pack. He then made for the clearer water off the coast.

Hugging the coast, Nordenskiöld steamed south-eastwards through waters marked as land on his maps to the mouth of the Lena river. 'If the coast had been followed the whole time,' he noted in his *Voyage of the Vega,* 'if the water had been clear, and the navigable water sufficiently surveyed so that it had been possible to keep the course of the vessel near the land, the voyage of the *Vega* to the mouth of the Lena would never have been obstructed by ice. . . .' This time they reached the New Siberian Islands with ease and Nordenskiöld was reminded of the discoveries by the early Russian explorers of ivory and other prehistoric remains when he dredged up, in his search for marine life, the decayed remnants of mammoth tusks. He rejected the temptation to land and explore, however, for fear of jeopardizing the expedition and turned instead southwards towards the mainland. There they met the first human beings since leaving the Kara Strait, dressed in reindeer skin, swarming out in their skin canoes and boats, laughing and gesticulating as Nordenskiöld distributed tobacco and Dutch clay pipes. Ethnographically, these tribes were akin to the Eskimoes and Nordenskiöld observed how closely their household implements resembled those he had seen from old Eskimo graves in Greenland. Their contemporary contacts, however, appeared rather to be with the south and east. They spoke no Russian but could count up to ten in English; and this and the possession of a Chinese coin and an American cent piece suggested trade with the American whalers of the Pacific rather than with Russia overland.

Winter now was almost upon them. Off North Cape the ice was closely packed around the ships and only one hundred and twenty miles from Cape Dezhnev, on the very threshold of the Arctic and Pacific Oceans overlooking Bering Strait, their way was barred by a belt of floes. It was only a few miles wide. But it was solid enough to stop the *Vega*.

Apart from violent movements of the ice in mid December which made Nordenskiöld hurriedly set up a depot on shore, it was a peaceful winter. And with the spring, caravans of sledges drawn by reindeer began to pass on their way to the Bering Strait. But there were still three months to wait. Then one July night, just as they were sitting down to dinner, convinced that the ice barrier would not move for some days, they suddenly felt a faint movement of the ship. Boilers were lighted at once and the *Vega* moved off. 'The sea was mirror-bright and nearly clear of ice, a walrus or two stuck up his head, strangely magnified by the fog; in our neighbourhood, seals swam around us in large numbers, and flocks of birds, which probably breed on the steep cliffs, swarmed round the vessel. The trawl net repeatedly brought up from the sea bottom a very abundant yield of worms, molluscs, crustacea, etc. A zoologist would have had a rich working field.'

Early on the morning of 20 July, dark heights could be seen to the east through the dispersing fog. 'These were the mountain summits of the easternmost promontory of Asia ... by 11 a.m. we were in the middle of the sound which unites the North Polar Sea with the Pacific, and from this point the *Vega* greeted the Old and New Worlds with a display of flags and the firing of a Swedish salute.'

Nordenskiöld's predictions about the value of his voyage to Russia have been more than justified. With the aid of powerful modern ice-breakers, with aircraft, with meteorological stations established along the coast to observe the variations of weather and of ice, with the aid of an elaborate hydrographic service to chart and light and buoy these dangerous and often, even now, impassable waters, the Soviet Union has maintained along Nordenskiöld's route a more or less regular highway for shipping under the Chief Administration of the Northern Sea Route ('Glavsevmorput'). New ports have sprung up, their vast hinterland has been exploited, and it was along this route during World War II that Lend-Lease supplies from the United States were shipped to the Soviet Union in her most critical hours.

The next to appear in this saga of Scandinavian exploration is the tall, fair-haired Norwegian, Fridtjof Nansen ('a true Viking', Admiral McClintock called him), a man who in daring, in endurance, and in intellectual stature is supreme among Arctic explorers. He was by training and by inclination a scientist, a zoologist who turned later to oceanography, mathematics, astronomy, and much else, and a scientist Nansen remained all his life, even when burdened in later years with grave national and international responsibilities. He was also in a very special sense an adventurer, loving exploration not only for its excitements, or for the satisfaction of physical achievement, but because he was convinced (with Ibsen whom he so greatly admired) that the key to man's destiny lay in the study of personality and in the development of individual character and that only in the silence and solitude of the wilds, alone with Nature, could man hope to discover himself. There was no doubt an element of escapism in this mind-searching Nordic approach, and indeed for Nansen escape was a necessity. Science alone was not enough; it was too cold, he said. But in the Arctic, Nansen wrote, 'I found the great adventure of the ice, deep and pure as infinity, the silent, starry night, the depths of Nature herself, the fullness of the mystery of life, the eternal round of the universe and its eternal death'. Only in the Arctic could Nansen find relief from the dark and sombre imaginings, the doubts and fears with which in the restless, turbulent, civilized world he was so constantly afflicted.

Nansen's Arctic career began in the summer of 1882 at the age of twenty-one when he joined a sealer working in Spitsbergen and Greenland waters to gain experience of zoology in the field. Two years later, while a member of the staff of Bergen Museum, he read of Nordenskiöld's landing on the east coast of Greenland and of his penetration of the ice sheet, and it was then, after reading Nordenskiöld's description of the ice sheet surface, that Nansen had those first daring and imaginative ideas which were to transform Arctic exploration. He planned to cross Greenland on ski.

Scientific work – postgraduate studies on the structure of the central nervous system – kept him busy for three years. He then started to put his plan into action. To many, the notion of a party of young men attempting to ski across the Greenland ice sheet seemed an irresponsible, indeed a laughable idea. Even Nordenskiöld was sceptical. In the end, however, the Swedish explorer came under the spell of this impulsive, blunt, but supremely confident young man. The risk he thought – and he had no illusion about the risk – was worth taking and he wrote in support of Nansen's application for funds, pointing out that 'the investigation of the real nature of Greenland is of such great and fundamental significance for science that it is scarcely possible at the present time to set a more important goal for a polar expedition. . . .'

Elsewhere Nansen received much discouragement. He was reminded of the disaster which had overtaken the German expedition, under Koldewey, on the east coast in 1869. He was reminded that even Nordenskiöld had failed, and that on the west coast, only two years earlier, a young American Robert E. Peary had suffered infinitely worse misfortune. Nevertheless, with funds from Denmark supplementing those from Norway, he went ahead with his plans; three Norwegians (one, a retired ship's captain, Otto Sverdrup) and two Lapps were selected; special pack sledges were designed; and Nansen took lessons in the Eskimo language from Dr Henry Rink, the specialist on Greenland. Simplicity and efficiency of equipment were characteristic of all Nansen's expeditions and he himself was largely responsible for its design. Indian and Norwegian snow-shoes, sleeping bags of reindeer skin, the famous portable Nansen cooker, all these appeared on his first expedition to Greenland.

Nansen himself, as always, personally supervised every detail, and made sure that every possible contingency was foreseen.

In May 1888 Nansen and his party of five expert skiers sailed in the Norwegian sealer *Jason* for the East Greenland coast but landed, because of gales and drift, two hundred miles south of their planned starting point. In the centre of the ice sheet, storms held them up in August and they found their planned route due west was too long, and even skis too slow, if they were to catch the last boat leaving the west coast for Norway. They then lashed the ski-sledges together and hoisted a tarpaulin sail. 'Our ship', wrote Nansen, 'flew over the waves and drifts of snow with a speed that almost took one's breath away. We were swirled over the rough surface, and often we simply jumped from the crest of one wave to another. . . . It was rapidly getting dark, but the full moon was rising, and she gave us light enough to see and avoid the worst crevasses. It was a curious sight for me to see the two vessels coming rushing along behind me, with their square Viking-like sails showing dark against the white snowfield and the big round disk of the moon behind. . . . Faster and faster I go flying on, while the ice gets more and more difficult. . . . The ground here is seamed with crevasses . . . crevasse after crevasse, running parallel with one another and showing dark blue in the moonlight.' When they reached the west coast, however, after a journey of over four hundred miles – a journey which had involved a climb to nine thousand feet above the level of the sea – the ship had gone.

After spending the winter of 1888–9 among the Eskimoes, Nansen returned to Norway and to immediate fame. For Nansen the scientist, the expedition brought its own rewards in his realization of the full significance of this great ice mass, reduced through the discharge of glaciers, renewed by continual precipitation. For Nansen the man, the journey was an unforgettable experience. '. . . When the moon came up and . . . played over the tops of the ice ridges, and bathed the whole of this stark world of ice in its silvery rays, then peace descended all about us and life became beauty.'

Nansen's was the first of many crossings of the Greenland ice sheet; by the American Robert E. Peary, by the Swiss de Quervain, by a Dane J. P. Koch who wintered (with Alfred Wegener) in Dronning Louise Land. Of these Peary's journey in 1871 when in eighty days he travelled fourteen hundred miles across the ice sheet at its northern end, moving in from the west, was the boldest venture, for almost nothing was known at that time about the northern or north-eastern parts of the interior of Greenland. Descending rapidly towards the east coast Peary reached the edge of a great rock cliff, overlooking 'Independence Bay'. This was not as he thought part of the East Greenland Sea but the western end of a deep fjord. Nevertheless, by this journey Peary virtually established the insularity of Greenland, even though it had yet to be completely proved. Peary's Greenland journeys, however, were essentially training exercises, rigorous tests to prepare himself and his equipment for a very much more ambitious project, the attainment of the North Pole and it is in that context that they will be described.

Nansen, meanwhile, had been contemplating an even more audacious and more controversial enterprise: his drift across the polar basin in the *Fram*. The idea first came to him long before his Greenland crossing when he happened to read an article by the Norwegian meteorologist Professor Henrik Mohn in a daily newspaper *Morgenbladet*. In this Mohn argued that the wreckage from De Long's ship the *Jeannette*, which had sunk three years earlier off the New Siberian Islands, could only have drifted across the polar sea to south-west Greenland on an ice-floe, moving with the current south down Greenland's east coast, round its southern extremity at Kap Farvel, and up the west coast as far as Julianehaab. Nansen saw the possibilities at once and in 1890, after his return from Greenland, published his plans. 'If', he declared, 'a floe could drift right across the unknown region, that drift might be enlisted in the services of exploration.' Using this trans-polar current, using a ship so slimly shaped that she could slip 'like an eel out of the embraces of the ice', Nansen was confident that in two years' time, he too, like the wreckage from the *Jeannette*, could cross the polar basin.

In February 1890 Nansen addressed the Norwegian Geographical Society and casting back to the labours of Parry and his men, of Nares and Markham, against the powerful Arctic drift, he drew attention to the fundamental principles on which his plans were based. 'If we pay attention to the actual forces of nature as they exist here, and try and work with them and not against them, we shall find the safest and easiest way of reaching the Pole. It is useless to work, as previous expeditions have done, against the current. . . .' He then marshalled his evidence. There was not only the drift of wreckage from the *Jeannette*. Had not a throwing stick used only by the Alaskan Eskimoes of the Bering Strait been found on the Greenland coast? Had not the drift-wood found all along the east coast of Greenland proved to be of Siberian origin? Even the sediment which he himself had collected from the drift ice east of Greenland had been proved to come from the Siberian rivers. About the existence of a trans-polar current at least there was no doubt. 'It may be possible', Nansen confessed, however, 'that the current will not carry us

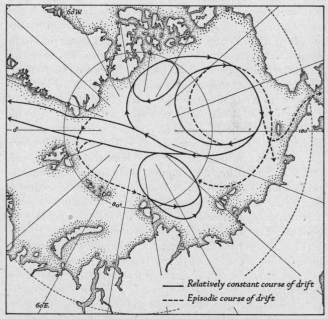

Ice Drift in the Central Polar Basin (after Burkhanov, 1955)

exactly across the Pole, but the principal thing is to explore the unknown Polar regions.'

Whether a ship could safely drift as the ice-floes drifted was to many, however, a very different matter. General Adolphus Washington Greeley, leader of the disastrous American expedition of 1881–4, a great admirer of the Arctic technique of the British Navy, expressed the strongest disapproval. 'It is doubtful', he declared, 'if any hydrographer would treat seriously his theory of polar currents, or if any arctic travellers would endorse the whole scheme ... arctic exploration is sufficiently credited with rashness and danger in its legitimate and sanctioned methods, without bearing the burden of Dr Nansen's illogical scheme of self-destruction.' In London, in 1892, Nansen boldly confronted an audience at the Royal Geographical Society and found the Arctic Admirals of the Franklin Search assembled in impressive strength. But his reception there was only slightly less discouraging. Admiral Sir George Nares, in calm disregard of the evidence, declared the chances of a northerly drift to be small. Sir Allen Young, the unsuccessful navigator of the North-West Passage, thought like Weyprecht that there would be land in all directions near the Pole and that this would be Nansen's greatest danger. Admiral Sir George Richards was not in favour of 'amateur nautical expeditions'. Even old Sir Joseph Hooker, the survivor of Ross's Antarctic Expedition, though he would not say that Nansen's project was impossible, considered nevertheless that it 'would not justify the exposure of valuable lives for its attainment' and expressed the hope that Nansen would 'dispose of his admirable courage, skill, and resources in the prosecution of some less perilous attempt to solve the mystery of the Arctic Area'. Only Admiral Sir Leopold McClintock and a merchant officer Captain Wiggins who had navigated the Kara Sea, had any praise for Nansen's vision and daring. 'This', McClintock declared, 'is the most adventurous programme ever brought under the notice of the Royal Geographical Society.' Nansen, encouraged by praise from so eminent an explorer, was quite unmoved by these earlier rebuffs. Expressing his gratitude to 'the eminent Arctic men', he declared 'I could get no better encouragement for my expedition, because their criticism has not been able to convince me that I am wrong in my opinion about the currents or about the expedition'.

In Norway there were also some critics, but Nansen received all the support he needed and he experienced none of the difficulties met with before his Greenland expedition. Two-thirds of the cost were provided by the Government and Storthing, private subscribers headed by King Oscar provided the remainder, and on 24 June 1893 the *Fram* (Forward), specially designed by a Scottish architect, sailed for the Arctic under the command of Captain Otto Sverdrup, Nansen's companion on the Greenland crossing, with the thirteen Norwegian members of the expedition. Food and scientific equipment had been most carefully selected with the advice of experts, Norwegian, Swedish, German, Dutch, in all the different scientific fields including that of the physiology of diet and nutrition. Russia too contributed, and Siberian sledge dogs were purchased and three supply depots in the New Siberian Islands were stocked at the expense of Nicolai Kelch of Irkutsk.

It was to the north of these islands in September 1893 that the *Fram*, after coasting along Europe and Asia, drove deep into the pack. The long drift then began. By the end of the month, the ship was frozen in and her crew resigned themselves to two, possibly three years of isolation and wandering. The *Fram*'s rudder was hauled up, her six-knot engine was dismantled, oiled, and stored away; and a joiner's shop was rigged up in the hold. There was constant distraction to while away the hours and days; soundings and temperatures had to be taken in the depths of the sea when leads or pools in the ice could be found; magnetic observations were recorded; Nansen in traditional polar style edited a weekly newspaper *Framsjaa*. Only the occasional unexpected appearance of a bear, clumsy but menacing alongside the ship, broke the monotony of this carefully organized routine. Though the *Fram* rose, as Nansen had foreseen, easily, indeed superbly, over the floes, sometimes her course was erratic and alarming. On occasions her bows would swing round to the south as if – Nansen thought – she was yearning for the southern shores. Then as suddenly she would swing round to the north again as if drawn forward by some invisible power towards the unknown. But despite these disconcerting, apparently random manoeuvres, they were in general moving with the current steadily north-west along the route of the wreckage from De Long's *Jeannette*.

Of the thirteen men on board, Nansen perhaps felt most acutely the monotony and confinement of the voyage. 'I long', he wrote in his diary, 'I long to return to life . . . the years are passing here. . . . Oh! at times this inactivity crushes one's very soul; one's life seems as dark as the winter night outside; there is sunlight upon no other part of it except the past and the far, far distant future. I feel as if I *must* break through this deadness, this inertia, and find some outlet for my energies. Can't something happen? Could not a hurricane come and tear up this ice, and set it rolling in high waves like the open sea?'

Two years had indeed almost passed since the *Fram* left Norway and it was becoming evident that despite her north-westerly course, she would not pass across the Pole. Early in the spring of 1895, therefore, Nansen decided upon one of the most daring exploits in the history of polar exploration; to leave the *Fram* to the skill and patience of her captain Otto Sverdrup and with one companion, H. Johansen, dogs, sledges, two kayaks, and a hundred days' food, to strike out across the floes to the Pole. Even Nansen, the dedicated scientist, could not refrain from seizing this chance to plant his country's flag at the northern extremity of the axis of the earth.

On 14 March 1895 Nansen and Johansen left the warmth and safety of the *Fram* and launched out into the Arctic wasteland, travelling at first swiftly and easily over flat ice, then laboriously and painfully over ice massed into immense ridges, so tumultuous and jagged that it overturned the sledges and slashed the thin skins of their Eskimo kayaks. 'Ridge after ridge', Nansen wrote, 'and nothing but rubble to travel over . . . and from the highest hummock only the same kind of ice was to be seen. It was a veritable chaos of ice-blocks, stretching as far as the horizon.' After twenty-three days, in cold so intense that their clothing froze and cut deep sores in their wrists, they reached a latitude of 86° 14′ N., two hundred and twenty-four nautical miles from the Pole, one hundred and sixty miles further north than had ever been attained before. But in such conditions they could do no better and on 8 April 1895 they turned south on the first lap of the long homeward journey over the ice to the nearest land, Franz Josef Land.

Through April, May, and June they travelled over ice becoming treacherous as it thinned and weakened under the warmth of the summer sun, and often they were forced into long detours to avoid open stretches of water. On 11 July 1895 Nansen wrote, 'A monotonous life this on the whole, as monotonous as one can well imagine it – to turn out day after day, week after week, month after month, to the same toil over ice ... no sign of land in any direction. . . . Our hearts fail us when we see the ice lying before us like an impenetrable maze of ridges, lanes, brash, and huge blocks thrown together pell-mell, and one might imagine oneself looking at suddenly congealed breakers. There are moments when it seems impossible that any creature not possessed of wings can get further. . . .' Shortly afterwards, however, the edge of the ice faintly appeared and beyond it the dark surface of the sea. In the distance, they saw land. 'At last the marvel has come to pass – land, land, and after we had almost given up our belief in it! ... So this was what land looked like now that we had come to it! I had imagined it in many forms, with high peaks and glittering glaciers, but never like this.' Lashing the kayaks together with the sledges, they rigged a sail and sped over the water, ecstatic at the sensation of dancing over the waves after so many months of heavy, unremitting toil.

After a winter in northern Franz Josef Land in a rough stone hut, living off bear's meat, getting their light and heat from walrus blubber, Nansen and Johansen headed south and there in May 1896 met Jackson of the Jackson-Harmsworth Expedition. There can never have been a more astonishing or more dramatic encounter. First they heard the barking of a dog, then unbelievably the sound of a voice, 'a human voice, a strange voice, the first for three years'. Only by reading Nansen's own description in his *Farthest North* can one sense to the full the tension and emotion of the scene.

Frederick Jackson, an Englishman who had been sponsored after the American fashion by Alfred Harmsworth (later Lord

Northcliffe), hoped like Weyprecht and De Long to find in Franz Josef Land the beginning of a land route to the Pole. In course of his explorations he was able to check the surveys of Weyprecht and those of an Englishman Leigh Smith (who visited the islands and lost his yacht the *Eira* in the ice in 1881–2) with results that were to change completely the map of Franz Josef Land. In another respect, too, Jackson's expedition deserves notice. He used ponies to pull his sledges instead of dogs – these were kept for hunting – and when men from the Jackson-Harmsworth Expedition joined Scott and Shackleton in the Antarctic they went full of praise for Jackson's sledging methods. To Scott and Shackleton these were greatly preferable to the methods used by Nansen, Amundsen, and other Norwegians which involved, as sledge loads lightened on the homeward journey, the killing of their dogs for dog-food; or even, to save the transport of other food, their slaughter for human consumption.

For Nansen and Johansen, who had only two leaking kayaks to carry them across the hundred and sixty miles to the nearest land, the meeting with the English expedition was an almost miraculous piece of good fortune. For Jackson, however, who was just about to start on another trip northwards to search for land leading to the Pole, it put an end to all his hopes since Nansen had proved that sea and only sea – sea not open as imagined by Kane and others but perpetually frozen over – lay around the Pole and filled the polar basin.

When Nansen and Johansen reached Norway on board Jackson's ship the *Windward* they seemed to all the world like men returned from the dead. But the first news, the day after their arrival, of the fate of the *Fram* was no less startling; after a drift of thirty-five months she had broken out of the pack north-west of Spitsbergen and undamaged, without the loss of a single man on board, had arrived in Tromsö. It was the last act, the wholly triumphant climax, to what General Greeley had described as 'Dr Nansen's illogical scheme of self-destruction'.

The *Fram* expedition was by no means only a great Arctic journey, created by the vision and genius of an extraordinary man. Its scientific work consisting of long and continuous observations in the highest northern latitudes, mainly in oceanography and meteorology, proved of fundamental importance for polar science, and indeed provided the basis for all future Arctic work. In this respect and in the new attention Nansen paid to scientific principles in such matters as diet and nutrition, the *Fram* expedition raised to a new level standards of polar exploration.

Nansen's subsequent career in political and diplomatic life, as the protagonist of Norwegian independence, as the League of Nations Commissioner after the First World War who organized the repatriation of prisoners and the relief of famine, is outside the scope of this book. The Nobel Prize was his reward for a lifetime of unceasing devotion to the cause of human knowledge, human freedom, and human happiness. In all these diverse activities he showed those same gifts of imagination and vision which he displayed in the realm of scientific exploration.

Nansen the scientist was also the scholarly historian of the early Viking voyages to the Arctic. But his mind was never confined by the past. Already, before the nineteenth century was out, he was reaching forward to the new instruments of polar exploration, to the submarine which would one day link the Atlantic and the Pacific by a voyage beneath the ice, to the use of balloons and aircraft. He was the founder and first president of an international society for the exploration of the Arctic by aircraft and in the summer of his death in 1930 he had planned to fly in the *Graf Zeppelin* over those frozen seas through which the *Fram* had drifted.

Fridtjof Nansen died with one geographical ambition unattained, an expedition to the South Pole. It had been in his mind ever since he returned from his Arctic drift and he kept the *Fram* in reserve for that purpose. In 1907 his fellow countryman Roald Amundsen pleaded to be allowed to borrow the *Fram* for another Arctic drift expedition, this time to cross over the Pole. To Nansen, this request faced him with one of the most difficult decisions of his life. He was getting on in years and it meant the final abandonment of all his Antarctic ambitions and it was with the greatest reluctance that he agreed. He little knew then that Roald Amundsen's Arctic expedition would be diverted, to the astonishment of Scott and indeed of the world, to the very project which he himself had for so long had in mind.

THE SCANDINAVIAN ASCENDANCY:
SVERDRUP AND AMUNDSEN

THE *Fram* arrived at Tromsö on 24 August 1896, and almost at once there was a fresh surging forward of exploration in the Arctic led again by Norwegians, both of whom owed their inspiration and one his whole Arctic training and career to the great Fridtjof Nansen. These explorers, Otto Sverdrup, captain of the *Fram*, and the much younger Roald Amundsen, had none of the high intellectual attainments, the scientific knowledge, the breadth of vision, the searching profundity of mind which were the marks of Nansen's genius. They had become, however, no less than he, masters of the technique of polar exploration and in the nine years 1898 to 1906 their voyages and discoveries added almost as much new land and sea to Canada's future Northwest Territories as all the ships of the thirty-year Franklin Search.

It was natural enough when the sponsors of the *Fram* expedition found Nansen unwilling to embark so soon on another extensive Arctic voyage that they should turn to Otto Sverdrup, his right-hand man on the first Greenland crossing and on the polar drift. Once again the *Fram* was to be the ship, but the destination this time was to be the north of Greenland where the inland journeys of the American Robert E. Peary had shown that there were many problems to be elucidated and new discoveries to be made. 'Together with Dr Nansen and my owner', Sverdrup afterwards wrote, 'I agreed on the following route, which was to be up Smith Sound and Kane Basin, through the Kennedy and Robeson Channels, and as far along the north coast of Greenland before wintering. From there we were to make sledge expeditions to the northernmost point of Greenland, and as far down the east coast as we could attain.' These expeditions, enlarging and consolidating Peary's discoveries, would settle any last remaining doubts about the insularity of Greenland and would complete the exploration of the northern and eastern coasts. 'There was no question', Sverdrup added, 'of trying to reach the Pole.'

For the unsuspecting Norwegians North Greenland was an unhappy choice since it provoked an immediate clash between Sverdrup and Robert E. Peary. Peary has already appeared on his first Greenland expedition of 1886. In 1891 he returned, accompanied this time by a very remarkable man, his Negro servant Matthew Henson whom Peary had first met serving in a hat shop in Washington. This was the expedition in which Peary, Henson, a young Norwegian hunter Eivind Astrup, and some Eskimoes reached 'Independence Bay' on the east coast after a journey of 1,200 miles. In 1894, blizzards and an epidemic among his dogs forced Peary back after 130 miles, but he started across the ice sheet again in 1895 and despite the loss of all his essential supplies in a snow-drift once again reached the east coast.

At the age of twenty-four Peary had written to his mother: 'I shall not be satisfied that I have done my best until my name is known from one end of the world to the other.' A year later he joined the Civil Engineering Corps of the United States Navy and while working on the Nicaraguan Canal happened to read Nordenskiöld's story of his Greenland ice sheet journeys. Peary at once saw in polar exploration his avenue to fame, an avenue leading to the most cherished of all geographical prizes, the North Geographical Pole. For many years these were secret ambitions. But in January 1897 as Sverdrup and Nansen were discussing their proposed explorations around North Greenland, Peary promulgated his plan 'for an extended scheme of Arctic exploration, having for its main purpose the attainment of the North Pole'. This was the motive, powerful and incessant, behind Peary's *Windward* expedition of 1898–1902. That Sverdrup's Greenland explorations were not, like his, ultimately directed towards the Pole seemed to Peary inconceivable. He saw only in such a famous and experienced Norwegian explorer a potential and highly dangerous rival, threatening to bring to nothing years of hardship, years of planning and laborious preparation, threatening to disrupt and ruin his whole life-work.

'The introduction of a disturbing factor in the appropriation by another of my plan and field of work. . . .' Such were the terms in which Peary bitterly referred to Sverdrup's plans for exploration.

Since Sverdrup intended to sail the *Fram* through Smith Sound, it was vital to Peary that he should get there first. The incident is worth recording as an illustration of the rivalries, the suspicions, and jealousies which obsessed the minds of some of the explorers of the new, professional, and independent kind in their overwhelming ambition to achieve personal fame and fortune through polar exploration. As it happened both Peary and Sverdrup were prevented by ice from penetrating to the north of Smith Sound in 1898 and the *Fram* withdrew for the winter south of the Bache Peninsula. The following spring, to save further embarrassing complications, Sverdrup switched his plans and retired into Jones Sound where the *Fram* passed a second winter. His new objective was the unexplored western parts of Ellesmere Island and in the spring not only was this long and deeply indented coast – King Oscar Land – mapped by Sverdrup's second-in-command Gunnar Isachsen with an accuracy seldom excelled on such reconnaissance exploration, but in the course of numerous long sledging journeys new lands were seen still further west.

In preparation for a fresh and extensive campaign, the *Fram* was then moved up to the head of Jones Sound for a third winter and in the spring Axel Heiberg Island, Isachsen Island, Amund and Ellef Ringnes Islands (so called after the brewers who supported the expedition) were mapped and their geology and natural history studied. These, known as the Sverdrup Islands, and the mountains and bays of King Oscar Land were discoveries which in their extent can only be compared with the discoveries made during the widespread manoeuvres of the Franklin Search. To have accomplished so much with a single ship; to have navigated her through such a maze of channels swept by violent and contrary currents, constantly imperilled by ice; to have brought his expedition – in common only with Sir John Ross – safely through four consecutive polar winters, these were achievements which marked Sverdrup as an outstanding leader and the greatest ice pilot of his day.

Otto Sverdrup returned to Norway in 1902. A year later Roald Amundsen embarked on an Arctic voyage. Amundsen like Peary was a professional explorer, a man for whom exploration was not an interlude, or a pastime, or an opportunity for research, but a profession which he had preferred to medicine as a career. Shrewd, far-sighted, methodical (in all except financial matters), he prepared himself with considerable care. He learnt seamanship in a sailing vessel. He learnt something of the technique of scientific exploration with de Gerlache's Belgian expedition of 1897, the first to winter in the Antarctic. And since magnetic studies seemed likely, from the point of view of grant-giving organizations, to be an essential adjunct to the project he had immediately in mind, namely the navigation of the North-West Passage, he studied terrestrial magnetism at Hamburg.

A quarter of a century had elapsed since the last attempt on the North-West Passage. In 1875 Allen Young, following McClintock's recommended route down Peel Sound, had been stopped by ice near the entrance to Bellot Strait (see map on inside back cover). In the following year he tried again but was diverted by the Admiralty (on the insistence of the Royal Geographical Society) to act as a relief ship to Nares's expedition. Amundsen decided to follow the route taken by Allen Young and because the North-West Passage itself aroused little interest, planned to combine with this voyage a year's magnetic observations in the vicinity of the North Magnetic Pole.

At midnight on 16 June 1903 Amundsen's ship the *Gjøa*, of 100 tons burden, cutter-rigged and equipped with an auxiliary motor, slipped out of Christiania Harbour; secretly it was said, to avoid a creditor who threatened to stop the expedition. Amundsen was then only twenty-nine. By August, Beechey Island (where Franklin had spent his first winter) was reached and Amundsen made good progress down Peel Sound. The critical moment came when the *Gjøa* neared the De la Rouquette Islands where Allen Young's yacht the *Pandora* had been stopped. But this time there was no massive barrier of ice, and as Amundsen in anxiety paced the narrow deck, he felt an irregular lurching motion of the ship, imperceptible at first, then as he waited for it, becoming more and more distinct. 'I would not have sold this slight motion for any amount of money', he confessed. 'It was a swell under the boat – a message from the open sea. The water to the south was open.'

After fogs and gales and snowstorms in Franklin Strait and Rae Strait, the *Gjøa* reached fair weather and smooth water to the south-east of King William Island and there in a small harbour, Gjøa Haven (excellently situated for Wiik the magnetic observer, in relation to the Magnetic Pole) Amundsen spent two winters, nineteen months in all. For Amundsen, Amundsen of the Antarctic, the man destined to be first at the South Pole, these months, sledging along the east coast of Victoria Island, learning from the Eskimoes their technique of travel, and most important for his future polar journeys, their methods of feeding and handling dogs, were months of priceless experience.

At the end of July 1905, the *Gjøa* sailed and by August was in the waters of Cambridge Bay reached by Collinson from the west in his much larger ship the *Enterprise* in 1852. 7 August, the day the *Gjøa*'s anchor dropped in the shallows west of Cape Colbourne was, wrote Amundsen, 'a significant day in the history of our Expedition – for we had sailed the *Gjøa* through the hitherto unsolved link in the North-West Passage'. After a third winter at King Point, north of the mouth of the MacKenzie River (where Wiik died) the *Gjøa* sailed in 1906 into the Pacific Ocean. Careful planning, great determination, luck, most of all perhaps the wise selection of so small a ship, had enabled Amundsen to achieve the first of his polar ambitions, the navigation of the North-West Passage.

These great Norwegian voyages belong like those of Nordenskiöld and Nansen to an era of Scandinavian exploration comparable with that of the Viking Age. One other and lesser Scandinavian venture, moreover, of the closing years of the nineteenth century is worth recalling because it introduced a new technique into polar exploration. This was the attempt by the Swedish technologist Salomon August Andrée to reach the Pole by balloon. Andrée, a zealous social reformer, a man who saw in technology the only means whereby the new discoveries of science could be properly applied for the betterment of mankind, was a typical product of the liberal tendencies which accompanied the remarkable industrial and technological advance of Sweden in the later nineteenth century. His balloon, the *Eagle*, the instrument by means of which the mysteries of the polar basin were to be revealed by methods less arduous than sledging journeys or the slow process of an Arctic drift, was an elegant affair, manufactured by M. Lachambre of Paris. Its envelope was of double Chinese silk. The car was of wicker work and Chinese cane. And it was equipped by Andrée with drag-lines and a steering sail, inventions which he was convinced would make it 'steerable to a high degree', even as far as the Pole.

The base for the ascent was Spitsbergen. After an abortive attempt in August 1896 (when Andrée and his companions, Knuth Fraekel and Nils Strindberg were the first to greet the *Fram* after her drift across the Pole) the journey started in the summer of 1897 in circumstances far from auspicious for this first polar flight. 'My comrades', wrote Andrée in his diary, 'insist on starting, and as I have no fully valid reasons against it, I shall agree to it, although with some reluctance.' The balloon rose, then fell again, then floated north-eastwards across Virgo Harbour, the trailing drag-lines furrowing the water. Half-way across the harbour, in full view of a crowd of tense spectators, the *Eagle* began to sink and its car to skim the surface of the water. Then as ballast was hurriedly thrown overboard, it bounded up like a great ball, leaving two-thirds of the drag lines, an essential element in Andrée's vaunted steering mechanism, lying along the beach. They had now lost all power of retarding the balloon in relation to the wind, since the steering sail set above the carrying ring had no longer any power of steerage. Thus freed from all contact with the earth the *Eagle* soared a thousand, two thousand feet, floating high above the edge of the pack, so high that the men in the car felt the heat of the sun. The air was still; only a melancholy whistling from the balloon valve broke the silence. As he watched the dark shape of a bird, perhaps a fulmar, gliding serenely on their starboard bow, Andrée reflected, 'It is not a little strange to be floating here above the polar sea. To be the first to have floated here in a balloon. How soon, I wonder, shall we have successors? Shall we be thought mad or will our example be followed? I cannot deny but that all three of us are dominated by a feeling of pride. We think that we can well face death, having done what we have done . . .'

In ten hours the *Eagle* travelled four hundred kilometres towards the north-east. Then loss of gas and cooling by cloud brought them down. The wind failed and the *Eagle* came to rest for an hour or so, then the wind rose again from the east and they travelled westwards into an icy fog and threw out knives, ropes, an anchor, scientific instruments, anything to gain height. Even so, the *Eagle*'s car began to hit the ice, and continued bumping, rising, falling, bumping, so incessantly that they could get no rest and were forced to descend and anchor to an ice-floe for twelve hours or so. Then they were off again. But almost immediately the sun vanished into the clouds, ice began to coat the envelope, and a fine drizzle froze on the ropes. On this stage of the journey in twenty-one hours they made two hundred and thirty kilometres but were only eighty kilometres north-north-east from their last starting point. On 14 July, though they were sailing high at the time, Andrée for some unknown reason brought the balloon down and anchored to the ice. It was the last flight of the *Eagle*.

Then began the long march over the sea ice by three men who were probably less well equipped to counter the ferocious advance of an Arctic winter than any in polar history. They had three choices of destination: Cape Flora on Franz Josef Land where Frederick Jackson of the Jackson-Harmsworth Expedition had left supplies; the Seven Islands off Nordaustland; or Mossel-bukta. They chose the first though it was twice as far away and spent twelve days marching to the south-east, making little headway against the contrary drift of the ice of which Andrée seems to have had little knowledge. Andrée then turned towards the Seven Islands. But still the drift was against him. Eventually, after journeying at an average speed of three miles a day, they reached White Island (Kirtøya) all utterly exhausted. It was then 17 September and White Island was the first land they had seen since 11 July. 'Our provisions', wrote Andrée in his diary, 'must soon and richly be supplemented, if we are to have any prospect of being able to hold out for a time'. By the middle of October all three men had died and thirty-three years later their bodies, their logs, their journals, Strindberg's daily shorthand letters to his fiancée, and a number of rolls of film subsequently developed with great skill by Swedish experts, were found by a Norwegian sealer.

In Sweden the news of the fate of Andrée and his companions assumed the proportions of a national tragedy, heightened as it was by the appearance in the printed films of the three men who had been the victims of this Arctic tragedy thirty years before. Though courageous, this first attempt to fly to the Pole was a premature and ill-planned adventure. 'Many people', Nansen told the Royal Geographical Society in 1892, 'think that the North Pole can be reached by balloons or balloon ships, and that it will be so reached one day. I do not deny the possibility of this; on the contrary I regard it as very probable. ...' Nordenskiöld who had been contemplating the use of captive balloons (a very different proposition) to reconnoitre above the pack ice of the Arctic went further and declared of Andrée's project, 'It is a long time since I embraced a proposal for a polar expedition with such enthusiasm'. This lavish expression of confidence by so experienced an Arctic explorer is astonishing. Andrée admittedly had been experimenting with balloon navigation ever since his first meeting with the American balloonist Wise in 1876 when he discussed the possibilities of using the trade winds for long ballooning journeys. But his earlier flights though numerous had all been brief. His steering equipment was rudimentary, its principles falsely based. His calculations of speed and course, on the evidence of his diaries, were wildly unreliable. His lack of precautions, too, against a forced landing, especially as regards clothing, contrast inexplicably with his forebodings at the start of the Eagle's journey. Nevertheless in this first use of flight, in the stress moreover which Andrée laid on the future importance of air photography and mapping from the air – these ranked high among the motives of his expedition – the voyage of the Eagle has its place in polar history. Ill-fated though it was, it foreshadowed the birth in the twentieth century of the air age in polar exploration.

THE TURN OF THE CENTURY: THE REVIVAL OF ANTARCTIC EXPLORATION

THE massive and exhaustive operations of the Franklin Search, the further explorations, British and American, springing from it, and the subsequent brilliant sequence of Scandinavian discoveries in the Arctic did not wholly divert attention from Antarctica. An early, indeed the earliest, protagonist of the resumption of Antarctic exploration in the second half of the nineteenth century was an American, Captain Matthew Fontaine Maury, Superintendent of the Hydrographic Branch of the United States Navy, and the occasion was a meeting of the Royal Geographical Society on 26 November 1860 when Maury read a paper, 'The Physical Geography of the Sea, in connexion with the Antarctic Regions'. Concluding his address, Maury, who had earlier promulgated a scheme for international cooperation in meteorology, pleaded in similar terms for a resumption of international effort in Antarctica. In this, he urged, Britain through the medium of the Royal Geographical Society should take the lead.

Maury in his determination to stir his audience into action used powerful and forthright language. In the Arctic, great strides had been made, but for the last twenty years, he declared, neither France nor England nor Russia nor for that matter the United States had done anything to advance Antarctic exploration though inner Antarctica was 'as little known as the interior of the moon'. The reproach was greatest in England's case. Did not the Antarctic continent now lie within eight or ten days' steaming of the nearest British possessions? Should it then, he asked, be any great matter to seek out a winter harbour for one or two vessels, and to explore from there by boat or over the ice? The Antarctic indeed lay at Britain's door. But if the British, Maury declared, 'made not haste to undertake the duty, it might be that the go-ahead American nation would yet be before them'.

Maury's eloquent allusions to Britain's duty to posterity, and to the last great British Antarctic explorer James Clark Ross, drew only a chilly response. Captain Washington, former secretary of the Royal Geographical Society who had become Hydrographer of the Navy, pointed out that Englishmen, Russians, and Frenchmen had done more to explore Antarctica than the United States and he demanded 'whether it might not rest with the United States to take up the question and to send out an expedition ...?' Maury, in reply, however, would commit himself no further than 'to give fair warning that if England did not undertake these explorations, the Americans would show the way'. As it happened, neither the United States nor Britain, as Washington admitted, seemed likely to be in any position to indulge in Antarctic exploration. The United States, as Maury spoke, was on the eve of a sanguinary and debilitating Civil War and in any event her government was still too hotly involved in congressional battles with Charles Wilkes to take kindly to any fresh projects for American exploration in the Antarctic. In Britain the prospect was no more hopeful. Lord Ashburton, the President of the Royal Geographical Society, closing the discussion after Maury's paper, expressed the hope that 'the Government would undertake the proposed exploration of the Antarctic Seas which would be as much for the general benefit of mankind as it was for the glory of this country.' But he knew very well since his own Society had for the past ten years been the centre of a vigorous and relentless pressure on the Government to provide funds for the Franklin Search, that after such heavy expenditure on exploration, fresh projects would be regarded with the utmost disfavour.

Nevertheless over the years Maury's plea, echoed in German rather than in international terms by Dr Georg Neumayer, Director of the Marine Observatory at Hamburg, had its effect. Ten years after Maury's visit to England, a great project of exploratory research was initiated by the Royal Society and the Admiralty in the very field of study, the physical geography and biology of the Antarctic seas, upon which Maury had addressed the Royal Geographical Society. This project, the *Challenger* oceanographical expedition was, however, exclusively concerned with maritime exploration. The land explorations 'over the ice', conducted from a winter anchorage as Maury proposed, were to wait until the turn of the century.

The Antarctic 'as far as the neighbourhood of the Great Ice Barrier' was included in the *Challenger* expedition's almost global programme of maritime research and exploration in deference to the deep-sea soundings and dredgings by Sir James Clark Ross which had laid the foundations of Antarctic oceanography. But these polar investigations represented only a small fraction of the work to be done and it was not until February 1874, two years and two months after her departure from England, that H.M.S. *Challenger* crossed the Antarctic Circle in approximately 78° 22′ E., opposite that part of Australia's future sector of Antarctica called Princess Elizabeth Land.

The *Challenger*, a wooden corvette of over two thousand tons and the first steam vessel to cross the Antarctic Circle, steered east and north-east, skirting the floating pack, and made soundings and dredgings as far almost as the charted position of Wilkes's (doubtful) 'Termination Land'. No sign of the coast was seen and by March the *Challenger*'s Antarctic explorations were over and her commander, Captain George Nares, R.N., turned towards England and, as we have seen, to fresh adventures in the Arctic. The civilian staff, meanwhile, under the direction of Professor C. Wyville Thomson of Edinburgh University, turned to the gigantic task of working up and publishing (in fifty volumes) the massive accumulation of observations.

The responsibility for this great work fell before long upon a young Canadian of Scottish origin, John Murray, who had been engaged as biologist for the voyage. But so enormous was the task of sifting, analysis, and interpretation that twenty years passed before he was able at a meeting of the Royal Geographical Society in November 1893 to give some account of the *Challenger*'s Antarctic findings.

It is a curious fact that the *Challenger* expedition which never touched, which indeed never saw, the Antarctic coastline was the first to demonstrate beyond reasonable doubt the existence of an Antarctic continent. The sequence of the ingenious argument which led John Murray finally to this conclusion is therefore worth recalling. On more than one occasion during the second quarter of the nineteenth century icebergs had been observed drifting northwards with rocks embedded in them. One had been seen by John Balleny in latitude 61° S. and the ever alert and inquisitive Charles Enderby had drawn Charles Darwin's attention to it. Darwin argued that since the iceberg had been sighted at least 450 miles from Balleny's admittedly doubtful discovery of Sabrina Land and since both Balleny and before him Cook had sailed some way south of that point without encountering land, the iceberg in question must have drifted northwards at least a hundred miles. The rock embedded in it, moreover, must similarly have travelled at least that distance from its parent source and since it was deeply embedded it had probably travelled a good deal further north before melting caused it to drop into the ocean or to be deposited on some distant shore. The boatswain of H.M.S. *Beagle* had already told Darwin of a similar rock-carrying iceberg which he had seen on a sealing voyage to the east of the South Shetlands. Furthermore, Dumont d'Urville, the French Antarctic explorer, had been told of the discovery of 'erratic boulders', probably dropped from icebergs, which had been found in 1830 by the naturalist of an American expedition on the shores of the same volcanic islands. On the basis of these facts and taking into account the large number of icebergs which had been observed in recent years drifting northwards as far even as 35° to 40° S., Darwin concluded that if 'but one iceberg in a thousand, or in ten thousand, transports its fragment, the bottom of the Antarctic Sea, and the Shores of its islands, must already be scattered with masses of foreign rock – the counterpart of the 'erratic boulders' of the northern hemisphere'.

It was soon evident that the dredging up of such rocks might provide valuable clues to the geological nature of Antarctic land and the *Challenger* expedition proved this to be the case. In the central parts of the great ocean basins only rocks of volcanic origin were dredged up. But in high latitudes in the South Atlantic and in the Central Pacific, just beyond the limit to which Antarctic icebergs had been seen to drift, fragments of continental rock, granite, and quartz, were found and as the *Challenger* approached the Antarctic Circle, rocks of similar origin – granites, diorites, schists, quartzites, sandstones, and limestones – increased in number until at the most southerly points reached they made up the bulk of the deposits. Further evidence that these rocks had originated from some great southern continental land-mass was provided by the discovery of a mineral, glauconite, in the blue muds of the Southern Ocean. Glauconite, it was known, was generally found in the muds along continental shores in association with the debris of continental rocks.

Recapitulating these arguments, Murray, on a foggy November evening in 1893, demonstrated to his audience at the Royal Geographical Society how the existence of an Antarctic continent could be deduced from the rocks dredged up by the *Challenger* expedition. But, he continued, the argument could be carried further than that, for not only the nature but also the size of the Antarctic land-mass could be deduced, in the latter case from the knowledge of the depths of the surrounding ocean. He then proceeded to show by means of an outline map (which remained without amendment for a good many years) the probable position and extent of Antarctica and to present his audience with a remarkable word picture of the continent, derived from all the evidence then available.

Facing one ocean, Murray postulated, were volcanic mountain ranges; facing others, lower hills and sweeping lowland plains while over most of the continent there lay a heavy and perpetual cap of ice and snow, the inner nucleus of rock being revealed only in adjacent islands and in mountain ranges fringing the coast. From the central highlands, ice and snow descended and accumulated in undulating fields and plains and terminated ultimately in one vast glacier which projected over the low lands into the ocean and formed the flat-topped ice cliffs with perpendicular walls which Wilkes and Dumont d'Urville and Biscoe had seen. When the forefront of this great creeping glacier projected in sufficient depth large blocks of ice broke off to form the wandering icebergs of the Southern Ocean. These, often some miles in length, floating sometimes a hundred to two hundred feet above the surface of the sea, would collide, their fragments mingling and merging with other land-ice, with salt-water ice, and with accumulations of snow to form the pack which had for generations filled with alarm the hearts of Antarctic mariners. Murray completed his ingenious and realistic picture of Antarctica with a vivid description of the life and journeyings of the rock-carrying icebergs whose significance Darwin had been the first to discern. 'Waves dash against the vertical faces of the floating ice-islands as against a rocky shore, so that at the sea-level they are first cut into ledges and gullies, and then into caves and caverns of the most heavenly blue from out of which comes the resounding roar of the ocean and into which the snow-white and other petrels may be seen to wing their way through guards of soldier-like penguins stationed at the entrances. As these ice-islands are slowly drifted by wind and current to the north, they tilt, turn, and sometimes capsize, and then submerged prongs and spits are thrown high into the air, producing irregular pinnacled bergs higher possibly than the original table-shaped mass. As decay proceeds, the imprisoned boulders, stones, and earth are deposited over the ocean's floor as far as sub-tropical regions.'

Murray did not confine his portrait of Antarctica to a description of land and ice. He talked also of the meteorology of Antarctica, of the zone of permanently high pressure which lay above the continent; he described how, deep below the cold waters of the Antarctic Ocean, were warmer waters which flowed southwards as the colder surface waters drifted north; and he spoke of the great profusion of animal and vegetable life which the *Challenger* Expedition had found in Antarctic seas, especially in the deepest waters above the ocean floor. From these depths they dredged up animals which could be recognized as descendants of those which once occupied the shallower waters washing the shores of a great continent.

Murray concluded his masterly reconstruction with a fervent appeal to his audience that, in the interests of science, Antarctic exploration be at once resumed so that the first landings could be made on the mainland. Little progress indeed had been made in this direction since the American Maury, in 1860, had so bluntly urged upon the British the task, indeed the obligation, to carry forward the great discoveries of Ross. In 1873–4 a sealing and reconnaissance expedition under Captain Edward Dallmann, the first German expedition to the Antarctic, made some minor discoveries in the vicinity of Graham Land. In 1880 Lieutenant Bove of the Italian Navy produced an abortive scheme for a two-year expedition to Antarctica which was to form part of the First Polar Year. Five years later the British Association set up a committee, which included in addition to the Arctic admirals, famous scientists like Sir William Thomson (Lord Kelvin) and Professor Huxley. This drew attention to the scientific importance of Antarctic exploration, its members discussed and argued. But nothing happened.

In the end it was the whalers, British and Norwegian, and not the scientists who gave the first boost to Antarctic exploration. By the last decade of the nineteenth century, the Greenland whale fisheries had reached their lowest ebb, for the Greenland whale – the bowheaded or 'right' whale – had by then almost disappeared. Remembering Ross's claims to have seen the 'right whale' in the Antarctic, a Dundee whaling firm in 1892 sent four whalers into this region and sent with them – largely on the advice of Leigh Smith, the explorer of Franz Josef Land – two naturalists (one, William Spiers Bruce, was to achieve eminence as an Antarctic explorer) equipped with instruments loaned by the Royal Geographical Society. The voyage, principally in the Weddell Sea, was profitless for Ross's 'right whale' was never found and the naturalists were given little chance to do scientific work. Nevertheless, the effort was not entirely wasted, for in the following year a Norwegian expedition under the same Captain C. A. Larsen, who had landed Nansen on the east coast of Greenland for his ice sheet crossing, was encouraged to make a voyage to the South Orkneys and Weddell Sea, and this in turn led to the first important step in the advance of Antarctic exploration.

When Larsen returned to Norway in July 1893 he gave an account of his voyage to old Commander Foyn, the doyen of the Norwegian whaling industry, a Norwegian Charles Enderby, who was an enthusiastic supporter of exploration and was greatly interested in Larsen's account of his voyage in little-known Antarctic seas. When, therefore, soon after he had seen Larsen, Foyn was approached by a young Norwegian, H. J. Bull, who had failed to arouse enthusiasm for Antarctic whaling in Australia, with a request that he should back a whaling and exploring voyage to the Ross Sea, Foyn was sympathetic. The result was that in September 1893 the whaling ship *Antarctic* sailed from Norway under the command of Captain Leonard Kristensen, with H. J. Bull on board. Among the crew of the *Antarctic* was a remarkable young Norwegian C. E. Borch-grevink who had been teaching languages and natural science in Australian schools. He was passionate about exploration and in him Bull found a fellow enthusiast. It was probably due to their joint insistence that the first landing was made on the coast of Victoria Land, a coast which had not been visited since the days of Sir James Clark Ross.

The landing was made on 24 January 1895 near Cape Adare. 'The sensation', wrote Bull, 'of being the first men who had set foot on the real Antarctic mainland was both strange and pleas-urable, although Mr Foyn would no doubt have preferred to exchange this pleasing sensation on our part for a right whale, even of small dimensions.' To commemorate the landing a pole was erected carrying a box painted with the Norwegian flag. Penguins were snatched, screaming and struggling, from a local colony for the naturalists at home; specimens of rock were col-lected for the geologists; and specimens of lichens and seaweed were brought on board in triumphant refutation of Ross's state-ments about the absence of vegetation in Antarctica. But vege-table life was the only sign of life they saw. On the sea-shore, as Bull and Borchgrevink left, there lay two dead seals, their skins hairless, smooth, and hard, preserved by the freezing air. Surely this, Bull thought, was proof that no land mammals could exist, for how could they have overlooked so luscious a meal?

The conclusions which the Norwegians drew from this first landing confirmed all the American Maury's expectations of nearly forty years before. 'During our exploration ashore', they wrote, 'we got a strong impression that the bay at Cape Adare inside the low promontory would provide many advantages as a landing place and station for a new expedition. It is probable, at least, that a vessel moored inside this promontory would lie protected against the outer floes as well as against the ice forming in the bay itself ... among the rocks of Cape Adare, a shelter could be found for a house, and the low promontory would furnish plenty of space for moving about, for an observatory, etc. ... and if by ill luck the relief party did not succeed in fetching away the explorers during the second season, the penguin colony would afford an inexhaustible larder and stock of fuel.' In the mind of one member of the crew of the *Antarctic*, Carl Borchgrevink, there had already formed a determination to put these possibilities to test.

While the *Antarctic*, southward bound, was lurching through heavy seas, there arose in the calm surroundings of the Royal Geographical Society a heated discussion about the revival of British Antarctic exploration. This took place in 1893 after John Murray's eloquent and persuasive address on the discoveries of the *Challenger* expedition and during it various proposals and plans were put forward, the most far-sighted (if one looks ahead to the circumnavigations of the United States Navy in the nineteen-forties) being those advanced by old Sir Joseph Hooker who half a century earlier had been with James Clark Ross in *Erebus*. Hooker proposed an expedition of two ships which would sail clockwise and anti-clockwise round the continent, charting the position of the pack, looking for 'water sky' or open water beyond it, and for possible avenues through the encircling ice. A year spent in such general exploration, he argued, would reveal the points at which a full-scale attack could most profitably be launched. After such matters of strategy had been debated, Murray revealed that he had personally been in communication with geographers and scientists all over the world. All, he declared, and none more so than his colleague the learned and prolific Dr Neumayer of the Marine Observatory, Hamburg, had enthusiastically acclaimed his suggestion that a great scientific expedition to the Antarctic be launched from Britain forthwith.

John Murray had not been alone in his efforts to recruit support for such a British enterprise for his Chairman, the President of the Society, Clements Markham, had also written a great number of letters; to learned societies, to influential men throughout the world and in particular to the Governments of Australia and New Zealand. He had moreover already set to work a committee of the Society to thrash out the best methods of renewing Antarctic exploration.

Markham's part in the Antarctic revival at the end of the nineteenth and early in the twentieth century is comparable with that played by the Society's earlier president John Barrow in promoting the revival of Arctic exploration after Waterloo. His name, no less indeed than that of his personal protégé and chosen leader Robert Falcon Scott, is indissolubly joined with the first great land explorations of the continent and so influential were his interventions, so massive and dominating his role, that some slight sketch of his career and personality is necessary for the understanding of this second great phase of Antarctic history.

Markham was born in 1830, four days after the foundation of the Society whose destinies, as an honorary secretary and as president, he was to govern in unchallenged supremacy for many years. Leaving school at an early age he joined the Navy and served as a midshipman in H.M.S. *Assistance* during the Franklin Search. It was an experience which like Barrow's boyhood voyage on a Greenland whaler inspired a lifelong enthusiasm for polar exploration and delicious memories of those early glorious days lingered with him all his life. Indeed when in later years he began to devote his great energies to the organization of polar affairs it was to the days of Franklin and the Search expeditions that he looked wistfully back, days when ships under billowing sail manned by men who were the pride of the Queen's Navy braved, like their forebears of Elizabethan times, the perils of the polar seas. It was in keeping with his veneration for the old naval tradition in polar exploration that Markham should have been the sturdiest supporter of Nares's Arctic expedition in 1875.

Markham resigned from the Navy at the age of twenty-one and after some adventurous wanderings among the Inca ruins of Peru became a clerk in the India Office. He achieved some

distinction later by leading an expedition to Peru which culminated in the transport of cinchona plants to India and the
establishment there of a flourishing quinine industry. Soon after
his return Clements Markham was elected an honorary officer
of the Royal Geographical Society and with one year of absence
in 1868 when he served as geographer and geologist to Lord
Napier's Abyssinian Expeditionary Force he served the Society
as honorary secretary and finally as president until 1905. In the
varied business of the Society Markham found a congenial outlet for his ambitions, his enthusiasm, and his formidable energy.
An astute committee man, a skilled exponent of all those complicated tactics and subtle manoeuvres whereby a resolute man
with time and patience can gradually gather into his hands the
reins of power, Markham and the Society soon become virtually
synonymous. Though there were doubtless some, casualties
along the line of his forward march to higher office, who found
him dominating, even ruthless, it was probably no bad thing
that the Society should have been ruled by so masterful a president at a time when through it the nation was involved in many
great projects of exploration. In all these projects, in Africa, in
Australia, and in the Arctic in the form of the Nares expedition,
Markham played a powerful though sometimes an invisible
part. However, with Nansen's revelation of the true nature of
the polar basin, the Arctic (which had in any event become
largely a Scandinavian preserve) lost some of its attraction. Towards the turn of the century, therefore, Markham like Murray
and Neumayer, decided to devote himself to the revival of exploration in Antarctica, almost untouched since James Clark
Ross and still the greatest unknown region of the world.

Markham's attitude towards Antarctic exploration, however,
was very different from that of the scientist Murray. Markham
was inspired by the romance of exploration, as he was inspired
by the romance of history, and of heraldry. For him, Antarctica
provided the stage for epic adventures, for episodes of personal
heroism and of national achievement no less glorious than those
of Elizabethan and earlier times which he himself had chron-
icled in flamboyant prose and with small regard for accuracy in
several imposing volumes. In the forefront of this pageant of

Antarctic endeavour there was always the vision of the fighting ships of the Royal Navy and of a splendid renaissance of British naval activity. This he was resolved must be the first result of the new efforts to revive Antarctic exploration.

An excellent opportunity to launch a world-wide appeal on behalf of Antarctic exploration came to Markham in 1895 when in his sixty-sixth year he presided over the meetings in London of the sixth International Geographical Congress. During these, Dr Neumayer of Hamburg read a paper on the past and future of Antarctic exploration, while John Murray and Sir Joseph Hooker gave strong support from the scientific point of view. As the Congress progressed, enthusiasm in favour of a new Antarctic expedition mounted. But the highlight of the proceedings was provided by the young Norwegian C. E. Borchgrevink who, having failed to persuade the Royal Geographical Society to pay his fare from Australia, had succeeded in raising funds for his passage so that he might describe to the Congress his landing at Cape Adare. Borchgrevink's announcement that he had discovered living plants on the coast of Victoria Land raised considerable excitement and altogether his youthful zest and passionate enthusiasm made a great impression, especially on Neumayer, Hooker, and Murray. To them Borchgrevink disclosed his plans for a new expedition which would attempt the first wintering on the mainland.

The climax of these international deliberations took the form of a unanimous resolution addressed to the world. 'The exploration of the Antarctic Regions', the Congress declared, 'is the greatest piece of geographical exploration still to be undertaken.' And it demanded that 'in view of the additions to knowledge in almost every branch of science which would result from such a scientific exploration the Congress recommends that the scientific societies throughout the world should urge in whatever way seems to them most effective, that this work should be undertaken before the close of the century'.

Armed with this impressive testimony of international support Markham for two years bombarded the Treasury and Admiralty with requests for funds to launch an Antarctic expedition manned by officers and men of the British Navy. But to no

avail. In 1897 therefore he turned with undiminished vigour
upon the Council of his own Society and persuaded them with
all the power and eloquence at his command that funds must be
made available from the Society's own modest resources to
launch an expedition on their own. A relatively large sum,
£5,000, was voted and it was agreed that a public appeal should
be made for further support.

No time could have seemed more favourable, no moment
more propitious, for such an appeal to the people of Britain on
behalf of a great national pioneering venture. The eighteen-
nineties was a renascent period, marked by a great quickening
of imagination. It was an era of hope and of action. It was char-
acterized also, perhaps because of that growing sense of personal constriction which seems so often to accompany rapid
industrial expansion and technological advance, by a hunger for
vicarious sensation, for romance by proxy; tastes which were
stimulated, exploited, and fulfilled by writers of current fiction
and above all by the mass journalism of the new 'Yellow Press'.

In literature these psychological needs were met by the works,
for example, of Rider Haggard, of Robert Louis Stevenson, of
Joseph Conrad; by the new romances of science of H. G. Wells;
and, most of all, by the writings of Rudyard Kipling whose
panegyrics of the British pioneer pitting himself against nature
or against barbarism at the ends of the earth recalled to those
then suffering from an overdose of *fin de siècle* the refreshing
spirit of Elizabethan days. More important, however, and especially so in the development of exploration, was the way in which
this hunger for vicarious sensation was catered for by the new
cheap and popular newspapers like the *Daily Mail*. These, because of a nation-wide circulation never before attempted or
achieved, could now bring romance to an increasingly indus-
trialized and urbanized land; a land where in the nineties, with
the first electric trams, tubes, and motor cars, the suburban
sprawl began.

The year 1897 in which Markham launched his public appeal
was also notably auspicious. It was the year of the Diamond
Jubilee, and all London was ablaze with pageantry in triumphant celebration of the greatest of all British adventures, the

adventure of Empire, symbolized in the person of the Queen. Nevertheless, despite these auspicious circumstances, Markham's appeal made little headway. Not even among Colonial premiers attending the First Colonial Conference could he arouse more than a formal interest though, as he did not fail to remind them, it was to just such voyages of exploration and discovery that they owed the territories which they represented. Abroad, however, and in England too in another direction, the agitations of the International Congress bore fruit. In Germany plans for an Antarctic expedition gained considerable support. In Belgium, an expedition promoted by a young lieutenant in the Belgian Navy, Adrien de Gerlache, sailed from Antwerp in 1897. And in that same year the young Norwegian C. E. Borchgrevink, after months of fruitless and disheartening effort in a strange city, found a patron for his Antarctic project in the person of the wealthy magazine proprietor Sir George Newnes.

The Belgian expedition, a parsimonious affair meagrely supported by the Belgian Government and the Belgian Geographical Society and made possible only by a generous donation from Madame Osterreith whose beneficence gained her the title of 'Mère de l'Antarctique', sailed in the *Belgica*, a Norwegian sealer of 250 tons. Among the sailors and scientists there was Roald Amundsen as first mate; an American surgeon and anthropologist Dr Frederick Cook who had joined on failing to promote an American Antarctic expedition; and (among the scientists) a Roumanian and two Poles. Reaching the South Shetlands early in 1898 de Gerlache sailed southwards to the Palmer Archipelago and in the course of some twenty landings carried out important geological and zoological investigations and made the first accurate surveys of the region.

In February the *Belgica* steamed farther south along the coast of Graham Land towards Bellingshausen's Alexander I Land. Twenty miles of impassable pack-ice bounded the coast and it was already late in the season but de Gerlache pushed on until early in March, in 71° 30′ S., just as he tried to turn back to the north, the *Belgica* was beset. In May the long night began and the first winter to be endured by explorers in the Antarctic. On the fifteenth the sun set at noon and disappeared for seventy

days and only the fitful brilliance of the moon or the occasional
glow of the Aurora Australis flooding over the dismal frozen
scene lightened the dejected spirits of the inexperienced men of
the *Belgica*.

Amidst the restless grinding of the floes, churned into violent
motion by frequent storms, the winter passed and in July daylight returned. But it was another six months before the ice re-
laxed its grip on the *Belgica* and then only by blasting and sawing through pack ten feet thick could the ship be released for
her homeward voyage in the spring of 1899. Considering how
inadequate were its resources the de Gerlache expedition was a
remarkable success, for apart from valuable work in the Palmer
Archipelago, it had, due to its unsought sojourn in the ice, been
able to carry out a longer series of continuous scientific observations in the Antarctic than had ever been achieved before.

To Markham whose own project for a National Antarctic
Expedition under the aegis of the Royal Geographical Society
was still held up for lack of funds, the departure of the Belgian
expedition brought little comfort. But the news of Borchgrevink's success the following year, received at the very moment
when Markham was making yet another urgent appeal for
government support, was infinitely less agreeable. Markham
when he first heard at the International Geographical Congress
of Borchgrevink's intention to lead an expedition to the Ross
Sea had realized at once that here was a determined and powerful competitor for the public support which he himself hoped to
gain for his National Antarctic expedition. He therefore used all
his influence to oppose Borchgrevink's ambitions. Admittedly
the latter's support came not from the Government nor from
any learned society but from the magazine proprietor Sir
George Newnes. Nevertheless, that this young man with his
raw colonial ways should have succeeded where he, Markham,
and the Royal Geographical Society had failed was a bitter blow.
Letting it be known that he considered Borchgrevink's ship the
Southern Cross to be unseaworthy, Markham was not among
those who saw her off from the Thames in August 1898.

The man who had come to Borchgrevink's rescue, enabling
him to launch his expedition, was a pioneer of the journalism

which after 1880 began to cater for the new class of reader emerging from the schools created by Forster's Education Act of ten years before. The founder of the weekly *Tit-Bits* and in 1891 of the more serious illustrated *Strand Magazine* Newnes, following Harmsworth's lead in supporting the Jackson expedition to Franz Josef Land, decided to back Borchgrevink for he saw in this first attempt by man to winter on the Antarctic mainland a story of pioneering adventure very much to the taste of the time. Borchgrevink's expedition, however, was by no means a mere journalistic exploit. His scientific staff included Sub-Lieutenant William Colbeck, R.N.R., a highly qualified magnetic observer, navigator, and surveyor; Louis Bernacchi, a Tasmanian trained at the Melbourne Observatory as meteorologist; and as naturalist and zoologist Nicolai Hanson of the British Museum of Natural History. But the expedition was not only well staffed for scientific work. The captain of the *Southern Cross,* a converted Norwegian whaler with new and powerful engines, was the experienced Jensen who had been second mate on the *Antarctic*. And the expedition for the first time in Antarctic history carried dog-teams in charge of two Finnish Lapps.

On 14 January 1899, just as the black pools between the ice floes were turning to blood red under the spreading rays of sunrise, the *Southern Cross* came within sight of the Balleny Islands. Ten days later they were in the thick of the pack with the ship groaning under an ice pressure so intense that Borchgrevink decided to turn back to the north and try again farther to the east. It was a successful manoeuvre. Open water was reached in latitude 70° S. and longitude 174° E. and by 17 February they were in Robertson Bay, off Cape Adare, where Borchgrevink had landed from the *Antarctic* in 1894. Looking up once again at the dark rocks of the Cape named by Sir James Clark Ross, Borchgrevink was deeply conscious that this was a historic moment. 'It was a moment', he wrote, 'which, I believe, will live in the memory of my staff and myself, as we slowly moved towards the low beach whereon man had never attempted to live before. At 11 p.m. for the first time in the world's history, an anchor fell at the last *terra incognita* on the globe.' But there was a striking difference in the scene from when he had last been there. Now the waters of the Bay were almost free from ice and the rocks of the Cape were dark and bare. Only an occasional ice-block stranded on the narrow pebbly beach reminded him of the frozen landscape he had seen five years before.

By 1 March unloading was completed, the Union Jack presented by His Royal Highness the Duke of York was hoisted, and the *Southern Cross* steamed away from Camp Ridley, the first winter camp on the Antarctic mainland. The building of a wooden hut, roofed with canvas and seal-skins weighted with sacks of coal; the setting up of meteorological and magnetic observatories nearby; these were the first tasks in what is now an established routine. Then, before winter set in, Borchgrevink and Bernacchi climbed 3,670 feet to the summit of Cape Adare.

Like the Belgian expedition beset in the pack far to the east, Borchgrevink and his men found their first Antarctic winter a dismal experience. 'During the gradual shortening of the days', Borchgrevink confessed, 'we experienced great depression, as if watching ourselves grow old. We were getting tired of each other's company and began to know every line in each other's faces ... the days were now very dark, though the horizon towards the north-west was slightly crimson. The darkness and the silence in this solitude weighs heavily on one's mind. The silence roars in one's ears. It is centuries of heaped up solitude. ...' For seventy-five days, from 15 May until 29 July, they were in darkness and then to deepen the gloom of their imprisonment Nicolai Hanson, the zoologist, died.

Spring was heralded by a slow and stately procession of penguins returning over the ice to summer quarters and then the first explorations began, confined by the mountain walls of Victoria Land to the vicinity of Robertson Bay. Excellent charting and mapping was done by Colbeck and two great glaciers were explored and gratefully named by Borchgrevink after Sir George Newnes and Sir John Murray who had so encouraged him at the International Geographical Congress. But it was not until 28 January when the *Southern Cross* returned that they could explore farther abroad; to Ross's Coulman Island, across Lady Newnes Bay and farther south into the region round Mount

Erebus and Mount Terror which Borchgrevink named Newnes Land. By the middle of February 1900, with freezing winds coating the *Southern Cross* with ice, they reached the 'Barrier' and by the middle of the month, at a point about longitude 164° W. where the ice cliffs were low above the water, Borchgrevink landed and set out on the first sledging journey across the surface of the Ross Ice Shelf. It was a momentous occasion, the first step towards the great explorations by Scott and Shackleton which during the next ten years were to reveal to a fascinated world the grim majesty of inner Antarctica. Of this first journey over the ice Borchgrevink, in an address to the Royal Geographical Society, surprisingly gave only a brief and laconic account. 'At this place', he stated, 'I affected a landing with sledges, dogs, provisions, and instruments; and leaving the vessel with the rest of the expedition in charge of Captain Jenson, I myself, accompanied by Lieutenant Colbeck and the Finn Savio, proceeded southwards, reaching 78° 50′ S., the farthest south ever reached by man.'

In the summer of 1900 Borchgrevink arrived in England from Australia to present the results of his expedition. These were far from negligible. Colbeck had made the first reliable chart of the edge of the Ice Shelf and showed that it had receded thirty miles since Ross's day; the first live insects had been recorded from the mosses and lichens which stained the rocks of Robertson Bay; and a useful series of observations in meteorology and magnetism had been made. More important than these discoveries, however, was the fact that Borchgrevink· had shown that wintering on the Antarctic continent was physically possible (Hanson's death having been not from exposure or cold but from an intestinal disease). He had shown, moreover, that from Ross's 'Barrier' land journeys into the interior could be made.

Borchgrevink's own reception was not enthusiastic. He was blamed for lack of tact in dealing with his staff; he was blamed for failing to press farther forward into the interior; and his articles in Newnes's magazines describing his adventures in the racy style of the new popular journalism provoked acid comments from eager critics. Nevertheless despite such shortcomings, despite every discouragement, and in the face of the active opposition of the most powerful of polar impresarios, Clements Markham, C. E. Borchgrevink had taken the first steps along the route to the South Pole. As even Clements Markham, in happy allusion to the days of the Franklin Search, was compelled to admit, 'hereafter the Continent may be penetrated by sledges on the principles adopted by McClintock, and important discoveries may be made there'.

SCOTT AND THE *DISCOVERY* EXPEDITION

DIFFICULT as he found it to adjust his mind to the new scientific approach, 'doctrinaire' though he considered the scientific men to be, Markham was well aware that the scientists – men like Murray and Neumayer – were among the most ardent champions of a new Antarctic expedition. He therefore decided to enlist their support through the medium of the national academy of science, the Royal Society, which had for generations advised the Government on all scientific matters, and as a first step in this new direction he invited the Royal Society to summon a special meeting to consider the scientific merits of such an enterprise.

This meeting, attended by Neumayer, Murray, and Sir Joseph Hooker, exceeded all Markham's expectations, so great was the enthusiasm, so numerous and varied the proposals for research. The support of the Royal Society was assured. It was now time to discuss operational plans. For the Royal Society, John Murray was the obvious spokesman; for the Royal Geographical Society, it could have been none other than Clements Markham himself.

At the start all went smoothly enough and Markham agreed broadly with Murray's outline plan. This was for an expedition of two ships which, after landing a wintering party on the shores of Bismarck Strait, Graham Land, would sail for Victoria Land. There, in McMurdo Sound, in the shadow of Mount Erebus, the principal base would be established for two Antarctic seasons. The ships themselves were not to winter; they would return to pick up both wintering parties in the third season, having spent the interval in refitting and in oceanographical observations.

The aims of the expedition, conceived on a grand scale, were to be exploration and research. The nature and extent of the continent was to be determined, its interior deeply probed.

The depth of the great ice sheet was to be discovered and the movements and composition of the ice were to be investigated. Observations were to be carried out in meteorology and magnetism, and gravity measurements were to be made. 'All this', Murray had earlier said, 'should be the work of a modern Antarctic expedition. . . .' Although the expedition would be expected to thrust forward into the interior, the South Pole should not be its goal. 'A dash at the South Pole', Murray declared, 'is not however what I now advocate, nor do I believe that is what British science at the present time desires. It demands rather a steady, continuous, laborious, and systematic exploration of the whole southern region with all the appliances of the modern investigator.'

To Clements Markham, this very sober analysis no doubt sounded a trifle anaemic but it was not here that their principal difference lay. This emerged as they began to discuss the composition of the wintering parties and in particular the leadership of the expedition. Markham favoured a predominantly naval expedition for work both on land and at sea. Murray, however, believed that the wintering parties should largely be composed of civilians who would, under the leadership of a civilian scientist, be entrusted with the scientific work. This division of responsibility between the Navy and civilian scientists had, Murray knew, worked admirably on the *Challenger* expedition. Why should it not work again? To Markham, however, who had behind him the admirals of the Royal Geographical Society, the mere suggestion that naval men, even though working on land, should be led by a civilian was anathema. On land as on the sea, he insisted, only to a naval officer could the safety of naval men be entrusted. It was more than a passing difference of opinion. It was a fundamental difference in approach which was soon to lead to an open breach between the two parties of the enterprise.

This, however, was not the only difference between Murray and Markham during their discussions about the organization of the National Antarctic Expedition. Murray maintained that only when funds sufficient to cover the whole cost of the expedition had been assured should any expenditure be incurred.

Markham again disagreed. If money to equip one ship could be collected, why, he demanded, should they not go ahead? No doubt there was logic in this argument. If discoveries came up to expectations, public enthusiasm would be aroused; if on the other hand some disaster befell them, was it conceivable that the Government would not come to the rescue of a naval and national expedition? Based though it may have been on such practical considerations, Murray found Markham's proposal unpalatable and from that moment he withdrew unobtrusively from further discussion of the arrangements.

Unruffled by these early dissensions Markham pursued his own undeviating way. Following the recommendations of the International Geographical Congress, he coordinated plans with Professor Erich von Drygalski's German expedition which was preparing to explore to the south of Kerguelen Island and with the organizers of a Swedish expedition destined for the Weddell Sea which was to be led by Otto Nordenskjöld, nephew of the conqueror of the North-East Passage. Then, despite his disagreements with John Murray, he secured the appointment of a joint committee of the Royal Society and the Royal Geographical Society. By 1899 he had succeeded in raising towards the cost of the expedition the sum of £15,000.

The Government still showed no signs of willingness to help either with money or with men but Markham's fund was now rapidly and handsomely augmented by gifts from two members of the Royal Geographical Society's Council. The first, for £25,000 – more than twice the cost of the *Belgica* expedition – came from Mr Llewellyn Longstaff, one of those generous benefactors of exploration whom Victorian capitalism had bred. The second large subscription came from Alfred Harmsworth, later Lord Northcliffe, who a few years earlier had financed the Jackson-Harmsworth expedition. The role of the Press as supporters of exploration has been so considerable in the twentieth century that Alfred Harmsworth, a pioneer in this field as far as Britain is concerned, deserves more than a passing reference in any survey of polar history. The founder of the first newspapers with a mass circulation, the *Evening News*, the *Daily Mail*, and, in 1904, the first illustrated daily newspaper, the

Daily Mirror, Harmsworth had brought about no less than a journalistic revolution. He had borrowed a good deal of his journalistic technique from the United States and it is interesting to recall in connexion with the serialization in his newspapers of articles from the polar regions that in America, James Gordon Bennett, owner and editor of the *New York Herald* and a member of the council of the American Geographical Society, had been the first, thirty years before, to provide first-hand accounts of exploration for his readers. These journalistic developments whereby that new phenomenon 'the man in the street' could follow daily the exploits of his countrymen in remote and dangerous regions had a twofold effect on polar exploration. On the one hand, the newspapers came to be in a powerful position to stimulate public interest and support. They were, moreover, able to provide large subscriptions to expeditions in return for exclusive articles. On the other hand, such articles were bound, if they were to satisfy popular demand, to be concerned with adventure rather than with research. For the more scientifically minded promoter or leader of an expedition this was sometimes a source of embarrassment for, valuable though the financial support of the newspapers was, there was the danger that it might compel an excessive emphasis on the adventurous side of exploration, on record-making journeys, on dashes to the Poles, rather than on less sensational scientific work. It was, moreover, a danger, or at least a dilemma, which became increasingly acute as not only the newspapers but the film, radio, and television moved into the field of polar exploration towards the middle of the twentieth century.

But to turn back to Clements Markham. With considerable funds now in hand and with the backing of the Royal Society, he once again approached the Treasury and they, impressed perhaps by such evidence of public and scientific support and no doubt by this time more than a little weary from such a continuous and intense bombardment, agreed to contribute £45,000, a sum equal to the total Markham had already collected. For Markham, this was a victory amply deserved and he immediately set about the selection of a ship and a leader. The matter of the ship was quickly settled for the Admiralty were prevailed upon to design a new wooden ship, the steam barque *Discovery*, and building started at once in Dundee. The problem of the leader was a more complicated and a more controversial matter.

Markham's own account in his *Lands of Silence* of how Robert Falcon Scott, then aged twenty-eight, came to be chosen reveals for how long he had been brooding over the prospect of a great naval Antarctic expedition. 'I had selected', he wrote, 'the fittest commander in my own mind in 1887, when I was on board the *Active* in the West Indies, the guest of my cousin Commodore Markham. . . . When we were at St Kitts, 1 March 1887, the lieutenants got up a service cutter race. The boats were to be at anchor with awnings spread. They were to get under way and make sail, beat up to windward for a mile, round a buoy, down mast and sail, pull down to the starting point, anchor, and spread awning again. The race tried several qualities. For a long time it was a close thing between two midshipmen, Robert Falcon Scott and Hyde Parker. However, Scott won the race and on the 5th he dined with us. He was then eighteen and I was much struck with his intelligence, information, and the charm of his manner.'

Indeed Scott was Markham's *beau idéal* of a young British naval officer, closely moulded by the training and discipline of a service to whose traditions he was dedicated with an almost religious fervour. When therefore Scott and Markham met by chance in a London street in June 1899, the meeting seemed to Markham providential. Here, just as the question of leadership of the Antarctic expedition was about to be decided, was the man of his choice. For Scott, too, the meeting seemed exceptionally fortunate. A young torpedo lieutenant, ambitious, on the alert for new opportunities, for new ways of advancement quicker than the routine channels of promotion seemed ever likely to provide, he saw in Markham's suggestion that he should apply for the post not only the chance of achieving rapid professional distinction but a splendid opportunity of enhancing through polar service, as many a British naval officer had done before him, the prestige of the Country and the Navy. Two days after his meeting with Markham, Scott applied for the post of leader of the National Antarctic Expedition.

Until this meeting Scott had never seen himself as a polar explorer. But he had ample time for reflection, for a year passed while committees discussed and the Admiralty considered his application. Meanwhile he returned to his ship, the *Majestic*, flagship of the Channel Fleet. Then in June 1900 he was promoted commander and a month later the post was his.

Scott, establishing at once his own high standards of professional efficiency, went furiously to work, bent on mastering all aspects of the expedition, including the plans for scientific research. He was by no means without technical and scientific training – the torpedo in which he had specialized was the most modern development of naval science – and in his grasp of scientific matters he showed a remarkable and to some a surprising quickness and ability. The most urgent task however was the selection of the members of the expedition and here those divergencies began to emerge among his employers on the Joint Committee just as they had emerged in the conversations between Markham and Murray. The Joint Committee envisaged only a small naval nucleus but both Markham and Scott would have preferred a predominantly naval expedition. In favour of this there was not only the general advantage voiced by Markham's Special Antarctic Committee (echoing Sir John Barrow) that 'apart from the valuable scientific results of an Antarctic expedition, great importance must be attached to the excellent effect that all such undertakings . . . have invariably had on the Navy. . . .' There was Scott's decided preference for a purely naval party. 'From an early date', he subsequently admitted, 'I had set my mind on obtaining a naval crew. I felt sure that their sense of discipline would be an immense acquisition, and I had grave doubts as to my ability to deal with any other class of men.'

In the end three officers of the Royal Navy were appointed, Royds, Skelton, and Barne. Then Markham intervened with a new proposal. By the 'Navy', Scott meant the 'Royal Navy' but Markham now added two officers of the Merchant Navy, one with previous knowledge of Arctic ice conditions, the other an expert in the handling of sails, a skill still essential in Antarctic conditions, as Markham knew. The first was Lieutenant Albert B. Armitage of the Peninsular and Oriental Line who had been a member of the Jackson-Harmsworth expedition. The second, Ernest Henry Shackleton, was a junior officer who had spent much of his roving and adventurous life in sailing ships; he was given a sub-lieutenant's commission in the Royal Naval Reserve. The first appearance of Shackleton on the polar scene is a curious occasion in that there was thus introduced, through the agency of Scott's own patron, the man who was to become Scott's greatest personal rival in Antarctic exploration.

The scientists were the next to be selected: Dr Koettlitz who had been, like Armitage, a member of the Jackson-Harmsworth expedition; Dr Edward Wilson, a biologist and a painter and draughtsman of unusual skill; and three other scientists, one of them, the physicist Louis Bernacchi, member of Borchgrevink's *Southern Cross* expedition, the only man who had ever been to the Antarctic before. A naturalist was needed and the post was offered to W. S. Bruce but he with the support of rich industrialists from Paisley was organizing a Scottish National Expedition to the Weddell Sea. So T. V. Hodgson of the Plymouth Biological Station was appointed and the scientific staff was completed by the selection (at the instigation of the Royal Society) of a geologist, Professor J. W. Gregory, whose work on the Great Rift Valley of Africa had brought him world renown.

No sooner had *Discovery* been launched by Mrs Clements Markham than a violent dispute broke out between the two societies about the leadership of the land parties. The Royal Society assumed, as indeed Gregory himself had assumed, that he, as the appointed leader of the scientific staff, would be in charge of all land explorations because he was after all not only a distinguished scientist but an explorer of long experience. But Markham would have none of it. Then as H. R. Mill, the historian of the Royal Geographical Society, describes, 'at the eleventh hour the crisis passed. Gregory resigned from the expedition, the centre of gravity of which shifted from research to adventure. This change did not mean that scientific work was suspended, merely that it was placed on a lower level in the general plan.' Despite this shift of emphasis, the scientific side was well looked after. The staff was reorganized by George Murray, Keeper of Botany at the British Museum, a geologist and a physicist were added, special training was given in magnetism, oceanography, and meteorology, and when the *Discovery* expedition sailed from Cowes in August 1901 it was probably better equipped for scientific work on land and sea than any previous expedition.

The *Discovery*'s destination was the Ross Sea where Scott's immediate tasks were to explore the Ice Shelf and to discover the mountainous land eastwards of it which James Clark Ross thought he had seen. But *Discovery* was a slow ship, carrying sails in order to economize in coal, and it was not until 1 January 1902, after visiting Australia and New Zealand, that she reached the pack almost on the Antarctic Circle. Though legally she was a merchant vessel, life on board during the slow outward voyage was governed by strict naval discipline. Ward-room and messdeck, to Shackleton's amusement, messed apart. No detail affecting the order of the ship or the behaviour of officers and men escaped the stern and meticulous eye of the young commander.

In little more than a week, *Discovery* was through the pack and off Cape Adare where Borchgrevink had landed. Then came the voyage southwards along the mountainous coast of Victoria Land through drifting ice towards the historic landmark Mount Erebus, proudly displaying her plume of smoke. After a landing there and another at Cape Crozier, *Discovery* turned eastwards, coasting along the front of the Ross Ice Shelf which in height as in depth, as Borchgrevink had found, had greatly diminished since Ross's day. Sailing beyond the limit reached by Ross to about 150° W., Scott saw in the distance the now bare rocks of the mountains which Ross had seen. He called the new territory King Edward VII Land. Dense pack-ice prohibited any close approach so Scott turned westwards again towards the inlet in the Ice Shelf ('Discovery Inlet') where Borchgrevink and his dog-teams had landed.

Here, where the lip of the great Ice Shelf was no more than fifteen feet above the level of the sea, Armitage and a sledging party landed. Scott meanwhile prepared for a reconnaissance by a new and exciting method, reconnaissance from a captive balloon. The Swedish explorer Baron Nordenskiöld had given much thought to the use of captive balloons for reconnaissance in the Arctic but the suggestion that Scott should use one came from old Sir Joseph Hooker. The balloon, a small Army balloon presented by an enthusiastic lady supporter of the expedition, could only take one passenger and Scott, in some trepidation, went up alone on this first Antarctic ascent. 'As I swayed about in what appeared a very inadequate basket', he wrote, 'and gazed down on the rapidly diminishing figures below, I felt some doubt as to whether I had been wise in my choice.' The balloon rose 500 feet, hovered, sagged uncertainly, then as Scott remembered to throw out the sandbags (not one by one but all together) it shot up to 800 feet and from this altitude, anchored only by the thin wire rope, he saw how the ice shelf rose steadily towards the south in a series of long and parallel undulations, alternating bands of light and shadow marking each rise and fall. Far away in the distance, eight miles away Scott calculated, Armitage and his party could be seen as black dots moving microscopically over the monotonous grey of the snow. After Shackleton had ascended to photograph this future field of exploration, Scott steamed westwards up McMurdo Sound to Ross Island to prepare for the first Antarctic winter.

Scott and his men did not winter on land as Borchgrevink had done. They wintered on the ship like Parry and his men off Melville Island, though there were observation huts on shore, on the south-western corner of Ross Island, and store huts sufficient to accommodate the whole expedition in case ice crushed *Discovery* at her winter moorings.

Then began a period of intensive training for the first sledge journeys the following spring. Skiing, sledging, the handling and feeding of dogs, all this had to be learnt from the beginning for although Scott and Markham, on a brief visit to Norway, had sought the advice of Nansen and Amundsen, these British sailors, stumbling heavily over the ice, bruised from innumerable falls, were the rawest of recruits by comparison with the Scandinavians used from childhood to speeding swiftly over the snows. But control over the dogs was their greatest problem. At the merest touch of their inexperienced hands, it seemed, an apparently docile dog-team would be transformed into a welter of snarling animals and tangled harness, exhausting their patience and defying their most ingenious efforts to restore discipline and peace. Man-hauling in the old traditional style soon appeared not only more reliable but infinitely preferable to these refractory and unpredictable beasts.

On 23 April 1902 the sun sank at noon, to disappear for four months. There was plenty, apart from work, to keep the men from moping during the winter darkness. Shackleton, a voracious reader, recited poetry, preferably the poems of his favourite Robert Browning, in an engaging Irish brogue, and having something of a flair for journalism, edited the *South Polar Times*, the lineal descendant of Sabine's *Winter Chronicle and North Georgia Gazette* on Parry's first North-West Passage Expedition. This was illustrated by the delicate drawings and water-colour sketches of Wilson, the first of many paintings and sketches by him which catch so dexterously not only the brilliant hues and changing lights but the darker, harsher moods of Antarctica. Another more boisterous publication was *The Blizzard*, now a collector's piece among Antarctic bibliophiles.

Midwinter's Day (which in fact was not celebrated until August) was marked by the opening of the Royal Terror Theatre, featuring as its first performance 'Ticket of Leave, a screaming comedy in one act', followed by a Nigger Minstrel Show, and one is reminded again of Parry and his men and of Lieutenant Beechey's Arctic production of 'Miss in her Teens' off the coast of Melville Island. Then for two months all hands concentrated on preparing for the first of the great land journeys in Antarctic exploration. The starting date was 2 November 1902, the time 10 a.m., when Scott, Wilson, and Shackleton set out with three sledges and all nineteen dogs on their first thrust across the 'Barrier'. For Scott, his mind constantly preoccupied with every detail of the preparations, it was a tense and anxious moment. As he well knew, he and his men were mere beginners in this business with equipment virtually untested, and what lay beyond in the way of weather or physical obstacles was quite unknown. Even the eternally optimistic Shackleton, jovial, buoyant, picturing already in his mind a triumphant return from the South Pole to permanent fame and fortune, had occasional misgivings.

On 15 November the last of the supporting parties which had been laying supply depots along the return route turned back towards the ship and the three men marched on alone for fifty-nine days, making fifteen miles or more each day but sometimes no more than five over the corrugated and often deeply snow-drifted surface of the ice shelf. In latitude 82° 17′ S., 380 miles beyond the point reached by Borchgrevink and within sight of a great mountain range far to the south, Scott decided they must return for he saw how the strain was telling. But the greater test was to come on their homeward journey. One by one their dogs died or had to be shot and to Scott, who had already found the slaughter of seals for dog-food an unbearable sight, this was a deeply painful and indeed unforgettable experience. On the homeward journey, hunger began to weaken them for their rations had been cut to a minimum and the depots, when they reached them, proved quite inadequately stocked. Snow-blindness attacked first one then the other and then, worst of all, scurvy set in, so seriously in Shackleton's case, with haemorrhage and breathlessness and paroxysms of coughing, that Scott had to forbid him to pull on the march. With Scott and Wilson pulling alone, and Shackleton keeping pace only by an immense effort of will, the ship was reached on 3 February 1903 after an absence of ninety-three days.

Much had happened during their absence. Skelton and Armitage had ascended a great glacier to the west of Ross Island – the Ferrar Glacier – to a height of 9,000 feet and there in latitude 78° S., they found themselves on a summit of a mountain range continuous with the mountains of Victoria Land, and joined, it seemed likely, with the distant mountains seen far to the south by Scott and his ice shelf party. This range of mountains buttressed a vast plateau of ice and snow which stretched out endlessly before them.

No less heartening as Scott, Shackleton, and Wilson approached Ross Island was the sight of the relief ship, the *Morning*, lying out beyond the ice in which *Discovery* was still locked. The dispatch of the *Morning* had been a personal triumph for Clements Markham and the Council of the Royal Geographical Society, for after the departure of the *Discovery* for the Antarctic

the joint committee of the two societies, the scene of so much
argument about the leadership of the land parties, had dissolved
and Markham had been left with the truly formidable task of
raising no less than £50,000 to equip the relief expedition. His
very eloquent allusions to the courage, the fortitude, and the
patriotism of the men isolated in Antarctica had left the Treasury
unmoved. New Zealand, with an eye perhaps to her future Ross
Dependency, had contributed, but no more than £1,000. It was
therefore left to Markham and the Royal Geographical Society
to raise almost the entire sum. The *Morning*, a Norwegian ship,
was purchased in November 1901; Captain Colbeck, the experienced first mate of the *Southern Cross* was in command; and
with Mr Rupert England, Lieutenant G. F. A. Mulock, R.N.,
and Lieutenant E. G. R. Evans, R.N. (later 'Evans of the *Broke*'
and Admiral Lord Mountevans) as officers, she sailed in November the following year. Markham, jubilant, celebrated his success
by composing an anthem, which was set to martial music,
entitled 'Intrepid Souls'.

> Intrepid Souls have these men I ween
> Who brave the Antarctic cold
> No dangers that threaten their lives are seen
> When they seek the brave and bold
>
> Seeking where the lost have been
> *Discovery*'s masts will soon be seen.
>
> Soon the *Morning* will start and the time draweth nigh
> To sail o'er the ice-clad main
> When they'll seek around with a watchful eye
> Nor at any toil complain.
>
> Seeking where the lost have been
> Brave Scott and his crew will yet be seen.

The joy with which the *Morning* was received at Hut Point,
however, was overshadowed by Scott's carefully weighed decision, based on medical advice, that he must send Shackleton
home. 'It has been a great blow to poor Shackleton', he wrote in

his diary, and Shackleton admitted years afterwards that it had indeed been the bitterest disappointment of his life. Physically, he appeared more robust than any on the expedition. Throughout his roving youthful life, he had in the barbaric conditions of sailing ships been accustomed to endure hardships and face dangers greater than any his companions had experienced. Yet it was he and not they who had been compelled to fill the humiliating role of passenger on the return sledge journey. This was not only a deeply wounding blow to his pride, it was a shattering of all those hopes of fame and fortune with which, in this new popular age of polar exploration, an admiring people and a grateful government seemed very likely to reward the victorious explorer. However, the order had been given and Shackleton, though he was convinced that a month would have seen him fit, surrendered his place to Lieutenant Mulock of the *Morning*. Psychologically it was the most critical moment in his career for, as he embarked disconsolately on board the *Morning*, he was filled with an intense determination to return. Next time he would return in triumph. Nothing less than the attainment of the Pole itself would compensate for this undeserved and humiliating retreat from Antarctica.

In October 1903, at the close of Scott's second winter, the land journeys started again and on 30th November Scott ascended another great glacier to the west and saw, as Skelton and Armitage had seen the year before, the infinite sweep of the polar plateau, lifeless, featureless, its grey monotonous surface merging imperceptibly with sullen skies. Far to the south lay the Pole. Once again the dogs failed them and much of the journey which carried them this time three hundred miles from the ship was made man-hauling sledges over the precipitous and tumbled ice slopes, hauling breathlessly with webbing harness round their waists and with braces over the shoulders, up and down through the thin and stifling air of the glacier.

At home, meanwhile, anxiety was growing about the expedition. And Markham especially, aged seventy-three and less vigorous and confident now after three years of constant work and worry, was seriously alarmed by Colbeck's report that he had left the *Discovery* frozen in. Supposing that during the coming second summer there was once again no break-up of the ice, what then would happen if he and the Society, as seemed all too likely, failed to raise the large sums required to fit out another relief expedition? It was a frightening prospect, so alarming indeed that Markham decided that even the Government this time might relent and come to the rescue of the National Antarctic expedition. The Government's reaction was swift, decisive, and in several respects astonishing and H. R. Mill, a contemporary, in his *Record of the Royal Geographical Society, 1830–1930*, has left a succinct though restrained account of the proceedings. 'Mr Balfour, then Prime Minister', he records, 'was roused from his usual philosophic calm. He made caustic remarks in the House of Commons on the way in which he conceived that the Government has been misled from the first as to the cost of the expedition. He sent an ultimatum to the Society, demanding the instant handing over of the *Morning*, and taking the rescue of the *Discovery* out of its hands, as the Admiralty was undertaking to bring back the naval members of the expedition.' There were many among Markham's colleagues who found these pungent disclosures uncomfortable. But Markham was unabashed. Had he not in his earlier conversations with John Murray firmly held to the belief that once sufficient funds to launch the expedition had been found, the rest would follow?

The Admiralty's arrangements for the new relief expedition were wasteful and extravagant to the point of absurdity. Not content with only the *Morning*, they purchased a Dundee whaler, the *Terra Nova*, and employed Shackleton to supervise her stores. They then rushed her out to New Zealand not under her own steam but towed by relays of warships through the Mediterranean, through the Suez Canal, and through the Indian Ocean. Scott meanwhile was wholly unaware of these hectic and extraordinary activities and when on 5 January 1904 the ships arrived at the ice edge with peremptory orders to him to abandon ship and return at once with his men, this proclamation he says 'descended on us like a bolt from the blue'. Confronted by this demand, of all demands the most intolerable to the captain of a ship, that he should thus precipitately abandon the *Discovery* to the mercy of the still encircling ice, Scott had no choice but to obey and the laborious work of carrying, piece by piece, stores and instruments and scientific collections ten miles across the ice to where the relief ships lay was gloomily begun. But all the while he was watching intently for the slightest sign of a break-up of the ice and early in February some thawing could be seen. Slowly, the *Discovery* edged forward until only six miles separated the ships. Then she was stopped. But there was some hope now that by ramming, sawing, and the use of explosives the ice might be loosened enough to enable her to get through before the new winter ice grew round her. The crews of all three ships then set to work. By 12 February there were three miles to go. On the 14th only yards remained. On the 16th, one last explosion and the *Discovery* was free. On 5 March, after a sojourn of two years and two months on the mainland, the expedition crossed the Antarctic Circle, the *Discovery* moving at a snail's pace, eking out the miserable allowance of coal which was all that the Admiralty's elaborate relief arrangements could supply.

Scott, after a long slow voyage round Cape Horn during which many oceanographical observations were made, returned triumphantly to England and on 7 November 1904 gave an account of his achievements to a crowded audience in the Albert Hall. His was a proud record. The great Ice Shelf had been followed to its eastern end beyond the limit reached by Ross. King Edward VII Land had been discovered. A range of mountains had been found stretching far southwards and buttressing a vast plateau and this Armitage had penetrated to 130 miles at an elevation of 9,000 feet while Scott, Shackleton, and Wilson, pushing forward towards its south-western base, reached 82° 17′ S., 207 miles beyond the previous 'farthest south'. In the second season Scott himself had ascended to the great plateau and penetrated even more deeply southwards. During both seasons a massive accumulation of scientific observations was made. Their subsequent publication in a series of magnificent volumes remains to this day a tribute to the great stride forward made by the expedition in the development of Antarctic science.

The large audience in the arena of the Albert Hall (including the American Ambassador) listened entranced to Scott's story.

The screen upon which the lantern projected photographs of the expedition's dramatic discoveries was flanked on both sides by the sledge flags of all the officers designed, as Mill records, 'by Sir Clements Markham with loving care according to strict heraldic rules'. To Markham the evening was the triumphant climax to all his efforts, not least because the expedition (to quote Mill again) 'had proved, to the delight of its promoter, that the officers and men of the British Navy could still go almost anywhere and do almost anything'. His monumental work accomplished he retired the following year from the presidency of the Royal Geographical Society.

The drama of Scott's first expedition must not be allowed to obscure the achievements of other, less sensational, expeditions at work simultaneously in the Antarctic with all of whose organizers Markham had been in touch following the exhortations of the International Geographical Congress. These were the German expedition of Professor von Drygalski; the Swedish expedition led by Dr Otto Nordenskjöld; the Scottish National Antarctic expedition led by the young Edinburgh naturalist W. S. Bruce; and finally the French expedition led by the scientist Dr Jean Charcot through whose initiative France returned to the Antarctic for the first time since Dumont d'Urville. Scientifically, the Swedish expedition was the most illuminating. All, their aims being severely scientific, form an interesting contrast to the *Discovery* Expedition.

The German expedition in which the scientist Drygalski was in charge both by land and sea was supported wholly by the Imperial Government. Sailing in the *Gauss*, named after the famous German mathematician whose calculations of the probable position of the South Magnetic Pole James Clark Ross had set out to confirm, Drygalski called at his base at Kerguelen Island where an observatory was being built and then made for the mainland in the general direction of Knox coast. Land was sighted in February 1902 but proved unapproachable, so magnetic and astronomical observatories built of ice blocks were established on the floes off the coast. The following spring sledging parties advanced across the ice towards a black hill fifty miles away on the mainland and here Drygalski, like Scott, used a captive balloon and ascended to fifteen hundred feet to photograph the distant and gently rising polar plateau. The land he named Kaiser Wilhelm II Land, a name retained today, and after another winter and more scientific journeys in the spring, the *Gauss* returned to Cape Town in February 1903.

Nordenskjöld's Swedish expedition, supported wholly by Swedish philanthropists, arose out of his work as a geologist in Tierra del Fuego when he developed the theory that the southern tip of South America was geologically connected with the northernmost extremity of Graham Land. After an unsuccessful attempt to penetrate the Weddell Sea in the same steam whaler, the *Antarctic*, which had carried Borchgrevink to Cape Adare, Nordenskjöld spent two winters in the north of Graham Land. The *Antarctic* foundered in the ice on her way to bring out the party, but the Swedes were rescued by an Argentine naval vessel which appeared by a strange coincidence on the very day on which the captain and five men of the *Antarctic* staggered into the camp, having made their way over the sea ice from the islet on which they and the entire ship's company had successfully survived the winter.

The rescue of Nordenskjöld and his men had provided the motive for Jean Charcot's expedition but when he heard that they were safe he turned to the exploration of Alexander Land and of the west coast of the Graham Land peninsula. Alexander Land proved no more accessible than it had been in Bellingshausen's day but between 1903 and 1905 Charcot charted many of the islands of the Palmer Archipelago and the British maps of this section of the Falkland Island Dependencies owe much to this first voyage by a French explorer whose subsequent explorations were to win for France great distinction in Antarctica.

In terms of discovery, the most ambitious of these expeditions was the Scottish Antarctic Expedition led by a fervent Scot and dedicated scientist, W. S. Bruce, into the unknown and dangerous Weddell Sea. Bruce who had served as a naturalist on the steam whaler *Balaena* in 1893 and had been a member of the Harmsworth–Jackson Franz Josef Land expedition, had recently taken part in a summer expedition to Spitsbergen supported by a man with whom he became close friends, the rich industrialist Mr Andrew Coats of Paisley. Bruce now enlisted the wealth of the Coats family in aid of his new and ambitious venture and by February 1903 in a Norwegian steam whaler renamed the *Scotia* he crossed the Antarctic Circle and moved freely into the Weddell Sea. But in 70° S., the *Scotia* was beset, escaped, and made for the north to find a harbour for the winter in Scotia Bay, on Laurie Island in the South Orkneys. When the *Scotia* left in November 1903 for her second attempt on the Weddell Sea, a meteorological party, later replaced from Argentina, was left behind.

This time the *Scotia* penetrated the rotating pack-ice of the Weddell Sea with no great difficulty and reached 74° S. in 22° W., slightly to the east of James Weddell's 'farthest south' early in the nineteenth century. Beyond, land could be seen, low and flat and featureless with a coastline of cleanly and deeply sculpted ice cliffs akin to those seen on the far side of the continent by Biscoe, Wilkes, Ross, and others. These were the termination of the great downpouring of ice from the central highlands which John Murray had so vividly described, and the source of the icebergs and ice islands of the Antarctic seas. No landing could be made, indeed no approach was possible nearer than two miles, but Bruce named the new territory Coats Land after James and Andrew Coats of Paisley. And Coats Land it is today, an inhospitable land but, with open water off its coast, a welcome sight to the few explorers, Filchner, Shackleton, Sir Vivian Fuchs, and a few more who have succeeded in reaching it through the ice of the Weddell Sea.

But Bruce's Scottish expedition will not only be remembered by this new and large addition to the Antarctic coastline. Failing to obtain support from his own government for the maintenance of the meteorological station on Laurie Island, Bruce handed this over to the Argentine Republic. It was an act of some significance in the subsequent political history of Antarctica for it provided a starting point for Argentina's future assertion of sovereignty over Laurie Island (and by extension over the South Orkneys as a whole) in defiance of earlier British claims.

PART IV

THE HEROIC AGE

THE CONQUEST OF THE NORTH POLE

WHEN the American Ambassador Mr Choate addressed Scott's audience in the Albert Hall on 7 November 1904, he declared, 'If you will only let Captain Scott continue his great work and complete the map of the world by planting the Union Jack upon the South Pole and let our Peary proceed with his disciplined followers and plant the Stars and Stripes upon the North Pole, why then you will make the two ends of the great world meet and leave the globe that we inhabit as it properly should be – in the warm and fraternal embrace of the Anglo-Saxon race.'

It was a timely preface to the events of the next eight years when the eyes of the public throughout the world were focused on the race for the poles. The scientists might say, as indeed they never tired of saying, that the geographical poles were no more than mathematical points in space, that their attainment could add little or nothing to human knowledge. To the public, however, and notably to the people of Britain, a country where the intellectual impact of science appeared to be imposing an increasingly materialistic and impersonal pattern of life, the prospect of these heroic and intensely personal endeavours was most exhilarating.

The nineties, it has been said, 'was a decade pre-eminently of the magazine supermen'. The same might be said of the first decade of the twentieth century which saw the beginning of what has often been called the 'Heroic Age' of polar exploration. The creation of the Heroic Age and of the concept of the polar hero owed much to the new journalism, to those newspapers and magazines with mass circulations which were greatly aided early in the twentieth century in the distribution of news by the telegram and the wireless message. Through these new means of national and international publicity, denied to the explorers of an earlier age, the polar leader could now become almost overnight a public hero, his name a household word. For many indeed, absorbed by the story of his romantic adventures, he became a dream figure with whom they could happily identify themselves in brief moments of escape from the new imprisonment of urban life.

Of the men who were to enjoy this new and widespread notoriety – Scott and Shackleton, Peary and Amundsen – none was more obsessed by his ambition to conquer, as he expressed it, 'the last great geographical prize' than the American Arctic explorer Robert E. Peary. From 1886 when he made the first of many expeditions to Greenland he had been fitting himself and perfecting his technique and equipment with this single end in view and in January 1897, on the eve of his *Windward* expedition of 1898–1902 , he openly avowed that his plan had 'for its main purpose the attainment of the North Pole'. Clements Markham had expressed the views of many explorers when he said 'Since Nansen's discovery that the Pole is in an ice-covered sea there is no longer any special object to be attained in going there'. But Peary's approach was different. He had no interest in scientific work. He was an engineer and a technologist, a military planner concerned with the strategy, tactics, and logistics of his polar campaign. However illuminating Nansen's geographical discoveries may have been, all that mattered to Peary was that Nansen had failed to reach the Pole.

The main achievement of Peary's first year of work, made the more anxious as we have seen by his fear that Otto Sverdrup might forestall him, was the establishment of an advanced base at Fort Conger, at the north-east corner of Ellesmere Island. Travelling according to plan through the darkness and cold of winter when the ice was hardest Peary reached Fort Conger by January 1899. By the autumn of that year fourteen tons of supplies had been deposited between Fort Conger and his ship the *Windward* which had been unable to approach any nearer because of the ice of Smith Sound. In the spring of 1900 further supplies were brought up until the base was fully stocked for the attempt on the Pole.

The first problem was the choice of a route. Fort Conger had one great advantage, that of flexibility, for from it there was the choice of two routes to the Pole; from Grant Land, the northern coastal district of Ellesmere Island on the west, or from Greenland on the east. Peary chose the Greenland route, arguing that if he failed to advance towards the Pole he could fall back on an exploration of the unknown Greenland coast east of Cape Washington, the limit reached by Lockwood of the Greeley Expedition. In the end, however, he decided to do this first. Only when he had reached Cape Morris Jessus (Kap Morris Jesup) in Peary Land and had thus identified the northernmost point of Greenland, did he turn northwards towards the Pole.

It was, even by Peary's rigorous standards, 'frightful going' in fog and over wave-like drifts of snow and he was soon forced to turn back. The attempt on the Pole had been a failure. But there was some compensation for Peary's supporters in the discovery of one hundred and fifty miles of new Greenland coast and in his justifiable claim that he had 'determined the northern limit of the Greenland archipelago or land group, and had practically connected the coast southward to Independence Bay'.

Meanwhile far to the east in Franz Joseph Land new competitors for polar honours appeared in an Italian expedition led by Prince Luigi Amadeo of Savoy, the Duke of Abruzzi, the distinguished Himalayan explorer and mountaineer. Inspired by Nansen's attempt to reach the Pole across the ice of the Arctic Basin, the Italians arrived in Franz Josef Land in 1899 in a Norwegian sealer, the *Stella Polare*. The following year, Abruzzi being incapacitated by severe frostbite, the leadership of the polar assault party fell to Lieutenant Cagni of the Italian Navy who set off with two supporting parties. One of these parties never returned. But Cagni and his men surpassed Nansen's farthest north by twenty-two miles and reached within 220 miles of the Pole. It was a gallant attempt magnificently led and the Italians were exultant. 'We have conquered! We have surpassed the greatest explorer of the century.' Nevertheless their leader concluded that this route to the Pole offered little prospect of success. The best hope he thought lay in a route northwards of Kennedy Channel and Ellesmere Island.

It was indeed the conclusion to which Peary himself had come. He had already discarded the Greenland route because of 'the comparatively rapid motion of the ice as it swung round the northern coast into the southerly setting East Greenland current' and in the spring of 1902 switched his starting point to Grant Land. In March he left Fort Conger, distant from the Pole by about 450 miles in a straight line, and left land behind him at Cape Hecla on 6 April. But once again he was defeated. In places the snow overlying the pack was so soft that 'the dogs wallowed belly-deep'. Continually he and his men were forced to double in their tracks or to make long and exhausting detours to find easier, less hummocky ground. In mid April, after a blizzard had set the pack-ice moving, two wide channels – one he called 'The Grand Canal' – opened across their path and forced them far off course. In such conditions, advancing at a rate of no more than six miles a day, Peary reached to latitude 84° 17′ N. on 21 April 1902. It was one more failure and one which Peary, so often described as the man who never failed, took greatly to heart. Nevertheless like the earlier Greenland venture it was not wholly unprofitable, for he had been able to establish a number of advance depots along this new route ready for another attempt and he had learnt one invaluable lesson. This was that even here, far to the west of the east Greenland current, the prevailing drift of the ice was from west to east (map p. 219). To offset this a course NNW. would have to be set. He learnt other lessons too that were to stand him in good stead; that a rapid return, a return which would leave him little time for sleep or camping, was vital if he hoped to follow the line of his outward tracks. 'I recognized', Peary wrote, 'that the entire pack was moving slowly, and that our trail was everywhere faulted and interrupted by new pressure ridges and leads, in a way to make our return march nearly, if not quite, as slow and laborious as our outward one.' There were improvements also that he could make in equipment and in the logistics and tactics of the assault. Sledges must be lighter to ride easily over the hummocky ice, and wider to bridge channels and water leads. A ship must be found that would penetrate through Smith Sound to the very edge of the polar sea, saving the long journey to the advance base. Finally a pioneer party was needed to push ahead and take the burden of breaking the trail. Through them the final assault party would pass, the energies of men and dogs being conserved for the last lap of the race. These were all lessons put to good use on his next and, as he hoped, his final expedition.

At the end of the *Windward* expedition in 1902, Peary returned to work in the naval dockyards. He had failed but nevertheless he was not too old to try again and he devoted every minute he could spare to raising funds for a new expedition incorporating all those improvements in equipment, in tactics, and in technique which his latest, most gruelling, and most bitter experience had taught him. The pivot of his national campaign was a group of wealthy New Yorkers headed by Herbert L. Bridgman who formed the Peary Arctic Club and by 1904 they had raised one hundred thousand dollars for a new ship, the *Roosevelt*, specially designed and built to penetrate the ice of Smith Sound and to carry the expedition far up the coast of Ellesmere Island to save the long journey over the ice to the advance base. Outlining his plans to the Secretary of the Navy Peary declared, 'I should expect to accomplish the distance to the Pole and return in about a hundred days or a little more, an average travel of about ten miles a day.' 'This plan', he added, 'is the result of some twelve years of travel in these latitudes.' Never indeed had he felt more confident of success. And in so far as a stimulus was needed to spur him on to victory it was provided by the news that the British under Captain Robert Falcon Scott had landed and advanced deeply into Antarctica. It might after all turn out that Britain and not the United States would be the first to conquer one of the poles of the earth.

In July 1905 Peary, now fifty, sailed from New York City in the *Roosevelt* which, after some damage to her bows, reached Cape Colombia on the north-east coast of Grant Island within ninety miles of the advanced base at Cape Hecla. The first party started off over the ice in February 1906 and the Peary system of Arctic tactics then took its classic form. The backbone of his force were the Eskimoes, men, women, and even children, the tribes from whom Peary, like the earlier American explorers Hall and Schwatka, had learnt in earlier days the basic techniques of Arctic travel and survival. They were employed to drive the dog-teams, Peary having over a hundred dogs. They were employed to build snow-houses (igloos) for use as staging camps along the route; these had great advantages for they saved the erection of cumbrous tents and were warmer and infinitely more wind-proof. The women, meanwhile, were employed to sew the seal and walrus clothing which Eskimoes and white men wore alike. There were five white men in Peary's expedition and as always of recent years, his devoted servant and the most trusted of all his companions, Matthew Henson, the only Negro explorer in Arctic history.

The essence of the Peary system was the dispatch of small advance parties to blaze the trail and set up camps and depots along the route to within striking distance of the Pole thereby saving the strength of the men and of the dogs reserved for the final dash. A very similar technique in a very different field was employed in 1953 by Sir John Hunt and the men of the British Everest Expedition. There too advance parties went ahead to prepare the route and to set up a camp within striking distance of the summit ready for the final assaults. 'To have a sufficient number of divisions, or relay parties, each under the leadership of a competent assistant; to send them at appropriate and carefully calculated stages along the outward journey ... and to return by the same route ... using the beaten trail and the already constructed igloos', these were the essentials of the Peary system. Each of these parties would 'knit together' the breaks in the trail created by any drift of the ice. They would thus keep it open for the assault party returning from the Pole.

After so many years of concentrated effort, after so much careful thought and meticulous preparation, it seemed only right that this time fortune should favour Peary. But again he had no luck. Not only the surface and drift of the ice but the weather were against him and with a record low temperature of −60° F. or 90° of frost his speed was reduced to half his estimate. At this rate there was no hope whatsoever that his provisions would last his journey to the Pole and back. Some record, however, had to be achieved not only to redeem his own name and reputation but to encourage his supporters of the Peary Arctic Club in New York. The Pole was clearly unattainable but he was only sixty miles behind Nansen's, eighty miles behind the Italian Cagni's, farthest north. Discarding almost everything from his sledges and collecting together the least exhausted of his dogs he plunged on, bending 'every energy to setting a record pace'. In a half gale and heavy drift he persisted until Cagni's record of 1900 had been beaten.

Peary returned safely, though as he admitted by the narrowest of margins, only to see the *Roosevelt*, despite the superb navigation of her British captain, Bob Bartlett, suffer such heavy damage from the ice in Smith Sound that she had to be reconditioned at enormous cost. However, once again the Peary Arctic Club came to the rescue and in July 1908 Peary sailed again on his last polar venture. The party, Peary's 'disciplined followers' as Ambassador Choate called them, consisted of Bob Bartlett, the captain of the *Roosevelt*, Matthew Henson, the doctor Goodsell, and two young men Borup and MacMillan. They called in at Etah in north-west Greenland (just north of the present United States Air Base at Thule) and collected fifty Eskimoes and two hundred and fifty dogs; by the autumn the advance land base at Cape Colombia had been stocked; and by February 1909 Peary was ready to move off.

Peary never ceased to learn from his previous failures and this time a course was set somewhat west of north to allow for the easterly drift. As a further precaution depots were left on the north Greenland coast so that in an emergency a return from the Pole could be made eastwards, diagonally with the set of the ice. In case the drift was found to be unexpectedly reversed, depots were also left to the west of Cape Colombia. As it turned out, however, these precautions were unnecessary for there was no strong westerly wind to reinforce the drift as there had been in 1906.

Throughout March they again had low temperatures and violent winds and were held up for days at a time waiting for the ice to close in over the broad black leads of water which they continually encountered. But they kept going, the advance parties, worked unmercifully by Peary, bearing the brunt of the strain. By 1 April they had reached 87° 47' N., the nearest man had reached to the Pole. Four of the advance parties each

led by a white man had already returned to the base with the
worst of the dogs harnessed to their sledges. Now, two hundred
and eighty miles from the base and one hundred and thirty-
three miles from the Pole, it was time for the last party to turn
back. This was the party led by Bob Bartlett, the British captain
of the *Roosevelt*. Peary trusted Bartlett as he trusted no one except Matthew Henson, the Negro, and he was anxious to show
the gratitude he felt for Bartlett's extraordinary skill as a navigator. He chose Bartlett's party therefore as the last to leave,
explaining afterwards: 'It seemed to me that, in view of the
noble work of Great Britain in Arctic exploration, a British
subject should, next to an American, be able to say that he had
stood nearest to the Pole.' The truth, however, was that he could
not bring himself to allow any other white man to share his
triumph.

Peary and five men – four Eskimoes and Matthew Henson,
who was almost as skilful as they in the technique of swift
Arctic travel – faced two great hazards as they set out on 2 April
on the last stage of the Polar journey. A twenty-four hour gale
might spring up and open wide and impassable leads in the ice,
dangerously delaying them. But more dangerous still was the
imminent approach of the full moon and of the spring tides.
These, Peary feared, might 'stir the great ice-fields around us
into restlessness' and create a network of water leads across the
path, some open, some perhaps thinly and deceptively coated
with new ice whose strength would have to be gauged to a nicety
if dogs and sledges were not to plunge into the deep and icy
water below. Nevertheless, as he climbed a great pressure ridge
behind his snow-house and looked towards the north he was swept
by a sudden surge of excitement. 'I felt', he wrote, 'the keenest
exhilaration, and even exultation, as I climbed over the pressure
ridge and breasted the keen air sweeping over the mighty ice,
pure and straight from the Pole itself. . . . It was a fine marching
morning, clear and sunlit, with a temperature of minus 25°, and
the wind of the past few days had subsided to a gentle breeze.
The going was the best we had had since leaving land. The floes
were large and old, hard, and level, with patches of sapphire-blue
ice (the pools of the preceding summer). While the pressure

ridges surrounding them were stupendous, some of them fifty feet high, they were not especially hard to negotiate, either through some gap or up the gradual slope of a huge drift of snow. The brilliant sunlight, the good going save for the pressure ridges, the consciousness that we were now well started on the last lap of our journey, and the joy of again being in the lead, affected me like wine. The years seemed to drop from me, and I felt as I had felt in those fifteen years before when I headed my little party across the great ice-cap of Greenland. ...'

In continuous daylight they travelled for ten hours at a stretch, racing against the approach of the full moon. The ice appeared motionless. But they could hear the floes grinding and groaning on all sides as they neared the 89th parallel. It was not the bitter wind they feared, though it lashed their faces like a whip of steel, nor the pressure ridges which rose dark and massive in the distance. The waterleads were the greatest menace. 'I was in constant dread', Peary confessed, 'lest we encounter an impassable one toward the very end. With every successive march, my fear of such impassable leads had increased', and indeed at every ridge he hurried forward fearing to see from its summit a broad, black stretch of water barring their way to the Pole. Early in April clouds obscured the sun and left them to march on in a grey and colourless and melancholy light. But they were not depressed, for they were near now, near enough to be certain of success.

On 6 April 1909 Peary with Matthew Henson and four Eskimoes reached the North Geographical Pole; 'The Pole at last. The prize of three centuries. My dream and goal for twenty years.' Five flags were planted, the American flag, the Navy League flag, the Red Cross flag, the 'World's Ensign of Liberty and Peace', and the colours of the Delta Kappa Epsilon Fraternity at Bowdoin College of which Peary was an alumnus. In a crack in a near-by ice ridge Peary then placed a bottle containing a strip of his national flag and a brief record of the journey, due credit being given to Herbert L. Bridgman and the Peary Arctic Club of New York City whose strenuous efforts had made possible the acquisition 'of this geographical prize for the honour and prestige of the United States of America'. In another document he, Robert E. Peary of the United States Navy, claimed the entire region in the name of the President of the United States.

On 7 April Peary turned south towards Cape Columbia and there sixteen days later he composed his message to the world. 'My life-work is accomplished. The thing which it was intended from the beginning that I should do, the thing which I believed could be done, and that I could do, I have done. I have got the North Pole out of my system after twenty-three years of effort, hard work, disappointments, hardships, privations, more or less suffering, and some risks. I have won the last great geographical prize of the North Pole for the credit of the United States. This work is the finish, the cap, and climax, of nearly four hundred years of effort, loss of life, and expenditure of fortunes by the civilized nations of the world, and it has been accomplished in a way that is thoroughly American. I am content.'

He was indeed content and when he had telegraphed his message from Labrador Peary was able at last to relax and to enjoy to the full the delicious prospect of his triumphant arrival in America. But he did not know that a few days earlier an even more dramatic message had astonished the world, this time from Copenhagen. This declared that the sender, the American explorer Dr Frederick A. Cook, accompanied only by two Eskimo youths, had reached the Pole on 21 April 1908; a year, therefore, before Peary. The strange case of Dr Cook is a subject for psychological rather than for historical study. For Dr Cook was no ordinary charlatan; if he had been, the Peary-Cook controversy would never have lasted as long as it did. He was, on the contrary, an experienced and respected polar traveller, who had been the anthropologist on Peary's Greenland expedition of 1892 and a few years later had served as doctor on de Gerlache's Belgian expedition, the first to endure a winter in the Antarctic pack. Nor was the lengthy and arduous journey so vividly described in *My Attainment of the Pole* by any means wholly imaginary. There is no doubt that in 1907 Cook with one white companion, Rudolfe Francke, sailed for the Arctic in the yacht *John R. Bradley*, named after his patron. There is no doubt that they wintered at Etah far up the north-west coast of Greenland, nor that in February 1908 they left with Eskimoes, dogs, sledges, and a canvas boat, crossed Smith Sound and crossed Ellesmere Island westwards to Cape Thomas Hubbard, the northernmost tip of Axel Heiberg Island. This was a tough journey of over five hundred miles and Cook deserves credit for it. But then the mystery begins. According to Cook's own account, he and two Eskimo youths started in March for the Pole five hundred miles away, reached it in April and after a stay of twenty-four hours returned by way of the Ringnes Islands to Grinnell Peninsula on North Devon Island, having been lost in fog on their way. There they wintered, then crossed Smith Sound to Greenland in the spring of 1909. What actually happened to Cook and his party after they left Cape Thomas Hubbard has only been elucidated over the years, notably by the distinguished Arctic explorer Vilhjalmur Stefansson who was able to check some of Cook's claims on the ground during his own explorations eastwards of the Beaufort Sea in 1913–18 while on the Canadian Arctic expedition. After leaving Cape Thomas Hubbard, far from travelling northwards to the Pole, Cook probably travelled south along the west coast of Axel Heiberg Island. He then passed an unobtrusive and uneventful winter in Jones Sound and calmly returned to Greenland. The journey to the Pole, so vividly described, seems to have been nothing but pure fiction.

What led Cook to indulge in such an elaborate fraud has never been discovered. Was it pure chicanery? Was it from some distorted, cynical sense of humour? Or was it perhaps sheer malice against Peary, guessing as indeed turned out to be the case, that in the absence of independent and reliable white witnesses on both sides, he, an experienced and quite reputable explorer, had at least as good a chance as Peary of being believed. There is still an interesting psychological problem to be solved in the strange case of Dr Frederick A. Cook.

Sufficient evidence to demonstrate the improbability of Cook's claims came only slowly to light. Cook's party photographed allegedly at the Pole in April 1908 are shown wearing musk-ox skins. But no such skins on their own admission were carried, nor was any musk-ox shot. Stefansson's findings were even more damning, for he showed by following his tracks that Cook could never have seen what he claimed to have seen if he had followed the northern route, and that certain inescapable landmarks along this route Cook never mentioned at all. At the time, however, the true facts were far from clear. Cook had on his side a great many supporters who pressed his claims against those of Peary and for years it seemed that the world was divided into the partisans of the two rival explorers. But if Cook's story could not be disproved, Peary's claims were no easier to substantiate. Bob Bartlett could testify that they had been within one hundred miles of the Pole. But thereafter what happened? And was it not strange, Peary's opponents were quick to ask, that no white man had been permitted to accompany him on the last and crucial stage of the journey?

The secrecy with which Peary, obsessed by his fear of competitors, had surrounded the expedition did nothing to strengthen his case. Preliminary announcements of his intentions had been of the most general kind. And no reports of his progress were allowed to be published for, as he said, 'I am not printing anything until I have got to the Pole'. Nor did the Congressional Investigating Committee set up to examine his claims do justice to them for the men composing it were for the most part quite unfitted to judge the merits of his case, and their ignorance and Peary's somewhat vague and unsatisfactory replies tended rather to increase the suspicion against him. Under more expert scrutiny however Peary's case grew in strength. The Royal Geographical Society in London, though it refused to adjudicate as between Cook and Peary, had earlier shown that they favoured Peary by their telegram of congratulation and they now proceeded to dispose of one important criticism against him, namely that at the date when Peary claimed to have been at the Pole the altitude of the sun there was too low to be observed by means of the sextant and artificial horizon which he used. More telling were the findings of the special sub-committee on research of the National Geographic Society in Washington. This panel of experts, meeting on 4 November 1909, reported its unanimous opinion that Peary had reached the North Geographical Pole.

Six months later, so convinced were they of the justice of Peary's claims, the Royal Geographical Society presented him with their rarest award, the Special Gold Medal, designed by

Mrs Robert Falcon Scott; an award, its President, Major Darwin, took care to point out, made not for the dash to the Pole alone but for Peary's services over the years to Arctic exploration. A replica of the medal in silver was presented to Captain Bob Bartlett. These awards, given only after the most careful consideration of Peary's case, might have been thought to have settled the matter, but over the next twenty years there were many, and they included one reputable polar historian, who not only continued to doubt Peary's claims, but harshly criticized his conduct as an explorer.

In certain respects, these critics were not unjustified. On his Greenland expedition of 1892, Peary had claimed to be the first to prove the insularity of Greenland when he reached his so-called 'Independence Bay'. But the *Danmark* expedition of 1906–7 and the later explorations of the Danish explorers Captain Ejnar Mikkelsen and Knud Rasmussen showed that 'Independence Bay' was not a bay but a deep fjord and that Peary's 'Navy Cliff' was a hundred miles from the sea. 'Peary Channel' was similarly disposed of by Rasmussen who found in place of it 'an extensive ice-free upland abounding in game'. As the result of these successive revelations, the United States Government in 1915 withdrew Peary's maps of this part of Greenland. If such rash and extravagant claims diminished the confidence of the exploring and scientific world, so also did Peary's published accounts of his polar journey. He published no scientific reports for although some desultory investigations were occasionally carried out by members of his expeditions, he himself had no interest in science. His books and articles accordingly were addressed to an exclusively popular audience and were written in a highly coloured prose with many a manifest exaggeration – fantastic heights of pressure ridges, for example – designed to add to their dramatic appeal. The first published accounts of his great polar journey appeared throughout 1910 in *Hampton's Magazine* in the United States and in *Nash's Magazine* in Britain. As stories of adventure they make exciting reading. But they offered nothing in the way of supporting evidence to substantiate Peary's claims.

It is not easy to be sympathetic towards a man so egocentric, so dominated by personal ambition, so jealous, and so ruthless in his treatment of possible competition as Peary appears to have been and it is all the more important that his achievements should be objectively assessed. No doubt on occasions as in Greenland he was careless or over-hasty. But he was also capable of very accurate work and the Royal Geographical Society, after a close inspection of the log of his polar journey, declared that 'one could not expect in the circumstances a much better set of observations to prove that a man had been within a few miles of the Pole'. Peary's greatest claim to distinction lay, however, in his mastery of the technique of polar travel which he had perfected over many years. 'Peary's great achievement', it has been said, 'was to have travelled over hummocky and often active pack-ice far from land at a speed far beyond his predecessors. His picked Eskimoes and dogs made it possible; his own will and ambition and knowledge that he was winning carried him through to his great triumph.'

Peary had not long been at home before he began to think of another polar adventure. The North Pole had been won for the United States. But the South Pole was still unconquered. He therefore started work on plans for an American Antarctic expedition which, since he felt himself to be too old, was to be led by Captain Bob Bartlett, the British captain of the *Roosevelt*. Peary had often pondered in his mind the relative difficulties of Arctic and Antarctic travel. In the Arctic, a sea surrounded by land, he had learnt to travel at the coldest and darkest time of year when the ice was firm and no open water barred the way. In the Antarctic, an ice-capped continent surrounded by ocean, travel was easiest during the comparative warmth and perpetual daylight of summer. The Antarctic had also another great advantage. Depots there, if properly marked, should be safer for neither drifting ice nor predatory bears or foxes were there to endanger them. Peary had carefully studied the reports of the British polar explorers and despite the great obstacles to travel in Antarctica, the physical strain imposed by the high altitude of the plateau, the sudden blizzards, the menace of crevasses formed by the slowly shifting ice sheet, he was optimistic about the chances of an American expedition to the South Pole led by a polar traveller of Bartlett's experience and ability, highly trained in Peary's sledging technique. In all these arguments, had not the Norwegian Amundsen intervened, Peary might well have been proved right. If he had been, the British leader of an American expedition would have been first at the South Pole.

SHACKLETON RETURNS

In 1904, the year of Scott's return from the Antarctic, the Eighth International Geographical Congress, meeting in New York, urged that new and greater efforts should be made to advance polar exploration. 'Realizing that the only untouched fields for geographical discovery are the regions immediately surrounding the poles of the Earth', the Congress declared its wish to 'place on record its sense of the importance of forthwith completing the systematic exploration of the polar areas'. It stressed, moreover, how important it was 'that the experience gained by men of science and officers in the recent Antarctic expeditions should be turned to account by following up without delay the successes they have obtained'. The Congress, furthermore, 'recognized that the Arctic regions possess a more immediate interest for the people of America, and expresses the confident hope that the expeditions now being prepared will be so supported as to secure early and complete success'.

In the Arctic, as we have seen, Robert E. Peary of the United States Navy had no need of encouragement from the International Geographical Congress to persuade him to persevere. Nor were his the only major Arctic explorations then in progress for further west Roald Amundsen, even as the Congress met in New York, had almost completed the first navigation of the North-West Passage. These were the major expeditions. But there was also much detailed exploratory and scientific work in progress elsewhere, in Canada's Northwest Territories and in East Greenland where Danish scientists had been very active.

In the Antarctic, however, exploration – apart from J. B. Charcot's important scientific work on the west side of the Graham Land peninsula – was coming to a halt and there was no talk of new plans, least of all in England though it had been the centre of the movement to revive Antarctic exploration at the turn of the century. There Scott, honoured not only by his own country but by France, Germany, Sweden, and many others, was touring the country on an exhausting lecture tour and receiving from each mayor and corporation a hero's welcome. In 1905 *The Voyage of the Discovery* was published. Soon afterwards *Discovery* herself, though she had been specially built and should have been retained for polar research, was sold to a commercial firm for a fraction of her cost. The members of the expedition, highly trained and experienced, were allowed to disperse into the relative obscurity of private or professional life. Scott returned to a new appointment in the Navy. And then a lull descended. It was as if the public, the Government, and the learned societies, exhausted by the efforts and the tension of the past few years, had suddenly tired of polar exploration.

But just as suddenly, towards the end of 1906, interest reawakened. The cause, however, was not Scott whom Ambassador Choate had foreseen sharing with Peary the honour of making 'the two ends of the great world meet', though it was known that he had been turning over in his mind fresh plans for exploration. This time the principal actor was E. H. Shackleton, the junior officer in the *Discovery*, the man whom because of his breakdown on the return southern journey, Scott had been forced to send home. If the news that Shackleton intended to promote and lead an Antarctic expedition was received generally with some astonishment it was received by Clements Markham with considerable indignation. As H. R. Mill recalls, 'Markham considered ambition in a subordinate as little less than mutiny and he did not dissemble his opposition to Shackleton's plans.'

The man who thus presumed to rival Markham's chosen leader was in background and in character as different from Scott as could be. Born of an Irish father and an Irish mother, he had left school at the early age of 16 and had joined the Merchant Navy. Thereafter he had been something of a rolling stone, moving from ship to ship and line to line in the merchant service, preferring always to take a chance rather than wait in tedious security for regular but slow advancement. He was by nature a gambler and an adventurer; a man, it has been said, who would have been as happy seeking buried treasure in the Pacific as he was to be among the hazards and excitements of Antarctic exploration.

Shackleton, bronzed and fit, a giant of a man astonishing to those who heard that he had been invalided home, had already made his mark lecturing on the first season's work of the *Discovery* expedition, for he had an Irishman's command of the English language (made the more attractive by a touch of brogue) and a magnetic platform personality. But marriage was in his mind and money was necessary. He thus embarked upon the first of an extraordinary variety of posts and projects which were gradually to lead him nearer to Antarctica to which he had all along been determined to return. He tried first to obtain a permanent commission in the Navy and when this failed – it was a rebuff Shackleton always remembered – he turned with considerable success to journalism, as sub-editor on Pearson's *Royal Magazine*. But journalism offered no golden prospects and when the post of Secretary to the Royal Scottish Geographical Society became vacant, he applied for it, realizing that while it offered scant hope of financial profit, it might easily lead to better things.

Shackleton had no mind for detail, whether in proof-reading, in the taking of minute scientific observations, or in matters of administration. But under the stimulus of his abundant vitality, his fertile imagination, and his personal charm, the Society prospered. Within a year, however – a year a little alarming and sometimes stormy for the more conservative members of the Society's Council – Shackleton was looking for fresh conquests and when the chance came to stand as Liberal-Unionist candidate for Dundee, he seized it with alacrity. Though he was immensely popular in the working-class districts he failed to win the seat; but it had not been waste of effort for as a candidate he had met many men of money and influence, one of them the great industrialist William Beardmore.

Dabbling in doubtful financial schemes, ingenious but always unsuccessful projects for getting rich quick, was a temptation which Shackleton could never resist and whether it was gold-mining in Hungary, a cigarette factory in the United States, or an international news agency, he plunged into each new gamble with the same exuberant optimism. Shackleton was about to launch another of these projects, the attraction this time being a lucrative contract for the transport of Russian troops from Vladivostock to the Baltic, when he received an offer of employment in Beardmore's great engineering works at Glasgow. This he accepted and it turned out to be one of the most profitable decisions of his life, for Beardmore was much impressed by Shackleton's drive and personality and after he had heard of the plans which the latter had nurtured all this while for a new Antarctic expedition, he was eventually persuaded (in the autumn of 1906) to guarantee most of the cost.

This large guarantee and those from many others, including the Misses Dawson Lambton who had bought the balloon for Scott's expedition, would of course have to be repaid. But Shackleton had no great anxieties on this score. The sale of the book, the sale of photographs, the lectures he would give, surely these together would yield a fortune. He did not hesitate, therefore, to embark immediately on active preparations; none too soon, he considered, for although he had no reason to anticipate any British rivals, both from France and Belgium there were rumours of impending Antarctic expeditions.

This time there was no delay in getting the expedition under way for there were neither sponsors nor supervisory committees to consult. Certainly they would have been valuable in shouldering the heavy burdens of financial responsibility which without them fell on Shackleton alone. But he was determined at all costs to be free. The Admiralty were invited to provide charts and instruments. The Royal Geographical Society, despite Markham's undisguised hostility to the enterprise, gave similar help. But that was as far as he was prepared to go towards entanglement with official or learned bodies.

His plans were relatively simple. From Hut Point where Scott had wintered, three parties were to operate; one eastwards across the Ross Ice Shelf and into the unexplored King Edward Land; one westwards across the mountains of Victoria Land to discover the South Magnetic Pole; and one, the main party southwards to the South Geographical Pole. Little as Shackleton was personally concerned with science – geology, someone remarked, was for him a matter of precious stones – much scientific work was planned and an excellent scientific staff was recruited. But for Shackleton the Geographical Pole was the thing. 'The money', he declared later, 'was given for me to reach the Pole. . . . I had a great public trust. . . .' All his efforts, all his ambitions, sharpened as they were by painful memories of his earlier failure, were focused upon this one single and supreme objective.

Since the expedition was due in the Ross Sea in the following February, Shackleton in April 1907 thought the time had come to announce his plans in *The Times*. Then came a wholly unexpected blow, a letter from Scott informing Shackleton that he too was contemplating an Antarctic expedition based on his old winter quarters at Hut Point and asking him therefore to select another winter base. Shackleton had no idea that Scott intended to return so soon to Antarctica and this letter, written from Gibraltar where Scott was in command of H.M.S. *Albermarle*, struck at the root of his plans. Seeking an area well beyond the frontiers of Scott's zone of activity, he thought that an alternative base and harbour might be found near the eastern end of the Ross Ice Shelf or in King Edward VII Land. But this would not only eliminate the South Magnetic Pole, it would involve much more hazardous ice conditions and mean therefore a larger, stronger, and inevitably a very much more expensive ship. These losses to the original plan were serious enough. But there was another more serious still; for a change to such a distant and less conveniently situated base, a base from which the approaches to the plateau would have first to be explored, would greatly diminish his chances of attaining the geographical Pole.

It was a hard, indeed a bitter decision to be forced to take and Shackleton thought deeply about it. In the end, however, he gave way and promised to plan his attempt on the Pole from near King Edward VII Land and to confine subsidiary explorations to that area.

The choice of ship was greatly complicated for he had now to find a vessel able not only to penetrate the familiar waters of McMurdo Sound but to thrust through the most ice-infested area of the Ross Sea to the unknown coast of King Edward Land. A new Norwegian ship, the *Björn*, of seven hundred tons and

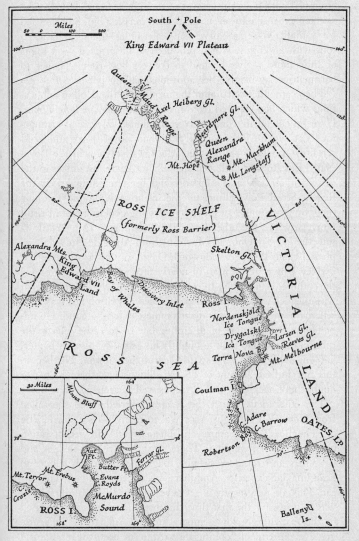

The Ross Dependency

equipped with powerful engines, would have been ideal; but she was too expensive for even Shackleton to risk a bid. So he settled for a smaller vessel, a Norwegian sealer of less than two hundred tons with an engine which produced so little speed – six knots or little more – that he had to convert her from schooner to barquentine rig to give her additional sailing power.

Then came the selection of the men out of the flood of applications which had resulted from his announcement in *The Times*. Here he cut adrift completely from the strictly naval arrangements at which Markham and Scott had aimed. Joyce and Wild certainly had been ratings and Mackay a surgeon in the Royal Navy. But Roberts had been a cook and Adams an officer in the merchant service, and Marston had been teaching art at the Regent Street Polytechnic. Of the scientists Raymond Priestley (now Sir Raymond Priestley) was a young geologist from Bristol University and the other two were Australians: Douglas Mawson (the late Sir Douglas Mawson) from Adelaide University as physicist and Professor Edgworth David, professor of geology at Sydney University, a man of nearly fifty who was recruited for the summer cruise only. In command of this heterogeneous team was a leader who was an adept at decentralization but was himself the hardest worker and the readiest to lend a hand. He imposed no formal code of discipline but those – the idle or the quarrelsome – who took too lightly his geniality, his easy banter, and his Irish ways very swiftly learnt their lesson. Neither on this nor indeed on any of his expeditions was there room for doubt that Shackleton was in fact as well as in name, 'The Boss'.

The equipment which the *Nimrod* carried when she sailed from Cowes on 7 August 1907 was in many ways characteristic of 'The Boss's' new approach. There were light-weight ration boxes, his own invention. There were Norwegian sledges and skis, furs and reindeer sleeping bags, a rare British tribute to Scandinavian expertise. And there was a specially adapted motor-car. This, though in practice it never moved far beyond the base, was to prove for the first time that petrol engines could be used in the exceedingly low temperatures of Antarctica. This progressive experiment, looking forward to the post-war mechanical age of polar exploration, contrasts oddly with Shackleton's choice of Siberian ponies for his chief means of transport. Nansen and Amundsen had advised dogs and Shackleton, according to his preliminary plans, had apparently decided to rely principally upon them. But British prejudices, stemming from the unhappy experiences of the *Discovery* expedition, were evidently too strong, and the arguments in favour of ponies put forward by the men of the Jackson-Harmsworth expedition who had been with Scott were too convincing. Shackleton seems therefore to have changed his mind and ponies were chosen. Though dogs were also taken, ponies remained the means of transport upon which the British were chiefly to rely not only on Shackleton's but on Scott's attempt on the Pole.

The *Nimrod* sailed from New Zealand (where Shackleton had been lecturing) on New Year's Day 1908. She was an absurdly small ship for so considerable an expedition, with so little storage space for coal that she had to be towed the whole way to the Antarctic Circle. Her decks were so crowded that several ponies had to be left behind. The weather was immensely rough, and the ponies plunged about in their wooden stalls as the *Nimrod* rose and swayed and fell in the heavy seas. The Ross Ice Shelf, however, was reached through mercifully ice-free waters and the *Nimrod* made for the inlet where Borchgrevink had landed and the *Discovery* had put in. But there was no inlet. Since Scott's visit great stretches of ice had calved away from the cliffs and there was now left a deep and extensive bay which Shackleton called the Bay of Whales.

But the Bay of Whales was a very different place from the one where, after Scott's intervention, Shackleton had resolved to set up winter quarters. Would any landing at all be now possible? And if it were, would there not be a great danger of further falls of ice from the Shelf which might precipitate camp and men and equipment into the icy water? Just as Shackleton was weighing up these risks the decision was suddenly taken out of his hands. A northerly wind sprang up, driving the ice and with the ice the *Nimrod*, headlong towards the cliffs and it was only by a matter of minutes that she escaped from being imprisoned in the bay.

Shackleton then moved eastwards along the front of the Ice

Shelf towards King Edward Land but very soon he again came uncomfortably close to disaster, and was forced to pull back from an easterly lead because of the tightening grip of the ice. At this point he was faced by a most complex and mind-racking decision. The Bay of Whales had proved too dangerous. King Edward Land, if Captain England of the *Nimrod* was right and he was already pleading with Shackleton to retreat to the west before it was too late, was unapproachable. Where then was he to go? To the one safe and obvious anchorage in McMurdo Sound? But this would mean breaking his promise to Scott. For forty-eight hours Shackleton, though the captain of the *Nimrod* was in constant anxiety, delayed the decision hoping always that the next hour might bring some possibility of a break through to the east. The ice, however, proved relentless and coal insufficient to allow lengthy manoeuvres against it. With ship and men, as Captain England continued to insist, in immediate danger, Shackleton had no choice but to turn westwards and make for McMurdo Sound. He guessed, and guessed correctly how Scott would take the news for it meant that he, Shackleton, would start for the Pole from a base from which considerable preparatory exploration had already been done. But intensely distasteful as it was, what other choice could he have made? He found comfort only in the thought that pangs of conscience and accusations of bad faith were preferable to hazarding the loss of the ship and his men.

The ice was still unbroken in McMurdo Sound when Shackleton arrived so winter quarters were established at Cape Royds at the western end of Ross Island and not at Scott's old site, Hut Point. This was no minor matter for Hut Point was two days' journey nearer to the Pole. More serious and more immediately important, however, was the problem of access to the Ross Ice Shelf from Ross Island so that preparatory depots along the line of advance to the Pole could be laid before the Antarctic winter set in. With these already laid, the spring journeys could start at the earliest possible moment. Only the western coast of Ross Island, however, afforded access to the Ice Shelf and then only when the intervening sound was frozen over. But just as the *Nimrod* was steaming away towards the open sea, the ice west of Ross Island broke up and made depot laying quite impossible.

The significance of this new misfortune lies in the requirements of time and space which governed a polar journey. For this in any average year only four months between October and March were available, major sledging journeys before the end of October being in those days too severe a test while a return to the main base was essential by early March at the latest if the relief ship was not to be imprisoned for the approaching winter by the newly-forming winter ice. The distance to the Pole and back which had to be covered in these four months of summer travel was 1,730 statute miles. And this in turn meant travelling at an average speed of little more than 14 statute miles a day, a speed which imposed heavy physical strain on men, man-hauling most of the way as the British were, at a high altitude, in thin air, and over unknown and dangerous country. In such conditions, weight was a vital consideration. If supply depots could be laid before or during the outward march ready for use on the tiring homeward journey, the weight on sledges could be greatly reduced. If these depots could be laid in advance, time would be saved, and time was the scarcest of all commodities on these polar journeys.

In these days when fast and powerful mechanized vehicles are the principal Antarctic transport, when aircraft can be summoned by radio to drop supplies, or can fly forward to drop supply dumps far in advance of the land parties, such logistic problems though they persist are less urgent. But to Shackleton they were vital and as winter approached and no advance depots could be laid because of the break-up of the ice, his mind was busy with such calculations. The autumn was not uneventful for in March Professor Edgeworth David, the geologist from Sydney University whom Shackleton had persuaded to winter despite his fifty years, together with Mawson, Adams and Marshall, and Mackay, made a first ascent of Mount Erebus to the edge of its active crater, over 13,000 feet above the level of the sea. Standing there on the verge of the abyss, they could see nothing 'on account of the huge mass of steam filling the crater and soaring aloft in a column five hundred to a thousand feet high. After a continuous loud hissing sound, lasting for some minutes, there would come from below a big dull boom, and immediately great globular masses of steam would rush upwards. . . .' The fumes of burning sulphur filled the air.

Winter passed without incident, all being occupied with incessant meteorological observations, with the preparation of sledges and equipment, and with seemingly endless discussions and calculations of the journeys to be made in the spring. It witnessed, however, one unusual event, the printing of an illustrated book, *Aurora Australis*, the first to be printed in Antarctica. But even before the full return of the sun when, above the line of the horizon, only the thinnest rays had begun to pierce the darkness, sledging began, up on to the surface of the Ross Ice Shelf and frequently to Hut Point, to lay depots for the spring journeys. Here, though it was useless in snow, Shackleton's motor car came into its own and towed sledges over the sea ice at six miles an hour.

The main depot-laying journey started towards the end of September and Depot A was established one hundred miles to the south of Hut Point. This was achieved by man-hauling mostly, at a remarkably high average speed of twenty miles a day, and it was a good augury for the southern journey. Then the summer plans had radically to be changed. Of the ten ponies shipped on board the *Nimrod*, six had succumbed either to the violence of the voyage or to the rigours of the Antarctic climate. Since Shackleton's dogs were intended mainly for work round the base, only four ponies were left for the major explorations and a drastic curtailment of the programme was essential. The journey eastward therefore across the Ice Shelf to explore King Edward Land was dropped so that everything could be concentrated on the great southern journey and on the simultaneous journey to the South Magnetic Pole.

The task which in October 1908 confronted 'The Boss' was no less than the accomplishment of the greatest land journey ever attempted in Antarctic exploration. It involved a long march across the wind-swept Ice Shelf, a long ascent to nine thousand feet and more over a precipitous and labyrinthine glacier surface to the polar plateau, then a long journey over the vast and shelterless plateau to the Pole, ascending to twelve or thirteen thousand feet above the sea. But this was only half the task. There was the return march of nearly eight hundred miles, and if the whole journey was to be accomplished within the four months of summer travel, an average speed would have to be maintained, twice, nearly three times, that achieved by the men of Scott's National Antarctic Expedition. This made no allowance for disasters or delays, for unforeseen obstacles, for the unpredictable onslaughts of Antarctic weather. It was a tremendous gamble, a gamble against odds, a gamble which appeared not merely acceptable but immensely exhilarating to Shackleton and the three men who were about to embark on this extraordinary enterprise.

Late in October they started with a supporting party who hauled their own sledges, east-south-east across the Ross Ice Shelf. The supporting party turned back on 6 November. Then they were on their own, four men, four ponies, two tents; the men, Lieutenant Adams, R.N.R., meteorologist; Dr Marshall, cartographer; Frank Wild of the *Discovery* expedition, and 'The Boss'. Twelve days later Wild's keen eye detected against the dazzling whiteness of the sunlit Ice Shelf the fluttering pennant of Depot A and by 19 November, despite heavy going through soft snow, they had exceeded Scott's limit for that date. Their first set-back occurred just as the western mountains which Shackleton had seen on his earlier, calamitous journey, came into view. The pony Chinaman, so weak that it could go no further, had to be killed. It saved their preserved foods – though as Shackleton remarked 'Poor old Chinaman was a particularly tough and stringy horse' – and it enabled them to leave an ample supply of meat at Depot B, a hundred miles south of Depot A, but it meant that they were left with three ponies only for the greater part of their seventeen-hundred-mile journey.

Shackleton's diary for the night of 26 November contains a reminder of the personal rivalries between the leading explorers which coloured, and sometimes disfigured, the explorations of the Heroic Age. As the great snow-clad heights of Mount Longstaff and Mount Markham (as Scott had named them) loomed ahead Ernest Shackleton celebrated – on a minute bottle of curaçao – the passing of Scott's southern limit on the Ice Shelf, with more than a month in hand. Beyond was new land, untouched, unseen by man, and Shackleton's mind responded instantly to the drama of the moment. '. . . It was with feelings of keen curiosity, not unmingled with awe, that we watched the new mountains rise from the great unknown that lay ahead of us. Mighty peaks they were, the eternal snows at their bases, and their rough-hewn forms rising high towards the sky. No man could tell what we would discover in our march south, what wonders might not be revealed to us, and our imaginations would take wings until a stumble in the snow, the sharp pangs of hunger, or the dull ache of physical weariness brought back our attention to the needs of the immediate present.'

Though men and ponies were now hauling together, the three remaining ponies were weakening fast under their loads of six hundred pounds a sledge. Grisi was the next to be shot. The meat, still bloody, was left at Depot C. On 1 December, at 83° S., Quan, The Boss's favourite, went. With one pony left, the four men marched on across the Ice Shelf, on a much more easterly course than Scott to avoid crevassed areas near the foothills, towards an isolated peak, three thousand feet high, which they named Mount Hope.

From Mount Hope, Shackleton could see stretching away in the distance a range of massive mountains, bare and sheer, buttressing an immense table-land of ice. Bisecting this range an enormous glacier swept down, a torrent of ice moving imperceptibly yet with such latent power within its frozen mass that the ice shelf at its foot was deeply cracked and split by its downward pressure. This Shackleton named the Beardmore Glacier after the man whose faith in him had made the expedition possible. It was in many respects the most important of his geographical discoveries in that it gave access to the polar plateau.

On 5 December, having struggled through a zone of pressure ridges and crevasses, they started to climb, two thousand feet in the first two miles, in breathless air and over a smooth and treacherous surface. Then a sudden shout broke the silence as Frank Wild, leading the last remaining pony over an apparently solid snow bridge, stepped into space and hung, by his left arm only, above a bottomless chasm. Wild and his sledge were saved. But Socks, the last pony, had gone. 'If we had been able to use Socks for food', Shackleton wrote afterwards, 'I have no doubt that we would have been able to get further south, perhaps even to the Pole itself. . . .'

On a ration quite inadequate to sustain such physical effort they rarely made more than five miles a day as they climbed in vapid air to a height of 5,600 feet on the glacier. The mountains which enclosed them here were of an unparalleled grandeur; one, an immense yellow sandstone cliff, being striated by a broad black seam of coal. At 6,000 feet another depot was laid containing everything they could spare to lighten the last stage of the journey, and by Christmas Day, at 9,500 feet, they had climbed to the edge of the plateau. From this point, in latitude 86° S., they had two hundred and fifty miles to go. Breathing was painful at this altitude. A biting wind, piercing their clothing and the thin walls of their one tent, had replaced the stale air of the glacier. Their hunger meanwhile was growing. Even the pony maize was finished, and their daily ration had to be reduced if their food was to last the journey to the Pole and back to the first depot.

'If the Barrier is a changing sea', wrote Shackleton on 28 December, 'the plateau is a changing sky. During the morning march we continued to go up hill steadily, but the surface was constantly changing. First there was soft snow in layers, then soft snow so deep that we were well over our ankles, and the temperature being well below zero, our feet were cold from sinking in. No one can say what we are going to find next, but we can go steadily on.' By the last day of the old year at an altitude which inflicted headaches so severe that it was, Shackleton wrote, 'as though the nerves were being twisted up by a corkscrew and then pulled out', they were in latitude 86° 54' S., with only three weeks' food and two weeks' biscuit to last five hundred geographical miles.

On 1 January 1909 Shackleton, looking across the world to where Peary was preparing for yet another attempt on the North Pole, noted that they had passed Peary's northern record of 87° 6'. But Shackleton, 'The Boss' whose leadership had urged them thus far, almost to the limit of their endurance, already knew that they could not safely carry the march south much farther. To a man of such impulsive and ambitious temperament, the temptation to continue, as they could have done, must have been almost irresistible. 'We can now', he declared, 'definitely locate the South Pole on the highest plateau in the world, and our geological work and meteorology will be of the greatest use to science; but all this is not the Pole.' Nevertheless he decided, and it was one of the great decisions of his life, to turn back. 'I must look at the matter sensibly', he wrote, 'and consider the lives of those who are with me. I feel that if we go on too far it will be impossible to get back over this surface, and then all the results will be lost to the world.'

The briefest excerpts from his diaries, extracted from some of the most vivid and stirring passages in polar literature, tell something of the tale of the next few days: 7 January, 'A blinding, shrieking blizzard all day, with the temperature ranging from 67° to 70° of frost . . .'. 8 January, wind, drift, cold, cramp, 'I feel this march must be our limit. We are so short of food, and at this high altitude, 11,600 feet, it is hard to keep any warmth in our bodies between the scanty meals.' 9 January, 'Our last day outwards. We have shot our bolt, and the tale is latitude 88° 23' South, longitude 162° East.'

On 9 January, at four o'clock in the morning, with the Queen's Union Jack, and documents and stamps (including New Zealand stamps) for burial in a brass cylinder, they started for the south 'half running and half walking over a surface much hardened by the recent blizzard' and, hoisting the flags, Shackleton took possession of the polar plateau in the name of King Edward VII. 'While the Union Jack blew stiffly in the icy gale that cut us to the bone, we looked south with our powerful glasses, but could see nothing but the dead white snow plain. There was no break in the plateau as it extended towards the Pole. . . .'

In appalling conditions they had sledged to within ninety-seven miles of their objective. But there was still the homeward journey to face; a journey rapid as far as the mountains, being downhill and with the wind behind them, then slowing up as dysentery (due, they thought, to the pony meat) attacked them. On the

Ice Shelf the southerly blizzard proved on unexpected blessing for, following Nansen's example on his Greenland ice sheet journey, they hoisted a sail on the sledge and sped over the surface so fast that by 18 February they were within sight of Mount Erebus and Mount Terror. Two days later they reached Depot A, within a hundred miles from Hut Point.

For most of the homeward journey Shackleton had been relying on food from the depots, reached with a margin not of days but of hours. But Depot A contained only tobacco. Their nearest food – and they had none left on arrival – was at Depot B, east of Minna Bluff, sixty miles south of Hut Point. The journey from Depot A to Minna Bluff and thence to Scott's old hut brought the party nearer disaster than at any time during the whole expedition. Only Wild's phenomenal eyesight could have seen the flag above Depot B and indeed at one moment in their exhausting and seemingly hopeless search they began to doubt whether it had been laid at all. Then Marshall fell ill and Shackleton and Wild, leaving Adams to look after him, set off for Hut Point on their own. At Hut Point, reached on 28 February, the worst of messages awaited them. The Magnetic Pole party had achieved their task. But the *Nimrod*, prepared to wait only until the 26th, had gone. Signals were frantically hoisted. Fires were lit. And when in the morning, as if by some miracle, the *Nimrod* appeared, it seemed the ultimate and crowning confirmation of all that had ever been said about Shackleton's luck.

The Northern Party of whose success Shackleton had learnt in the letter left at Hut Point had started, under the leadership of Professor Edgeworth David, on 25 September 1908, using the motor car to carry stores across the ice of McMurdo Sound to a depot ten miles out. The first two hundred miles of their journey to the Magnetic Pole lay over the coastal ice of South Victoria Land, a coast of which Mawson made a careful triangulation since until then it had only been roughly charted from the sea. The party was strong in geologists and the geology of this stretch of coast they found exceptionally exciting. After crossing two great ice tongues, one hundred feet high, which projected far out to sea (the Nordenskjöld and Drygalski Ice Tongues), David made for Terra Nova Bay and then aimed to strike westwards by one of the gigantic glaciers which led (like those which Scott and Shackleton had ascended) up through the mountains to the lofty inner polar plateau. Reeves Glacier was tried but proved too steep for sledges. They then tried Larsen Glacier to the south-west and by the end of December they were up on the plateau, ready to move westwards over its ice waves to the Magnetic Pole.

The Northern Party reached the main position of the Magnetic Pole on 16 January 1909 within a week of the climax of Shackleton's southern journey and, as Shackleton had done, Professor David took possession of the whole region in the name of the British Crown. By 4 February, when they met the *Nimrod* on the coast, they had travelled a distance over unexplored country of 1,260 miles, more than two-thirds of the mileage travelled by Shackleton's party. But this Northern Party achieved much else besides this remarkable journey for a great deal of new land was mapped for the first time and the complicated geological structure of South Victoria Land was now revealed.

While the Northern Party was engaged in these scientific explorations, other scientific work had been in progress nearer the base. Joyce and other members of Shackleton's supporting party, returning to the coast, explored the rocks on the north side of Mount Erebus. Geological explorations were also carried out to the west of McMurdo Sound and of these Priestley's survey from the Ferrar Glacier was the chief event. These scientific investigations, building upon the work of the *Discovery*'s scientific staff, prepared the way for the scientists on the Northern Party of Scott's last expedition. Yet, important as they were in the systematic unfolding of Antarctic geography, it is not by these that the *Nimrod* expedition will be remembered. To have discovered five hundred miles of new mountain ranges flanking the Ross Ice Shelf; to have ascended the Beardmore Glacier; to have brought his men in such conditions and with such in-adequate equipment to within ninety-seven miles of the Pole; these were the historic achievements by which Shackleton's return to Antarctica will be remembered.

THE RACE TO THE SOUTH POLE

'I CONGRATULATE you and your comrades most warmly on the splendid result accomplished by your expedition, and in having succeeded in hoisting the Union Jack presented you by The Queen within a hundred miles of the South Pole, and the Union Jack on the South Magnetic Pole. I gladly assent to the new range of mountains in the far south bearing the name of Queen Alexandra.'

With this message King Edward VII greeted the returning Antarctic hero. When he arrived on Monday, 14 June 1909, at Charing Cross Station, foremost among those in the large crowd which welcomed him was Captain Robert Falcon Scott. When Scott first heard of Shackleton's move to Cape Royds, he wrote to a friend '... The result to me is most important for it makes it impossible to do anything till he is heard of again. There are far consequences. I won't discuss them now, but you can guess something of my thoughts. ...' There was now no sign of jealousy, no word of reproach about Shackleton's use of a base so near Hut Point. Yet it can have been no comfortable experience thus to witness the triumph of this merchant service officer, the one member of the *Discovery* expedition who had failed and had then demolished Scott's own southern record by three hundred and sixty-six miles.

A fortnight later, Shackleton lectured to the Fellows of the Royal Geographical Society in the Albert Hall in the presence of the Prince of Wales (later George V). The lecture, a *tour de force,* was delivered with all the fluency, the artistry, and the dramatic sense of the accomplished lecturer which Shackleton had become. The kinematograph, used for the first time to illustrate polar exploration, brought so vividly to the large audience assembled in Kensington that summer evening the white sweep of the Ice Shelf, the grim majesty of glaciers and mountains, the cold and desolation of the polar plateau, that they felt themselves to be part of the great Antarctic drama. The Society, influenced by Markham's hostility towards Shackleton and a little incredulous when they first heard the news, had been cautious in their first messages of congratulation. But that evening the fullest amends were made and Shackleton was presented with the coveted Special Gold Medal to commemorate his new discoveries and his initiation of new methods of polar travel and equipment.

But the most welcome of all rewards came from Mr Asquith, the Prime Minister, who promised that the Government would pay off all the expedition's debts for which Shackleton was, of course, personally responsible. The cost of the expedition had been extraordinarily low, less indeed than the cost of the *Discovery* alone. Nevertheless, half the total of £54,000 was still due to William Beardmore and Shackleton's other guarantors. Freed from this debt, Shackleton's optimism was again unbounded. The book, the global lecture tour, would after all make his fortune. There was no limit, he was convinced, to the possibilities in store.

While Shackleton was thriving on increasing public admiration, and looking forward to fortune now that fame had been achieved, there were other less sensational explorations in progress in the Antarctic, led by Dr Jean Baptiste Auguste Charcot, Director of the French Laboratory of Maritime Research. Charcot, the first Frenchman (in 1903–5) to explore Antarctica since the great days of d'Urville, had returned in 1908 on a two-year expedition supported by the Government of M. Briand and the Geographical Society of Paris. He was a scientist with no interest in record-breaking journeys, and was preoccupied only with the systematic exploration of the west coast of Graham Land. This peninsula, together with South Georgia, the South Orkney Islands, the South Shetland Islands, and the South Sandwich Islands had been defined as the Falkland Islands Dependencies by the British Government in 1908 when they issued Letters Patent consolidating earlier claims dating from the late eighteenth century. These, however, were political matters with which Charcot was not concerned.

Charcot wintered in the *Pourquoi Pas?* at Petermann Island

off the west coast of Graham Land and then in 1909 continued with his systematic charting of the complicated coasts and archipelagos to the south, combining this survey – the basis of later British charts – with much other scientific work. The insularity of Adelaide Island, discovered by John Biscoe, was proved. Marguerite Bay, a familiar name to Antarctic explorers after the Second World War, was discovered, together with the adjacent Fallières Coast and Charcot Land; the latter, which was proved by Hubert Wilkins in 1929 to be an island, was named after the French explorer's father, a famous Paris neurologist. Charcot Island lay to the west of Alexander Land. But Charcot sailed even farther west, to within sight of Peter I Øy seen for the first time since Bellingshausen's ships approached it in 1821, and on through the Bellingshausen Sea as far as Cook's *Ne Plus Ultra* in longitude 106° 54′ W. Charcot's expedition was not only a landmark in terms of the scope and accuracy of his coastal mapping and the wide range of the expedition's scientific work. The French explorer also introduced a number of technical innovations which in the field of polar exploration were quite revolutionary for the first decade of the twentieth century. His ship, the *Pourquoi Pas?*, carried a searchlight and a De Dion motor boat, and was equipped with telephones. And electric light was used to light not only the laboratories on board but the scientific stations established on the islands.

While these French explorations were in progress in Graham Land, the pace of polar exploration elsewhere was steadily accelerating towards the climax of the ambitions of the leading polar explorers of pre-War days, the attainment of the Poles. In the north, just as Peary was preparing to move over the drifting sea ice towards his final triumph, Roald Amundsen the Norwegian announced his plans for a drifting expedition in Nansen's famous *Fram* across the North Pole. This expedition which in depriving Nansen of his ship meant the sacrifice of Nansen's own Antarctic ambitions was planned to last, so Amundsen declared, seven years if necessary. It sailed – and there is a certain irony in the fact in view of Amundsen's later change of destination – with some financial support from Scott's patrons in the Royal Geographical Society.

A few months later the message from Peary, following swiftly on the spurious claims of Cook, brought to an end a great phase of Arctic exploration. The public, when the messages from Cook and Peary broke upon the world, had barely recovered from the news that Shackleton had been within one hundred miles of victory. Now all eyes were turned to the south again. The Arctic race was over. Who would be first at the South Pole? At sea in the *Fram* Roald Amundsen, the whole incentive for his expedition removed by Peary's sudden announcement, was planning secretly his descent upon the Antarctic. At home, in Britain, Captain Robert Falcon Scott speeded up his plans for his last South Polar expedition.

For two years and more Scott had been contemplating another expedition. In March 1908 when he first heard the deeply disturbing news of Shackleton's landing in McMurdo Sound he had been on his way to south-eastern France to try out, with Charcot's help, a newly invented motor sledge with flexible tracks, the forerunner of the tanks of the First World War. Throughout that year and again in 1909 when Scott, out of touch and urgently needing more time for preparation, managed to get himself transferred to the Admiralty, experiments and planning went on and in September 1910 three months after Peary had so dramatically described his North Polar journey to the audience in the Albert Hall in London, Scott judged the moment most favourable for an announcement of his plans. These were centred on an attempt to reach the South Geographical Pole. But combined with this there was, he insisted, to be an extensive programme of scientific exploration in the region west of the Ross Sea, mainly in South Victoria Land.

Organization this time followed the lines of Shackleton's expedition rather than those of Scott's first polar venture. There were no official sponsors, no administering committees; a public appeal for funds was launched but the financial responsibility for the whole expedition was, as it had been with Shackleton, the leader's and the leader's alone. Large grants were obtained from the United Kingdom and the Dominion governments. The Admiralty gave leave to all officers and men selected. The Royal Geographical Society also made a generous donation from its funds. Its President, however, took care at the same time to make quite clear the Society's traditional attitude towards these races for the geographical poles. 'So far as the attainment of the Pole is concerned,' he declared, 'it is well known that only about a hundred miles remain to be covered. ... This spot may not exhibit any features of exceptional scientific interest, and the Royal Geographical Society could hardly advocate an expedition with the South Pole as its sole objective.'

The Pole, however, was what the public wanted and it was the public who were principally providing the funds. For Scott too, though he had all the interest in scientific work which Shackleton privately and so disarmingly disavowed, the Pole had become an overwhelmingly powerful incentive. After Peary's feat, national and professional prestige were both involved and as Scott's biographer, Stephen Gwynn, has said, Antarctic exploration for Scott was 'one chapter in the romance of England on the seas. ... He was called from the routine of his profession to a new adventure, and his thought from the first was not so much to make the adventure part of his profession as to make his profession part of the adventure.' Added to this there was the latent, but none the less deep-felt and sharpening spur of rivalry with Shackleton. This was to have a profound influence on the conduct of Scott's last expedition.

It is impossible in this context not to compare, on the basis of their published biographies, the characters of these two gallant and ambitious men. The one, the dedicated naval officer, an anxious man always 'scrutinizing', a biographer asserts, 'his own performance to see if it could be bettered, and how, and for what reason, it had fallen short of the standard which might be reached by proper strength and judgement'. The other, Shackleton, the extrovert and the unconventional, the irrepressibly optimistic gambler, endowed with both audacity and luck, whose exuberant attitude to polar exploration reminded his companions of the buccaneering sea-captains of Elizabethan days.

It would be superfluous to attempt to retell in any detail the story of Scott's last expedition. The ship selected was the *Terra Nova*, an old Scottish whaler which had been one of the ships on the second *Discovery* relief expedition, and Lieutenant E. G. R. Evans, R.N., who had been south in the *Morning*, was appointed second-in-command. There was a strong scientific staff which included Dr E. A. Wilson, Scott's chief of staff and the expedition's artist, as zoologist; Dr George Simpson, meteorologist; and as geologist and surveyor R. Priestley and F. Debenham. Two members of the expedition, Captain Oates, an Army officer, and A. Cherry-Garrard, made generous donations to the expedition's funds. On 1 June 1910, three weeks after the death of King Edward VII, the *Terra Nova* sailed from London, with Scott a little tired and harassed by all the work of preparation to which had been added the (to him) new, exhausting, and distasteful task of stumping the country to raise funds. The Royal Geographical Society organized an official farewell luncheon before the *Terra Nova* left. And at this, as H. R. Mill the Society's historian recalls, 'Sir Clements Markham pronounced a moving eulogy on his chosen explorer. ...'

The expedition reached Melbourne on 12 October and there Scott received the terse cable from Madeira which read: 'Beg leave to inform you proceeding Antarctica. Amundsen.' Forestalled at the North Pole by the American Peary, Amundsen had resolved to forestall Scott in Antarctica, and until that moment had with remarkable skill kept secret this private intention, informing the press that he was going north, by way of Bering Strait, on a strictly scientific expedition. When therefore the news reached the men of the *Terra Nova* the effect was all the more staggering and Scott had a hard task controlling their indignation and their anger. But he himself determined to put aside all thought of this unexpected and very formidable competitor and continued, with every appearance of serenity, on his way.

On 2 January 1911, Mount Erebus was sighted and at Cape Evans in McMurdo Sound seventeen ponies, thirty dogs, and two of the new tracked motor sledges (the third having dropped through the ice) were disembarked in delightfully sunny weather. As Shackleton had hoped but failed to do, the autumn months were spent depot-laying, the most important depot being One Ton Camp in approximately 70° 26′ S. and near the 170th meridian east of Greenwich; a geographical position of some significance in the unfolding of the expedition's story (see map p. 293).

These autumn depot journeys had taken a heavy toll of the ponies upon which Scott like Shackleton was relying for the polar journey and especially for hauling stores to the foot of the glacier leading to the plateau. One died, one had to be shot. Six more were lost when the ice of the Sound broke under them. There were, of course, the motor sledges and the dogs; but the former were experimental, useful auxiliaries perhaps, but never intended for lengthy journeys, while the dogs, five lost before the journeys started, two rescued by Scott from a crevasse on one of the depot journeys at great personal risk to himself, proved as intractable as ever. Scott once again was disheartened by their performance and on 12 March wrote, 'Bit by bit I am losing all faith in the dogs. I am afraid they will never go the pace we look for.' Yet both Nansen and Amundsen out of their great experience had urged him to take only dogs on the expedition.

Something of Scott's attitude to the use of dogs in polar exploration was described by Sir Clements Markham in *The Lands of Silence*. 'With regard to the use of dogs', he wrote, 'there were two ways of treating them. There was the idea of bringing them all back safe and well, which was McClintock's way, and there was the way of getting the greatest amount of work possible out of them, regardless of everything else, and using them as food, which was Nansen's and Peary's way. If dogs are treated with humanity, they are in the writer's opinion not so good as men in a long journey, and Scott had an unconquerable aversion to the employment of them in the second way.' But Scott's aversion was not wholly on humanitarian grounds. In his *Voyage of the Discovery*, in a passage which Markham regarded as one of the noblest he had written, Scott describes other feelings, symbolic one might think of the spirit of Antarctica's Heroic Age. 'To my mind,' he declares, 'no journey ever made with dogs can approach the height of the fine conception which is realized when a party of men go forth to face hardships, dangers, and difficulties with their own unaided efforts, and by days and weeks of hard physical labour succeed in solving some problem of the great unknown. Surely in this case the conquest is more nobly and splendidly won.'

While the depot laying was in progress the *Terra Nova* had carried a party eastwards to explore King Edward VII Land and, off the same ice cliffs of the Bay of Whales which Shackleton had rejected as too dangerous to use as a base and starting point for his southern journey, they found securely anchored Amundsen's ship, the *Fram*. To Scott's men, it was a most disturbing discovery. He was nearer to the Pole than they by sixty miles. His dog transport – he had no other – was safely on the Ross Ice Shelf and in excellent condition. And with these dogs (Greenland dogs used to ice conditions and not Siberian dogs as Scott's were) Amundsen could start earlier, for the ponies had already shown how vulnerable they were to bad weather so early in the season.

As soon as the Antarctic winter of 1911 was over, Scott hastened on with preparations for his journey which was to be across the Ice Shelf, up the Beardmore Glacier which Shackleton had already ascended, and thence across the polar plateau. There were to be three support parties, of four men each, who would sledge across the Ice Shelf to the Beardmore Glacier. One would then return and two, one of them including a Russian boy who was in charge of the Siberian dogs and ponies, would accompany Scott's main party to within striking distance of the Pole. All the parties made unexpectedly good progress across the Ice Shelf. Then on 4 December a great summer blizzard struck. For four days they were held up and this was bad enough with a time-table so finely balanced between the limits of the Antarctic travelling season. But much worse was the effect on their route over the lower slopes of the Beardmore Glacier which they found to be utterly transformed by thunderous avalanches and deep and cavernous movements of the ice.

Up the Beardmore Glacier, harassed by this maddening delay and without ponies now that the last had been shot, not Amundsen but Shackleton haunted Scott's mind for he carried with him the diary of Frank Wild who had been with Shackleton on his southern march. 'Throughout the outward journey', wrote Raymond Priestley, geologist on the expedition, some years later, 'Shackleton's team naturally played the part of a ghostly pacemaker in the race. Urged on by a leader of tremendous physique, of impatient temperament, and for the time being obsessed with one dominating idea, the sledge parties toiled early and late until at last Scott was able to record in his diary that the loss of time on Shackleton's schedule had been made good.' But, he added, 'at what cost this had been accomplished was not realized until later, on the return journey, the polar party itself began to fail'.

The loss in fact was more than made good for the plateau was reached in three days less than Shackleton had taken. The first supporting party was sent back from the Upper Glacier Depot at a height of eight thousand feet and the two remaining parties, led by Scott and Evans, then went forward with Dr Wilson, Captain Oates, and the seaman Edgar Evans accompanying Scott, while Lieutenant Bowers and two seamen Lashly and Crean were with Evans. At an altitude of nine thousand feet and over the worst surface they had struck, they had now to man-haul all the way.

On 30 December, Scott wrote, 'A very trying tiring march. ... We have caught up Shackleton's dates'. Five days later, on 4 January 1912, Bowers, a man of immense strength and powers of endurance, was at the last moment told by Scott to join the polar party. He took no skis. His addition meant overcrowding their one tent and disorganizing a carefully prepared routine. And his selection involved, as Priestley has pointed out, the man with the shortest legs in the party having to trudge on foot for over two hundred miles over the deep soft snow of the plateau. However, with four officers instead of three and with one seaman, Edgar Evans, living, Priestley commented, 'in a thought-tight compartment by himself', Scott set out for the Pole one hundred and seventy-eight miles due south. Evans meanwhile led the supporting party back down the Beardmore Glacier. Suffering from snow-blindness on the return journey, he developed an acute and nearly fatal attack of scurvy on the Ice Shelf and was only brought to safety after a record journey (without dog-teams) of over fifteen hundred miles by the gallant efforts of the seaman Crean.

Such are the bare facts of Scott's approach to the Pole. The rest of the story, the exhausting march across the plateau, man-hauling all the way; the sight of Amundsen's black flag tied to a sledge-bearer at the Pole; the tell-tale marks of sledge tracks, skis, dogs' paws; the death of Evans, Oates's self-sacrifice, the utter dejection and tragic end of the homeward journey; these deeply moving events are part of our heritage. In January 1912 Shackleton had written to a friend in New Zealand, 'I suppose that we shall soon hear of Scott. I am inclined to think that we will hear from Amundsen first.' Five days later, on 17 January, Scott reached the Pole. And on 30 October of that same year a search party from the *Terra Nova* led by Dr Atkinson found the bodies, all except that of Oates, in a snowed-up tent on the Ross Ice Shelf eleven miles south of the well-stocked One Ton Depot. Already weakened by scurvy, they would still have had one hundred and sixty-five miles to go.

'It is strange', wrote Nansen in his preface to a posthumous edition of Scott's *Voyage of the Discovery*, 'that with our common friend, Sir Clements Markham, he [Scott] seemed to be opposed to the use of dogs for the more strenuous sledge travelling. Had he used more dogs and less man-haulage, he might have made an easy and brilliant journey to the Pole and back.' This indeed was what the Norwegian Amundsen was about to achieve when he started on 19 October 1911 from his base at the Bay of Whales, with four sledges each drawn by thirteen Greenland dogs. Unlike the British, he and his men were highly expert in the selection and handling of dog teams, techniques which Amundsen himself had learnt from the Eskimoes on King William Island during his winters there from 1903 to 1905 on his North-West Passage expedition. For the rest, he had since his own last visit to Antarctica as a member of de Gerlache's *Belgica* expedition, studied with the greatest care the reports of Shackleton's southern journey and of Scott's National Antarctic Expedition and his choice of base, every detail of his meticulously planned campaign, had been scrutinized in the light of their experiences.

After the drama of Scott's attainment of the Pole, ending in a tragedy whose circumstances as profoundly shocked as they aroused the deepest admiration of the world, the ease and speed and uneventfulness of the Norwegian operations come as an anti-climax. The depot-laying which preceded the main assault had started in February with dog-teams moving at twenty-five miles a day, and with the men sometimes riding on the sledges, sometimes ski-driving on a rope from behind. One depot party laying a depot a hundred miles from Framheim, the Norwegian base, covered the return journey in two days at an average speed of fifty miles a day. By April the depots had been established as far as 82° S. and contained between them 7,500 pounds of stores including large quantities of seal meat; a food known to Norwegians and British alike as an effective antidote to scurvy.

Starting out on 19 October, Amundsen's four sledges and fifty-two dogs reached the southernmost depot on 3 November. Ahead were the mountains and the ascent of these to the level of the plateau was to prove far the hardest stretch of the journey. There was no means of direct ascent such as Shackleton and Scott found in the Beardmore Glacier farther to the east. Instead there was a tangle of ice-streams, the largest the Axel Heiberg Glacier curving away at right angles to Amundsen's course, all of them rent by chasms or barred by towering ice blocks which time and again forced the parties reconnoitring ahead of the sledges to turn back and start afresh. The heat within these ice falls was almost torrid and the Norwegians climbing roped together, Amundsen says, 'sweated as if running races in the tropics'. By 4 December, however, they had reached the level of the polar plateau.

There, at the Butcher's Shop as the Norwegians called it, the slaughter of redundant dogs began. Out of the double teams which had been employed for the ten-thousand-foot ascent, forty dogs were shot, providing food for the remaining dogs and for the men in accordance with Nansen's system (for saving weight on the remaining crucial part of the journey) which Markham and Scott found so savage and repellent, though the shooting of ponies and the eating of pony meat appeared to the British quite tolerable. On this same day, 4 December, ten thousand feet up on the lip of the plateau, the summer blizzard which was holding up Scott and his men for four days on the Ice Shelf below, struck the Norwegian party. But Amundsen would not wait. And three days later Shackleton's southern record was surpassed. That night Amundsen wrote in his diary, 'Sir Ernest Shackleton's name will always be written in the annals of exploration in letters of fire. Pluck and grit can work wonders, and I know of no better example of this than what that man has accomplished'. On 14 December 1911, in perfect weather, the Norwegian flag was unfurled at the Pole fluttering above, as Amundsen named it, 'King Haakon VII's Plateau'. Messages were left for Scott. Then the return journey, even more speedily accomplished, began.

The Pole had been conquered, but what else was achieved? In the south, Queen Maud Range had been discovered and Amundsen reported also the discovery of 'Carmen Land' though its existence was subsequently disproved by the late Admiral Richard E. Byrd's United States Antarctic Expedition of 1928–30 during which Byrd made the first flight over the South Pole. While Amundsen was crossing the polar plateau, however, K. Prestrud made other geographical discoveries to the east of the Ross Ice Shelf. Travelling over the ice from the Bay of Whales, where unexpectedly a Japanese expedition led by Choku Shirase had appeared, Prestrud reached King Edward VII Land (where the Japanese also landed) and after some exploration claimed it on 7 December 1911 in the name of King Haakon VII. But little scientific work was done by this or by Amundsen's party. A shrewd and infinitely careful planner, a master like Peary of the technique of polar travel, Amundsen, like Peary, was wholly preoccupied by his one ambition, the attainment of the Pole; an ambition the more intense and pressing because of the fear that in the Antarctic as in the Arctic he might yet be forestalled. From this main task no diversion was permissible. No more attention was paid to science therefore than on Peary's North Polar expedition.

The situation on Scott's expedition was very different. Its work indeed – in biology, geology, glaciology, meteorology, and geophysics – which was published in several volumes at the expense of the Scott Memorial Fund, formed a new landmark in Antarctic science. Many of the scientific investigations covered by this mammoth publication were carried out by Scott's Northern Party which, under the command of Lieutenant Campbell, the Chief Officer of the *Terra Nova*, set off in mid February 1911 to explore South Victoria Land, as Shackleton's northern party under Mawson had done. The first winter was spent at Cape Adare and Borchgrevink's huts there were found to be in good enough condition to be used as workshops and storehouses. After a winter of gales and hurricanes which broke with great violence upon their hut on the open shore, the party of six – Campbell for magnetic observations, Murray Levick, surgeon and zoologist, Priestley, geologist and meteorologist, two petty officers, and a seaman – embarked in January on the *Terra Nova* for Terra Nova Bay, where they were due to conduct a six weeks' sledging reconnaissance from which they were later to be picked up by the ship.

By mid February, when the men were already on half rations, no ship had arrived, and indeed none could have reached them for ice stretched as far as the eye could see and even by mid March there was still ice stretching twenty-five miles from the coast. They were forced to winter, therefore, in an ice cave, lined with snow and insulated with gravel and dried sea-weed, and in this the six men passed the months of the winter night, bombarded incessantly by gales which swept in from the sea. In September, painfully after so long a spell of immobility, they began their march southwards to Cape Evans and were lucky to pick up old food depots on the way to relieve their hunger. They reached Hut Point on 12 November 1912, and there heard the first news of the expedition's great disaster.

The explorations of this northern scientific party, and those carried out from the Main Base over the glaciers and coast to the west of Ross Island, do not complete the list of geographical discoveries. In 1911, on her way home to New Zealand, the *Terra Nova* turned, as Shackleton in the *Nimrod* had done, north-eastwards at Cape Adare and discovered the coast of Oates Land, now on the border between New Zealand's and Australia's Antarctic territory. Despite the vast distances travelled by the land parties, this was the most extensive new discovery made on Captain Scott's last expedition.

COAST AND CONTINENT

THE attainment of the Poles, Arctic and Antarctic in succession, seemed to many to be the end of polar exploration. But a glance at the map would have shown how much remained to be done before even the geographical outline of the polar regions was complete. The Poles had attracted a multitude of expeditions. They had drawn support for polar exploration which would never have been forthcoming for some less dramatic and exciting objective. Nevertheless, the constant preoccupation with their attainment and the great effort this demanded, had inevitably restricted the scope and range of polar exploration. In the Antarctic thousands of miles of coastline were still undiscovered. Even the broad arrangement of the continent – was it divided to the east and west perhaps by a great channel linking the Weddell and the Ross Seas? – was still unknown.

In the Arctic too, though exploration had been in progress long before a Southern Continent had been as much as sighted, large gaps remained to be filled. One gap was in the coastline of north-east Greenland where a stretch of four hundred miles or more awaited discovery and charting before Peary's work could be completed and the insularity of Greenland proved. But more important, as being the last great zone of the Arctic still to be explored, was the north-western sector of the archipelago now known as the Queen Elizabeth Islands. The discovery of lands there and the exploration of the adjacent Beaufort Sea remained to complete the work begun in the south by Parry and the many British naval expeditions of the nineteenth century and continued in the north and east by Captain Otto Sverdrup, the Norwegian, at the beginning of the twentieth.

The discovery and charting of the north-east corner of Greenland was the achievement of an audacious band of Danish explorers, Mylius-Erichsen, J. P. Koch, Ejnar Mikkelsen, and

Knud Rasmussen between 1906 and 1912. Mylius-Erichsen, leader of the *Danmark* Expedition of 1906-8, was the promoter and inspiration of this enterprise but he and Lieutenant Hagen and an Eskimo, Brönlund, perished on the inland ice during the winter darkness and it fell to Ejnar Mikkelsen, leader of the *Alabama* Expedition of 1909-12, to reveal and confirm his findings. Some maps and a diary describing Mylius-Erichsen's discoveries had been recovered by J. P. Koch of the *Danmark* Expedition when, searching for Erichsen, he found the body of Brönlung on the ice sheet. Other diaries were found by Mikkelsen and these and Mikkelsen's own remarkable journeys, and those of Knud Rasmussen who led a relief expedition to northeast Greenland in 1912 (when Mikkelsen was overdue), showed how wrong Peary's maps of north-east Greenland had been. Peary's 'Navy Cliff', far from overlooking the Greenland Sea, was well inland, at the western end of the long and deep 'Independence Fjord'. Peary's 'Channel' which he had supposed divided Greenland from Peary Land was proved to be a myth. South of 'Independence Fjord', far from the coast receding, a gaunt and formidable headland was discovered, 'North-East Foreland', projecting a broad and menacing front far out into the Arctic Sea.

In addition to their coastal explorations, Danish explorers wandered widely over the inland ice in the years before the First World War and crossed and recrossed the ice sheet by routes farther north than Nansen. Rasmussen, on his First Thule Expedition of 1912 (sent to search for Mikkelsen), crossed from Kane Basin to the north-east coast. The following year J. P. Koch and Alfred Wegener crossed the northern ice sheet from east to west, starting from Dronning Louise Land. This, a peculiar ice-free nunatak region lying inland from the east coast, had been discovered by Wegener during the *Danmark* Expedition while Mylius-Erichsen was following in Peary's tracks, and from it Wegener and Koch set out in April 1913 to make the 700-mile journey to Upernavik on the west coast. In one respect this was a particularly remarkable journey in the history of Scandinavian exploration for their five sledges were drawn not by dogs but by ponies. The last had to be killed just as the Danes reached the western edge of the ice sheet early in July.

These Greenland discoveries, however, were dwarfed in extent by the far ranging explorations of the Canadian anthropologist Vilhjalmur Stefansson, leader of the Canadian Arctic Expedition of 1913–18. Stefansson, who was to become, in the tradition of Rae and Hall and Schwatka, the exponent and the protagonist of Eskimo methods of travel and survival, had spent several years living with Eskimo tribes. He had with him, as captain of his principal ship the *Karluk*, Bob Bartlett whose Antarctic ambitions had been abruptly ended by Amundsen's attainment of the South Pole; Dr R. M. Anderson as chief scientist; and Hubert Wilkins, a daring and imaginative man who was to emerge after the First World War as a pioneer of Arctic aviation and submarine navigation. They were the principal participants in a six-year expedition which in boldness of concept, in endurance, and in the range of its journeys resembles the great expeditions of Nansen and Peary.

Stefansson's plan until the moment when he and a few companions were to strike north-eastwards over the ice of the Beaufort Sea was, on paper, simple, with one group of scientists established near the mouth of the Coppermine River, the other including Stefansson himself being on board the *Karluk* which was to sail eastwards round Point Barrow and join them. Off the Point, however, the *Karluk* was beset and while Stefansson and Wilkins were hunting she was swept amid the ice far out to sea and after a drift of four months and a thousand miles sank sixty miles to the north-east of Wrangel Island. Only Bob Bartlett and a few survivors were rescued. Stefansson, meanwhile, had reached the Coppermine and from there in March 1914 set off over the frozen Beaufort Sea. He had two companions, Storkerson and Andreason, one sledge and six dogs. After a journey of three months, advancing first across the drifting pack-ice and then from floe to floe as the pack dissolved with the warmth of spring, they reached an island outlier off the north-west corner of Banks Island; a coast sighted sixty years before from the sailing ships of the Royal Navy.

Between 1914 and 1917, while Europe was plunged in the

chaos of the First World War, Stefansson and his men dressed in caribou skins and living in tents made of musk-ox skins roamed widely over the ice of the Beaufort Sea, visiting Banks Island, exploring Prince Patrick Island, and linking up with the explorations of Otto Sverdrup in the north-east of the archipelago by their discovery of Brock and Borden Islands. They linked up also with the voyages of an American explorer Donald Mac-Millan, one of Peary's men, who had between 1913 and 1917 been searching for Peary's quite mythical 'Crocker Land' which Peary thought he had seen to the north-west of Ellesmere Island during his expedition of 1906. In the course of these great sledging journeys, made against the contrary drift of the ice or through the thick and bewildering fog of the Arctic spring, Stefansson found many relics of the British naval explorers of the nineteenth century, of McClure and McClintock, and one year he visited Winter Harbour where Parry's ships had lain at anchor during the first wintering of a naval ship in the Arctic. Stefansson had little use for the rigidly conventional methods of Arctic exploration which the British were so loath to abandon and nothing was more characteristic of his refreshingly progressive approach than the last act of the Canadian Arctic expedition, the establishment of a scientific station on an ice-floe. Stefansson himself was ill with typhoid fever at the time so the party was led by Storkerson. With four companions he set up a camp on an ice-floe seven miles in diameter and fifteen miles or more in length and for six months drifted north-westwards for over four hundred miles, making regular oceanographical and glaciological observations. It was a very daring and very profitable experiment, a technique which was adopted by the Russian explorer Papanin in his North Polar drift of 1937–8. It was the prototype, moreover, of the scientific stations set up by both Russians and Americans on drifting ice islands in the Arctic after the Second World War.

Stefansson's explorations, the turning of the last corner of Greenland and, for the Arctic record, the first east to west navigation of the North-East Passage by Commander Vilkitski of the Imperial Russian Navy in 1913–15, almost closed the list of the few great Arctic enterprises which remained to be com-

322 A HISTORY OF POLAR EXPLORATION

pleted after Peary's attainment of the Pole. But in the Antarctic
the prospects and possibilities of pioneer discovery when the
polar race was over were inevitably on a much greater scale.
'The discovery of the South Pole', wrote Shackleton in March
1912 when he heard the news of Amundsen's victory, 'will not
be the end of Antarctic exploration. The next work of importance to be done in the Antarctic is the determination of the
whole coastline of the Antarctic Continent, and then a trans-
continental journey from sea to sea crossing the Pole.'

Even as Shackleton wrote, new discoveries of Antarctic coastline were being made. The zone of exploration this time lay not
in the Ross Sea area, the scene of the Scott and Shackleton
dramas, nor in the Graham Land peninsula where the Frenchman Charcot had done magnificent work, but in the region
between Oates Land discovered by Scott's expedition and Wilhelm II Land discovered by the German Antarctic Expedition
under Erich von Drygalski in 1902. Indeed the whole object of
the new expedition, the first to be launched from Australia, was
to link up these two areas by exploring a coastline which had
not been visited since the days of Wilkes and Dumont d'Urville.

The leader of these Australian explorations was Douglas
Mawson, a Yorkshireman whose parents had migrated to Australia. He was already an experienced Antarctic traveller for he
had been with Shackleton in the *Nimrod* and with Edgeworth
David had reached the South Magnetic Pole. In 1910 Scott had
invited him to join his British Antarctic Expedition, and indeed
had intended to include him in the polar party. But Mawson
had declined. He was not interested in taking part in any race
to the Pole. He was a scientist, and in any event he was most
anxious to break new ground. Mawson asked Scott, therefore,
whether he would land him and a party west of Cape Adare so
that they could explore as an independent unit. This, however,
appeared impracticable so, with the encouragement of Shackleton and the Royal Geographical Society in London, Mawson
decided to launch an expedition of his own. Australia, unlike
her sister dominion New Zealand, had shown little interest in
Antarctic exploration, as Borchgrevink and Bull and indeed even
Clements Markham had found. But now, strongly influenced by

the veteran geologist Professor Edgeworth David who had seen with his own eyes a great future for Australia in Antarctica, the Australian Association for the Advancement of Science backed Mawson's project and the Australian Government made him a grant covering more than half its cost.

Mawson's aim was scientific investigation and geographical exploration of that 'steady, continuous, laborious, and systematic kind' advocated by Sir John Murray in his famous address of 1893 to the Royal Geographical Society. To this end, to save time and ensure as complete a coverage as possible, exploration was planned from four bases simultaneously, three on the mainland, contact between the bases and with the outer world being maintained by wireless telegraphy for the first time in Antarctica. Mawson's ship was the *Aurora*, an old sealer which had gone to the relief of Greeley's Arctic expedition in 1884. She was commanded by one of the most distinguished of Antarctic navigators, Captain John King Davis.

Dogs, for the first time on a British Antarctic expedition, were to be the principal means of transport; a motor boat such as Charcot, the French explorer of western Graham Land, had used a year or two before was taken; and Mawson also planned to take an aeroplane, a bold experiment in 1911 only two years after Blériot had made the first aeroplane crossing of the English Channel. This, however, crashed on a trial flight near Adelaide and was converted into, but never used as, an air tractor sledge.

After disembarking a party of scientists to map Macquarie Island, since permanently occupied by Australia, the *Aurora* steamed southwards along the 159th meridian east of Greenwich in the direction of Oates Land. In January 1912 the ice cliffs of the continent, seventy to a hundred feet high, were seen. The *Aurora* then turned westwards and followed the ice coast of a new land which Mawson called King George V Land until they hit upon a site for their main winter base, on Cape Denison in Commonwealth Bay.

By contrast with Victoria Land away to the east with its noble mountains, its curving and glistening glaciers and tumultuous ice-falls, this was a monotonous scene, a vast and flat expanse of ice-shelf rising towards the south, broken only by the shadowed scars of crevasses or the black shapes of a few bare and solitary rocks. Winds unceasing and more furious than any in Antarctica swept this melancholy land. In September 1912, as the Northern Party of Scott's expedition were leaving Terra Nova Bay, the Australians embarked on their explorations. There were four parties, led by C. T. Madigan, F. L. Stillwell, F. H. Bickerton, and Douglas Mawson himself, all except Mawson's party man-hauling their sledges because of a shortage of dogs. While these were engaged in exploring King George V Land, a fifth party concentrating on magnetic research advanced under Lieutenant Bage south-eastwards towards the Magnetic Pole.

Between September 1912 and February, 1913 King George V Land was systematically explored. Coast and coastal highlands and the slopes of the inland ice sheet were mapped, the movement, depth, temperature, and composition of the ice was investigated and the rocks of the snow-free outcrops were examined. From these rocks and from the cliffs, lichens, algae, and mosses were collected and in some beacons of white sandstone fossilized plant remains were found, relics of a tropical Antarctica. Apart from this sparse and anaemic vegetation and a few exceptionally hardy microscopic insects which had survived the deadly cold, there was no sign of land life. But seals and penguins, skuas, Cape pigeons, and other petrels abounded and the rocky islets off the coast especially were the haunts of countless birds. In the course of these journeys, not only King George V Land but the adjacent Terre Adélie, claimed by Dumont d'Urville for France in 1840, was explored and Bage reached within 175 miles of Edgeworth David's turning point in 1909 in the vicinity of the South Magnetic Pole.

Mawson, a reserved and modest scientist, had not the least ambition to star as an Antarctic hero but one of his journeys nevertheless, a journey from Cape Denison towards Oates Land belongs, like the land journeys of Peary, Scott, and Shackleton, to the literature of the Heroic Age. His companions were B. E. S. Ninnis, a young Royal Fusilier, whose father had been surgeon with Nares's Arctic expedition of 1875, and Dr Xavier Mertz, a young Swiss mountaineer and ski champion. Their way led over two of the most gigantic of Antarctic glaciers, the Mertz and Ninnis glaciers, which poured like 'a solid ocean rising and falling in billows two hundred and fifty feet in height' down through deep valleys from the continental plateau and far out into the sea. In the midst of this ice shambles Ninnis, with sledge and dogs and most of the food, fell beyond the reach of any rope into the echoing darkness of a seemingly bottomless crevasse. A few days later, Mertz, who had been weakening fast, died in his sleep one night as he and Mawson lay close together sheltering in their makeshift tent. Mawson was then left to struggle on alone, his feet gashed and blistered, his eye-sight dimmed and confused by his exhaustion. Man-hauling a half-sledge, more than ample for the remnants of his food and gear, he survived blizzards, escaping death in a crevasse only by the narrowest of margins. He arrived at Cape Denison after a solitary journey of one hundred and sixty miles over some of the most treacherous and wind-lashed ice country in Antarctica, only to see the *Aurora* sailing out of Commonwealth Bay.

The *Aurora* under her captain, John K. Davis, had been exceedingly active during Mawson's long and alarming absence. After he had disembarked the wintering party at Cape Denison, Davis had sailed westwards, anti-clockwise round the continent, aiming to explore the coast between King George V Land and Drygalski's Kaiser Wilhelm II Land, and then to land a party under Shackleton's former right-hand man, Frank Wild, near the region of the earlier German explorations. To Davis, this linking voyage proved most instructive for it showed how the ice front had receded, just as the Ross Ice Shelf had receded, since the cursory explorations in the first half of the nineteenth century by Dumont d'Urville, John Balleny, and Wilkes. Dumont d'Urville's Côte Clarie, much of Wilkes's coast, and John Balleny's Sabrina Land were in turn sailed over and as the *Aurora* reached longitude 106° East where Wilkes's Knox Land (now Knox Coast) should have been, pack-ice held them fifty miles from the shore. Beyond Knox Coast lay 200 miles of ice-free sea – the Davis Sea – washing the shores of new land, Queen Mary Land, later claimed for the Crown. Projecting 180 miles from this new coast was an immense ice shelf,

150 miles wide. On this, the Shackleton Ice Shelf, Frank Wild and his party of seven men established their winter base.

The *Aurora* sailed northwards on 21 February 1912, Davis promising to return in January 1913 to pick up the whole expedition. Wild and his men set about their three main tasks. These were to travel south as far as the rim of the continental plateau – a journey they completed before the onset of winter – and to travel east and west from Shackleton Ice Shelf; 200 miles to the east to reach Drygalski's camp at Gaussberg and a similar distance to the west to reach the presumed position of Wilkes's Knox Coast. These journeys, begun in October and November 1912 over country riven and distorted by giant crevasses, where avalanches thundered and glaciers cracked like gun-fire, were completed by February 1913 when the *Aurora* once again appeared off the Shackleton Ice Shelf. Queen Mary Land, like Terre Adélie, proved to be a region of constant winds, gales, and blizzards which hurled down the wireless masts during the winter and on one occasion held up a sledging party led by Dr Jones for a record period of seventeen days. But for the naturalists of Wild's party it had many compensations. Near one of the numerous rocky islets off the coast they came upon an Emperor penguin rookery of 7,500 birds covering nearly five acres of fast ice. Adélie penguin rookeries were numerous. A rookery of 300 petrels was the first that had been found in Antarctica.

The *Aurora* arrived, a month overdue, on 23 February and her captain, John K. Davis, had a story to tell no less eventful than that of Frank Wild and his men. Planning to relieve Mawson's base first before going on to relieve Wild, he had anchored off Cape Denison on 13 January and one by one the sledging parties – Madigan and Stillwell, Bage and Bickerton – had come in. But of Mawson there was no sign. Davis waited until, indeed until after, 15 January when Mawson had told him that if by chance he was missing he was to take over leadership of the expedition. But there was still no news. He had therefore to decide what to do. The relief of Wild's party on the Shackleton Ice Shelf – they had expected him on 30 January – was obviously an immediate duty, so he placed Madigan in charge of the search for Mawson and sailed for Queen Mary Land. On the way, however, a wireless message told him of Mawson's safe return and of the death of Ninnis and Mertz. Madigan asked him to turn back to Cape Denison and he tried, despite dense mist followed by heavy seas. But he could not possibly have landed. He turned back again therefore to the Shackleton Ice Shelf to bring off Wild and his men. But it was now far too late in the season to risk another journey to Cape Denison to take off Mawson and the rest of the Australasian Antarctic Expedition and the *Aurora* sailed for Australia. There and in England, meanwhile, a Mawson Relief Fund had been launched and Davis was able to return to Cape Denison in December 1913 to rescue Mawson and his men after their second winter in Antarctica.

It was characteristic of Mawson that even after so long and so harrowing a campaign he refused to turn north until the whole coastline between the Mertz Glacier and Gaussberg had been charted from the sea. This survey of a great arc of Antarctic coast was the last link in the chain which Mawson had forged and by it the discoveries of Wilkes and Dumont d'Urville, Scott and Drygalski, were joined. At each end were the newly discovered regions of King George V Land and Queen Mary Land, the first lands to be acquired there by the British Crown.

Shackleton had placed next in importance to such coastal discoveries as these, a trans-continental journey from the Weddell Sea to the Ross Sea crossing the Pole. It was no new idea for in 1910 William Spiers Bruce, the discoverer of Coats Land in the Weddell Sea, had circulated a printed prospectus appealing for funds for just such an expedition, but without result. Moreover, the idea of a trans-continental crossing had also been taken up by a German explorer Wilhelm Filchner who was attracted like Bruce by the possibility that it might settle a problem of absorbing interest to Antarctic explorers and geographers, whether a channel divided the central Antarctic land-mass between the two great embayments of the Weddell and the Ross Seas. But for Filchner too a trans-continental expedition, involving two widely separated ships and land bases, proved far beyond the resources he could raise. Rather than abandon the scheme altogether however he decided to restrict himself to a landing on the Weddell Sea coast, since this, if it succeeded, would at least establish a starting point for an attempt to cross the continent and would be a landing on a coast which, apart from the stretch cursorily examined from the sea by Bruce, was totally unexplored.

Filchner's ship, the *Deutschland*, a Norwegian sailing ship with auxiliary engines, left Hamburg harbour on her way to Buenos Aires in May 1911. And from Buenos Aires, where Filchner talked with Amundsen on board the *Fram*, she sailed, her decks alive with Manchurian ponies and Greenland dogs (and oxen, sheep, and pigs presented by Argentine admirers), for South Georgia. Her captain was Richard Vahsel and she carried two doctors and a scientific staff of five, equipped for special research both on land and at sea. On 14 December, the pack was sighted and entered well to the east as Bruce had recommended. The ice increased in density as they moved southwards but by 24 January they were through it and off Bruce's Coats Land in a relatively open sea. As they moved westwards they saw projecting towards the north and west the long monotonous line of an ice front, the frontal edge of a vast iceshelf whose limits could nowhere be seen. Filchner was now well beyond the range of Bruce's explorations and in a region never explored. He therefore named the new territory 'Prinz Regent Luitpold Land' (Luitpold Coast) and the ice-shelf the 'Kaiser Wilhelm Barrier'. This name, at the Kaiser's command, was subsequently changed to Filchner Ice Shelf, the name which is retained today.

As the *Deutschland* edged her way cautiously along the ice front a bay appeared and was named after the *Deutschland*'s captain Vahsel Bay. This desolate stretch of ice shelf Filchner chose as the site for his winter base, 'Stationseisberg', the base from which he proposed to explore both westwards and southwards as far as the junction with the continental land. By dawn on Sunday, 18 February, the hut was almost ready when, with a crash and a rumble like the sound, Filchner said, of a hundred guns, the ice front to the south fell away into the sea. The men of Stationseisberg were in immediate danger for the ocean swell and the high spring tide created a chaos of floating ice blocks round the berg and set it slowly drifting out to sea. Men and stores, ponies and dogs, were rushed on board the *Deutschland* which then moved out into the open water. But when she returned Vahsel Bay as first seen by Filchner and his men had disappeared.

The collapse of the ice front, however, had left a landing place and from this early in March the Germans sledged southwards as far as the inland ice. This first landing on the coast of the Weddell Sea so late in the season allowed no time whatever for extensive exploration. As it was, the Germans had left their departure too late and the *Deutschland* was beset and compelled to drift for nine months north and west with the ice. It was a high tribute to her builders that the Norwegian ship should have survived an experience which three years later was to crush and obliterate another exploring vessel. The long drift through the lugubrious winter darkness was singularly uneventful. Health was excellent; dogs and ponies were comfortably housed in stables built on the drifting pack; and Filchner was even able to launch a number of sledging expeditions. These at least made one valuable contribution to Antarctic geography for they disproved the existence of 'New South Greenland', land reported by the imaginative American sealing captain Benjamin Morrell in 1823. On 26 November 1912 the *Deutschland* moved gently through decaying pack into open water in the direction of South Georgia after a drift of 600 geographical miles of latitude. The only loss was the death of her captain who was buried at sea near the Antarctic Circle.

Filchner's landing place, Vahsel Bay, had – as he realized – one great advantage from the point of view of a trans-Antarctic crossing. It was the point on the Weddell Sea coast nearest the Geographical Pole. The German landings there had indeed placed the whole trans-Antarctic project in a far more favourable light than at the time of Bruce's original proposals. The coast at both the start and the finish of the crossing was now known, the Ross Sea side with all the intimate, detailed knowledge which had accumulated during the Scott and Shackleton expeditions. All that now remained was to organize the trans-Antarctic expedition, starting on the least familiar and terminating on the best known coast, in accordance with Bruce's plan.

In Germany Filchner set about the promotion of an Austro-Hungarian trans-Antarctic expedition. In England Shackleton at Bruce's suggestion took over his plans and used the threat of foreign competition with excellent effect in his campaign to whip up support. This was a good deal easier to win now than in Bruce's day when the attention of the world had been wholly concentrated on the Pole. Except by a few captious critics, the great hazards of a trans-continental expedition – in a pre-air and pre-Sno-Cat age – were forgotten. The narrow escape of the *Deutschland* from the ice in the most dangerous of Antarctic seas, the lack of provision for any reconnaissance of the wholly unknown stretch between Weddell Sea and the Pole, the narrow time limits within which a sledging journey of over two thousand miles would have to be accomplished, these risks and dangers, like the cost and complications of so elaborate an expedition, were submerged in the rising tide of public enthusiasm.

Filchner's schemes for an Austro-Hungarian expedition met no such encouragement, the resources of Germany and her allies, on the eve of the First World War, not being allowed to be diminished by even the cost of an Antarctic expedition. In England it was otherwise. The early days of the Imperial Trans-Antarctic Expedition admittedly were anxious, with Shackleton in debt to the extent of £50,000. But, to his astonishment and relief, a wealthy but dour and cautious Scot, the jute manufacturer Sir James Caird, came to the rescue with a donation equal to half this sum. With this support, with a grant of £10,000 from the Government, generous donations from two of his most faithful admirers, Miss Elizabeth Dawson Lambton and Dame Stancomb Wills, and substantial assistance from the Royal Geographical Society, the Imperial Trans-Antarctic Expedition was firmly established.

In its essentials Shackleton's plan was just what Bruce had proposed, namely the landing of a crossing party on the Weddell Sea coast and the landing of a support party in the Ross Sea. The latter would lay depots across the Ice Shelf up to the Beardmore Glacier for the use of the crossing party descending from the Pole. There was, however, one difference. Shackleton did not intend that any scientific work should be done by the crossing party. Science was to be the function of two subsidiary parties, one (geological) moving westwards towards Graham Land, the other travelling eastwards towards Enderby Land.

The ships of the Trans-Antarctic Expedition were the *Polaris,* a new Norwegian vessel renamed the *Endurance* after Shackleton's family motto, and the *Aurora* from Sir Douglas Mawson's expedition. The *Endurance,* destined for the Weddell Sea, was equipped with a primitive wireless receiver, but not with a transmitter, although a transmitter had been very successfully used on Mawson's expedition. This equipment (which never worked) was accepted by Shackleton with the greatest reluctance. Wireless might mean the intervention of sponsors, or tiresome directions, or reminders of those problems and complexities of civilized life by which he found himself so constantly baffled at home. In the Antarctic at least he was at peace and master of his destiny. He did not welcome means, however valuable from a safety point of view, whereby this peace could be disturbed.

No sooner were the two ships prepared, the *Aurora* in Australia, the *Endurance* in England, than the First World War broke out. Shackleton was quick to act. Without even consulting the donors, Sir James Caird and others, who had made the expedition possible he offered it, ships, men, dogs, and equipment, to the Government as a single unit. Mr Winston Churchill, then at the Admiralty, thanked him for the offer. But he instructed him nevertheless to carry on with his Antarctic plans and on Saturday, 8 August 1914, four days after Britain's declaration of war on Germany, the *Endurance* sailed from Plymouth Harbour, bound for the Weddell Sea. Shackleton could not have done more than offer his entire expedition to the Government. Nevertheless, the departure of the men of the *Endurance* at so critical a moment in British history did not fail to arouse comment and this sharpened considerably two years later when urgent demands for a relief expedition arrived.

In South Georgia Shackleton heard from the whalers that it was an exceptionally bad ice year in the Weddell Sea. He decided nevertheless to try and reach Vahsel Bay but to postpone the start of the crossing journey until the Antarctic summer

(October–March) of 1915–16. As Bruce and Filchner and the whalers at South Georgia advised, Shackleton entered the Weddell Sea as far east as possible, as far indeed as the fifteenth meridian of west longitude, and by New Year's Day 1915 the *Endurance* had steamed through nearly five hundred miles of pack into the clear blue water which washed the flat and featureless ice front of Coats Land. By the middle of January 1915, Bruce's farthest south was exceeded, then a new coastline, no less flat, no less monotonous, appeared, presenting an ice front rising forty feet above the water. This new coast apparently linked Coats Land with Filchner's 'Luitpold Land' and Shackleton named it after his principal benefactor, Sir James Caird. A giant glacier tongue projecting from it – it has since disintegrated – he named after Dame Stancomb Wills.

Shackleton had no intention of landing north of Filchner's Vahsel Bay on Luitpold Coast if he could possibly avoid it for to do so would mean adding two hundred miles to the journey to the Pole. Nevertheless, as a precautionary measure he looked for landing places and found one in a bay sheltered from the southeasterly winds by a glacier towering four hundred feet high. There in 'Glacier Bay', as he called it, he could have landed; it was a chance which, if (with aircraft) he could have seen what lay ahead, he would perhaps have taken. But he rejected it. 'I had reason later', Shackleton wrote, 'to remember it with regret.'

From this point on Caird Coast Vahsel Bay was a hundred miles away. But the *Endurance* had covered little more than half this distance when she was beset, on 19 January 1915, in the ice. Then the long and ultimately disastrous drift, longer even than the drift of the *Deutschland*, began. South-west, north-west, once within forty miles of the Filchner Ice Shelf, then away to the north-west again, for nine months the *Endurance*, her timbers cracking and groaning in the tightening grip of the ice, drifted towards her inevitable doom. Then the climax came, the death of a ship destroyed by the pack. 'At last,' wrote Shackleton, 'the twisting, grinding floes were working their will on the ship. It was a sickening sensation to feel the decks breaking up under one's feet, the great beams bending then snapping with a noise like heavy gunfire. . . . Just before leaving I looked down the engine room skylight as I stood on the quivering deck, and saw the engines dropping sideways as the stays and bed-plates gave way. I cannot describe the impression of relentless destruction which was forced upon me as I looked down and around. The floes, with the force of millions of tons of moving ice behind them were simply annihilating the ship.'

Shackleton had his plans well prepared and the disembarkation of men and dogs and equipment went without a hitch. But where should they now make for? For Nordenskjöld's hut three hundred and twelve miles to the north? For Robertson Island, the nearest land to the west? Could they indeed move at all over ice too soft and too broken for sledges, yet with too little open water to enable them to launch the boats? From Ocean Camp, near the spot where the ice had closed over the shattered top-masts of the *Endurance*, they moved to Patience Camp and from there they tried to sledge to the nearest land to the west. But in seven days, with dogs and sledges pulling only two out of the three cumbrous ship's boats they made no more than seven miles; a rate at which they would have taken three hundred days to reach the nearest land. All they could do was to wait for the ice to break up so that they could launch the boats. Meanwhile they could eat and sleep, sleep and eat, meals mostly of seal and penguins though varied on one memorable occasion by some un-digested fish from the stomach of a leopard seal. The weather over the Weddell Sea was astonishing in its variety. In the first half of January it had been warm and calm, with their ice floe almost stationary. Then a succession of south-westerly gales rising to blizzards swept them across the Antarctic Circle to within one hundred and fifty miles of land. March 1916 was a month of constant and extraordinary change; continuous gales and blizzards, days when the air was still but intensely cold, then sunshine, then the strangest of Antarctic sights, hours of rain. By March, they had drifted far to the north, beyond the northern extremity of the Graham Land peninsula. Clarence Island and Elephant Island, outliers of the South Shetland group, were only a hundred miles away.

Shackleton and his men sighted Clarence Island in the early days of April 1916. Nevertheless, though land was in sight and a barely perceptible swell beneath the ice told them that the open sea was near, those days were more dangerous than any they had so patiently endured because the pack, due to the action of wind and swell, was slowly disintegrating. Yet they hesitated to launch the boats for the swell, lengthening as they approached the open sea, had begun to drive the floes together in great confusion. Past Clarence Island, however, with the edge of the pack in sight, they dared wait no longer and as they launched the boats they were met by 'a rush of foam-clad water and tossing ice' which swept towards them like a tidal bore.

Shackleton's objective was Elephant Island. By day they rowed and sailed through a maze of drifting and colliding floes and bergs, uncomfortably conscious all the time that the killer whales which wallowed and blew around them with a hissing noise like the jets of a steam engine might mistake the white bottoms of the boats for their familiar ice. By night they camped on the floes. But rest was not easy for at any moment the floes without warning might open up beneath their tents. Indeed on one occasion Shackleton, warned by some sixth sense of danger, was only just in time to snatch a man in his sleeping-bag out of the sea before the two halves of a floe, as suddenly as they had opened, crashed together again.

Shackleton had not been long on Elephant Island before he decided that the health and mental condition of his men and the shortage of food made it essential that he should try somehow to reach South Georgia for help before winter froze the sea around them. Leaving the men on Elephant Island in charge of the ever-reliable Frank Wild he set off across 800 miles of ocean in one of the ship's boats the *James Caird*. The story of this voyage, comparable only with the wonderful open boat journey of Barents's men in the Arctic in the sixteenth century, is an epic of maritime adventure retold in one of the most stirring of all books of adventure, Shackleton's *South*. The *James Caird* had only a makeshift decking of canvas. Often the whale boat was half-full of water and shuddering under the blows of gigantic waves. But by superb seamanship and navigation, fortified by the dauntless, invincible spirit of a man who remained unshaken by even such mountainous and destructive seas, they made a landfall and after crossing (for the first time in history) the mountains of South Georgia they reached the safety of a whaling station.

The year 1916, the year of the massacres at Verdun and on the Somme, was not a time when the people of Britain were readily inclined to turn their thoughts to the Antarctic, and Shackleton's urgent appeals that an immediate relief expedition be launched fell in some quarters on unsympathetic ears. In the end, however, not one but four relief expeditions were organized – two British, one Uruguayan, and one Chilean – and these between May and August 1916 attempted in turn to reach the men on Elephant Island. On 30 August 1916 the fourth and last of the relief expeditions on the Chilean ship *Yelcho* got through with Shackleton, of course, on board, as he had been on all the previous but unsuccessful attempts.

The 800-mile boat journey, the desperate scramble over the mountains, and these four successive voyages were not the end of Shackleton's unceasing efforts to rescue the men of the Imperial Trans-Antarctic Expedition. At the other side of the continent the Ross Sea party had been in scarcely less desperate straits. They at least had carried out their allotted task, that of laying depots southwards to the Beardmore Glacier. But in May 1915 as the *Endurance* was drifting towards disaster in the Weddell Sea, the ice moorings of the Ross Sea ship, the old *Aurora*, parted in a blizzard leaving stranded the ten men who had wintered at Cape Evans on Ross Island. For nine months, the *Aurora* under her first officer Lieutenant J. R. Stenhouse drifted in the ice of the Ross Sea, battered, rudderless, and with little coal. But she escaped and established wireless contact with New Zealand. Shackleton reached New Zealand in December 1916. Within three weeks, the *Aurora*, chartered by the British, Australian, and New Zealand governments, was refitted and sailed under her former commander John K. Davis, with Shackleton again on board, to rescue the Ross Sea survivors.

Shackleton's Imperial Trans-Antarctic Expedition was a failure. But it was a failure distinguished by a display of courage and endurance and, on Shackleton's part once again, of powers of leadership unparalleled in polar exploration. Geographically it had added little to the discoveries of Bruce and Filchner beyond the short southern stretch of the Caird Coast but even so, seen in the perspective of history, the expedition made a contribution, and possibly a decisive one, to future Antarctic achievement. Throughout the ten-month drift of the *Endurance* and during the long sojourn on the drifting pack, a young Scottish geologist from Cambridge, J. M. Wordie (now Sir James Wordie) Shackleton's chief of scientific staff, had made careful and continuous observations of the movement and nature of the sea ice. More than forty years later when the ships of the British International Geophysical Year expedition and of Sir Vivian Fuchs's trans-Antarctic expedition entered the Weddell Sea the course they took, the course which brought them safely through the pack to the clear blue waters of the ice-bound coast, was dictated very largely by the intimate knowledge of sea ice conditions gained by Wordie during the drift of the Imperial Trans-Antarctic Expedition.

For the historian of the Antarctic, the year 1916, the year of the Shackleton relief expeditions, is memorable also because during it Sir Clements Markham, to whom more than anyone the revival of Antarctic exploration at the turn of the century had been due, died at the age of eighty-six. Born in 1830 he had lived long enough to remember the great days of sail when the ships of the British Navy had battled in Arctic seas and by his death the link with the Franklin search, with the dramas and the tensions which had so stirred the mid-Victorian emotions, was broken. Of recent years, he had been a little out of touch, uncomfortably aware of new trends, of the new language and pervasive influence of science which he instinctively distrusted, and because of this perhaps had clung with even greater obduracy to his reactionary ways. It was so even at the moment of his death, from injuries due to burning in his house in Eccleston Square. As a midshipman he used to read in his hammock, holding a candle in one hand and a book in the other. He was reading like this in bed one night when the candle dropped and the bed caught fire. Above the bed an electric light bulb hung unlit.

PART V

POSTSCRIPT TO POLAR HISTORY

23

BETWEEN THE TWO WORLD WARS

THE polar events of the forty years which divide Shackleton's
Trans-Antarctic Expedition from the great concentration on
polar science during the International Geophysical Year of
1957–8 are too close to be seen in historical perspective. However, the briefest survey shows how the end of the war marked
the closing of an old, the opening of a new, era marked by certain distinctive trends, developments, and influences. Indeed
almost at once the dividing line, the break with the past, was
symbolized by a calamitous event. This was the death in the
Antarctic of Ernest Shackleton, on board his ship the *Quest*, on
5 January 1922, off the island of South Georgia during a voyage
to discover new coastlands in the region of Enderby Land. By
his death the world was deprived of the greatest individual
leader in polar exploration, a man whose spirit, brave and generous, gay and adventurous, had illuminated a great era of Antarctic exploration.

In the technical field, the most important new development
after the war, more important by far than the introduction of
steam-powered ships in the nineteenth century, was the entry
of the polar regions into the Air Age; not only in the sense of
the use of air power in exploration, for reconnaissance, for transport and supply, for communication, but in providing (in the
Arctic) motives for research – especially in meteorology – which
would directly benefit polar aviation. There were, too, important developments in the political field leading in the years
between the two world wars to the partitioning among the interested powers of almost all the discovered polar areas. Governments claiming sovereignty over polar territories became enthusiastic patrons of polar exploration, seeking to consolidate
their claims by establishing land bases or by fostering research
and development projects. Occupation, administration, plans for

research leading to the development of natural resources, mapping, these were all evidence of state activity supporting claims to sovereignty; evidence which an international court would be very likely to require in cases of disputed or overlapping claims as in the Antarctic. These new incentives to exploration, like the old incentive, rivalry for the Poles, were valuable – even if they were not particularly attractive – to the explorers and scientists concerned because, even though only incidentally, they aided the advancement of exploration and research.

Parallel with these technical and political developments were important developments in the scientific field, brought about by the demand for a greater coordination and exchange of information about polar exploration, scientific discovery, and techniques. In the national field this led to the establishment of polar centres or institutes, such as the Scott Polar Research Institute founded in 1920 out of the proceeds of the Scott Memorial Fund; or, among government organizations, the 'Chief Administration of the Northern Sea Route' set up by the Soviet Government in 1932. In the international field this same need for greater integration of effort, the more urgent as exploring expeditions multiplied and specialization increased, led to the launching of the Second International Polar Year of 1932–3. The First International Polar Year, of 1882–3, too often remembered only by the calamity which befell the Greeley expedition, had added substantially to knowledge of geomagnetism and meteorology. The Second International Year, which was concentrated like its predecessor in the Arctic, made further advances in these branches of geophysics and in addition embarked upon studies of the ionosphere, the ionized region of the upper atmosphere responsible for the reflection of radio waves. This was research for which the polar regions are particularly important because of the long alternating period of daylight and darkness. It became increasingly important as radio communication developed rapidly after the First World War. The most important advances during the Second International Polar Year were made, however, in meteorology, vitally important to the progress of polar aviation in peace and in war. During the Second International Polar Year, ninety-four meteorological stations were manned in the Arctic (as against thirteen during the First Polar Year) and for the first time reliable information was provided about Arctic weather and the relation between ice drift and movement and the behaviour of the winds.

The realization that commercial aircraft, if they could be safely navigated across the Arctic by Great Circle routes, could greatly shorten the flying time between the great centres of population in the eastern and western hemispheres led many exploring expeditions between the wars to study the meteorology of the Greenland ice sheet not only because it lay in the track of future air routes but because its great mass of ice, like the even greater mass covering the Antarctic continent, had a profound influence on weather. Studies of Arctic weather and Arctic ice were no less important to sea navigation, particularly for the new Soviet Government of Russia whose northern coast is especially vulnerable to the circular and branching ice movements of the Arctic Ocean. Thus the beginnings of an organized effort by Russia to promote and expand Arctic research was a development of the first importance between the wars.

The impact of air power did not greatly affect the pattern of polar travel until after the Second World War. This remained, in the classic tradition established by the North American and Scandinavian travellers, as firmly based as ever on the dog and sledge. Even the British, opposed as their leading explorers had for so long been to the use of dogs in exploration, had learnt their lesson and not only adopted but now strove hard to improve upon the sledging techniques which had won for America and Norway the Poles.

One of the earliest Arctic expeditions after the First World War, the Fifth Thule Expedition led by Knud Rasmussen the Danish explorer, was very much in the pattern of pre-war days. This traversed for the first time by dog-sledge the North-West Passage. Accompanied only by an Eskimo woman and an Eskimo youth, Rasmussen started in March 1923 from Repulse Bay (in the northern waters of Hudson Bay, near Southampton Island) and travelling by way of Rae Isthmus, Boothia Peninsula, King William Island, and the Arctic coast of Canada reached in August 1924 the eastern shores of Bering Strait. As a feat of endurance and an exposition of sledging technique this was a remarkable performance and by this single continuous journey Rasmussen linked together many of the discoveries arduously won by Canadian trappers and traders and British naval officers during the nineteenth century.

There was, however, little scope left in the Arctic in the second quarter of the twentieth century for record-breaking journeys of such magnitude. Indeed only within the great ice sheet covering Greenland was there scope for exploration on anything like the grand scale. For this reason and because of its great significance in ice and weather research, innermost Greenland in the nineteen-thirties attracted a succession of expeditions, German, British, and American, the most important between the wars. In each case, as the earlier Danish explorers had advised, a central weather station in the heart of the ice sheet for continuous observations was the core of the scientific programme.

Between 1926 and 1931 three expeditions established stations of this kind: the University of Michigan Expedition led by a vigorous controversialist in Antarctic history, Professor William H. Hobbs; the German Greenland Expedition led by the fifty-one-year-old Professor Alfred Wegener who had been with Mylius-Erichsen in Greenland; and the British Arctic Air Route Expedition led by an adventurous and volatile young Cambridge Arctic traveller, H. G. (Gino) Watkins. Of these Wegener's was scientifically the most productive and, in the use of motor-sledges and new instruments for measuring the thickness of the ice cover by echo-sounding (seismic) methods, was technologically the most advanced. A central weather station was built on the 71st parallel, some 250 miles from the west coast, but in November 1930 the expedition had its tragedy for on a journey, a necessary but dangerous journey at the onset of winter, from this station to the coast, Wegener and a companion, Willemsen, died of exhaustion and exposure.

The British Arctic Air Route Expedition, led by Gino Watkins, was the most ambitious Arctic expedition sent out from Britain since the Scott and Shackleton days. Its motive was meteorological research and survey against the day when commercial aircraft flying over Greenland would accomplish a

North-West Passage by air. The most promising air route from England to Canada and the Pacific coast, which lay over Greenland, Baffin Island, and Hudson Bay, crossed the least known part of Greenland. The coast, moreover, for two hundred miles north of Angmagssalik was unsurveyed and the interior was unknown. To survey this coast, to explore the interior, looking especially for high mountains, and to make observations of weather conditions from a central station as both the Germans and Americans had done were the aims of the expedition.

Its members were for the most part young men from Cambridge which had since the war become Britain's chief centre of polar activity and the breeding ground for her polar leaders of the future. This was no accident. Living there were no less than three polar veterans, men who had served with Scott and Shackleton, men who had personally shared in the adventures, the dramas, the tragedies, and disappointments of British polar exploration in the pre-war Heroic Age; all of them in an excellent position to stimulate, advise, and instruct the younger generation. Two, Raymond Priestley and Frank Debenham, had been largely responsible for the foundation in Cambridge of the Scott Polar Institute. A third, J. M. Wordie, chief of scientific staff to Shackleton on the Trans-Antarctic Expedition (he was to play a leading part in the promotion of polar exploration in Britain after the Second World War), organized and led a number of summer expeditions of young men from Cambridge and elsewhere during the thirties; to Greenland, to Baffin Island, to Ellesmere Island. The value of such training was clear from those who gained distinction later in the nineteen-thirties and became the leaders after the Second World War when Britain once again took a foremost part in polar exploration. The release from the long isolation and restrictions of war has always been a spur to travel and adventure. Of the young men who thus emerged after the First World War none seemed to his elders to personify more completely the spirit of youthful adventure, none seemed to show greater promise of being the leader of the future, than the twenty-three-year-old Gino Watkins.

The British Arctic Air Route Expedition sailed in July 1930

in Shackleton's old ship, the *Quest*. Watkins had become a passionate advocate of Eskimo methods of travel, which had indeed
been the secret of American and Scandinavian success, and dogs
and sledges were to be the chief means of transport as well as
Eskimo skin canoes (kayaks) in the handling of which Watkins
had learnt to display extraordinary skill. Two motor boats were
also carried in the *Quest* and two De Haviland aircraft for reconnaissance and air photography to aid the land surveyors. This
was a sign of the times. But it was not the first use of aircraft
by a British Arctic expedition. Six years earlier a party of young
men led by George Binney (now Sir George Binney) from Oxford had been pioneers in this respect and had made a number
of successful flights in a seaplane over Spitsbergen and Nordaustland.

The expedition's most important contribution was probably
their very careful survey of the eastern coastal strip. Two long
sledging trips were also made westwards across the ice sheet,
one carrying kayaks for use in the fjords and streams between
the ice edge and the coast. But the most adventurous journey
was one in open boats (also carrying kayaks) made by Watkins,
Augustine Courtauld, and Captain Lemon of the Signals along
the ice-infested east coast from Angmagssalik southwards to
Prins Christians Sund, a distance of seven hundred miles. One
episode at the inland station was reminiscent of the feats of
endurance and fortitude of the Scott and Shackleton days. Watkins's plan, based on absurdly optimistic meteorological fore-
casts, had been to relieve the central weather station on the ice
sheet every month. But the blizzards, blandly prophesied as in-
frequent by the weather experts, blew weekly during October at
over a hundred miles an hour. In such conditions repeated
journeys to the heart of the ice sheet were impracticable and
Courtauld volunteered to remain at the station alone, to maintain observations throughout the winter. On 6 December he
began his solitary watch. On 5 May the following year he was
relieved. Snowed up towards the end of this lonely sojourn, his
submerged hut swept by blizzards which roared across the ice
and snow above his head, without fuel for either heating or
cooking for weeks before relief arrived, Courtauld survived and

returned in perfect health after a physical and psychological experience unique in polar history.

While in Greenland Watkins talked much of a great Antarctic project he had in mind, a trans-Antarctic expedition in the form of a sledging journey from the head of the Weddell Sea to the Bay of Whales. However, he failed to raise funds for this and returned to Greenland but there was drowned while hunting, as the Eskimoes hunted, in one of the kayaks in whose use he had shown such skill.

Allied to the meteorological studies which had been the central purpose of all these Greenland expeditions was the study of ice, its thickness, its composition, its movement and drift in relation to climatic factors. The study of ice drift and ice movement over the sea was an urgent matter for Russia's Administration for the Northern Sea Route and in May 1937 Soviet scientists led by Ivan Papanin embarked on an expedition which in its use as a scientific base of an ice floe drifting with the Arctic currents looked back to Stefansson's pioneer drift over the Beaufort Sea and forward to the air-supported Russian and American ice-drifting stations after the Second World War. In May 1937 Papanin's expedition was landed by aircraft on an ice-floe near the Pole and on this Papanin and three companions began a drift of nine months, southward with the cold currents flowing down past the north-east coast of Greenland. More than once, as when their floe collided with some grounded ice and was split apart, they were in great jeopardy but their slowly diminishing base lasted long enough to bring them to 70° 54′ S., midway between Scoresby Sund on the Greenland Coast and Jan Mayen island. There they were picked up by Soviet ice-breakers on 19 February 1938. Soundings near the Pole revealed an ocean depth of 14,000 feet and, throughout the drift, ice and weather observations were made, the latter enabling Russian pilots in 1937 to fly non-stop across the Pole to the North American Pacific coast.

Courtauld's five months of self-imposed imprisonment in the ice and this adventurous Russian enterprise greatly stimulated public excitement about polar exploration. But it was in the air rather than at sea or on land that the most spectacular, the most ambitious, and the most costly Arctic undertakings took place, though many of them contributed more to the progress of aviation than to geography. The Scandinavians, Salomon Andrée the Swedish balloonist, and none more than the great Norwegian Nansen, had all along been enthusiastic about the possibilities of trans-Arctic aviation and the first pioneer after the war was Nansen's protégé Roald Amundsen, the conqueror by sea of the North-West Passage and the first man to reach the South Pole overland. In May 1925 Amundsen and the American explorer Lincoln Ellsworth, who was later to gain distinction in Antarctic flying, left Kongsfjorden, Spitsbergen, in two Dornier flying boats and landed amidst high and hummocky ice 120 miles from the North Pole. They managed to get only one of their aircraft airborne again and in this returned to Spitsbergen, having made soundings of the Arctic Ocean near the Pole and accomplished a reconnaissance of over 12,000 square miles of the polar basin.

The following year Commander R. E. Byrd of the United States Navy, who was to be first since Wilkes to lead an American Antarctic expedition, joined in these Arctic flights. He had already gained experience of Arctic aviation with MacMillan's 1925 expedition to Peary's mythical 'Crocker Land', and on 9 May 1926 he flew from Spitsbergen to the North Pole. The next flight, the same year and again by Amundsen and Ellsworth, was indirectly to lead to one of the earliest disasters in Arctic aviation. The aircraft was an airship, the *Norge*, designed by an Italian designer, Colonel Umberto Nobile, and in this, the first flight by airship over the Arctic, Amundsen, Ellsworth, and Nobile tried to fly from Spitsbergen to Alaska. The first stage of the flight was remarkably successful and three flags, American, Norwegian, and Italian, were thrown down on the tumbled sea ice around the Pole. But during the flight onwards to Alaska they were constantly in imminent danger. Ice thickly encrusting the side of the ship was torn loose by the whirling propellers and flung against the gas-bags. Ice heavily encrusted the bows of the *Norge*. Their radio equipment had long ceased to function, and even their sun compass was heavily coated in ice. Nevertheless, navigating almost blind and without contact with the ground, they made an exceedingly fortunate landfall in Alaska on 14

May. They had flown non-stop from Europe to America over a distance of 3,400 miles.

The year 1928 was a notable year in the history of Arctic aviation both for the flights of the Australian explorer Hubert Wilkins and for the disaster which befell the airship *Italia* launched by the Italian North Polar Expedition. Wilkins had learnt to fly in the early experimental days of 1910–12 when aircraft seemed little more than a transparent pattern of fragile wires and struts. He was also an experienced Arctic traveller having been with Vilhjalmur Stefansson on his Canadian Arctic Expedition during the First World War. He had all along been convinced of the value of aircraft in polar reconnaissance but more important from the point of view of his backers, a group of Detroit business men, was his conviction that the day was not far off when commercial airways would fly on schedule across the Pole. Wilkins's trans-Arctic flight of 1928 was the climax to numerous earlier efforts, as costly as they were discouraging. On one of these, in 1927, he and his pilot Carl Ben Eielson crashed five hundred miles from Point Barrow, their starting point, and marched for fourteen days over the ice; an experience they would never have survived had it not been for the lessons Wilkins had learnt from Stefansson on their long journeys over the sea-ice of the Beaufort Sea. The flight in 1928, in a Lockheed Vega, began on 16 April from Point Barrow and Wilkins nearing Spitsbergen was almost within sight of victory when he was forced, after a continuous flight of 20 hours 20 minutes, to land on Likholmen – 'Dead Man's Island' – off the west coast of the archipelago. It took both men a week to become airborne again, with Eielson in the cockpit and Wilkins pushing with one foot on the ice. But they succeeded and within half an hour landed at Grønfjorden, Spitsbergen.

The Arctic flight of the Italian airship, the *Italia*, which followed a quarrel between Umberto Nobile and Roald Amundsen, was in many ways an unfortunate affair, and led afterwards to bitter controversy. Nobile, designer of the airship which he specially adapted for polar use, persuaded the Italian government to launch an Italian North Polar Expedition, and in order to add a scientific purpose to the flight declared that he would not

only land and moor three weeks at the Pole but would also survey from the air islands off the north Russian coast and in the
Canadian archipelago. The Russian part of the programme was
completed successfully. Then Nobile set out across the Arctic
Ocean for the Pole. The *Italia* was forced down one hundred
and eighty miles north-east of Spitsbergen and the subsequent
search for Nobile and his men lying with their wrecked airship,
no one knew where, in the heart of the Arctic Ocean was the
sensation of the year. At first there seemed no hope that they
would ever be found. Then a Russian wireless amateur near
Archangel, on the basis of a garbled and puzzling message,
tracked them down and the search started. Norwegian sealers,
Swedish sealers, Italian, Norwegian, and Swedish aircraft all
joined in, and at Amundsen's personal request a French seaplane was put at his disposal to search for the man whose
quarrel with him had preceded this most unfortunate enterprise.
After many failed attempts, Nobile at length was rescued by
one of the Swedish pilots and the remainder of the party were
picked up by the Russian icebreaker *Krassin* after they had been
sighted by the ship's light aircraft. But of Amundsen no trace
was ever found, except a float from the aircraft picked up off the
Norwegian coast in September 1928. It was evidence enough
that yet another link with the Heroic Age had finally and
tragically been broken.

One more but quite different attempt at a trans-polar crossing
must be mentioned because it is the antecedent of a remarkable
achievement still fresh in the memory. This was the attempt by
Sir Hubert Wilkins in 1931 to cross the Arctic Ocean, as far as
the Pole, by submarine. Wilkins's vessel, the submarine *O 12*
renamed the *Nautilus*, was lent to him by the United States
Navy and he crossed the Atlantic in her to his starting base at
Longyearbyen, Spitsbergen. In August Wilkins set out. He had
no luck. He encountered violent storms, his diving gear was
damaged, and after a voyage of three weeks he returned to Spitsbergen. Nevertheless, he managed to reach 82° 15′ N. during this
first voyage; a voyage which contributed more to Arctic science
than his aeronautical expeditions, for his chief scientist was a
distinguished Norwegian oceanographer, Professor Harald

Sverdrup, whose observations of ice movements and currents were to prove of lasting value. Despite this failure Wilkins remained optimistic about the prospects for under-ice navigation and about the commercial possibilities of a Northern Passage route for cargo-carrying submarines. But almost thirty years were to pass before Commander W. R. Anderson of the United States Navy in another *Nautilus*, this time atomic-powered, achieved in 1958 the first submarine trans-polar crossing.

These flights and land explorations added no new lands to the Arctic map. Indeed, it was little changed from that of the end of the First World War. But in the Arctic as in the Antarctic there was some consolidation of political geography as this phase of primary, pioneer exploration drew to a close; notably in the case of Greenland whose north-eastern coast had been the last major Arctic coastline to be explored. For some years the United States had claimed certain parts of north-west Greenland. These rights, however, she surrendered to Denmark in 1916 when the Danish West Indies were ceded to the United States. The ownership of East Greenland gave rise to more complicated problems. The Danish title to East Greenland, challenged by Norway in 1921, appeared to be confirmed in 1924 when a treaty between the two powers was signed, reserving for Norway (and subsequently also for Britain and France) certain hunting and scientific rights. In 1931, however, Norway occupied parts of East Greenland and Danish sovereignty over the whole country was only finally recognized after the dispute had been submitted in 1932 to the International Court at The Hague.

Sovereignty over the territories known as Svalbard – Spitsbergen with Bear Island (Bjornøya) – and over Jan Mayen island was also settled at this time, the former being awarded to Norway in 1920 by international agreement, the latter annexed by Norway in 1929 after she had maintained a weather station there for several years. All signatories of the Svalbard Treaty, nine nations in all, were awarded equal economic rights and the Soviet Union (which now has extensive coal mines in Spitsbergen) adhered to the Treaty in 1924. Curiously enough, entangled though their strategic situation was to be in the Arctic after the Second World War, there were no political disputes about Arctic sovereignty between the North American and Russian powers. The United States purchased Alaska outright from Russia in 1867, and since that time the boundary between Russia and Alaska has never been in question. Nor has the Canadian claim to ownership of the Arctic mainland and islands between Greenland and 141° W. longitude ever been disputed. Even the so-called Sector Principle (with all its possibilities of clash), whereby Canada in 1925 and Russia the following year officially declared that their Arctic claims extended (and therefore converged) at the Pole, was tacitly accepted by both sides.

Relatively soon after the First World War, the Arctic under these various responsible powers began to move out of the realm of primary exploration into that of exploitation and development, notably of mineral resources which were to replace the fur trade as the key to Arctic economy. During this second phase projects for mapping on a far-ranging and intensive scale, geological prospecting, weather, and many other detailed scientific investigations replaced the journeys and voyages of reconnaissance and discovery characteristic of the exploring days. In these movements towards the exploitation of national territories in the Arctic the new aircraft greatly speeded progress. The day when the Arctic would be mapped from the air, when long journeys would be by air and not by dog-sledge, when indeed not only dog-teams and sledges but snow-vehicles would be carried great distances by air to key points for local use, was already approaching fast.

This was the position in the Arctic between the wars. The Antarctic was in a very different situation. At the end of the First World War at least half of the coastline of a continent between five and six million square miles in total area was still, apart from some uncertain sightings in the first half of the nineteenth century, undiscovered. As for the interior, only the spaces flanking the well-worn track from the Ross Sea to the Pole could be described as known. Yet, with so much to be done, by the first years of the Second World War, the whole of the remaining coastline had been reconnoitred and often mapped and deep reconnaissances made in many directions into the interior. This was an achievement in twenty years which would never have been possible had it not been for the new air power.

Though during this period great advances were made not only in Antarctic geography but in many other sciences, the motives behind these great exploring efforts, motives which secured the funds which made them possible, were basically political rather than scientific. It was the same in the Antarctic as in the Arctic. With the advance of exploration the partition of discovered territories began.

An early example of the way in which science was to reap much benefit from the entry of Antarctica into the realm of international politics was seen in the programme of sustained oceanographical research and exploration undertaken by the British Discovery Committee. This was set up by the Colonial Office in 1923 (on a recommendation of 1917) to inquire into the prospects of research and development in Britain's new Antarctic Dependencies of the Falkland Islands. The establishment of this Committee, and of the research it promoted, followed logically enough the issue of letters patent in 1917 proclaiming for the first time sovereignty over a whole sector of Antarctica (following Canada's example in the Arctic). This sector included not only the various island groups specified in the letters patent of 1908 – the South Shetlands, the South Orkney Islands, South Georgia, and the South Sandwich Islands – but also the Antarctic mainland between longitude 20° and 80° W. Between 1925 and the outbreak of war 'Discovery Investigations', as the Discovery Committee's expeditions were called, made thirteen separate voyages to the Antarctic, lasting one or two seasons each, including several circumnavigations of the continent; one, of 1931–2, being the first to be made during the winter. These voyages, the first real efforts at sustained research in the Antarctic, were mainly concerned with oceanography, marine biology, and whale-marking. But on the land side, numerous island groups in the Dependencies were scientifically charted for the first time and surveys and landings were also carried out on Bouvetøya (Bouvet Island), the Balleny Islands, and Australian Antarctic Territory.

In 1925–7, but more extensively in 1937, a rival to Britain in Antarctica appeared, Argentina, claiming first the South Orkney Islands, then South Georgia, then in 1937 extending her claims to all of the territories in the British Falkland Islands Dependencies. These rival claims gave a new urgency to British activity in the Antarctic. A further development which, in providing a spur and incentive, directly or indirectly benefited exploration was the remarkable expansion of the whaling industry, due to the world shortage of fats after the War. In this Norway, as she had done before the First World War, played a leading role. New Norwegian inventions, the whaling factory ship and the stern slipway which enabled whales to be hauled on board and rendered down, made land bases for whalers unnecessary. This greatly extended the range of whaling ships after 1925 and led, in the search for new and distant whaling grounds, to new geographical discoveries, notably by Norwegian whalers in 1930–1.

These were some of the trends and developments in the Antarctic between the Wars. What, briefly, was the sequence of events? After the Shackleton-Rowett Expedition of 1921–2 on which Shackleton died and on which Frank Wild, the new leader, failed to discover new coast in the Enderby Land region, there was a lull in major voyages of exploration for five years. There was however, as already described, much whaling and oceanographical activity and geological and other scientific work, especially in the Falkland Islands Dependencies and one notable event, the first landing, by a Norwegian expedition in 1928–9, on Peter I Øy in the Bellingshausen Sea. This island (like Bouvetøya on which Norwegians had landed in 1927–8) was surveyed and claimed for Norway in 1929. Meanwhile, France moved nearer to the Antarctic continent in a programme of research and development in certain sub-Antarctic islands, notably the Îles de Kerguelen to which in 1924 she consolidated earlier claims.

In 1928, the year of the Arctic search for the *Italia*, the Antarctic too entered the Air Age with the first use, by the Arctic explorer Sir Hubert Wilkins, of the aeroplane on his joint British and United States Wilkins-Hearst Expedition. Wilkins's original intention had been to make a trans-Antarctic flight from Graham Land to the Ross Sea. But bad weather preventing this, the flight was limited to the east coast of Graham Land as far as 71° S. The flight was a warning of the errors which might be made by aviators in the often obscure and deceptive conditions of Antarctic flying for Wilkins returned with the news that Graham

Land, far from being a peninsula of the mainland, was an archipelago separated from the mainland by 'Crane, Casey, and Lurabee Channels' and by 'Stefansson Strait'. If this had been true, all the claims by explorers in the nineteenth century that in Graham Land they had discovered the Antarctic Continent would have been nullified. Five years passed before Wilkins's assertions were disproved. That they were, was due to the British Graham Land expedition of 1934–7 led by John Rymill; an expedition which carried out by land and air one of the most comprehensive exploring and scientific programmes (in geology, meteorology, glaciology, and biology) of any mainland expedition between the wars. Rymill's survey of the coast and islands off the peninsula as far as Alexander Land not only showed Wilkins's channels to be glacier streams and his strait not to exist but also went some way towards showing on a series of long sledging journeys that Bellingshausen's Alexander Land was in reality an island. The one new discovery of land made by Wilkins, Hearst Land, was also proved to be an island. In 1929–30 Wilkins made another attempt to fly across to the Ross Sea. Again he did not succeed but in a number of flights over Graham Land and over the adjacent pack as far as 73° S., he proved the insularity of Charcot Land discovered by the French explorer J. B. Charcot in 1908–10.

These first events of Antarctica's Air Age however did not touch upon the three great unexplored areas of coast: those between the Bellingshausen Sea and the Ross Sea, between the Weddell Sea and Enderby Land, and between Enderby Land and Kaiser Wilhelm Land, adjoining the coast explored by Mawson in 1911–14. These three great stretches of coastline in the ten years between 1928 and 1938 were explored by American, Norwegian, and British expeditions, led respectively by the American aviator Richard E. Byrd; the Norwegians Lars Christensen, Hjalmar Riiser-Larsen, and Gunnar Isachsen; and by Sir Douglas Mawson and John K. Davis for the British Commonwealth. In all of them, the new air power made it possible to reconnoitre and often to photograph vast expanses of Antarctica and thus to prepare the way for detailed exploration on the ground.

The United States expedition of 1928–30, led by Richard E.

Byrd, was the first American expedition (though on this occasion privately sponsored) since the stormy days of the irate and insubordinate Charles Wilkes ninety years before. It was, moreover, the first of a long line of American expeditions to Antarctica, predominantly transported and manned by the United States Navy, increasing yearly in size and in the mass and complexity of their equipment, which culminated in the largest Antarctic enterprise ever undertaken by one nation, the United States contribution to the International Geophysical Year. The part played by Byrd in all these expeditions (until his death in 1957) was not only that of a leader who became, like Wilkes, the American Antarctic hero of his day; he was also the instigator and promoter, the man who more than any other was responsible for the return of the United States to Antarctica and for focusing the attention of the American people for nearly thirty years on the geographical exploration of the Antarctic continent.

Though his aircraft carried him well beyond this region, Byrd's attention was centred for the most part on the unknown Pacific sector of Antarctica, between the Bellingshausen and the Ross Sea. On his first expedition, 1928–30, he discovered the western coast and hinterland of this region, Marie Byrd Land, and claimed it for the United States. Then in 1929, in the still hazardous conditions of polar aviation of those days, he made the first flight over the South Pole. Byrd's next expedition was in 1933–5. Wintering as before on the Ross Ice Shelf in the Bay of Whales, where more than a dozen buildings were erected, Byrd on this occasion by sledging journeys and flights proved beyond doubt the continental nature of Marie Byrd Land and in consequence settled a problem which had preoccupied both Bruce and Filchner, namely whether any sea connexion existed between the Weddell and the Ross Seas. Byrd's third expedition, 'The United States Service Expedition', took place during the first two years of the Second World War and again extensive additions were made to the geography of the continent. New coast (the Walgreen Coast) was added, overlooking the Amundsen Sea; earlier discoveries, notably in the neighbourhood of the Edsel Ford Ranges found in 1928–9, were greatly enlarged; and explorations, both land and air, were extended for the first time to the Graham Land peninsula. There, continuing the work of the British Graham Land Expedition, American sledging journeys far to the south proved for the first time the insularity of Bellingshausen's Alexander Land.

At intervals over these same ten years another great segment of Antarctic coastline was being explored by the Norwegians. This lay between the Weddell Sea and Enderby Land, a coast first sighted by the Russian Captain Bellingshausen early in the nineteenth century. These expeditions, promoted since 1927 by Consul Lars Christensen with resources incomparably more modest than those available to Byrd, made coastal discoveries no less extensive than those of the Americans though unlike them the Norwegians made little attempt to penetrate the hinterland either by land or air. In 1929–30 the eastward and westward limits of this long coastline were defined when Hjalmar Riiser-Larsen discovered and roughly charted Kronprins Olav Kyst and Kronprinsesse Märtha Kyst from the air. In 1930–1 Isachsen and Riiser-Larsen attacked the central portion of the coast and discovered and charted, again only roughly, Prinsesse Ragnhild Kyst. In the season 1936–7, yet another expedition, led this time by Lars Christensen himself, the promoter of all these Norwegian enterprises, filled the intermediate gaps by the discovery of Prins Harald Kyst and Prinsesse Astrid Kyst.

The third and last stretch of undiscovered coast to be explored, only slightly less extensive than those discovered by these American and Norwegian expeditions, was the stretch between Drygalski's Kaiser Wilhelm II Land, discovered early in the twentieth century, and Enderby Land and Kemp Land, sighted by the British sealers, Biscoe and Kemp, early in the nineteenth. This gap was filled by the British-Australian-New Zealand Antarctic Research Expedition (B.A.N.Z.A.R.E.) in a matter of two years, 1929–31, under the leadership of Australia's greatest explorer, the late Sir Douglas Mawson. Enderby and Kemp Land to the east were shown to be joined. MacRobertson Land was discovered, and between it and Kaiser Wilhelm II Land, Princess Elizabeth Land. No trace of Balleny's landfall was found but between King George V Land and Kaiser Wilhelm II Land two new stretches of coast emerged and were named

Sabrina Coast (in honour of Balleny) and Banzare Coast after the initials of the title of the expedition. Much charting and surveying from ship and aircraft was accomplished but perhaps the most important act of the expedition following these discoveries was to agree on a boundary, longitude 45° E., as the dividing line between British and Norwegian activities and between Enderby Land and Prins Olav Kyst. Mawson then proclaimed British sovereignty over the whole region, and in 1938 named it Australian Antarctic Territory. Yet another stretch of new coast was added to Australian Antarctic Territory in 1933–4. This was the work of aviators of yet another Lars Christensen expedition. They discovered 'Prinsesse Astrid Land', now known as King Leopold and Queen Astrid Coast, adjoining Kaiser Wilhelm II Land to the east. They also flew over part of the coast of MacRobertson Land where the name of the Norwegian leader is commemorated in Lars Christensen Coast.

Like the Arctic, the Antarctic (following the lead given by Wilkins in 1928) was the scene of numerous attempts to fly across it once the Pole had been reached by air. The first attempt by Lincoln Ellsworth who had flown across the Arctic with Amundsen, was from the Ross Sea to Graham Land, the reverse direction to Wilkins, but Ellsworth's plane was wrecked on the sea ice of the Bay of Whales. This was in 1933–4. The following year Ellsworth tried again starting this time from Graham Land, but he was foiled by incessant bad weather. In 1935, however, he succeeded, with H. Hollick-Kenyon as pilot, and made in November of that year the first flight across the continent from Dundee Island to the Bay of Whales. The flight was not continuous (there were four landings), nor was it by way of the Pole. The first continuous and trans-polar flight in a single-engined aircraft was accomplished only in 1958 by Squadron-Leader John Lewis of the Commonwealth Trans-Antarctic Expedition. In the course of his flight Ellsworth discovered James W. Ellsworth Land, renamed Ellsworth Highland, and claimed it for the United States.

As already described, a powerful motive inducing governments to provide funds for Antarctic exploration was their anxiety to consolidate or establish claims to Antarctic territory and indeed, by the beginning of the Second World War, only one sector, the Pacific sector, the focus especially of American activity, remained formally unclaimed. The British had given the lead in this partition of Antarctica when in 1908 and 1917 they issued letters patent claiming and defining the territory of the Falkland Islands Dependencies. These were followed in 1923 by the establishment of the Ross Dependency (between longitudes

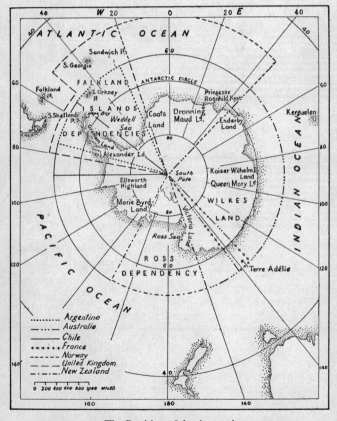

The Partition of the Antarctic

160° E. and 150° W.) which was placed under New Zealand administration. The French followed suit, and although no French expedition had been active in the neighbourhood of Terre Adélie since Dumont d'Urville, and indeed was not active until after the Second World War, they nevertheless included Terre Adélie in the decree of 1924 claiming the sub-Antarctic islands and it was accepted by the British and Australian Governments in 1933 as an enclave of Australian Antarctic Territory.

The next stage in the partition of Antarctica was the claiming by Norway of the sector between the Weddell Sea and Enderby Land; the sector which had been discovered by the expeditions of Consul Lars Christensen. Norwegian sovereignty had been proclaimed over Peter I Øy in 1931 but no comparable proclamation was made about this vast mainland territory, later named Dronning Maud Land, until 1939. The Norwegian Government was then spurred to action by the activities of a German expedition under Captain Alfred Ritscher which arrived in 1938 off the shores of Prinsesse Astrid Kyst and Kronprinsesse Märtha Kyst. Personally sponsored by Field-Marshal Goering, plentifully staffed by German Air Force and Naval personnel more interested perhaps in obtaining hydrographical and meteorological information valuable to Antarctic-based raiders in wartime than in geographical exploration, the expedition's two aircraft in a three-week visit flew over and photographed 350,000 square kilometres of territory. This was named by the Germans Neu-Schwabenland and was formally claimed by Germany in January 1939, three days after the Norwegian Government in Oslo had registered its claim.

The position of the Pacific sector at the beginning of the Second World War remained (and indeed still remains) unclarified. Numerous personal claims had been made by Byrd and other members of his expeditions, and by Lincoln Ellsworth. Byrd's expedition of 1939–41, the United States Antarctic Service Expedition, had indeed been instructed to establish permanent bases in Antarctic territory as evidence to support later formal claims. However, since Congress failed to provide funds, this expedition was withdrawn. After the war (in 1946), while Byrd's fourth expedition was still in the field, the United States position was made plain. This was that she neither made claims nor recognized the claims of others over the territories which one hundred and fifty years of Antarctic exploration had revealed.

This rapid survey of events and trends leads directly to the period of the Second World War and after. Nevertheless the two periods were in one respect markedly distinct. Between the wars, individual enterprise in exploration was still characteristic, as it had been of the decades before the First World War. After the Second World War, there was a change, with individual enterprise very largely giving way to government explorations on the mid-nineteenth-century pattern.

24

THE SECOND WORLD WAR AND AFTER: THE SIGNIFICANCE OF THE POLAR REGIONS

IT is remarkable how often, in Britain at all events, the Arctic is still thought to be the realm primarily of the dog-team and the sledge. Yet the aircraft and the helicopter are more appropriately the symbols and the instruments of Arctic progress today. Commercial airways navigating along or near Great Circle routes fly regularly across the Arctic, spanning in hours the stark mountains, the tumbled and hummocky sea ice, the vast and empty surface of the Greenland ice sheet over which Nansen and Peary and so many others painfully trudged. Air power, too, is the key to the economic and industrial expansion upon which Canada is now embarking in her Arctic territory. It is the key, moreover, to the strategic significance of a region where potentially hostile powers, in North America and the Soviet Union, confront each other across an Arctic 'Mediterranean' and prepare elaborate and costly defences against the possibility of air attack; defences in Canada's case more than anything responsible for the widespread opening up of her Arctic regions since the last war. Greenland also, since 1954 no longer regarded as a colony but as part of Denmark, has been brought through air power into closer contact with the outer world and has moved, in the west and south at least, out of a hunting into a fishing and monetary economy in which her mineral resources, of cryolite especially, play an important part. No doubt comparable developments have also taken place in the Soviet Arctic. The secrecy which surrounds Russia's Arctic possessions, however, allows little information to escape.

It is impossible here, for these are contemporary events, to give more than a rapid sketch of the broad trends and developments which have led to this Arctic transformation. The period opens with an exploit in the old style, the traversing of the North-West Passage by one of the outstanding pioneers in Arctic Canada today, Sergeant (now Inspector) Henry Larsen, R.C.M.P. In a little ship, the *St Roch*, one hundred and four feet long, he made (see map inside back cover) the North-West Passage twice, passing on his voyage in 1940–2 through the swirling ice of Bellot Strait, then on his second voyage in the summer of 1944 along Prince of Wales Strait and along Melville and Lancaster Sounds. Stopping at Winter Harbour in Melville Sound, he saw, carved on a high rock, the names of Parry's seamen and of Her Majesty's ships *Hecla* and *Griper* which had wintered there in 1819. Larsen's was a truly audacious achievement, one indeed which Parry himself would have been the first to admire.

Larsen's voyages in the *St Roch* stand out in romantic contrast to the network of air, land, and sea operations, economic and strategic, which since the War have covered Canada's Arctic sector. Those directed to the exploitation of the Canadian North have been based first and foremost on an extensive programme of air survey, supplemented by ground parties working mostly, not with dogs and sledges (though on occasion these too have been flown to key points for local use), but with aircraft, including helicopters. The aim has been to exploit the rich mineral resources of the Canadian Arctic, petroleum, graphite, coal, iron, nickel, copper, and gold; and, just south of the Arctic Circle, radium and uranium at Great Bear Lake. Geological prospecting in Canada's North West Territories, greatly speeded by the use of devices such as the airborne magnetometer, has been so widespread – as indeed have other scientific investigations basic to economic, industrial, and strategic development – that a Canadian geographer has lately remarked, 'It is probably true that no single part of the Canadian Arctic, even including remote islands not visited since they were first placed on the map long ago, has escaped the recent attention of the geologist, geographer, or other scientist. . . .'

An even more important factor in this transformation of the Canadian Arctic and in the opening up of many territories explored but unvisited for generations has been the Air Defence Programme focused on the so-called D.E.W. Line (Distant Early

Warning Line), once known under the Orwellian name, 'Project 572'. This radar fence, with more than forty manned stations stretching from East Greenland to Alaska, has meant the making of innumerable airfields, the building of small townships of scientists and technicians, the bulldozing of Arctic highways, and the employment of around twenty thousand men. The names of some of these prefabricated, air-conditioned, electronic stations – Frobisher, for example, in Frobisher Bay on Baffin Island – recall the debt which those responsible for this spectacular if gloomy project owe to the early explorers. All this rapid development of course has inevitably brought in its train sociological problems concerning the Eskimoes who have been brought into contact with the diseases and the temptations as well as the benefits of civilization. They are at the same time fast losing the native skills which have enabled them for so long to survive.

Greenland too, mainly along its west and south-west coast, the site of the earliest settlements and European explorations, has been brought into the stream of world affairs; largely because of its importance as a landing stage and weather observatory along a polar air route. Greenland's key role in the future of polar aviation had been foreseen as far back as the early thirties by the British Arctic Air Route Expedition sent out to test possibilities by the Royal Geographical Society. But the British were not the first to be so far-sighted. In the nineteen-twenties, the Norwegian Arctic explorer Bernt Balchen, who flew with Amundsen and Wilkes in the Arctic and piloted Admiral Byrd to the South Pole, forecast the role of Greenland as 'the great aircraft-carrier of the Arctic'. The urgent needs of war saw his forecast realized. In 1941 an agreement was signed between the United States and Denmark. This, while reaffirming Danish sovereignty over Greenland, granted the United States the temporary use of certain bases in west and south-west Greenland for defensive purposes, but in particular as staging points for the ferrying of aircraft to Britain. The first airports, planned by Balchen himself as Arctic adviser to the U.S. Air Force, were at Julianehaab, in southern Greenland, and at Søndre Strømfjord in the south-west. After the war, following an agreement in 1951 between the

United States and Denmark covering the use of N.A.T.O. bases in Greenland, the greatest of these Arctic airports was established at Thule, far up the west coast near the entrance to Smith Sound, the 'Sir Thomas Smith's Sound' discovered in 1616 by the Englishman William Baffin. Thule, with its airfields, its aluminium buildings, its radio and radar tower lower only than the television mast on the Empire State building in New York, is now a pulsating modern Arctic town. The pioneer days of trans-Arctic flying belong, as we have seen, to the period between the wars when the flights of Amundsen, Byrd, and Wilkins were succeeded by the survey flights of von Gronau of Germany and of the U.S. aviator Lindbergh; and by one of the most courageous flights of those early days, the British pilot John Grierson's solo single-engined flight to Ottawa by way of the Faroes, Iceland, and the Greenland ice sheet. But it was not until the airfields in south-west Greenland had been built that the first commercial air service between Europe and the west coast of North America could begin. This took place in November 1954 when the Scandinavian Airlines System, true to their national tradition of Arctic pioneering, made the first commercial flight from Copenhagen to Los Angeles by way of the airfield at Søndre Strømfjord.

While West Greenland was thus fast developing under the impact of war and air power and the energetic measures of the Danish Government to develop the settlements north and south of the capital, Godthaab, Greenland's ice sheet and its northern and eastern coasts (where the musk-ox and the kayak could still be seen) continued to attract exploring expeditions. First among these after the Second World War were the expeditions known as the Expéditions Polaires Françaises, launched by the French ex-parachutist and anthropologist Paul-Émile Victor who, more than anyone, has been responsible for the remarkable revival of French polar exploration, both Arctic and Antarctic, since the last war. These French expeditions, working between 1948–57 and supplied very largely by air direct from France, have been concerned chiefly with the seismic investigation of the central and southern parts of the ice sheet. Seismic and other glaciological investigations also preoccupied the British North Greenland Expedition of 1952–4, working in Dronning Louise Land. This, led by a naval officer, Commander C. J. W. Simpson, has a special place in the history of recent British exploration. Like the French expeditions, it relied greatly on supply by air, using aircraft of the Royal Air Force, but one of its aims was to bring about the re-entry of the Navy into polar exploration. This was a reminder that in Britain belief in the traditional role of the Navy in polar enterprise, so staunchly held by Clements Markham in the nineties, still survived. Another large expedition working in Greenland since the Second World War was the Danish Peary Land expedition, led by Count Eigil Knuth. This too, working in the extreme north-west of Greenland, relied considerably upon air support and was involved in survey and in investigations of the ice sheet. The latest of these large Greenland expeditions to study the conditions and history of the ice sheet is the International Expedition to Greenland of 1959–61, organized and led by M. Paul Émile Victor.

Before turning to different forms of Arctic exploration since the Second World War one other aspect of Arctic activity must be mentioned because it is so characteristic, in Britain especially, of this period. That is the annual flow of undergraduate expeditions to the Arctic, which have greatly increased in number since the first of their kind, from Oxford, in the early twenties. Easily and cheaply accessible, with a climate at its best during the months of the summer vacation, Iceland, Spitsbergen and Nordaustland, Greenland, Jan Mayen island, have all been targets of such undergraduate parties combining adventurous travel with scientific work. The Svalbard archipelago has been especially popular and a more or less continuous series of small expeditions from Cambridge have, in proportion to their size and resources, added considerably to the detailed geological mapping of these islands.

Since the war, however, not land expeditions but those travelling on or even under the ice, particularly the floating ice which covers almost throughout the year the central polar basin, have made the most important and exciting geographical discoveries in the Arctic. Until the year 1937–8, the year of Papanin's Russian drift expedition, knowledge of this region was still based upon the work of Nansen in the *Fram* and upon evidence from the drifting *Jeannette* (both of the late nineteenth century) as well as upon Amundsen's drift in the *Maud* in 1922–4. Following Papanin's drift, however, there were other Russian drift expeditions on the eve and during the first two years of the war, and then from 1948 a whole series of expeditions, Russian and American, drifting on ice floes and ice islands over most of the central polar basin. Aircraft cooperated with these drifting stations not only in manning and supplying them but also in supplementary ice reconnaissance and observation. In this curious world of floating ice laboratories and floating air-fields, circulating round and about the Pole regardless of any political sector boundaries radiating from it, the Russians have been most active. Geographically, the most dramatic discovery by the Russian ice floe parties since 1948 has been that of the great submarine Lomonosov Ridge (so called after the famous Russian inventor of the eighteenth century) which was found to range below the sea ice from Canada's Ellesmere Island to the New Siberian Islands (Novosibirskiye Ostrova). This divides the central polar basin into an 'Atlantic' and a 'Pacific' sector; a division which must powerfully affect the movement of surface currents and the drift of ice.

Much else has been discovered by these post-war expeditions about the relations between wind and ice drift and about the history, the growth, and the decay of sea ice; that in the Atlantic sector, for example, the ice drifts much faster than in Nansen's time whereas it is slower in the Pacific sector; that ice floes in the course of a three-year period, while retaining the same overall thickness, diminish on top but increase below. The Russians obtained clear proof of this steady process of growth and decay in 1954 when they rediscovered a camp-site on their drifting station S.P.–2, abandoned three years earlier. Their old tents were still standing but they were standing isolated on pillars of ice, 1·6 metres high, pillars which the presence of the tents had prevented from melting.

Submarine discoveries almost comparable, it appears, with that of the Lomonosov Ridge were made more recently by Commander W. R. Anderson of the United States Navy when in

August 1958, following the lead given by Sir Hubert Wilkins twenty-seven years before, he navigated the nuclear-powered submarine *Nautilus* under the ice of the central polar basin and under the North Pole. This was the first submarine navigation of the North-West Passage. Submerging under the ice off Point Barrow, Alaska, the *Nautilus* travelled 1,830 miles in 96 hours, surfacing at a point (79° N.) between Greenland and Spitsbergen. Watching the ice overhead through the periscope and on a television screen but navigating 'blind' and with no certainty that some lofty mountain range might not suddenly loom up from the sea-bed to meet the ice above, Anderson by this exploit achieved one of the great voyages of polar history. Off Point Barrow, a deep and narrow sea valley was discovered leading into the deep waters of the central polar basin. There, below the Pole, a depth of 13,410 feet was recorded, two thousand feet deeper that expected. The voyage of the *Nautilus* did more than illuminate the submarine geography of the Arctic. It showed that nuclear-powered, freight-carrying submarines could by using this Arctic route cut almost by half the sea voyage between London and Tokyo. An even faster trans-polar voyage was made in March 1959 by the nuclear-powered submarine U.S.S. *Skate*, the first submarine to surface (breaking through thin ice) at the Pole.

The Antarctic during and after the Second World War followed much more closely the pattern of pre-war exploration, a pattern coloured in the United Kingdom's sector of Antarctica by the wrangles which broke out during the War between Britain and both Argentina and Chile about the ownership of these scattered lands. Argentina, having in 1937 extended her claims to all the United Kingdom's Antarctic territory, in 1940 set up a national commission to handle her polar interests. That same year, Chile, in a belated display of nationalism, claimed Territorio Antártico Chileno (between longitudes 53° and 90° W.), thereby, as the map on p. 357 shows, overlapping the claims of Argentina. Then, Britain being occupied with more vital issues elsewhere, the battle for the frozen wasteland, the cold war in its most literal sense, began and is still being waged. Cold but courteous memoranda exchanged between London, Buenos Aires, and Santiago, have been accompanied by a spate of expeditions, British and Argentine, with the Chileans later joining in, asserting and counterclaiming sovereignty by means of notes delivered, mostly in peaceful fashion, by explorers across the intervening ice. National emblems painted on lonely huts or on the few rock faces free from the perennial cover of snow and ice have been obliterated and repainted by the rival Antarctic powers in turn. Science, however, has benefited from this peculiar tussle over the rocks and ice and snow of Antarctica, for in 1943 the British Admiralty launched Operation *Tabarin* under which permanent meteorological stations were established in the Falkland Islands Dependencies. In the following year a programme of scientific research and exploration, in geology, biology, and survey, was started and was continued and widened in 1945 when the whole project was taken over by the Colonial Office under the name 'Falkland Islands Dependencies Survey'. Thus began a scientific enterprise (placed three years later under the Governor of the Falkland Islands) which, however political its origin and basis, has through its yearly expeditions rendered great services to Antarctic science; an enterprise indeed in terms of years of continuous effort probably unique in Antarctic history. Inevitably these exploring activities have had their political slant, leaders of the various bases, numbering a dozen or more, being enrolled as magistrates, postmasters, and the like. They have thus been able to display those signs of 'state activity', clear evidence of which would be required if this Antarctic dispute, at British or South American instigation, ever came before an international court of law.

While the United Kingdom was thus striving to consolidate her position in the Dependencies and British and South American expeditions were manoeuvring for bases there, the United States reappeared on the Antarctic scene with Operation 'Highjump' commanded by the veteran explorer Richard E. Byrd. Comprising a Task Force of thirteen ships and four thousand men, this was then the largest exploratory venture attempted in Antarctica. Byrd divided his fleet into three groups, two concentrating on the coastal waters of the Ross Dependency and adjoining Pacific sector, the third steaming westwards from Oates Land round to Prinsesse Astrid Kyst. During these Antarctic circumnavigations, photographic and reconnaissance flights were made deep inland and in February 1947 Byrd made his second flight over the South Pole. Science played a relatively small part in this elaborate naval expedition and no wintering parties remained in Antarctica. Its chief object indeed was not science at all but, by photographic reconnaissance, to create a basis for subsequent United States claims to a large sector of Antarctica, and – having in mind no doubt the strategic situation *vis-à-vis* the Soviet Union in the Arctic – to give polar experience to a large number of men. As already noted, the United States has not yet made claims to Antarctic territory. Instead she has adopted the paradoxical attitude that while neither making claims nor recognizing those of others, she reserves any rights arising out of claims made by her own explorers. In contrast to this, however, she proposed in 1948 that the whole region be placed under United Nations Trusteeship. This was the first effort to rationalize the political position of Antarctica. But it came to nothing partly because the Soviet Union, which had not been consulted, made it plain in 1950 that she would recognize no decisions about the future of Antarctica in which the Soviet Union had had no part.

The turn of the half-century saw some striking developments in the evolution of Antarctic exploration. It saw the Australian Government in 1949 signify its intention to take a practical and permanent interest in its Antarctic territory by the setting up of an Antarctic division of the Department of External Affairs. This was followed five years later by the establishment of Australia's first permanent base on the mainland, at Mawson in MacRobertson Land; an achievement of the Australian National Antarctic Research Expedition which had since the War been active in the scientific exploration of the sub-Antarctic islands, Heard Island, Macquarie Island, and Kerguelen. Since then these Australian expeditions, advised by the veteran explorer Sir Douglas Mawson and energetically promoted and led by the physicist Phillip Law, have been annual events, comparable in terms of cost and continuous effort only with the United Kingdom's programme of research and development in the Falkland Islands Dependencies.

The turn of the half-century saw also, as the result of Paul-Émile Victor's efforts, the return of France to the Antarctic Continent; to France's traditional section, Dumont d'Urville's Terre Adélie. It also saw (in 1947–8) yet another United States Expedition, the Ronne Antarctic Research Expedition, at work from Byrd's old base of 1939–41, Stonington Island, west Graham Land. This marked a new departure in Antarctic exploration in that it included two women, the first to winter in Antarctica.

In 1949 a venture was launched which presaged a new attitude and a new outlook towards Antarctic exploration, the Norwegian British-Swedish expedition to Norway's Dronning Maud Land; the first international expedition to Antarctica. The man at the back of this idea, which was refreshingly free from political or strategic motives, was the Swedish geographer, Professor Hans W. Ahlmann. He had for several years been investigating possible causes for the recent recession of ice cover in the Arctic, and he argued that if this recession was due to some global climatic change and not merely to a local fluctuation, confirmation should be forthcoming from the Antarctic, as reports of ice-free areas from Alfred Ritscher's brief German expedition to Dronning Maud Land in 1939 had indeed already suggested that it might. Norway bore the brunt of the cost and organization of the expedition, but both Sweden and Britain (through the Royal Geographical Society and the Scott Polar Institute at Cambridge) played considerable parts. Due largely to the genius of its principal organizer, the late Harald Sverdrup, director of the Norwegian Polar Institute at Oslo, it was, in the range and intensity of its scientific work, probably the most productive scientific expedition to Antarctica until the greatest international venture in science ever undertaken, the International Geophysical Year of 1957–8.

In 1905, the historian of Antarctica, the late Dr Hugh Robert Mill, pleaded in his book *Siege of the South Pole* for the establishment of an international committee which 'should plan, not an expedition, but a system of research by means of simultaneous and consecutive expeditions and fixed observatories'. This was precisely the idea behind the Antarctic operations of the International Geophysical Year, the successor on a global rather than a polar scale to the International Polar Years of 1882–3 and 1932–3. Unlike these earlier Years, which concentrated almost entirely on the Arctic, the Antarctic this time was to receive the greatest attention. The influence of its great ice mass on weather, and on oceanographical and atmospheric dynamics; the problems posed by the relatively unstudied Antarctic aurora whose brilliance had amazed so many generations of explorers; the possibility of conducting research from the South Polar plateau into the ionosphere during the sunless hours of the long winter night; these were some of the scientific advantages of concentration on Antarctica.

The I.G.Y., involving a dozen nations and fifty scientific bases, was concerned less with exploration than with research, of a kind largely outside the geographical scope of this book. Nevertheless, because of the new techniques employed, new departures in transport and supply which seemed to forecast a new future for polar travel, certain events must be included. Of these, the most dramatic were the first direct air flights from New Zealand to the Antarctic Continent in 1955–6, and the establishment in 1956–7, entirely by air, of the United States 'Amundsen–Scott' Station at the South Geographical Pole. The establishment and the supply by air of this station, which housed the first wintering party at the South Pole, involved the airmen of the United States in many remarkable and courageous feats of aviation in, conditions relatively little known, and seemed to point the way to a new pattern of Antarctic exploration. This appears likely to be based on the swift transport of men and dogs, vehicles and supplies, by air to selected strategic points from which intensive local ground explorations can be conducted as had already been done in the Arctic.

The year 1953 may be regarded as the dawn of the third and in some respects the greatest of the main periods of Antarctic endeavour; the first being the mid nineteenth century, the days of James Clark Ross, of Dumont d'Urville, of Wilkes; the second, the opening years of the twentieth century when Sir Clements Markham and the Royal Geographical Society led the international revival of Antarctic exploration to which the

American, Matthew Fontaine Maury, had forty years earlier pointed the way. It was not only the year when the international committees of the I.G.Y. were laying plans for their great combined scientific onslaught on Antarctica. It was also the year in which J. M. Wordie, the president of the Royal Geographical Society and a former shipmate of Shackleton's, provided a link with the past by reviving the idea, in striking contrast to these international and largely static operations, of a wholly British trans-Antarctic expedition.

The idea of a trans-Antarctic expedition on the lines of Shackleton's from the Weddell Sea to the Ross Sea via the Pole had been brewing for some time in the minds of British explorers, among them the future leader of the expedition Dr (now Sir Vivian) Fuchs. But 1953 seemed a most appropriate time at which to ventilate the scheme. The British Commonwealth in the person of Sir Edmund Hillary had only that summer shared in the first ascent of Mount Everest, and the public seemed very likely to welcome no less enthusiastically an attempt at the first land crossing of the Antarctic continent by a British expedition. The expedition itself is too recent, its story too well known, to need detailed description. After receiving the initial support of the Royal Geographical Society in 1954, the project hung fire, then the United Kingdom Government made a considerable grant towards its cost and the following year saw the departure of a reconnaissance expedition which, though by a rather narrow margin, penetrated the Weddell Sea and established 'Shackleton' Base. This was not the first base to be set up in this part of the United Kingdom's sector of Antarctica, for an Argentine expedition, using for the first time the ice-breaker the *General San Martin*, had already established a meteorological station on the Filchner Ice Shelf in 1954–5.

The first land crossing of the Antarctic continent by Fuchs and his men, Sir Edmund Hillary having previously laid depots and reconnoitred the route from the Ross Sea to the Pole, was achieved between 24 November 1957 and 2 March 1958, the United States South Pole station being visited on the way. Despite great difficulties near the Weddell Sea coast where the expedition's 'Sno-Cats' were caught in a maze of deep, concealed

crevasses of unparalleled extent, the crossing was completed with
an almost military precision within a day of the planned date.
But this first crossing overland, so ably and so resolutely conducted, was not the only, or even perhaps the most important,
of the expedition's achievements. The unknown stretch between
the Weddell Sea to the Pole was for the first time explored.
Furthermore, within the limits imposed by the Antarctic season
upon a motorized caravan engaged in a journey of over two
thousand miles, much scientific work was done; in particular, a
seismic traverse across the continent. This revealed ice depths
of 9,000 feet, with many high mountain peaks rising up below
the ice, and a deep valley underlying the South Geographical
Pole. Before and during this mammoth polar journey aircraft
were available for reconnaissance and support, including the
laying of advance dumps, and on 6 January 1958 an Otter aircraft piloted by J. H. Lewis flew nonstop across the continent.
Multi-engined aircraft of the United States I.G.Y. Operation
Deepfreeze had previously made a number of trans-continental
flights, but this was the first single-engined aircraft to do so.

Sir Vivian Fuchs's trans-Antarctic journey has sometimes been
described as 'the last great journey in the world'. But already
as this book goes to press another, even longer, trans-Antarctic
journey is being planned by the Soviet Union which, as a
participant in the I.G.Y., entered Antarctic exploration in 1955
for the first time since the days of the great Russian explorer
Bellingshausen. This will be a journey of 3,700 miles through the
South Pole, the South Magnetic Pole, and the Pole of Relative
Inaccessibility, the point on the Antarctic continent farthest
from the coast. And no doubt there will be more to follow. The
Arctic, as we have seen, has already passed from exploration to
the phase of exploitation. But it will be many years before the
six million square miles of the Antarctic continent can be said
to have been completely explored.

What meanwhile is to be the future of Antarctica? In terms
of the contemporary struggle for power, it seems likely to be of
slight importance. It may be useful as a military training ground
in polar techniques, a training ground remote from prying eyes.
The ice-free water of Drake Passage, north of the South Shetland

Islands, might afford a welcome alternative route between the Atlantic and Pacific to the ice-bound North-West Passage, should enemy action close the Panama Canal. But by comparison with the vital strategic importance of the Arctic, bounded by great and antagonistic powers, these are minor matters. Though the commercial advantages seem doubtful at present, in the near future the Antarctic may, like the Arctic, be the scene of transpolar flights by commercial airways linking the cities of Australia and South America across the South Pole. These may involve intermediate airfields and permanent meteorological stations on the continent.

Economically, the wealth of Antarctica at present lies in its seas, in a highly profitable and highly competitive whaling industry. But the Antarctic continent too, still only partially explored, may yet produce surprises. Coal, tin ore, lead, copper, iron, even gold and silver have been found. Oil and nuclear ores are still a possibility in a continent of such tremendous size. But economic exploitation in the harshest of all environments, over distances so great and with relatively few rock faces easily accessible and free from ice, is unlikely to prove profitable, or even possible, unless world shortages elsewhere drive men to invent new and startling techniques. It has been suggested that the Antarctic might be useful for storage of the world's food surpluses, that atomic-powered settlements might be used to transform the cold as well as the hot deserts of the world, that the Antarctic blizzards and gales which have menaced so many generations of explorers might be harnessed as a source of power. It has even been suggested that man may in time find the means to harness the latent heat of the enormous mass of Antarctic ice. But these are Wellsian ideas. One day perhaps they may be translated into fact. Meanwhile science rather than strategy or economics is the key to the future of Antarctica; scientific research and scientific exploration in the greatest geophysical laboratory in the world. The Antarctic, like the Arctic, may even have its place in the new Space Age, for radiation, so perilous to man, is thinnest over the Poles and there is said to be a strong case for making manned space launchings from high latitudes.

With the Antarctic at present offering such meagre material rewards, one wonders why it should cause so much international rivalry, and why the problems of sovereignty over this wasteland seem so impossible to solve. As we have seen, an effort to do so was made by the United States in 1948 with her suggestion of a United Nations Trusteeship. In 1956, inspired it seems by New Zealand, India made a similar proposal. In 1958 the President of the United States made a fresh attempt to settle the Antarctic problem. Addressing a memorandum to eleven countries, including this time the Soviet Union, he drew attention to the smooth and easy cooperation which had marked the International Geophysical Year and proposed in extension of it an international treaty to cover freedom of scientific investigation in Antarctica, and indeed its free use for any peaceful purposes. This proposal, however, contained a suggestion of certain provisos upon which the Soviet Union was quick to jump. Not only would the United States, it appeared, reserve all their own rights over Antarctica, including the right to assert territorial claims; they also suggested that other nations might maintain their historic rights and claims to sovereignty. In reply the Soviet Union, while drawing attention, as indeed the United States had done, to the discoveries of her earlier explorers, and reserving all rights, again like the United States, based on those discoveries, rejected any such suggestion of provisions safeguarding existing claims. And there the situation stood. Even the dispute between Britain and Argentina and Chile, which has bedevilled all political discussions about the future of Antarctica, had yet to be settled, for the South American countries, basing their claims to the Falkland Islands Dependencies very largely on the highly doubtful grounds of geographical contiguity and rights inherited from Spain, have (unlike the United Kingdom) consistently refused to submit their case to the jurisdiction of the International Court at The Hague. Some temporary progress was later made, however, when all the countries with Antarctic interests, including the United Kingdom, Argentina, and Chile, signed the Antarctic Treaty (in Washington, on 1 December 1959). This treaty, to run for thirty years, will ensure that Antarctica is used for peaceful purposes only and will ensure freedom for and facilitation of scientific research. While signature of the treaty implies no renunciation by the contracting parties of any claims to territorial sovereignty, it does prohibit new claims or enlargement of existing claims. Under this treaty, therefore, the existing political situation in Antarctica will temporarily be 'frozen' in the interests of international peace and scientific cooperation.

These international frictions, far from impeding the progress of exploration, have tended rather to advance it, for there are few Antarctic expeditions these days which do not depend heavily on government subsidies, and these are probably seldom granted unless some political advantage, such as the reinforcement of sovereignty, can be seen. Indeed, with distances so great, with the cost of chartering ships so high, with aids to speedier exploration such as aircraft so costly, an Antarctic expedition on modern lines is well beyond the means of any unsubsidized private organization, even with industrial and commercial backing. In the Arctic there is still much valuable field research awaiting, in glaciology, biology, geology for example, which can be done by small parties at low cost. On rare occasions, as in the case of the British explorer Duncan Carse's South Georgia Survey of 1951–7 which remapped the island, there have been expeditions of this kind in Antarctica. But, generally speaking, the day of the purely private Antarctic expedition is over.

Meanwhile, what is happening geographically to the polar regions? Superficially, the polar scene is unaltered. Arctic snow and ice appear to be no less. On the Antarctic continent, where the world's lowest surface temperature of —125° F. has recently been recorded, the enveloping ice sheet is known in places to be three miles deep. Nevertheless both Arctic and Antarctic, it seems, are slowly, almost imperceptibly changing, for their ice cover is melting and adding minutely to the volume of the oceans. In the remote future perhaps, in terms of geological time, when low-lying shores have crumbled and have been submerged under new levels of the sea, the Arctic may return to the Mediterranean climate it enjoyed before the Ice Age, while luxuriant vegetation may flourish once again within the Antarctic circle. But until then the polar exploration will remain the challenge it has always been to those who seek knowledge and adventure.

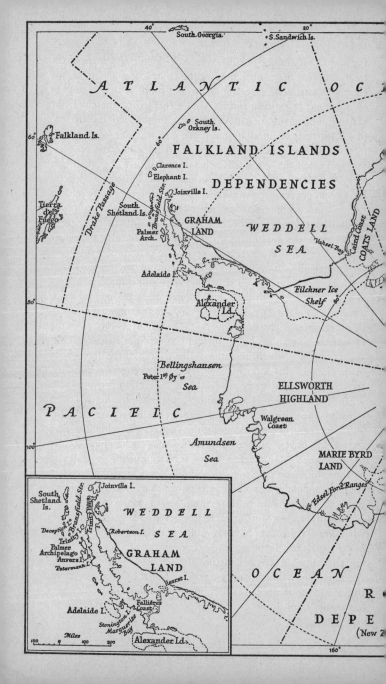

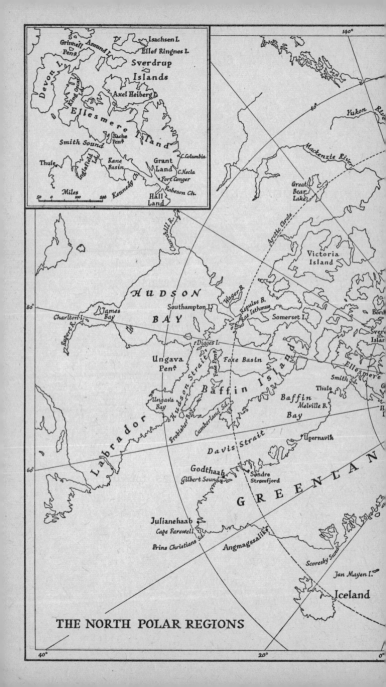

THE NORTH POLAR REGIONS

160°
180°
165°

BERING SEA

ALASKA

E.Cape
Bering St.
Chukchi
Pen.
Gulf of
Anadyr
Anadyr

Kamchatka Pen.

Anadyr R.

Sea of
Okhotsk

Chukchi
Sea

Point Barrow

Wrangel I.

Herald I.

Kolyma R.

Okhotsk

145°

East
Siberian
Sea

Yakutsk

LL.

A R C T I C

80°

New
Siberian
Is.

Lena River

120°

rock
I.

up
s

O C E A N

North
Pole

Severnaya
Zemlya

C. Washington
Peary
Land
C. Morris Jesup

ant
d

Franz Josef
Land

Wilczek I.

Walden I.
Mosselbukta
Kings Bay

Seven Is.
White I.
North East Land

L. Flora

Novaya

Spitsbergen

Matochkin Shar

Bear I.
B

Zemlya

Vaigach I.

North Cape

Vardø

Kola Pen.

Archangel

20°
40°
60°

S.

108°

S.

Kara Sea

Yenesey River

Gulf of Ob

Ob River

80°

60°

R.

Arctic Circle

20°

BIBLIOGRAPHY
(WITH NOTES)

The list which follows contains a selection of the books, papers, etc., which have been chiefly used, and references to original documents. Where permission has kindly been given by publishers to reproduce substantial extracts, acknowledgement of this is indicated by the asterisk after their names. For the last two summary chapters, I have referred mainly to a few secondary works and to works on the politics, economics, and future of the Antarctic. (Abbreviations of periodicals are in accordance with the *World List of Scientific Periodicals*, Third Edition, London, 1952.)

GENERAL

JEANETTE MIRSKY, *To the Arctic* (Allan Wingate, London, 1949). Arctic exploration to 1937.

HUGH ROBERT MILL, *The Siege of the South Pole* (Alston Rivers, London, 1905). Antarctic exploration to 1905.

BRIAN ROBERTS, 'Chronological List of Antarctic Expeditions' (*Polar Rec.* 59, May 1958, pp. 97–134, and 60, Sept. 1958, pp. 191–239). A very valuable annotated list, based on recent research, to 1957–8.

POLAR GEOGRAPHY

RUDMOSE BROWN, *The Polar Regions; a physical and economic geography of the Arctic and Antarctic* (Methuen, London, 1927).

GEORGE H. T. KIMBLE and DOROTHY GOOD, *Geography of the Northlands* (American Geographical Society of New York and Chapman and Hall, London, 1955).

W. H. C. KNAPP, *Antarctica* (Haarlem, 1958). A conspectus of the geography, geology, botany, etc., of the Antarctic; in Dutch.

J. K. CHARLESWORTH, *The Quaternary Era* (1957). For the history of glaciation.

TERENCE ARMSTRONG, 'The Ice of the central polar basin' (*J. Glaciol.* 22, Oct. 1957, pp. 103–110).

TERENCE ARMSTRONG and BRIAN ROBERTS, 'Illustrated Ice Glossary' (*Polar Rec.* 52, Jan. 1956, pp. 4–12).

The *Polar Record* of the Scott Polar Research Institute and the *Proceedings* and the *Journal of the Royal Geographical Society*, and the *Geographical Journal* of the same Society, are mines of information.

ANTHOLOGIES

GEORGE MURRAY, *Antarctic Manual* (Royal Geographical Society, 1901). With valuable bibliography of early works.

V. STEFANSSON, *Great Adventures and Explorations* (Robert Hale, London, 1947). With stimulating comments linking polar passages.

AUGUSTINE COURTAULD, *From the Ends of the Earth* (University Press, Oxford, 1958). An uneven selection but with some unusual passages.

Chapter 1

E. G. R. TAYLOR, *The Haven Finding Art* (1957).

M. CARY and E. H. WARMINGTON, *The Ancient Explorers* (1929).

J. OLIVER THOMSON, *History of Ancient Geography* (1948).

STRABO, *Geography*, 1, 233, 399, 441, and 519 (Loeb ed., trans. H. L. Jones, 1932). For the voyage of Pytheas.

T. D. KENDRICK, *A History of the Vikings* (1930).

P. NÖRLUND, 'Buried Norsemen at Herjolfnes' (*Meddelelser om Grønland* 67, 1924), pp. 1–267.

HANS AHLMANN, *Glaciological Research on the North Atlantic Coasts* (Royal Geographical Society, 1948). For climatic changes affecting medieval Greenland, see pp. 25–76.

E. G. R. TAYLOR, 'The Northern Passages' (in A. P. Newton ed., *The Great Age of Discovery*, 1932).

Chapter 2

E. G. R. TAYLOR, *Tudor Geography 1485–1583* (1930).

R. HAKLUYT, *The Principal Navigations, Voyages, Traffiques, and Discoveries of the English Nation. . . .* (Hakluyt Soc., 1903–5).

HAKLUYT SOCIETY, *The Voyages and Works of Davis* (1880).

Chapter 3

GERRIT DE VEER, *The three voyages of Willem Barents to the Arctic Regions* (Hakluyt Soc., 1876).

LLEWELYN POWYS, *Henry Hudson* (1927).

HAKLUYT SOCIETY, *Voyages of William Baffin* (1881).

Chapter 4

A. L. ROWSE, 'Sir Richard Grenville's place in English history' (*Proc. Brit. Acad.* 43, 1958, pp. 79–95. Raleigh Lecture).

R. T. GOULD, 'The charting of the South Shetlands, 1819–28' (*Mariner's Mirror* 27, 1941, pp. 206–42). For Dirck Gerritz and the Antarctic.

E. W. H. CHRISTIE, 'The supposed discovery of South Georgia by Amerigo Vespucci' (*Polar Rec.* 40, July 1950, pp. 560–64).

EDWARD LYNAM (ed.), *Richard Hakluyt and his successors* (Hakluyt Society, 1946). For trends and public taste in travel literature.

E. E. RICH, *The History of the Hudson's Bay Company 1670—1870* (Vol. I: 1670–1763. Hudson's Bay Record Soc., 1958).

CAROLA OMAN, *Nelson* (1947). Also the journals of Thomas Floyd, R.N. (in the possession of Brigadier Sir Henry Floyd) published in A. H. Markham, *Northward Ho!* (London, 1879).

B. H. SUMNER, *Survey of Russian History* (1944).

J. MIRSKY, *To the Arctic* (pp. 68–85).

Chapter 5

J. C. BEAGLEHOLE (ed.), *The Journals of Captain James Cook*. Vol. I (Hakluyt Soc., 1957); Vol. II (1961).

J. C. BEAGLEHOLE, 'On the Character of Captain James Cook' (*Georg. J.* 122, Dec. 1956, pp. 417–29).

J. C. BEAGLEHOLE, *The Exploration of the Pacific* (1947).

J. COOK, *A Voyage towards the South Pole and round the World* (1777).

J. COOK and J. KING, *Voyage to the Pacific Ocean . . .* (1784).

H. C. CAMERON, 'The Failure of the Philosophers to sail with Cook in the *Resolution*' (*Geogr. J.* 116, July–Sept. 1950, pp. 49–54).

R. A. SKELTON, *Explorers' Maps* (1958).

CHARLES DE BROSSES, *Histoire des navigations aux terres australes* (1751).

ALEXANDER DALRYMPLE, *An historical collection of the Several Voyages and Discoveries in the South Pacific Ocean* (1770–71).

Chapter 6

H. G. SCHENK, *The Aftermath of the Napoleonic Wars* (1947).

F. A. KIRKPATRICK, *History of the Argentine Republic* (1931).

MICHAEL LEWIS, *History of the British Navy* (1957).

Chapter 7

SIR JOHN BARROW, *An Autobiographical Memoir ...* (1847).

BRIAN ROBERTS, 'Notes on the Barrow Collection of Arctic Equipment' (*Geogr. J.* 95, May 1940, pp. 368–80). Sir John Barrow's second son John – 1808–98 – with whom he is often confused, followed his father to the Admiralty, became Keeper of the Records, and also contributed to Arctic exploration.

JOHN ROSS, *A Voyage of Discovery in H.M. Ships Alexander and Isabella* (1819).

SIR EDWARD PARRY, *Journal of a Voyage for the Discovery of the North-West Passage ... in 1819–20* (1821).

SIR EDWARD PARRY, *Journal of a Second Voyage ... in 1821–23* ... (1824).

SIR EDWARD PARRY, *Journal of a Third Voyage ... in 1824–25* ... (1826).

SIR EDWARD PARRY, *Narrative of an Attempt to reach the North Pole ... 1827* (1828).

SIR JOHN FRANKLIN, *Narrative of a Journey to the Shores of the Polar Sea, in 1819–22* (1823).

SIR JOHN FRANKLIN, *Narrative of a Second Expedition ... in 1824–27* (1828).

SIR JOHN ROSS, *Narrative of a Second Voyage in Search of a North-West Passage* (1835).

SIR GEORGE BACK, *Narrative of the Arctic land Expedition to the Mouth of the Great Fish River* (1836).

THOMAS SIMPSON, *Narrative of Discoveries on the North Coast of America* (1843).

DR JOHN RAE, *Narrative of an Expedition to the Shores of the Arctic Sea in 1846–47* (1850).

E. E. RICH and A. M. JOHNSON (ed.), *Rae's Arctic Correspondence, 1844–55* (Hudson's Bay Record Society, London, 1953). See also review of above by V. Stefansson in *Geogr. J.* 120, Dec. 1954, pp. 486–93.

Chapter 8

A. HOWARD CLARK, 'The Antarctic fur-seal and sea-elephant industries' (George Brown Goode, *The Fisheries and Fishery Industries of the United States*. Vol. II, Part 18, Washington, 1887).

S. E. MORISON, *Maritime History of Massachussetts* (Boston, 1941).

'John Miers' Account of the Discovery of the South Shetland Islands'

(*Polar Rec.* 40, July 1950, pp. 565–75. Reprinted from *Edinburgh Philosophical Journal*, Vol. 3, No. 6, 1820).

R. T. GOULD, *op. cit.*, Chapter 4 above.

'Edward Bransfield's Antarctic Voyage, 1819–20, and the Discovery of the Antarctic Continent' (*Polar Rec.* 32, July 1946, pp. 385–93). Text of original documents.

LAWRENCE MARTIN, 'Antarctica Discovered by a Connecticut Yankee, Captain Nathaniel Brown Palmer' (*Geogr. Rev.* 20, Oct. 1940, pp. 529–52. American Geographical Society of New York).

W. H. HOBBS, 'The Discoveries of Antarctica within the American Sector . . .' (*Trans. Amer. Phil. Soc.* 31, Jan. 1939, Part I).

A. H(INKS), 'On some Misrepresentations of Antarctic History' (Review of Hobbs *op. cit.*, in *Geogr. J.* 94, Oct. 1939, pp. 309–30).

Chapter 9

F. DEBENHAM (ed.), *The Voyage of Captain Bellingshausen to the Antarctic Seas, 1819–21* (Trans. from the Russian. Hakluyt Soc.,* 1945).

TERENCE ARMSTRONG, 'Recent Soviet interest in Bellingshausen's Antarctic Voyage of 1819–21' (*Polar Rec.* 39, July 1950, pp. 475–8).

TERENCE ARMSTRONG, 'Four Eye-witness accounts of Bellingshausen's Antarctic voyage of 1819–21' (*Polar Rec.* 41, Jan. 1951, pp. 85–7).

N. NOZIKOV, *Russian Voyages round the World* (Trans. E. and M. Lesser, 1945).

Chapter 10

GEORGE MURRAY, *Antarctic Manual.* For voyages of Biscoe and Balleny. The *Biscoe Papers* in R.G.S. Archives.

CHARLES ENDERBY, 'Discoveries in the Antarctic Ocean, in February 1839' (*Journal of the Royal Geographical Society* 9, 1839, p. 517).

H. R. MILL, *Siege of the South Pole* (1905).

B. ROBERTS, 'Chronological List . . .' (*Polar Rec.* 59, May 1958, pp. 99–112). The most complete list of sealing expeditions.

Chapter 11

CHARLES WILKES, *Narrative of the U.S. Exploring Expedition, 1838–42* (Philadelphia, 1845).

DANIEL C. HASKELL, *The United States Exploring Expedition and its Publications, 1844–74* (New York Public Library, 1942).

Chapter 12

A.Z., *A Letter to the President and Council of the Royal Geographical Society on Antarctic Discovery* (Privately printed, 1836). In R.G.S. archives.

M. J. DUMONT D'URVILLE, *Voyage au Pôle Sud ...* (1846).

JAMES CLARK ROSS, *A Voyage of Discovery and Research in the Southern and Antarctic Regions, 1839–43* (John Murray*, London, 1847).

For Hooker's description of the third voyage, see *Geogr. J.* 3 (Jan.– June 1894), p. 29.

Chapter 13

E. M. GELL, *John Franklin's Bride* (1930).

FRANCES J. WOODWARD, *Portrait of Jane* (1951). Biography of Franklin's second wife.

The Franklin Papers in the Scott Polar Research Institute, Cambridge, England.

R. J. CYRIAX, *Sir John Franklin's last Arctic Expedition* (1939).

R. J. CYRIAX and J. M. WORDIE, 'Centenary of the Sailing of Sir John Franklin with the *Erebus* and *Terror*' (*Geogr. J.* 106, Nov.– Dec. 1945, pp. 169–97). References to Command Papers, etc.

Memoir of Lieutenant John Irving, R.N. (ed.) Benjamin Hall (Edinburgh, 1881).

SIR JOHN BARROW, *Voyages of Discovery and Research within the Arctic Regions* (1846).

CAPTAIN LEOPOLD MCCLINTOCK, *The voyage of the Fox in the Arctic Seas* (5th Edition, 1881). The acquisition from Ireland of the McClintock papers by the National Maritime Museum, Greenwich, was too recent for use.

J. R. BELLOT, *Journal d'un voyage aux mers polaires* (1851).

CHARLES FRANCES HALL, *Arctic Researches* (1864).

Chapter 14

JOHN WRIGHT, *Geography in the making; the American Geographical Society, 1851–1951* (A.G.S., New York, 1952).

ELISHA KENT KANE, *Arctic Explorations* (Philadelphia, 1856).

CHARLES FRANCES HALL, *Life with the Esquimaux* (1864).

CHARLES FRANCES HALL, *Narrative of the North Polar Expedition. ...* (Washington, 1876).

SIR GEORGE NARES, *Narrative of a voyage to the Polar Sea during 1875–6* (1878).

EMMA DE LONG, *Voyage of the Jeannette* (Boston, 1883).

A. W. GREELEY, *Three Years of Arctic Service* (New York, 1886).

JULIUS VON PAYER, *New Lands within the Arctic Circle* (London, 1876).

Chapter 15

A. E. NORDENSKIÖLD, *The voyage of the Vega round Asia and Europe* (Trans. Alexander Leslie. Macmillan and Co.*, London, 1881).

TERENCE ARMSTRONG, *The Northern Sea Route; Soviet exploitation of the North East Passage* (1952).

F. NANSEN, *The First Crossing of Greenland* (Trans. Hubert Majendie Gepp. Longmans Green and Co.*, London, 1890).

JON SÖRENSEN, *The Saga of Fridtjof Nansen* (Trans. J. B. C. Watkins, 1932). See H. R. Mill's review article 'The Life of Nansen' *Geogr. J.* 71, March 1933, pp. 260–2).

F. NANSEN, *Farthest North* (Constable*, London, 1897).

FREDERICK JACKSON, *A thousand days in the Arctic* (1889).

The Jackson Diaries, etc. In Scott Polar Research Institute, Cambridge; formerly in R.G.S.

Chapter 16

GORDON HAYES, *Robert Edwin Peary; a record of his explorations, 1886–1909* (1929). An unbalanced, biased book, hostile to Peary, but with useful source material.

OTTO SVERDRUP, *New Land* (1904).

MSS. in R.G.S. archives relating to Young's recall from North-West Passage attempt. (See also R. J. Cyriax and J. M. Wordie, *op. cit.*, Chapter XIII.)

ROALD AMUNDSEN, *The Northwest Passage* (Constable*, London, 1908).

The Andrée Diaries. English edition (John Lane*, London, 1931). See analytical review by A. R. H(inks) (*Georg. J.* 77, April 1931, pp. 362–6).

Chapter 17

M. F. MAURY, 'The Physical Geography of the Sea, in connection with the Antarctic Regions' (*Proc. Royal Geographical Society*, 5, 1860–61, pp. 23 ff.).

CHARLES DARWIN, 'Note on a Rock seen in an Iceberg in 61° S. Lat.' (Cf. Murray, *Antarctic Manual*, p. 346).

JOHN MURRAY, 'The Renewal of Antarctic Exploration' (*Geogr. J.* 3, Jan.–June 1894, pp. 1–42 with discussion).

H. R. MILL, *The Record of the Royal Geographical Society, 1830–1930* (R. G. S.*, 1930).

SIR CLEMENTS MARKHAM, *The Lands of Silence; a history of Arctic and Antarctic exploration* (1921).

ADMIRAL SIR ALBERT H. MARKHAM, *The Life of Sir Clements R. Markham* (1917).

ADRIEN DE GERLACHE (DE GOMERY), *Voyage de la Belgica* (2nd edition, 1902).

C. E. BORCHGREVINK, 'The *Southern Cross* Expedition to the Antarctic, 1899–1900' (*Geogr. J.* 16, 1900, pp. 381–414). For an assessment of Borchgrevink and for his relations with Markham, see *Geogr. J.* 83, June 1934, pp. 534–7. Also, Borchgrevink, *First on the Antarctic Continent*, 1901.

Chapter 18

STEPHEN GWYNN, *Captain Scott* (1929).

SIR CLEMENTS MARKHAM (*op. cit.*, above).

ROBERT F. SCOTT, *The Voyage of the Discovery* (1929). With preface by Dr F. Nansen.

ERICH VON DRYGALSKI, *Zum Continent des Eisigen Südens; Deutsche Südpolar Expedition 1901–3* (Berlin, 1904).

N. OTTO G. NORDENSKJÖLD and J. G. ANDERSSON, *Antarctica* (London, 1905).

J. B. CHARCOT, *Journal de l'expédition antarctique française, 1903–5* (Paris, 1906).

The Voyage of the Scotia. By Three of the Staff (1906).

SIR CLEMENTS MARKHAM, *Intrepid Souls*. Words by Sir Clements Markham, K.C.B., President R.G.S. Music by Herbert Schartau. Privately printed. R.G.S. archives.

Chapter 19

ROBERT E. PEARY, *Northward over the Great Ice* (1898).

DUKE OF ABRUZZI, *On the Polar Star in the Arctic Sea* (1903).

ROBERT E. PEARY, *Nearest the Pole* (1907).

ROBERT E. PEARY, *The North Pole* (Hodder and Stoughton*, London, 1910).

BRADLEY ROBINSON, *Dark Companion* (1943). The biography of Matthew Henson.

Dr Frederick Cook, *My Attainment of the Pole, being a Record of the Expedition which first reached the Boreal Center, 1907–09.* ... (London, 1911). For Cook's probable route, see J. Mirsky, *To the Arctic*, pp. 301–2.

W. H. Hobbs, *Peary* (London, 1936). For an evaluation of Peary's claims, see review of above by A. R. H(inks) and J. M. W(ordie), 'Peary's Journey to the Pole' (*Geogr. J.* 89, March 1937, pp. 255–9).

Chapter 20

H. R. Mill, *The Life of Sir Ernest Shackleton* (1923).

Margery and James Fisher, *Shackleton* (1957). With review of this by L. P. Kirwan, 'The Rise of the Polar Hero' (*Geogr. J.* 124, March 1958, pp. 90–2).

E. H. Shackleton, *The Heart of the Antarctic* (Heinemann*, London, 1911).

Chapter 21

J. B. Charcot, *The Voyage of the* Why Not? *in the Antarctic, 1908–10* (London, 1911).

L. Huxley, *Scott's Last Expedition* (1913).

A. Cherry-Garrard, *The Worst Journey in the World* (1922).

R. E. Priestley, 'The Scott Tragedy' (*Geogr. J.* 68, Oct. 1926, pp. 340–2). A review of G. C. Simpson, *Scott's polar journey and the weather* (Halley Lecture, 1925. Clarendon Press, Oxford).

Roald Amundsen, *The South Pole* (London, 1912).

Chapter 22

Ejnar Mikkelsen, *Lost in the Arctic* (London, 1913).

Knud Rasmussen, *Greenland by the Polar Sea* (London, 1921).

V. Stefansson, *The Friendly Arctic. The story of five years in polar regions* (London, 1921).

'Bob' Bartlett, *The Log of 'Bob' Bartlett* (London, 1928).

Sir Douglas Mawson, *The Home of the Blizzard; the story of the Australian Antarctic Expedition, 1911–14* (1915).

W. Filchner, *Zum Sechsten Erdtheil: Die sweite Deutsche Südpolar Expedition* (Berlin, 1922).

E. H. Shackleton, *South* (Heinemann*, London, 1919).

Chapters 23 and 24

A. W. Greeley, *The Polar Regions in the Twentieth Century; their discovery and industrial evolution* (1929).

GORDON HAYES, *The Conquest of the North Pole; recent Arctic Exploration* (London, 1937).

GORDON HAYES, *The Conquest of the South Pole; Antarctic exploration, 1906–31* (London, 1932).

ANDREW CROFT, *Polar Exploration* (1939). An account of mainly twentieth-century exploration, reprinted with some additions in 1947.

G. R. CRONE, *Royal Geographical Society. A Record 1931–55* (1955).

UMBERTO NOBILE, *My Polar Flight* (London, 1961).

HENRY LARSEN, *The North-West Passage, 1940–2 and 1944* (City Archives, Vancouver, Canada, 1954). Also *Geogr. J.* 110, Jan. 1948, pp. 1–16.

J. M. SCOTT, *Gino Watkins* (1935).

L. P. KIRWAN, 'The Partition of Antarctica' and TREVOR LLOYD, 'The Political Geography of the Arctic' (Chapters on political and economic geography in W. Gordon East and A. E. Moodie, *The Changing World*, 1956).

C. H. M. WALDOCK, 'Disputed Sovereignty in the Falkland Islands Dependencies' (*Year Book of International Law*, 1948). Indispensable for a proper understanding of the legal background. Many official documents on this and other Antarctic political issues have been published in recent issues of the *Polar Record*.

J. F. DA COSTA, *Souveraineté sur l'Antarctique. Expéditions polaires françaises* (Paris, 1958). The official text of the Antarctic Treaty (see pp. 374–5), which arose from President Eisenhower's proposals, is given in *Cmnd* 913 (H.M.S.O., London) and in *Polar Rec.* 65 (May 1960), pp. 157–62.

SIR RAYMOND PRIESTLEY, 'Twentieth Century Man against Antarctica' (Presidential Address to the British Association for the Advancement of Science. *Advanc. Sci.* 13, 1956).

C. G. L. BERTRAM, 'Antarctic Prospect' (*International Affairs* 33, April 1957, pp. 143–53).

INDEX

Aberdeen, 192
Abruzzi, Duke of, 275
Académie des Sciences, 60
Active, 257
Adams, John Quincey, 143–4
Adams, Lieutenant, 294, 299, 303
Adare, Viscount, 168
Adelaide, 323
Adelaide Island, 140, 307
'Administration of the Northern Sea
    Route, Chief', 340
Advance, 200
Adventure, 80–3
Africa, 22–3, 24, 154, 244
African Association, 62, 88
Ahlmann, Hans W., 369
Aigle, 73
Alabama Expedition, 319
Alaska, 70, 71, 86–7, 92, 99, 113,
    125, 346, 350, 362, 366
Albany, 47
Albermarle, 293
Albert, Prince Consort, 170, 192
Albert Hall, 267, 273, 305, 308
Alfred the Great, 19, 32
Alert, 204
Aleutian Islands, 126, 189
Alexander, 98
Alexander I, 122, 125–9, 177
Alexander VI (Pope), 18
Alexander Land, 133, 135, 247,
    269, 307, 353–4
Amadeo, Prince Luigi. *See* Abruzzi,
    Duke of
America, North, *passim*
America, South, 25, 38, 57, 93–4,
    117, 120, 269, 357, 373, 374
American Geographical Society,
    188, 199–201, 256
Amsterdam, 40–2
Amund Island, 228
Amundsen, Roald, 166, 197, 224–5,

226, 229–30, 247, 261, 274, 288,
    295, 307–8, 310–16, 320–1, 327,
    346–7, 356, 362–4
Amundsen Sea, 354
Amundsen–Scott Station, 370
Anadyr, Gulf of, 70
Anadyr Peninsula, 72
Anadyr River, 68–70
Anadyr'skiy Zaliv. *See* Anadyr, Gulf
    of
Anderson, G. W., 62
Anderson, James, 192
Anderson, R. M., 320
Anian, Straits of, 56
Andrée, Salomon August, 230–3,
    346
Andromache, 117
Angmagssalik, 17, 343, 344
Ann, Tzarina, 70
Antarctic, 241–2, 249, 269
Antarctic Circle, 82–3, 86, 131, 133,
    138, 141, 235-8, 260, 267, 270,
    329, 333, 375
Antarctic Continent, *passim*
Antarctic Ocean, 125, 127, 164, 235,
    237, 239–41, 270, 330, 341, 348
Antwerp, 40, 246
Anvers Island, 140, 145
Archangel, 32, 348
Arctic, *passim*
Arctic Circle, 16, 55, 65, 361
Arctic Ocean, 70, 97, 125, 201, 205,
    214, 346–8
Arctic Seas, 15, 16, 68, 98, 106,
    188–9, 192, 319
Argentine, 270, 351, 367, 374
Aristotle, 15, 24, 34
Armada, 27, 33, 38
Armitage, Albert B., 258–9, 260–1,
    263, 265, 267
Arnold and Barraud, 130
Ashburton, Lord, 235

Asia, 28, 34, 40, 58, 68–72, 79, 86, 92, 213–14, 221
Aspasia, 115
Assistance, 188, 243
Astrolabe, 160–1
Asquith, Herbert Henry, 306
Astrup, Eivind, 227
Atkinson, Dr, 313
Atlantic Ocean, 15, 22–3, 40, 56–7, 99, 106, 126, 177, 183, 197, 201, 224, 348, 373
Aurora, 323, 325–7, 331, 335
Austin, Captain, 188, 190
Australia, 78, 121, 133–4, 148, 162, 172, 236, 241, 242, 244–5, 251, 260, 322–3, 327, 331, 351, 355–6, 368, 372
Australian Antarctic, 129, 133, 154, 317, 327, 356
Australian Association for the Advancement of Science, 323
Axel Heiberg Glacier, 315
Axel Heiberg Island, 228, 283

Bache Peninsula, 228
Back, Commander, 111–13, 181
Back River. *See* Great Fish River
Baffin, William, 45, 49–50, 55, 91, 97–8, 199, 363
Baffin Bay, 38, 55, 98–9, 105–6, 181, 192, 202, 342
Baffin Island, 18, 33–6, 38, 49, 55, 99, 208, 343, 362
Bage, Lieutenant, 325
Balaena, 266
Balchen, Bernt, 362
Balfour, Arthur, 266
Balleny, John, 137, 141, 148, 151, 237, 324
Balleny Islands, 141, 148, 150, 249, 351
Baltic, 279
Banks, Sir Joseph, 77, 81–2, 97
Banks Island, 188, 320
Banzare Coast, 355
Barents, William, 41–6, 49

Barents Sea, 31, 42, 55
Barne, Naval officer, 257
Barrier Land, 251
Barrington, Hon. Daines, 67
Barrow, Sir John, 92–3, 96–7, 102, 111, 114, 157, 176–80, 183, 188, 242, 257
Barrow Strait, 102, 168, 177, 182, 190
Bartlett, Bob, 279–80, 284–5, 286–7, 320
Basques, 43
Bathurst Lane, 182
Bay of Whales, 296, 312, 314–15, 344, 356
Bayley, William, 81
Beagle, 237
Beaglehole, Dr, 76
Bear Island, 42, 45–6, 55, 349
Beardmore, W., 290–1
Beardmore Glacier, 300, 304, 312–15, 330, 335
Beaufort Sea, 50, 86, 99, 102, 283, 318, 320–1, 345, 347
Beaufoy, 137
Beechey, Lieutenant (later Captain), 100, 103, 176, 184
Beechey Island, 182, 186, 190, 191, 229
Belcher, Sir Edward, 190, 199
Belgian Geographical Society, 247
Belgica, 247, 255, 314
Belgium, 246–7, 249, 291
Bellingshausen. *See* Von Bellingshausen
Bellingshausen Land, 354
Bellingshausen Sea, 134, 136, 140, 307, 352–3
Bellot, 190
Bellot Strait, 110, 186, 190–1, 229, 361
Bennett, James Gordon, 199, 207, 256
Bereg Aleksandra I. *See* Alexander Land
Bergen Museum, 215
Bering, Vitus, 69–72, 86

Bering Island, 71
Bering Sea, 71
Bering Strait, 41, 58, 68–71, 86, 97, 99, 101, 112, 176, 184–5, 187–8, 189, 206, 207, 211–13, 219, 310, 341
Berlin, 89
Bernacchi, Louis, 249, 258
Bessels, Dr, 203
Bickerton, F. H., 323, 326
Binney, Sir George, 344
Biscoe, John, 137–41, 145, 148, 162, 238, 270, 307, 355
Bismarck Strait, 253
Bjorn, 293
Black Sea, 129
Blossom, 176
Bona Confidentia, 29
Bona Esperanza, 29, 31
Bone, Thomas Main, 118–19
Booth, Felix, 109–10
Boothia, Gulf of, 105
Boothia Felix, 110, 113, 157, 192, 341
Boothia Peninsula. *See* Boothia Felix
Boston, 201
Bourbon, 80
Borchgrevink, C. E., 170, 241–2, 245–6, 248–52, 259–63, 268, 295, 322
Borden Islands, 321
Borough, Stephen, 29, 32, 36
Borup, 279
Bouvet de Lozier, 73, 85
Bouvet Island, 73, 85, 351
Bouvetya. *See* Bouvet Island
Bove, Lieutenant, 240
Bowers, Lieutenant, 313
Brainard, Sergeant, 209
Bransfield, Edward, 117–18, 121–2, 132, 160
Bransfield Strait, 121
Brentford Bay. *See* Bellot Strait
Briand, Monsieur, 306
Bridgman, H. L., 277
Brighton, 186

Bristol, 20, 22, 28, 63
British Arctic Air Route Expedition (1930), 342–3, 362
British Association for the Advancement of Science, 89, 158–9, 169, 240
British–Australian–New Zealand Antarctic Research Expedition (1929–31), 355
British Everest Expedition, 278, 281, 306
British Graham Land Expedition, 353, 355
British International Geophysical Year Expedition, 336
British North Greenland Expedition (1952–4), 363
Britons, 15
Brittany, 15
Brock Islands, 321
Brown, Captain, 130
Browning, Robert, 262
Bruce, William Spiers, 240, 259, 268–70, 327–30, 331, 332, 335, 354
Brunel, Oliver, 38–40
Buffon, William, 62
Buchan, Alexander, 77
Buchan, David, 97–8, 106, 111
Buenos Aires, 222–3, 366
Bull, H. J., 241, 322
Button, Sir Thomas, 48–9
Bylot, mate, 50
Byrd, Richard E., 316, 346, 353–4, 358, 362–3, 367–8
Byron, Charles, 73–4
Byron, Lord, 200

Cabot, John, 22, 29
Cabot, Sebastian, 29, 32
Cagni, Lieutenant, 275, 279
Caird, Sir James, 330–2
Caird Coast, 332, 336
Calais, 109
Cambridge, 27, 364, 369
Cambridge Bay, 189, 230

Cameron, Simon, 155
Camp Ridley, 250
Campbell, John, 62, 74
Campbell, Lieutenant, 317
Canada, 28, 45, 55–6, 63, 72, 91–2, 93, 343, 350, 351, 360–1
Canadian Arctic, 20, 35, 47, 49–50, 58, 62, 92, 108, 111, 113, 182, 185, 283, 288, 320–3, 347, 350, 361
Canadian Arctic Archipelago. See District of Franklin
Canadian Northwest Territories, 226
Candlemas Islands, 131
Canning, George, 93
Cape Adare, 168, 172, 241–2, 245, 249, 260, 269, 317, 322
Cape Ann, 139
Cape Bowles, 120
Cape Bristol, 131
Cape Colbourne, 230
Cape Cod, 47
Cape Columbia, 205, 277, 279, 282
Cape Crozier, 260
Cape Denison, 323, 325–8
Cape Dezhnev, 214
Cape Dundas, 177
Cape Evans, 310, 317, 336
Cape Farewell (Kap Farvel), 37, 218
Cape Flora, 232
Cape Hearn, 103
Cape Hecla, 277
Cape Herschel, 193
Cape Horn, 35, 58, 78, 116, 143, 162, 267
Cape Melbourne, 169
Cape Montague, 131
Cape Morris Jessup (Kap Morris Jesup), 275
Cape of Good Hope, 22, 24, 149, 163
Cape Royds, 296, 305
Cape Thomas Hubbard, 283
Cape Town, 82, 85
Cape Washington, 275
Carcass, 67
'Carmen Land', 316

Caroline Islands, 56
Carse, Duncan, 375
Catherine the Great, 72, 210
Cartaret, Philip, 73
Cartier, Jacques, 28, 33
Casey Channel, 352
Cathay, 21–3, 25, 29, 31, 34, 35–6, 38–41, 44–5, 56, 61, 91
Cathay Company, 34–6
Challenger, 204, 235–9, 242, 254
Chancellor, Richard, 26, 28, 31–2, 41
Charcot, Jean Baptiste Auguste, 268–9, 288, 306–7
Charcot Land, 322, 353
Charlton Island, 48
Chaucer, 20
Chelyuskin Peninsula, 213
Cherry-Garrard, Apsley, 310
Chesapeake Bay, 47
Chesterfield Inlet, 66
Chile, 366–7, 374
China, 21, 41, 45, 68, 79–80, 92, 96, 145
Chirikov, Captain, 71
Choate, 269, 273, 289
Christensen, Lars, 354, 355–6, 358
Christiana Harbour, 229
Chukchi Peninsula, 68
Chukchi Sea, 185
Chukchi Tribes, 68–70
Chukotskiy Poluostrov. See Chukchi Peninsula
Churchill, town, 49
Churchill, Winston, 331
Churchill River, 49, 63
Cicero, 24
Cincinatti, 203
Clarence Island, 120, 333
Coats, Andrew and James, 270
Coats Land, 270, 327–8, 332
Colbeck, William, 249, 250–1, 264–5
Collinson, Captain, 187–90, 197, 230
Columbus, Christopher, 22, 156
Commerson, Philibert, 74
Commonwealth Bay, 323, 325

Commonwealth Trans-Antarctic
 Expedition, 170, 356
Congressional Investigating
 Committee, 284
Connecticut, 115, 202
Conrad, J., 246
Copenhagen, 129–30, 282, 363
Cook, Frederick A., 247, 282–4,
 307–8
Cook, James, 59, 61–2, 66, 73–90,
 93–4, 115–17, 129
Coppermine River, 111–13, 320
Cornelison, Jan, 43
Cornwall, 15, 34
Cornwallis Island, 102, 182
Cortereal, Miguel and Gaspar, 28
Côte Clarie, 162, 325
Coulman Island, 250
Courtauld, Augustine, 344–5
Cowes, 260, 294
Cowley, Ambrose, 57
'Crane Channel', 353
Crean, seaman, 313
'Crocker Land', 321, 346
'Crocker Mountains', 98–101, 109
Crozier, Francis Rawdon Moira, 106,
 163, 172, 174, 183, 191
Crozier Strait, 182
Cumberland Sound, 36

Da Gama, Vasco, 22, 24
Danes, 63
Dallmann, Edward, 240
Dalrymple, Alexander, 74–5, 78–80,
 84–6
Dampier, William, 57, 61–2
Danish West Indies, 349
Danmark Expedition, 320
Darwin, Charles, 237, 239
Darwin, Major, 285
David, Edgeworth, 294, 297, 303–4,
 323, 324
Davis, Edward, 57
Davis, John, 36–9, 47, 50, 55
Davis, John King, 323, 325–7, 335,
 354

Davis Sea, 325
Davis Strait, 36, 50, 55, 97–8, 183
De Bougainville, The Chevalier, 67,
 74
De Brosses, Charles, 62, 74–5, 78–9,
 84
De Gerlache, Adrien, 229, 247–8,
 282
De Haven, E. J., 188, 190, 199
De Kerguelen-Trémarec, Yves
 Joseph, 79–80
De La Roché, Antonio, 58
De La Roquette Islands, 229
De Lesseps, 211
De Long, George Washington, 207,
 218, 224
De Mendana, Alvara, 56
De Quervain, 217
De Quiros, Pedro Fernandez, 56
De Traversay, Marquis, 127
De Veer, Gerrit, 41–4
Dead Man's Island, 347
Dease, Peter Warren, 111–13
Debenham, Frank, 310, 343
Deception Island, 121–2, 134, 150
Dee, John, 27, 32, 34
Denmark, 285, 349, 359, 361
Deslisle, Guillaume, 71
Deslisle de la Croyère, Louis, 71
Deptford, 30
Derwent River, 172
Deutschland, 328–30, 332
Devon Island, 100, 102
Dezhnev, Simon, 68–70, 86
Diaz, Bartholomew, 22, 24
Dickens, Charles, 180
Dickerson, Mahlon, 146
Dickson, Baron Oscar, 210, 212
Dickson Island, 213
Digges, Sir Dudley, 48
Digges Island, 48
Dijon, 62
Discovery, William Baffin, 51;
 Henry Hudson, 49, 51; Captain
 Middleton, 65; George S. Nares,
 204; Robert Falcon Scott, 257,

259–61, 263–7, 289, 295, 304–6, 310

Discovery Committee, 351

District of Franklin, 182

Dobbs, Arthur, 65–6

Dorlton, 77

Dorothea, 97

Dove, 123

Dover, 109

Drake, Sir Francis, 35, 57

Drake Passage, 58, 372

Dronning Louise Land, 218, 319, 364

Dronning Maud Land, 132, 136, 358, 368

Drygalski, 324, 354

Drygalski Ice Tongue, 303

Dublin, 158

Dundee, 257, 290

Dundee Island, 356

Durforth, Cornelius, 29

D'Urville, Jules Sebastien César Dumont, 149, 154, 159–62, 165, 166, 168, 238, 268, 306, 322, 324–5, 358, 369, 370

Dutch East India Company, 45–7, 57

Dutch White Sea Trading Company, 40

Dvina River, 32

Eagle, 231–3

East Cape, 68, 70, 86

East Greenland, 216, 276, 349, 351

East Greenland Sea, 218, 276, 288

East India Company of the Chamber of Amsterdam, 45–6

East Siberian Sea, 68, 101

Edsel Ford Range, 354

Edward VII, 305

Edward Bonaventure, 29, 31–2

Egerton, Lord Francis, 184

Eielson, Carl Ben, 347

Eira, 224

Elephant Island, 120, 333–5

Elizabeth I, 33, 38

Ellef Ringnes Island, 228

Ellesmere Island, 197, 199, 201, 203, 205, 208, 228, 274–5, 277, 283, 320, 344, 365

Ellsworth, Lincoln, 346, 356–8

Ellsworth, Highland, 356

Empire State Building, 363

Endeavour, James Cook, 77–81; Edward Parry, 106

Enderby Brothers, 90–1, 137–8, 141

Enderby, Charles, 90–1, 124, 137–8, 141, 240

Enderby Land, 133, 139, 141, 148, 150, 152–3, 164, 331, 339, 351–6, 358

Endurance, 331–3, 335–6

England, 25–8, 32, 33, 36–40, 45–7, 50–1, 55–6, 58–60, 61–5, 66–7, 71, 77, 83, 92–3, 96, 104–5, 110, 130–1, 140, 157–60, 162–3, 164, 169, 175, 177, 186, 234–6, 246, 251, 257, 267–8, 288, 309, 327, 330–1

England, Rupert, 264, 296

English Channel, 323

English Muscovy Company, 32, 40, 45–7

Enterprise, Captain Martin, 182; Edward Parry, 106; Sir James Clark Ross, 186, 187–9, 230

Equator, 24

Erebus, 163–9, 172–3, 176, 180–4, 190–2, 242

Eric the Red, 17–18

Ericsson, Leif, 18

Eskimoes, 17–18, 20, 34–7, 56, 65, 95, 102, 105, 110, 180, 185, 187, 189, 191, 202–5, 213–14, 217, 227, 230, 277, 279–83, 286, 314, 319–20, 341, 344, 362

Essex, 34–5

Etah, 279, 282

Europe, 21, 27, 37, 69, 89, 93, 121, 126, 186, 198–9, 204, 211, 220, 347, 360, 363

Evans, E. G. R., 264, 310, 313
Everest, 369

Falkland Islands Dependencies (British Antarctic Territory), 84, 269, 351–2, 357, 367–8, 374
Falkland Islands Dependencies Survey (British Antarctic Survey), 367
Fallières Coast, 307
Fanning, Edmund, 115, 122–3, 134, 144
Faroe Islands, 16–17
Felix, 188
Felix Harbour, 110
Ferrar Glacier, 304
Fiji, 149
Filchner, William, 123, 270, 327–30, 332, 354
Filchner Ice Shelf, 328, 332, 371
Finland, 210
Finnmark, 31
Fitzjames, James, 183
Flawes and Wood, 50
Floyd, Midshipman Thomas, 67
Flying Fish, 147, 150
Forster, Johann Reinhold and son, 82–3
Forsythe, Commander, 190
Fort Conger, 274, 276
Fort Resolution, 183
Fort Sumter, 201
Fortune, 69
Foyn, Commander, 240–1
Fox, 192, 197
Fox, Margaret, 201
Foxe, Luke, 49, 63, 65
Foxe Basin, 49, 105
Foxe Peninsula, 49
Fraekel, Knuth, 231
Fram, 218, 221–5, 226, 228, 231, 307–8, 311, 328, 365
Framheim, 315
France, 24, 47, 58, 62–3, 64–5, 66–7, 73–4, 79–80, 91, 93, 127, 154, 159–61, 234–5, 269, 289, 291, 308, 324, 349, 351, 358, 363, 369

Franche, R., 282
Franklin, Benjamin, 144
Franklin, Lady Jane, 179, 188, 190–1, 199
Franklin, Sir John, 96, 108, 111–13, 164–5, 170, 178–94, 199, 202, 229
Franklin Strait, 182, 186, 230
Franz Josef Land, 197, 206–8, 223–4, 232, 240, 249, 269, 275
Frederick the Eskimo, 209
French Canada, 66
French East India Company, 73–6
French Laboratory of Maritime Research, 306
Frisius, Gemma, 27
Frobisher, Martin, 33–6, 39, 203
Frobisher Bay, 33, 35–6, 203, 362
Frobisher Station, 362
Fuchs, Sir Vivian, 270, 336, 371–2
Furness, 65
Fury, 105–6, 110
Fury Beach, 110, 186
Fury and Hecla Strait, 105, 113

Gabriel, 34
Garda, 17
Gaul, 15
Gauss, 268–9
Gauss, Johann Karl Friedrich, 157, 161, 164, 167–8
Gaussberg, 326, 328
Gefferson, William, 29
General San Martin, 371
Geographical Society of London, 89–91, 92, 96–7, 99, 116. *See also* Royal Geographical Society
George, 36
George III, 67, 146
George IV, 130
George V, 305
George's Bay, 118–20
Georgia Isle. *See* South Georgia
German Scientific and Medical Association (Groz), 208
Germany, 221, 239, 247, 255, 268, 289, 330–1, 343, 358

Gerritz, Dirck, 57
Gesellschaft für Erdkunde, 89
Gibraltar, 293; Straits of, 15
Gilbert, William, 60
Gilbert Sound, 36–7
Gjøa, 229–30
Gjøa Haven, 230
Glasgow, 291
Gloucester, 187
Goddard, William Henry, 120
Godthaab, 36, 363
Goering, Hermann, 358
Golden Hind, 35, 57
Golovnin, Captain, 128, 129
Gonçalves, Lope, 24
Goodsell, Dr, 279
Goodsir, Dr, 201
Goupil, Monsieur, 160
Graf Zeppelin, 225
Graham, Sir James R. G., 140
Graham Land, 120–1, 140–1, 145, 149, 164, 174, 240, 247, 253, 269, 288, 306–7, 322–3, 330, 333, 352–5, 356, 369
Grand Canal, 275
Grant Land, 273, 275–6
Gravesend, 32
Great Barrier Reef, 80
Great Bear Lake, 96, 358
Great Britain, 49, 73, 75, 79, 88–92, 94, 115, 127, 144, 155, 157, 160, 175–6, 192, 204, 208, 234, 242, 245–6, 254–5, 273, 276, 280, 285, 297, 335, 341–4, 349, 351–2, 362, 364, 367–9, 371, 374
Great Fish River, 112–13, 183–4, 191
Great Ice Barrier, 236
Great Ice Valley, 259
Greece, 19, 21
Greeks, 15
Greeley, Adolphus Washington, 208–9, 220, 224
Green the Astronomer, 77, 81
Greenhythe, 181
Greenland, 17–21, 33–4, 36–8, 42,

45–6, 50–1, 51, 91, 96–7, 99, 116, 169, 197, 199–200, 203, 205, 208–9, 211, 214, 216–21, 226–7, 240, 274–6, 281, 282–3, 285, 303, 318–19, 320–1, 341–2, 344–5, 349, 360, 362–4, 366
Greenland Sea, 319
Greenwich, 30–1, 102, 138, 181
Greenwich Hospital, 86
Gregory, J. W., 262
Greig, Sir Alexis Samuilovich, 129
Greig, Sir Samuel, 129
Grenville, Sir Richard, 56–7
Grey, Earl, 184
Grierson, John, 363
Grinnell, Henry, 96, 188–90, 199, 201–4
Grinnell Land, 200, 209, 283
Grinnell Peninsula. *See* Grinnell Land
Griper, 99–104, 361
Grønfjorden, 347
Gulf Stream, 206
Gunbjorn, 17, 19
Gwynn, Stephen, 309

Haakon VII, 316
Haddington, Lord, 177
Hadley, John, 61
Hagen, Lieutenant, 319
Haggard, Rider, 246
Hague, The, 349, 374
Hakluyt, Richard, 27–9, 33, 41, 44, 57
Hall, Charles Francis, 193–4, 201–5, 277, 320
Hall Land, 203
Halley, Edmund, 60, 75
Hamburg, 208, 229, 235, 242, 328
Hampton Roads, 149
Hanseatic League, 18
Hanson, Nicolai, 249, 250–1
Harmsworth, Alfred (Lord Northcliffe), 223–4, 255–6
Harrison, John, 61
Hawthorne, Nathaniel, 147

Hayes, Isaac Israel, 201–2
Heard Island, 368
Hearne, Samuel, 97
Hearst Land, 353
Hecla, 99–106, 361
Helgoland, 19
Hendrick, Hans, 204
Hendricus, Albert, 43
Henry III, 19
Henry VI, 20
Henry the Navigator, Prince, 22
Henson, Matthew, 227, 278–81
Herald, 185
Herald Island, 185, 207
Hercules, 15
Herjolfness, 18
Hero, 121–2
High Island. *See* Ross Island
Hillary, Sir Edmund, 371
Hobart, 140, 163–6, 172, 179
Hobbs, William H., 342
Hobson, Lieutenant, 192
Hodges, William, 82
Hodgson, T. V., 259
Holland, 23, 25, 40–1, 43–7, 55, 58–9, 221
Hollick-Kenyon, H., 356
Holy Land, 89
Hooker, Sir Joseph, 163, 170, 174, 220, 242, 245, 253, 261
Hopewell, 46
Hoppner, Lieutenant, 100
Hudson, Henry, 45–9, 55, 62
Hudson, Lieutenant, 150
Hudson Bay, 48–50, 55, 62–8, 72, 105, 111–13, 203, 341–2
Hudson River, 47
Hudson Strait, 38, 47, 55, 64, 86, 104
Hudson's Bay Company, 47, 49, 56, 63, 64–5, 97, 109, 111–13, 183–4, 188, 191–2
'Hudson's Tutches'. *See* Jan Mayen Island
Humboldt Glacier, 200
Hungary, 290

Hunt, Sir John, 278
Hut Point, 264, 291, 296, 297, 303, 305, 317
Huxley, Professor, 240

Ibsen, 215
Ice Haven, 43–4, 46
Iceland, 16, 18–21, 37
Icy Cape, 87
Île de France, 80
Imperial Academy of Sciences, 60
Imperial Admiralty College, 72
Imperial Trans-Antarctic Expedition, 330–5
Independence Bay, 218, 227, 275, 285
Indispensable, 130
India, 68, 79, 244, 374
Indian Ocean, 79, 126–7, 141, 164
Indies, 21–3
Inglefield Land, 200
International Expedition to Greenland (1959), 364
International Geographical Congress (1895), 245, 246, 247, 248, 250, 268; (1904), 288
International Geophysical Year (1957–8), 136, 198, 339, 354, 369–74
International Polar Conference (1879), 208
International Polar Year (1882–3), 198, 208, 340–1, 369; (1932–3), 340–1, 369
Intrepid, 188, 190
Investigator, 186, 187–9
Ireland, 16–18
Irving, Dr, 67
Irving, Lieutenant, 179–80
Isabel, 199
Isabella, 98, 110
Isachsen, Gunnar, 228, 354, 355
Isachsen Island, 228
Islam, 21
Isle of Georgia. *See* South Georgia
Italia, 347–8, 352

Italian North Polar Expedition (1928), 347–8
Italy, 279
Ivan the Terrible, 32

Jackman, Charles, 36, 40–1, 44
Jackson, Frederick, 223–4, 232, 249
Jackson, President, 144
Jackson–Harmsworth Expedition, 222, 249, 255, 259, 269, 295
Jacquinot, Captain, 162
James, Thomas, 49, 63
James Bay, 48–9
James Caird, 334–5
James W. Ellsworth Land. *See* Ellsworth Highland
Jan Mayen Island, 45, 55, 345, 349, 364
Jane, 137
Japan, 21, 71, 149
Jason, 217
Java, 78
Jeannette, 207, 218–19, 222, 365
Jensen, Captain, 211, 249, 251
Jerjulfsson, Bjarni, 18, 21
Johansen, H., 222–4
John R. Bradley, 282
Johnson, 147–8
Jones, Dr, 326
Jones, Thomas ap Catesby, 145–6
Jones Sound, 50, 98, 228, 283
Joyce, naval rating, 294, 304
Juet, Robert, 46, 48
Julianehaab, 328, 362

Kaiser Wilhelm Barrier, 328
Kaiser Wilhelm II Land, 269, 322, 325, 353, 355
Kamchatka, 128–30
Kamchatka Peninsula, 69–72, 92, 101, 126
Kane, Elisha Kent, 199–202, 224
Kane Basin, 200–1, 226, 319
Kara Sea, 32, 36, 40–2, 45–6, 55, 208, 212, 220
Kara Strait, 41–3, 46, 213

Karlsefni, Thorfinn, 18
Karluk, 320
Keilhau, Professor, 210
Kelch, Nicolai, 221
Kelham, Professor, 210
Kellet, Captain, 185, 187, 207
Kemp, John, 137, 141, 355
Kemp Land, 141–2, 355
Kendall, Larkum, 82
Kennedy, Captain of *Prince Albert*, 190
Kennedy Channel, 200, 203, 226, 275
Kerguelen Island, 79–80, 255, 268, 352, 368
King, Richard, 181, 184, 190
King Edward VII Land, 174, 260, 267, 291–3, 296, 298, 305, 312, 316
King George III Island, 77
King George V Land, 154, 323–5, 327, 355
King Haakon VII Plateau, 316
King Leopold and Queen Astrid Coast, 356
King Oscar Land, 228
King Point, 230, 240
King William Island, 110, 113, 182–3, 192, 193, 230, 314, 341
Kipling, Rudyard, 246
Knight, James, 64
Knox Coast, 153, 268, 325–6
Knox Land. *See* Knox Coast
Knuth, Count Eigil, 364
Koch, J. P., 218, 318–19
Koettlitz, Dr, 259
Kola Peninsula (Kol'skiy Poluostrov), 19, 31, 40, 44
Koldewey, 216
Kolyma River, 68, 70
Krassin, 348
Kristensen, Leonard, 241
Kronprins Olav Kyst, 355
Kronprinsesse Märtha Kyst, 132, 355, 358
Kronshtadt, 127

Kruzenstern, A. J., 126, 129
Kuntze, Dr, 128
Kurile Islands, 71

Labrador, 18, 22, 28, 55, 204, 282
Lachambre, M., 231
Ladoga. See *Mirnyi*
Lady Franklin, 188
Lady Newnes Bay, 250
Lambton, Elizabeth Dawson, 330
Lambton, The Misses Dawson, 291
Lancaster Sound, 50, 98–102, 105, 111, 177, 182, 187–8, 361
'Land of Desolation.' *See* Kerguelen Island
'Land of Fires.' *See* Tierra del Fuego
Lander, Richard, 141
Lars Christensen Coast, 356
Larsen, C. A., 240–1
Larsen, Henry, 360
Larsen Glacier, 304
Laurie Island, 270
Lashly, seaman, 313
Law, Philip, 368
Lazarev, Mikhail, 128–9, 132, 136
Lemon, Captain, 344
Lena, 212
Lena River, 69, 207, 212–13
Leningrad, 127
León, 85
Lever, 180
Levick, Murray, 317
Lewis, John, 356
Lewis, J. H., 372
Liddon, Lieutenant, 99
Lincoln, Abraham, 201
Lincoln Sea, 203
Lind, James, 61, 81
Lindbergh, Charles A., 363
Linnaeus, 79
Linnean Society, 61–2, 88
Lively, 138–40
Liverpool, 96
Livingstone, 199
Lockwood, 209, 275

Lomonosov Ridge, 365
London, 26, 32–4, 36, 40, 46–7, 63–4, 66, 89, 93–5, 98, 101, 109, 117, 145, 179, 186, 220, 245, 246, 257, 310, 366
London, Port of, 36
Longstaff, Llewellyn, 255
Longyearbyen, 348
Loper, Mrs, 123
Los Angeles, 363
Louis XV, 71
Louis Philippe, 159–60
Louis Philippe Land, 160
Louisburg, 66
Louvain, 27
Ludwig, Archduke, 92
Luitpold Coast, 328, 332
Lunardi, 96
Lurabee Channel, 353
Lutwidge, Skeffington, 67
Lyall, scientist, 163
Lyon, Israel, 67

McClintock, Sir Leopold, 186, 190–4, 202, 220–1, 311, 321
McClintock Channel, 182
McClure, Captain, 187–92, 197, 199, 321
McCormick, 163
Mackay, surgeon, 294, 297
Mackenzie, Alexander, 97
Mackenzie River, 96, 111–12, 230
MacMillan, Donald, 279, 321, 346
McMurdo Bay, 163, 253
McMurdo Sound, 172, 261, 293, 296, 303–4, 308, 310
Macquarie Island, 133–4, 323, 368
MacRobertson Land, 355, 368
Madeira, 310
Madigan, C. T., 322, 325
Magellan, Ferdinand, 25, 57
Magellan, Strait of, 25, 39, 56–7
Maine, 47
Majestic, 258
Mandeville, Sir John, 24
Margate Roads, 164

Marguerite Bay, 307
Marian Islands, 56
Marie, 73
Marie Byrd Land, 150, 354
Markham, Albert, 205, 209, 218
Markham, Clements, 96, 242–8, 252–8, 261, 264–8, 274, 289, 294, 306, 310–11, 314–15, 322, 336, 364, 370
Markham, Mrs Clements, 259
Markham, Commodore, 257
Markland, 18
Marquis de Traversay Islands. *See* Sandwich Land
Marseille, 15
Marshall, Dr, 299, 303
Marston, 294
Martin, Captain, 182
Mary Ann, 130
Maryland, 18
Maskelyne, Nevil, 61
Mason, Commissioner, 155
Massachusetts, 115
Massilia, 15
Matochkin Shar, 41, 46
Maud, 363
Maurice of Nassau, 45
Maury, Matthew Fontaine, 234–6, 240, 242, 369
Mawson, Sir Douglas, 121, 294, 297, 303, 322–7, 331, 333, 335, 354, 355
May, Jan, 45–6
Mediterranean, 15, 266, 375
Mela, Pomponius, 24
Melbourne, 140, 162, 310
Melville, Lord, 97
Melville Bay, 50
Melville Island, 102, 104, 107, 177, 188, 261–2
Melville Peninsula, 105, 203
Melville Sound, 102, 104, 182, 188, 361
Mercator, Gerhard, 21, 27, 32
Mertens, Dr, 128
Mertz, Xavier, 323–5

Mertz Glacier, 323, 326
Middleton, James, 65–6
Miers, John, 116–17
Mikhailov, Paul, 128–31
Mikkelsen, Ejnar, 285, 318–19
Mill, Hugh Robert, 141, 259, 266, 268, 289, 310, 369
Minna Bluff, 303
Mirnyi, 128, 131–3, 136
Mohn, Professor Henrik, 218
Moluccas, 80
Montevideo, 116
Montreal, 66
Moonshine, 36–7
Moore, Captain, 66
Morning, 263–6, 310
Morrell, Benjamin, 124, 328
Moscow, 32
Mosselbukta, 232
Mount d'Urville, 149
Mount Erebus, 170–1, 251, 253, 260, 297, 303, 304, 310
Mount Hope, 149, 300
Mount Longstaff, 300
Mount Markham, 300
Mount Melbourne, 171
Mount Terror, 170, 251, 303
Mullock, G. F. A., 264–5
Munck, Jens, 49
Murchison, Sir Roderick, 181
Murmansk, 31
Murray, George, 259
Murray, Sir John, 236, 238, 242, 245, 250, 252–4, 258, 266, 270, 322
Mylius-Erichsen, 318–19, 342
Mys Dezhneva. *See* East Cape
'Mysterie and Companie of the Marchants Adventurers for the Discoverie of Regions, Dominions, Islands, and Places Unknowen, The', 28

Nansen, Fridtjof, 208, 211, 216–25, 226–7, 233, 240, 261, 274–8, 295, 303, 309, 311, 314–15, 360, 365
Napier, Lord, 243

Nares, Sir George, 21, 204–5, 209, 218–20, 236, 243, 323

Nassau Bay, 149

National Antarctic Exhibition, 254, 257, 266, 268–9, 299, 314

National Geographic Society of Washington, 284

Nautilus, W. R. Anderson, 348–9, 366; Sir Robert Williams, 348–9

'Navy Cliff', 285, 319

Ne Plus Ultra, 150, 307

Nelson, Lord Horatio, 67

Netherlands, 26, 40

'Neu-Scwabenland', 358

Neumayer, George, 235, 242, 244, 253

New Amsterdam. *See* New York

New England, 121, 187

New Guinea, 78

New Hebrides, 56

New Siberian Islands, 207, 213, 218, 221, 364

New South Britain. *See* South Shetland Islands

'New South Greenland', 328

New South Shetland Islands. *See* South Shetland Islands

New York, 47, 122, 188, 203, 276, 278, 288, 363

New York Chamber of Commerce, 200

New Zealand, 78, 83–5, 133, 141, 170, 172, 242, 260, 263, 268, 314, 317, 322, 335, 358, 360, 374

Newcastle, 162

Newland. *See* Spitsbergen

Newnes, Sir George, 247, 249, 250

Newnes Land, 251

Nicholas of Lynn, 20

Nimrod, 294–6, 298, 303–4, 317, 322

Ninnis, B. E. S., 324, 327

Ninnis Glacier, 324

Nobile, Umberto, 346–8

Nordaustland (North-East Land), 211, 232, 344, 364

Nordenskiöld, Baron Nils A. E., 197, 210–16, 233, 260

Nordenskjöld, Otto, 255, 269, 333

Nordenskjöld Ice Tongue, 303

Norge, 346–7

Norsemen, 16–19, 35, 38, 45

North Cape, 9, 27, 214

North Devon Island, 283

North Foreland, 138–9

North Greenland, 226–7, 279, 318–19, 349, 364

North Magnetic Pole, 101, 104, 110, 154, 157, 159, 163, 229–30

North Polar Sea, 214

North Pole, 16, 20, 45, 50, 55, 97, 105, 107–8, 163, 176, 197, 199–200, 203–9, 211, 218–20, 221–4, 227, 230–1, 233, 256, 273–85, 286–8, 301–2, 307–8, 310, 316, 318, 322, 340–1, 345–9, 365–6, 373

North Sea, 77

North-East Foreland, 319

North-East Passage, 25–6, 31–2, 35–6, 40–1, 46–7, 51, 55, 59, 68, 72, 197, 211–12, 321, 372

North-West Company, 36, 111

North-West Passage, 27–8, 33, 34–5, 38, 49–50, 55–6, 63–6, 72, 86, 91–3, 96–7, 104–6, 108–9, 111, 114, 125, 159, 167–8, 176–7, 180, 182, 185, 189–93, 197, 207, 229–30, 288, 314, 341–2, 346, 361, 366, 373

Norton, Captain, 66

Norway, 17–21, 31, 40, 46, 133, 212, 216–17, 221–2, 224, 229, 240–1, 261, 349–50, 352–3, 358, 369

Norwegian Antarctic, 131

Norwegian Geographical Society, 218

Norwegian Polar Institute, 368

Nova Scotia, 18, 83

Novaya Zemlya, 32, 40–7, 55, 206–7, 212

Novosibirskiye Ostrova. *See* New Siberian Islands
Novosil'skiy, P. M., 133

Oates, Captain, 310, 313–14
Oates Land, 151, 317, 322–3, 367
Ob, Gulf of, 70
Ob River, 27–8, 40, 72
Obsskaya Guba. *See* Ob, Gulf of
Ocean Camp, 333
Ochtere, Viking, 19, 33
Ohio, 202
Okhotsk, 69–70, 126
Okhotsk Sea, 126
Ommanney, Erasmus, 188, 190
One Ton Camp, 310, 314
Operation 'Deepfreeze', 372
Operation 'Highjump', 367
Orange Harbour, 149
Orkneys, 16
Orleans Channel, 160
Orontius, 24
Orosius, 19
Ortelius, 21, 33
Oscar, King of Norway, 221
Oslo, 358, 369
Osterreith, Madame, 247
Ottawa, 363
Oxford, 344, 364

Pacific Coast, 69, 75
Pacific Ocean, 25, 28, 56, 59, 62, 68, 74, 86–7, 92, 99, 106, 126–7, 143–4, 146, 149, 150, 153, 160, 168, 177–8, 184, 197, 201, 212, 214, 223, 230, 237, 289, 343, 354, 357–8, 373
Palestine Association, 89
Palmer, Nathaniel, 121–5, 134–5
Palmer Land, 123, 135, 140, 145, 148, 245, 269
Palmer Peninsula, 121
Panama Canal, 211, 373
Pandora. See *Jeannette*
Papanin, Ivan, 321, 345, 364–5
Paramour, 60

Paris Geographical Society. *See* Société de Géographie
Parker, Hyde, 257
Parkinson, Sydney, 77
Parry, Sir Edward, 66, 95, 98–111, 125, 176–9, 184, 205, 261, 318, 321
Patience Camp, 333
Patrick, St, 16
Pavlovich, Alexander, 125
Payer, Julius, 206–7
Peacock, 147, 150–4
Peary, Robert E., 107, 209, 214, 217–18, 226–9, 273–89, 308–9, 311, 316, 319, 322, 360
Peary Arctic Club, 273–9, 281
'Peary Channel', 285
Peary Land, 275, 319, 364
Peel, Sir Robert, 178
Peel Sand, 182, 229
Peglar, Harry, 193
Pelican, 57
Pendleton, Benjamin, 122, 144
Peninsula & Oriental Line, 258
Penny, William, 188
Persia, 32, 92
Peru, 244
Pet, Arthur, 36, 40–1, 44
Peter I Øy (Ostrov Peter I), 133, 135, 307, 358
Peter the Great, 51, 58–60, 68–9, 128
Petermann, A. H., 206–7
Petermann Island, 306
Philadelphia, 66, 144, 200
Philadelphia Philosophical Society, 146
Philip of Spain, 38
Philippine Islands, 199
Phipps, Hon. Constantine, 45, 67, 97, 106
Piner's Bay, 152
Pioneer, 188
Plate River, 116
Plover, 185, 187
Plymouth, 76, 330

Point Barrow, 86, 113, 189, 320, 347, 366
Point Turnagain, 112
Point Victory, 193
Polar Basin, 206–8, 218, 222, 244, 275
Polaris (Charles Francis Hall), 203
Polaris (Ernest Shackleton), 331
Pole of Relative Inaccessibility, 372
Polo, Marco, 21, 33
Porden, Eleanor, 179
Porpoise, 147, 149–50, 152–4, 162
Port Mary, 130
Port Philip, 140
Portsmouth, 95, 130
Portugal, 22–3, 26–7, 40
Possession Island, 170
Pourquoi Pas?, 306–7
Powell, George, 123, 137
Powell's Group. *See* South Orkney Islands
Prestrud, K., 316
Prickett, Abakuk, 48
Priestley, Sir Raymond, 294, 310, 312–13, 317, 343
Prince Albert, 188, 190
Prince Patrick Island, 321
Prince Regent. *See* George IV
Prince Regent Inlet, 101, 104–5, 109–11, 184
Prince of Wales. *See* George V
Prince of Wales Strait, 189, 358
Princess Astrid Land. *See* King Leopold and Queen Astrid Coast
Princess Elizabeth Land, 236, 355
Prins Christians Sund, 334
Prins Harald Kyst, 355, 367
Prins Olav Kyst. *See* Kronprins Olav Kyst
Prinsesse Astrid Kyst, 355, 358, 366
Prinsesse Ragnhild Kyst, 132, 355
Prinz Regent Luitpold Land, 328, 332
Ptolemy, 22
Puchas, Samuel, 49
Pytheas, 15–16, 34

Quebec, 66, 76
Queen Alexandra Mountains, 305
Queen Elizabeth Islands, 318
Queen Louise Land, 218
Queen Mary Land, 235–7
Queen Maud Bay, 130
Queen Maud Gulf, 113
Queen Maud Range, 316
Quest, 339, 344

Racehorse, 67
Rae, John, 185, 188–92, 320
Rae Isthmus, 203, 341
Rae Strait, 230
Rasmussen, Knud, 285, 319, 342
Reeves Glacier, 304
Relief, 147
Renovation, 183
Repulse Bay, 65, 341
Rescue, 202
Resolute, 188
Resolution (Sir Thomas Button), 48
Resolution (James Cook), 80–5
Reynolds, John R., 96, 144–7, 157
Richards, Sir George, 220
Richardson, Sir John, 111, 112, 185
Richmond, 77
Riiser-Larsen, Hjalmar, 132, 353, 355
Ringgold, Lieutenant, 154
Ringnes Islands, 283
Rink, Henry, 211, 216
Rio de Janeiro, 130, 134
Ritscher, Alfred, 358, 369
Robertson, scientist, 163
Robertson Bay, 249–51
Robertson Island, 333
Robeson Channel, 226
Ronne Antarctic Research Expedition, 368
Roosevelt, 277, 279–80, 286
Roosevelt, Theodore, 156
Ross, Sir James Clark, 109–10, 113, 150, 154, 157, 159–60, 163–76, 178–9, 184, 236, 242, 244, 249, 260, 267–8, 369

Ross, Sir John, 98–101, 105, 109–12, 125, 228
Ross Dependency, 151, 264, 357, 367
Ross Ice Shelf, 171–3, 251, 260, 262–3, 267, 291, 295, 298–9, 302, 304–5, 322
Ross Island, 171, 261, 263, 296–7, 317, 335
Ross Sea, 174, 241, 260, 293, 308, 318, 322, 327, 329, 335, 350, 352–4, 356, 371
Ross Sea Dependency, 151, 170, 264, 357, 367
Royal Geographical Society, 130, 137, 141, 158, 169, 175, 181, 184, 192, 220–1, 229, 233–6, 238, 240, 243–6, 248, 251, 253–4, 259–60, 264, 266–8, 284–6, 289, 305–10, 313–16, 322–3, 325, 330, 354, 362, 369–71. See also Geographical Society of London
Royal Scottish Geographical Society, 290
Royal Society, 60, 63, 65–7, 75–6, 81, 97, 130, 159, 162, 169, 178–9, 185–7, 235, 253, 255–6, 259
Royal Terror Theatre, 262
Royal Victoria Theatre, 172
Royds, 258
Rupert River, 48
Russia, 19, 31, 32, 35, 40, 51, 55, 59–60, 62, 66–9, 71–2, 87, 91–3, 96, 109, 113, 125–7, 131–3, 135–7, 169, 177, 198, 210–12, 214–15, 220, 234–5, 321, 341, 345, 348, 350, 360, 364, 368, 372–4
Russian-American Company, 72, 123
Rymill, John, 353

Sabine, Captain, 99–100, 104, 157–9, 163
Sabrina Coast, 356
Sabrina Land, 141, 153, 237, 325
St Gabriel, 70
St Helena, 163
St Kitts, 257

St Lawrence Island, 70
St Lawrence River, 26, 30, 64, 66, 76, 111
St Paul, 71
St Peter, 71
St Petersburg, 69–71, 101, 125–6, 129
San Francisco, 92
San Jacinto, 155
Sandwich, 4th Earl of, 67, 81, 85
Sandwich Land, 85, 115, 131, 134, 149, 306, 351
Santiago, 366
Saunders Island, 131
Savio, 251
Scandinavia, 20, 212, 234, 242, 344
Scandinavian Air-Lines System, 362
Schwatka, Frederick, 193, 199, 207, 277, 320
Scientific Committee of the Imperial Naval Staff, 125
Scoresby, William, 90
Scoresby, William, the younger, 90, 97, 106, 210
Scoresby Sound, 345
Scotia, 220
Scotia Bay, 270
Scotland, 16
Scott, Robert Falcon, 59, 121, 224, 243, 251, 257–58, 273–4, 277, 288–9, 291–6, 299–300, 304–5, 308–17, 323, 327, 329, 339, 343
Scott, Mrs R. F., 285
Scott Memorial Fund, 316, 340
Scott Polar Research Institute, 340, 343, 369
Scottish National Antarctic Expedition, 259, 265, 268
Scythia, 28
Sea-Gull, 146–7, 149
Seal Island, 120
Searchthrift, 32
Seven Islands, 232
Shackleton, Ernest Henry, 204, 224, 251, 259–67, 270, 274, 289–306, 308–17, 322, 329–35, 343–4

Shackleton Base, 371
Shackleton Ice Shelf, 326
Shannon, 16
Sharpe, Bartholomew, 57
Shetland Islands, 16
Shirase, Choku, 316
Shirreff, Captain, 117
Short, Captain, 130
Siam, 45
Siberia, 59, 68–71, 126, 211–12, 219
Sibiriakov, A., 212
Sibiriakov Island, 212
Sieur de Joinville's Island, 160
Simanov, Ivan, 128, 132
Simpson, C. J. D., 363
Simpson, George, 310
Simpson, Thomas, 111, 113
Simpson Strait, 182, 193–4
Singapore, 148
Skate, 366
Skelton, 258, 263
Skelton Glacier, 263
Slidell, Commissioner, 155
Smith, Leigh, 223, 240
Smith, William, 116–21, 132, 134
Smith Sound, 50, 98, 199–200, 203–5, 226, 228, 274, 277, 282, 363
Société de Géographie, 89, 159, 306
Solander, Dr, 77, 81
Solomon, 56
Solomon Islands, 56, 74
Somerset Island, 106, 110, 186
Søndre Strømfjord, 362
Sophia, 18
South Africa, 96
South Atlantic, 23, 60, 73, 130, 138, 164, 237
South Georgia, 58, 85, 115, 306, 328–9, 334, 339, 351
South Magnetic Pole, 157–8, 161, 164–8, 171–2, 174, 268, 291–4, 303–4, 305, 322, 324, 372
South Orkney Islands, 123, 148, 240, 270, 306, 351

South Polar Basin, 364–6
South Pole, 56–7, 81, 84, 125, 137, 159, 175, 224, 230, 252, 254, 256, 262, 265, 273, 286–8, 291–2, 295–8, 301–2, 304–5, 307–9, 311–16, 318, 320–1, 327, 329–30, 340–1, 345–7, 350, 354, 356, 361, 365, 367, 369–73
South Sandwich Islands. See Sandwich Land
South Sea, 47–9, 57, 80, 141, 143–4
South Shetland Islands, 57, 94, 125, 134–5, 144, 149–50, 240, 247, 306, 333, 351, 372
South Victoria Land, 303–4, 308, 317
Southampton Island, 49, 341
Southern Continent. See Southland
Southern Cross, 248–51, 259, 264
Southern Hemisphere, 75
Southern Ocean, 73, 115, 133, 138, 143, 238
Southland, 73–5, 78–80, 118–19, 134
Soviet Northern Sea Route, 212
Spanberg, Martin, 70
Spain, 22–3, 25, 37, 43, 45, 57–8, 75, 374
Spithead, 85
Spithead Road, 130
Spitsbergen, 40–1, 43–4, 47, 55, 67–8, 98–9, 106, 197, 207, 210–11, 214, 224, 344, 346–9, 364, 366
Sporing, Hermann, 77
Stanley, 199
Starvation Cove, 194
Stationeisberg, 328–9
Stefansson, Vilhjalmur, 283, 320–1, 347
'Stefansson Strait', 352
Stella Polare, 275
Steller, Georg Wilhelm, 71
Stenhouse, J. R., 335
Stevenson, Robert Louis, 246
Stillwell, F. L., 324, 326
Stockholm, 210

Stonington, 121
Stonington Island, 368
Storkerson, 320–1
Strabo, 16
Strindberg, Nils, 231–2
Suez Canal, 266
Sunshine, 36
Svalbard, 349
Svalbard Treaty, 349
Sverdrup, Harald, 348, 369
Sverdrup, Otto, 185, 216, 221, 226–7, 273, 318, 321
Sverdrup Islands, 227
Sweden, 212, 220, 231, 233, 255, 269, 289, 369
Sydney, 133–4, 149, 150–1, 153, 163
Syria, 89

Tahiti, 74–6, 78
Tartary, 28
Tasman Sea, 133
Tasmania, 140, 148, 178–9
Tasmanian National History Society, 164
Tegethoff, 206, 212
Teneriffe, 130
Termination Land, 236
Terra Nova, 266, 309–12, 317
Terra Nova Bay, 303, 317, 324
Terre Adélie, 153, 161–2, 324, 326, 358, 369
Territorio Antártico Chileno, 366
Terror (Francis Moira Crozier), 163–9, 172–6, 180–4, 190, 193
Terror Bay, 193
Thames, 46, 65, 99, 140, 248
The Terror (Back), 183
Thomson, C. Wyville, 236
Thomson, Sir William, 240
Thorne, Robert, 23
Thule, 15–16, 48, 279, 363
Tierra del Fuego, 25, 57, 84, 148–9
'Tilberie Hope', 46
Tokyo, 366
Toombs, Senator, 155
Torell, Professor, 210

Torrington, John, 190
Toulon, 159, 164
Tower Island. *See* Trinity Island
Trent, 97
Trinity Island, 119–21
Trinity Land, 119–21, 132, 140
Tromso, 212, 224, 226
Troughton, 130
Tula, 138–40
Turkey, 79
Twain, Mark, 156

Undine Harbour, 130
Ungava Bay, 48
Ungava Peninsula, 48
United States, 202
United States Service Expedition, 342
University of Michigan Expedition, 342
Upernavik, 50, 319

Vahsel, Richard, 328
Vahsel Bay, 328, 329, 332
Vaigach Strait, 46
Valparaiso, 116–18, 149, 150
Van Heemskerck, Jacob, 40–1
Vardö, 31
Vasilev, Commander, 125
Vauxhall, 186
Vega, 211–14
Venus, 75, 77
Verron, 74
Vespucci, Amerigo, 58
Victor, Paul-Émile, 363–4, 368
Victoria, Queen, 170
Victoria Barrier. *See* Ross Ice Shelf
Victoria Island. *See* Victoria Land
Victoria Land, 113, 168–70, 172, 188–9, 230, 241, 245, 253, 285, 290, 307, 323, 354, 372
Victoria Strait, 182–4, 189
Victory, 109–10, 181
Vikings. *See* Norsemen
Vilkitski, Commander, 321
Vincennes, 147, 151–3

Virgo Harbour, 231
Vladivostok, 291
Von Bellingshausen, Baron Fabian Gottlieb, 121–4, 127–38, 140, 145, 158, 161, 166, 169, 177, 240, 247, 269, 307, 353–5, 372
Von Drygalski, Erich, 255, 268, 322, 327
Von Gronau, 363
Von Humboldt, Alexander, 129, 160
Von Kotzebue, Otto, 127
Vostok, 128, 131–3, 136

Wager River, 66
Walden Island, 106
Wales, William, 81
Wallis, Samuel, 73–4
Walsingham, Secretary, 37
Wardhouse, 31
Warwick, Lord, 34
Washington, 145
Washington, Captain, 158–63, 169, 235
Watkins, H. G. (Gino), 342–4
Weddell, James, 137–8, 148, 170, 270
Weddell Sea, 123, 137, 148–9, 159–60, 174, 240, 259, 318, 327, 329–32, 335–6, 345, 354–5, 358, 371–2
Wegener, Alfred, 217, 319, 347
Welles, Gideon, 155
Wells, H. G., 246
Wellington Channel, 102, 176, 178, 182, 188
West England. *See* West Friezeland
West Friezeland, 33–4, 36, 55
West Indies, 257
Weyprecht, Karl, 205–8, 212, 220, 223
Whitby, 77, 90
White Island (Kirtøya), 232
White Sea, 19, 31
White Sea Trading Company, 40
Wick, 230

Wiggins, Captain, 220
Wilczek, Count, 206
Wilczek Island, 206
Wild, Frank, 294, 299–301, 303, 312, 326–7, 334, 352
Wilhelm II Land, 322
Wilkes, Charles, 145–55, 158, 161, 164, 166, 168, 201, 203–4, 236, 238, 270, 322, 326, 354
Wilkes, John, 146
Wilkins, Sir Hubert, 307, 320, 347, 352–3, 362
Willemsen, 352
William, 36
William of Nassau, 40, 44
Williams, 116–17, 120, 132, 134
Willoughby, Sir Hugh, 28–32, 42
Wills, Dame Stancomb, 330
Wilson, Edward, 259, 262–3, 267, 310, 313
Windward, 224, 274, 277
Wineland, 18
Winter Harbour, 103, 321, 361
Wise, American balloonist, 232
Wood and Flawes, 51
Woolaston Land, 188
Woolwich, 180
Wordie, Sir James, 336, 343, 370
Wrangel Island, 185, 207, 320

Yakutsk, 69
'Yankee Harbour', 122
Yelcho, 335
Yenisey River, 41, 208, 212–13
Young, Sir Allen, 197, 207, 220, 228–9
Yukon, 99

Zeeland, 41
Zélée, 160–1
Zeno, Nicolo and Antonio, 21, 28
Zeno Maps, 27, 33–4, 55
Zoffany, 81
Zoological Society, 89